STUDIES IN
IMPERIALISM

General editor: Andrew S. Thompson
Founding editor: John M. MacKenzie

When the 'Studies in Imperialism' series was founded by
Professor John M. MacKenzie more than thirty years ago,
emphasis was laid upon the conviction that 'imperialism as
a cultural phenomenon had as significant an effect on the
dominant as on the subordinate societies'. With well over
a hundred titles now published, this remains the prime
concern of the series. Cross-disciplinary work has indeed
appeared covering the full spectrum of cultural phenomena,
as well as examining aspects of gender and sex, frontiers
and law, science and the environment, language and literature, migration and patriotic societies, and much else.
Moreover, the series has always wished to present comparative work on European and American imperialism, and particularly welcomes the submission of books in these areas.
The fascination with imperialism, in all its aspects, shows
no sign of abating, and this series will continue to lead the
way in encouraging the widest possible range of studies
in the field. 'Studies in Imperialism' is fully organic in its
development, always seeking to be at the cutting edge,
responding to the latest interests of scholars and the needs
of this ever-expanding area of scholarship.

Sounds of liberty

MANCHESTER
1824

Manchester University Press

Sounds of liberty

MUSIC, RADICALISM AND REFORM IN THE ANGLOPHONE WORLD, 1790–1914

Kate Bowan and Paul A. Pickering

MANCHESTER
UNIVERSITY PRESS

The rights of Kate Bowan and Paul A. Pickering to be identified as the authors of this work have been asserted by them in accordance with the Copyright, Designs and Patents Act 1988.

Published by MANCHESTER UNIVERSITY PRESS
ALTRINCHAM STREET, MANCHESTER M1 7JA

www.manchesteruniversitypress.co.uk

British Library Cataloguing-in-Publication Data
A catalogue record for this book is available from the British Library

Library of Congress Cataloging-in-Publication Data applied for

ISBN   978 0 7190 8274 0   hardback
ISBN   978 1 5261 3833 0   paperback

First published 2017

Typeset by
Servis Filmsetting Ltd, Stockport, Cheshire

For Jenny Bowan and Don Pickering

CONTENTS

LIST OF FIGURES

FOUNDING EDITOR'S INTRODUCTION

Britain, a German music critic once disparagingly remarked, is a land without music. The reality could not have been more different. Both Britain itself and the overseas settler territories positively teemed with musical events, as did the 'Indian Empire' and the so-called dependent territories. Indeed, it could be said that imperialism itself was a phenomenon which was pursued with musical accompaniment. Almost all regiments had their bands which travelled and performed on colonial campaigns. The Scots never moved without their bagpipes and drums. Music both consoled and energised fighting forces. In more peaceful circumstances, regimental bands performed in public parks, on civic occasions and at government houses, as did naval bands when ships of the Royal Navy visited ports. If the ceremonial lay at the heart of the imperial experience, then music was a crucial aspect of ceremonies everywhere. Exhibitions, large and small, were show-cases for music, sometimes even 'exotic' indigenous music. Parades, durbars, sporting events, the welcoming of distinguished visitors and the opening of colonial parliaments all brought music into the public realm. If these were exterior expressions, then theatres, halls and other buildings were settings for what we might call 'interior' music. All of this music often indulged in early forms of 'cross-over', combining the popular with the western classical tradition, either through light classics or even performances associated with opera or ballet. In addition to all of this, worship in the Christian church was nothing without music, in the form of organ or harmonium 'voluntaries', choral anthems and of course hymns. Missions everywhere regarded music not only as a crucial part of their proselytising activities but more broadly as a means, as they saw it, of civilising indigenous peoples whom they sought to convert. Music was taught in schools, while musical performances, including programmes of song and light operettas (notably Gilbert and Sullivan in the second half of the nineteenth century), became a distinctive characteristic of public performances in most cities, ports and hill stations of the empire. Thus, the British Empire included many lands which resounded with music.

This book shines a spotlight on one very important area of all this musical activity, namely the role of music in radical and reform movements. It does so in the context of what the authors describe as the 'Anglophone world', particularly Britain itself, North America, Australia and New Zealand. The United States is included along with

Canada since so many musical aspects of radical activity can be found on both sides of the forty-ninth parallel, while the complex of interactive influences embraced the USA as well as the British 'Dominions'. The authors demonstrate that music was an integral part of radical, reformist and libertarian activity everywhere, of political movements like Chartism, of trade union activism and strikes, of Labor Day celebrations, of temperance, secular and freethinking societies, as well as of churches and missions that set out on more liberal and sympathetic approaches to Christian conversion. Music, of course, was generally the accompaniment to lyrics and texts; language designed to convey the ideological messages of these movements, thereby rendering the words more striking, more easily recollected, as well as more powerfully projected, through melody and rhythm.

The book's significance, however, lies in much more than its focus on such radical movements. It offers a distinctive approach to the cultural understanding of the British Empire, demonstrating the manner in which the cultural expressions of political activity should never be seen as radiating outwards from Britain but as creating much more complex and interactive trans-continental and trans-ethnic networks. It also highlights the distinctive role of women in so much of this activity as well as in its musical expression. Indigenous peoples in Canada, Australia and New Zealand swiftly adopted, while also adapting, western musical forms, notably the brass and other bands, as well as hymn-singing. These aspects of trans-culturation are analysed with a degree of sympathetic understanding in that such transfer of musical expression is seen as often becoming a matter of exchange rather than simply the practice of cultural hegemony. Indigenous peoples everywhere had their own significant musical experience and their acquisition of new instruments and forms of singing could be culturally enlarging rather than a case of the replacement of one form by another. New musical forms, in other words, were assimilated in pursuit of hybridity. The authors demonstrate an awareness of the potential gulf between intention and effect, even of the ways in which radical ideas can be subverted both through wider participatory experience in terms of class or race and through the simple yearning for entertainment. Thus the book is a contribution to much more than musicological studies. It provides significant extra dimensions to the understanding of radical movements in their social, cultural, gender and anthropological contexts.

John M. MacKenzie

ACKNOWLEDGEMENTS

The list of individuals and organisations deserving of our acknowledgment is a long one, accumulated over the several years during which this book was researched and written. We would like to offer our sincere thanks to Joan Allen; Richard Allen; Owen Ashton; Yann Beliard; Fabrice Bensimon; Jim Chandler; Malcolm Chase; Brad Cummings; Liz Fitch; Nev Kirk; Keith Laybourn; Susan Manning; Gordon Pentland; Robert Poole; Katie Stevenson; Mike Saunders; David Worrall; and Emma Brennan of Manchester University Press (for seemingly inexhaustible patience). We are grateful to librarians and staff of the following institutions: National Library of Australia; Noel Butlin Archives, Australian National University Library; Australian Institute of Aboriginal and Torres Strait Islander Studies; Mitchell Library, State Library of New South Wales; State Library of Victoria; John Oxley Library, State Library of Queensland; State Library of South Australia; University of Wollongong Library; National Library of Scotland; University of Edinburgh Library; Mitchell Library, Glasgow; Manchester Central Reference Library; Working Class Movement Library, Salford; Greater Manchester County Record Office; Labour History and Archives Study Centre, Manchester; National Co-operative Library, Manchester; British Library, St Pancras; Bishopsgate Institute, London; South Place Ethical Society Library, London; Cambridge University Library; Newcastle City Library, Newcastle upon Tyne; Modern Record Centre, Warwick; Newport Museum, Art Gallery and Library, Wales; Huntington Library, San Marino; New York Public Library; University of Chicago Library; Toronto Reference Library; Thomas Fisher Rare Book Library, University of Toronto; Archives Centre, McMaster University Library, Hamilton, Ontario; National Library and Archives Centre, Ottawa; Workers' History Museum, Hamilton, Ontario; Rare Book and Special Collection, McGill University, Montreal; Bibliothèque et Archives Nationales du Québec, Montreal; University of British Columbia Library, Vancouver; Hocken Library, Dunedin; Alexander Turnbull Library, Wellington; International Institute for Social History, Amsterdam; Bibliothèque nationales de France and officials of the Edith Nesbit Society and the British Socialist Party. The project was funded by generous support from the Australian Research Council, supplemented by assistance in the form of fellowships and travel bursaries from the College of Arts and Social Sciences, Australian National University; Australian

ACKNOWLEDGEMENTS

Academy of the Humanities; Institute for Advanced Study in the Humanities, Edinburgh University; Institute for Scottish Historical Research, University of St Andrews; Andrew Mellon Foundation; Sorbonne Paris-V; University of Newcastle upon Tyne.

The sounds of liberty

We're low – we're low – we're very very low,
And yet when the trumpets ring,
The thrust of a poor man's arm will go
Through the heart of the proudest king!
We're low, we're low – our place we know,
We're only the rank and the file,
We're not too low – to kill the foe,
But too low to touch the spoil.

Ernest Jones, *Song of the 'Lower Classes'*, 1852.

Among the priceless and seemingly boundless collection in the British Library is a slightly careworn programme entitled *Festival of Music for the People*.[1] Published in 1939, the pamphlet anticipated a series of concerts to be held over three nights in April at the Albert Hall, located in London's leafy suburb of Kensington, at Conway Hall in Red Lion Square and in Queen's Hall in the West End. Although the events occurred more than two decades beyond the years covered in our study of music and music-making in radicalism and reform throughout the Anglophone world during the long nineteenth century (1790–1914), they are an ideal way to introduce it. The principal drawcard for the concerts was undoubtedly the bass-baritone, Paul Robeson, regarded as the most famous African American in the world and, according to Hazel Carby, the 'first internationally acclaimed Black icon', not only as a vocalist but also as an actor on stage and screen and as a political activist.[2] Robeson had resided in Britain since the late 1920s, having fled his native America in disgust at the racism he encountered during his rise to fame. In Britain, like many political émigrés before him, Robeson rubbed shoulders with the leading radicals, reformers and socialists of the day and his political instincts were increasingly channelled into a range of progressive causes, from opposition to imperialism in India to support for the Left Theatre Movement and the republican struggle against fascism in Spain. In 1937, with Spain at the forefront of his mind, Robeson made the pronouncement that would underpin the remainder of his career. 'There are no impartial observers,' he told an audience at a relief concert in aid of Spanish children. 'The artist must take sides. He must elect to fight for freedom or slavery. I have made my choice.'[3] Robeson's place on stage during the Festival of Music for the People was justified, therefore, not only because of his prodigious talent and his mellifluous voice but also by his politics. Here was a man of the people.

Of course, Robeson was not the only person standing there. The tenor was a Welshman, Gwynn Parry Jones, highly regarded at that time. The narrators were Ronald Kelley and Wilfrid Walker, the latter a well-known Shakespearean actor who also dabbled in cinema. The People's Festival Wind Band and two dance troupes numbering 100 – the Woodcraft Folk group and the Unity Theatre Dance Group (probably the noted groups of that name from Aberdeen) – participated. Finally, Robeson and Jones were supported by 500 choristers. This mass chorus brought together members of discrete labour, co-operative and socialist organisations. The Bromley Labour Choir was there, as were the Labour Choirs from Ashford, Clapham, Eltham, Epsom and Ewell. Numerous co-operative choirs and choral societies were listed as participants: from Greenford, Laindon (Ladies'), West London, Bexley Heath, East Ham, Enfield Highway, Kentish Town, Redhill and Reigate, Surbiton, Tooting, Tottenham and Edmonton. The Edgware Co-operative Musical Society performed, as did the Hendon Left Singers and the New Progress Choir. Members of friendly societies also sang: the Unity Male Voice Choirs and the Rhondda Unity Male Voice Choir (presumably the well-known troupe from Wales). Alan Bush, a well-known pianist and composer and Communist Party activist would conduct.[4] The event was billed as a pageant entitled *Music and The People in Ten Episodes* and followed a scenario developed by Randall Swingler, a well-known poet, literary critic and political activist who had been a member of the Communist Party since the early 1930s.[5]

The premise upon which the production was developed was summarised with eloquent simplicity in the programme notes:

> After a flourish on brass and drums, the Speaker enters and introduces the theme of the Pageant. Music, he says, is not a drug or a world of fantasy to which men can escape from the real problems of their life. Rather it is part of the pattern of life they wish for, and a guide and inspiration to their efforts to attain it.

The flourish on bass and drums, as it was described, had been written for the occasion by Ralph Vaughan Williams and, indeed, every episode

[2]

contained music penned by a cavalcade of well-known composers in the ranks of British modernism, from Elisabeth Lutyens to Bush himself,[6] laced with numerous well-known political songs, old and new.

Episode One of the pageant was devoted to an idyllic depiction of a village green in fifteenth century: 'Feudal England'. The first note of conflict was in Episode Two, which included references to the peasant uprising of 1381 and Jack Cade's rebellion seventy years later. The title given to Episode Three continues the theme: 'Peasants in Revolt'. 'This time we see the Peasants massing for the long planned revolt', the programme notes continue, 'under the leadership of John Ball and Wat Tyler'. As the rebels march on London in 1381 they sing the *Cutty Wren*, 'one of the most interesting and powerful songs in English. The words are cryptic, as indeed they are meant to be,' we are told, 'for they hide a design and objective of a revolutionary character.' The subject of Episode Five requires a jump forward of more than 250 years to the 'Soldiers of Freedom' in 1649 with a particular focus on the Levellers and the Diggers. The former, we are told, were men who believed in 'greater democracy than Cromwell was able to establish'. The Diggers 'made an experiment in communal ownership and government' for which they were prosecuted. As they are led away under arrest they sing the 'most famous of the many of the songs of their leader, Gerald Winstanley, "Stand up now, Diggers All"'.[7]

Part Two of the pageant begins with an episode entitled 'Changing Europe' devoted to the French Revolution and built around the iconic songs the *Marseillaise* and the *Carmagnole*. 'We see here', the programme states, 'how the music which had been through centuries the secret bond of unity among the peasant people flowered into an open expression of their rights and demands at this historic moment.' Episode Seven follows directly on: as the last of the revolutionaries departs the stage, we are told, Beethoven ascends the rostrum and reads from 'his notebooks'. Beethoven's 'uncompromising statements' on the idea of freedom are answered by a chorus from *Fidelio*, sung by 'prisoners', which, linking past and present, is followed by a song composed and sung in a Nazi concentration camp. Episodes Eight and Nine promised the first appearance of Robeson in the evening's entertainment. Robeson was described 'one of the foremost champions of freedom and international brotherhood' and, supported by a 'Negro choir', he was slated to sing a 'Chain-gang song, then a Cotton-picking song, and some songs of freedom' drawn from the 'rich and vigorous musical culture' of the 'Negro people'. In a seamless transition from Robeson's rendition of *Kneelin' Low* was a massed rendition of a 'historic song of the British working-class', Ernest Jones's 'We're Low'.

'Every union had its song, and singing was an integral part of every meeting,' the programme noted, and Jones's song stands as representative of this culture. This song was offered as a 'token of the widespread musical activity in the early days of the Trades Union movement.' Bookending Jones's emblematic song was a rendition of William Morris's tribute to Alfred Linnell, an anonymous protester killed 'as a result of injuries received from police brutality' at a rally in Trafalgar Square in 1887.

To summarise the Finale – 'For Peace and Liberty' – the author of the programme notes links past struggles to those continuing in Germany, Italy, China and Spain, drawing attention to the place of music and music-making: people 'sing their determination to resist and conquer oppression'. To emphasise the corporeal ties between present and past the actors were to be joined on stage by 'men who are playing representative parts in the life of our time' to 'say his word on our theme of MUSIC FOR THE PEOPLE': Fred Copeman, a veteran of the International Brigade, the Dean of Canterbury and a 'worker and workers' leader', Tom Mann (then in his eighty-third year). Paul Robeson and the entire chorus would close the show by singing *Land of Freedom* (the 'great song of liberated Soviet humanity') by the Russian film composer Isaak Dunayevsky and 'America's Song of Democracy', *Men, Awake!* from the politically charged Broadway show *Pins and Needles*, which premiered in 1937.

The festival provoked a shrill reaction from the gatekeepers of the music establishment. On the one hand, they doggedly promulgated the long-standing trope that music was intrinsically apolitical. Music, insisted one churlish correspondent to the leading trade journal, the *Musical Times*, 'is the one art that can define nothing'.[8] Admittedly, conceded another commentator in retrospect, 'music can heighten the effect of words'; nevertheless, 'it can have no political meaning in itself'. For example, he continued, the 'tune of the most ferocious song of the French Revolution, "Ça ira", is a prattling country dance which is as genial as the words are bloody-minded'. *The Red Flag*, he insisted, has a tune 'that is not even palely pink'.[9]

Many sensed that there was grave danger in political association. 'We believe that we express the views of most musicians', fumed the editor of the *Musical Times*, 'when we say that art will lose much and gain little or nothing by being associated with politics.' 'Party politics is a dirty game,' another correspondent argued, 'let's keep music out of it.' Indeed, 'we don't want composers to attempt tonal tub-thumping, with diatribes and philippics in symphonic form.'[10] 'What is to become of the significance of vocal music', commented a contributor, 'if politicians are to adapt the texts they sing to their particular brand of party

[4]

politics? The practice is to be condemned, whether indulged in by the Labour Party, the British Union of Fascists, or the Primrose League.'[11] For others, such as Richard Capell, music critic for the conservative *Daily Telegraph*, what rankled was the festival's 'naïve Jacobinism'.[12] *The Times* extended the argument by suggesting that the quality of the performance was diminished by an echo of ideology: the 'artistic results of burning zeal may be no more than tepid if artistic principles are abandoned for the sake of pointing a moral, rewriting history, or making political gestures. And this is what happened.' The 'procession of the years', he continued, 'passed too slowly before our ears and eyes.'[13]

This response takes its place in what is effectively the long-standing debate between art for art's sake and utilitarian art with a social, moral or political purpose. *The Times*'s editor was in eminent company; German philosopher and sociologist Theodor Adorno later took up the cudgels again in important ways. The leading figure of the Frankfurt School, Adorno had also studied composition with one of the twentieth century's most important and iconoclastic composers, Arnold Schoenberg, and his aesthetic and philosophical ideas about music were profoundly shaped by this relationship. In his significant body of writings on music, Adorno espoused a high modernist musical philosophy, articulating complex connections between modernist art music and society while decrying popular music and jazz, both of which he saw as irrevocably tainted by the demands of capitalism.

Despite or even because of Adorno's contemptuous dismissal of twentieth-century protest music as *Unterhaltungsmusik* (entertainment music) that was 'nicht zu ertragen (unbearable)',[14] a vast body of scholarship has emerged in recent decades exploring the diverse genres that constitute popular music. Of course, this is central to our purpose in this book but it is important to note (and it will quickly become clear) that none among our cast of music creators is waiting to be elevated to the century's musical pantheon. The reader will encounter no virtuosos. Except in cases where it mattered to the social actors themselves, questions of aesthetics and abstract elegance are not discussed in the pages to follow. In other words, our case about the importance of music and music-making has nothing to do with the question of whether it was art – however defined – or not. In fact, in aesthetic terms – and this is the last of our aesthetic judgements – much of the music we recover was thoroughly pedestrian; some of it twee, some simply awful. The sounds of liberty were typically to be heard in the faint strains of 'rough music' played on the streets of Toronto – increasingly regarded as what we would today call noise pollution – and the wonderfully 'middle-brow' performances within the walls of a

secularist coven in Christchurch; in cacophonous election songs swirl-
ing around the hustings in Glasgow and Sunday afternoon chamber
music concerts in the heart of radical Holborn; in the defiant anthems
blaring slightly out of tune on picket lines in Broken Hill and in the
hymns warbled by choirs in Winnipeg. Nicholas Mathew has recently,
and revealingly, rescued the 'political Beethoven', reintegrating him
into the broiling social and political world in which he lived. The
reader will find no Beethovens here.[15]

Among scholars of popular music are many who have explored
its myriad intersections with various forms of oppositional politics
and resistance both within and outside the political nation. The literature is too extensive to explore here in any detail; suffice to say
that the last several decades have seen not only a plethora of articles
and monographs but also the appearance of a dedicated journal and
book series devoted to the broad subject of music *and* politics (we
will return to the significance for us of the conjunction). A couple of
points are relevant here, however. First, the extensive reference list in
John Street, Seth Hague and Heather Savigny's 'Playing to the Crowd:
The Role of Music and Musicians in Political Participation' clearly
demonstrates that the overwhelming preponderance of this work has
been devoted to the twentieth and twenty-first centuries.[16] Having
said that, several important studies focusing on the long nineteenth
century deserve notice. In addition to the ground-breaking study of
nineteenth-century working-class British musical culture by Dave
Russell there is important work by leading socio-cultural historians
such as Michael Pickering, Vic Gammon and Peter Bailey to name
just a few.[17] Although politics is not their primary focus, it is never far
from their gaze. There are also many valuable studies of British radicalism by historians such as Chris Waters, Eileen Yeo and more recently
Michael Davis which consider song as part of their subject.[18] Waters's
excellent account of socialist politics provides a detailed account of
late nineteenth-century socialist song culture.[19] In terms of chronology Duncan Hall's account of the musical culture of interwar British
socialism follows on from our research.[20] Given the close relationship
between poetry and song, studies of British demotic literature and
poetry within the broader context of radical British culture by literary scholars such as Michael Sanders, Anne Janowitz, Ulrike Schwab
and Solveig Robinson have offered important analytical frameworks
for considering the relationship between words and music.[21] Beyond
Britain, Laura Mason and Ralph P. Locke have made important contributions to the study of French revolutionary song.[22]

What these studies have in common is that they are almost entirely
bounded by the borders of the nation state. This is also true of the

essentially curatorial work that started in earnest in the late eighteenth century. Notwithstanding the highly charged political edge to cultural nationalism, preservation has been at the heart of the drive to collect ballads and folk music down to the present day. Some of those hard at work both in the archives and in the field were antiquarians interested in music and history for its own sake. In some cases, however, there was a distinct political agenda. Despite this, the overt political commitments of those involved were often subsumed by the impulse to record the past as if a repository had political purchase in and of itself. Roy Palmer in Britain, Rona Bailey and Herbert Roth in New Zealand, Joe Glazer and Edith Fowke in Canada, Philip Foner and Vera Brodsky Laurence in the United States and John Meredith and Hugh Anderson in Australia are just a few of the many individuals who have produced compilations of national song, the contents of which have been inspired and shaped by questions and anxieties around national identity.[23] In this way, even collections of political music have become separated from their own history. As Ron Eyermann and Andrew Jamison have pointed out, one consequence of the antiquarian impulse is that the 'empirical material is separated out from broader patterns and conceptions of social change, and, indeed, separated from the other domains of social life, becoming part of a sociological subfield, the sociology of music, art, or culture.'[24] In terms of the vast archive they have created, the labours of the dedicated and tenacious collectors are invaluable and we draw upon them throughout our book.

Most of these collections include political songs. In addition, there have been explicit attempts to gather and publish the music of the people specifically in the area of labour history. However, for many researching in the area of labour or working-class song culture the interface between 'folk' and labour and 'folk' and left-wing politics is often blurred. In *Song and Democratic Culture*, Ian Watson acknowledges and draws heavily upon the work of earlier collectors, particularly A. L. Lloyd, the renowned folk song collector and communist. In so doing he attempts to reconcile the anti-industrial, anti-commercial sensibility of folk music with the music made by the industrial working class and offers the somewhat convoluted categories of 'industrial folk song' and 'labour anthem'.[25] Clark D. Halker's study, *For Democracy, Workers and God: Labor Song-Poems and Labour Protest 1865–95*, in some ways stands as an American counterpart to Watson's study.[26] Halker uses 'song-poetry' as a 'lens onto the larger world of Gilded-Age workers and labor protest'.[27] His largely undefined term 'song-poem' nevertheless is a reminder of the close relationship between music and words; orality, aurality and print, or what has usefully been called 'transmediality', whereby cultural production is typically and often

[7]

simultaneously available across multiple platforms.[28] The contents of songsters, for example, frequently appeared as slip ballads or in the columns of the popular press (or both) and were subsequently republished in cheap compendiums. At each point they were sung or played or hummed, copied, taught or committed to memory. We will return to this point often in the pages to follow.

Again, however, it is important to emphasise that the concept of the nation hangs over collecting like an intellectual pall. Although Halker acknowledges the different countries that many song-poets came from he is only interested in them in so far as they are American immigrants. In identifying the range of sources that fed the musical culture, he recognises the presence of Scottish and Irish songs, hymns, broadsides, ballads and minstrel songs, and also takes account of the importance of British and German poetry but he does not draw any conclusions about the transnational networks this repertoire reveals. Rather, this eclectic collection of music is of interest only in so far as it contributed to what he has called the US 'labor song-poem', a genre he calls 'indigenous' to the United States.[29] In so doing, he produces a form of uncritical American exceptionalism. A glance at the contents pages of the plethora of songbooks produced in North America during the long nineteenth century highlights many familiar English, Scottish and Irish melodies, either with the original lyrics or as the basis of contrafacta. However, running an eye down the lists also shows a growing corpus of songs generated in America (particularly during the Civil War) which quickly became staples in the performance of radicalism and reform in the 'old world' and in the wider Anglophone world. *John Brown's Body, Tramp! Tramp! Tramp!* and *Marching Through Georgia*, to take three of the most obvious examples, provide eloquent testimony to the existence of a shared cultural pool and a shared process of cultural production that defies fragmentation. Michael Pickering, working in the same area at the same time as Watson and Halker, offered an important interpretative framework addressing the 'lived realities of popular song' and 'understanding its meaning, significances and gratifications in the social and cultural contexts to which it belongs'.[30] In so doing Pickering problematised the categories of 'folk song' and 'folk culture', noting that they were 'often empirically at variance with the range of content, modes and procedures of everyday culture', but his focus is firmly fixed on the 'rhythms of labour' in Britain.[31]

Where scholars have looked beyond national borders they have done so often in a comparative rather than transnational or inter-colonial sense. Thomas Turino, for example, offers a fascinating comparison of the uses of popular song in the American Civil Rights movement and

Nazi Germany;[32] William Weber explores middle-class musical taste in the important metropolitan centres of Europe and America; and Derek B. Scott also looks to New York as well as to Paris and Vienna in his consideration of important types of nineteenth-century popular music in *Sounds of the Metropolis*.[33] Ian Peddie's *The Resisting Music: Music and Protest* looks at popular music from different parts of the world but not with any overarching sense of the transnational.[34] Likewise, Annie J. Randall's edited collection *Music, Power and Politics* has a wide geographical sweep from Mexico to Serbia to Barbados to China to Iran. But, again, these stand as discrete studies.[35] On the basis of the tantalising title alone special mention needs to be made of Jeffrey Richards's *Imperialism and Music: Britain 1876–1953*. Perhaps surprisingly, his is not an inter-colonial study, nor is it actually intended to be: it is about 'the expression in music of the ideology of the British Empire'.[36] Richards investigates music written for the Empire but not across the Empire.[37]

In 2002 Eric Hobsbawm combined nostalgia with prescience to offer a sweeping synopsis of historical approaches past and present. Of particular relevance for the present study, he identified history's 'failure ... to emancipate itself from the framework of the nation-state' as 'probably the major weakness of the subject' in his lifetime.[38] In an important sense Richards embraces Hobsbawm's admission of a lifetime of failure. Our book is an attempt to grapple with his frustrated apophthegm. To do so we are driven beyond the horizons of distance (and calendrical measurement) into the realm of the inter-colonial, trans-oceanic and transnational. Notwithstanding the fact that music is sinuous and polysemous (and, as we have seen, for some churlish naysayers, ontologically apolitical), meeting Hobsbawm's challenge involves listening for stable, didactic signifiers of a shared radical and reformist culture, which were not out of earshot across space or time. We join Hobsbawm in chafing against the bonds of the nation.

Over the past two decades much has been written and said to help us in this. A crucial point of entry was a conference convened in 1998 to explore a new paradigm – the British world – within a broader impulse towards transnational history. As Kent Fedorowich and Andrew Thompson, themselves progenitors, have written, the stated goal of the inaugural 'British World' conference was to 'escape from the static confines and parochial constraints of "national" historiographies in order to provide a more integrated and comparative approach to the British world'.[39] What distinguished the idea of a British world from the traditional idea of imperial history conceived in the rarefied air of metropolitan certainty was twofold: an understanding that the imperium was characterised by perpetual circulation and

[9]

roundaboutness; it was not only or even principally a rusty hub and spokes. Indeed, as Alan Lester and David Lambert argued, it is important to see the British world as 'networked or webbed', 'an interconnected space' at the intersection of a 'new' imperial and postcolonial history.[40] Secondly, it highlighted the importance of what one of the present authors has called 'globalisation from below'.[41] The agents of the British Empire were not only those in receipt of imperial honours or the troops dispatched to protect them. On the contrary, the participants in the official Empire comprised a tiny proportion of the 13.5 million Britons who departed the United Kingdom for extra-European ports as migrants in the second half of the nineteenth century or the millions of expatriate Britons waiting for them at their point of disembarkation or, indeed, passing on their way elsewhere in the British world like proverbial ships in the night. Before he took his seat on the platform at the Festival of Music for the People, to take one extraordinary example, Tom Mann had plied his trade as a political and trade union activist in (in order) Birmingham, London, Battersea, Newcastle, Lanark, London, Wellington (New Zealand), Melbourne (Victoria), Broken Hill (New South Wales), Liverpool, Cape Town and Durban in Southern Africa before living out the remainder of his active public life in Britain. He also travelled widely to conferences and symposia. Mann was accompanied every step of the way by his equally pugnacious and committed partner, Elsie Harker. Admittedly, Harker and Mann were outliers in any index of peripatetic radicals but they were not exceptions that prove the rule.

As is well known, even when the peregrinations were between metropole and periphery it is important to note that the flow was not always or even predominately in one direction and was often repeated many times over. For example, Scottish-born John Dunmore Lang, Australia's first republican and the most prominent radical activist of his generation under southern skies, undertook nine return passages between Scotland, England and the Australian colonies between 1824 and 1874.[42] Starting his journey – physical and political – at the opposite end of the axis, however, was Harry Atkinson, a trade unionist and Fabian socialist born in Urenui on the North Island of New Zealand in 1867. Having established a reputation as a trade union organiser in Wellington, Atkinson travelled to Manchester in 1890 where he became a stalwart of the Labour Church and helped to establish the local branch of the Independent Labour Party before returning to New Zealand in 1893 to resume his role as a Labour and socialist activist the minute he disembarked.[43] Dora Montefiore, one of the most prominent radical suffragettes in the British world, was London-born but first came to prominence when the Women's Suffrage League was formed in her home in the Sydney suburb of Paddington in 1891. Having returned to London, in 1898 she became an executive member of a number of women's suffrage organisations and was imprisoned for her activities. Upon her release Montefiore joined the Social Democratic Federation and, later, the British Socialist Party. She went back to Sydney and became editor of the *International Socialist* before again returning to London where she was elected to the council of the United Communist Party of Great Britain.[44] Vida Goldstein, on the other hand, was born in Portland, Victoria. Of all the prominent Australian campaigners for women's rights, notes her biographer, Goldstein was the one who gained a truly international reputation. On tours of both the United States and Britain her public speeches drew massive crowds.[45]

With these kinds of people and a cast of many others like them in mind, this project was conceived within a 'British world' paradigm, a choice that quickly proved problematic, however. Simply following in the footsteps of relentlessly travelling activists took us beyond the borders of the Empire on which the sun never set, especially into the north-east of the United States (and French Canada). Not only did they insist we follow wherever they went, but in these places we met citizens (many of them first- and second-generation migrants) who, in turn, insisted that they take their place in the pages to follow.

There were places, however, where we could not go, notably Ireland but also the Cape Colony and Britain's many Crown colonies. This decision was essentially forced upon us for two reasons: practical and historical. The scope of the project was already ambitious, chronically and geographically, and to extend it would have required more time and words than we were able to give it. Many of our radicals visited the Cape – some settled there and participated in domestic struggles for reform across a broad front – but southern Africa remains, relatively, a shadow in the work of historians of nineteenth-century radicalism and thus there are few guides into the continent to help ward off egregious error and to allow us to make a meaningful contribution. The same is true of Britain's Crown colonies where the so-called 'subject' peoples vastly outnumbered their British governors. There were radicals there, to be sure, but it was beyond our capacity to find them.

Ireland presented a particular problem in terms of scope. The nexus between music and politics in Ireland has generated important scholarship (and is worthy of more study). From this it is abundantly clear that the context in which music was composed, shared and performed across St George's Channel was fundamentally cross-cut by issues of religion and nationalism, which demand comprehensive attention within a differently calibrated framework. And it is a vast canvas. Of course, many thousands of radicals and reformers from Ireland or of

Irish descent settled in Greater Britain and beyond where they became embroiled in the struggles of their adopted home(s). They were musical in every sense and a rich musical culture travelled among their meagre possessions and in their hearts and minds. They neither could nor should be excluded from the ink spilled below.

Notwithstanding the pragmatic reasons underpinning some of our decisions in respect of scope, their historiographical implications seemed to be manifold as we put them into effect. On the one hand, our research suggests that a rethink of what has been accepted as American exceptionalism, particularly as it applies to the nineteenth century, is overdue. A fellow Australian, Ian Tyrrell, has been making this point in a string of important publications.[46] Our work lends support to this view: many American radicals were self-consciously and determinedly part of a transatlantic political world; many radicals in the Empire wandered in and out of the United States without bumping into anything alien or experiencing a cultural epiphany. The same is true of Australia. J. G. A. Pocock, an eminent New Zealand historian nestled among the turrets in Cambridge, has long since advocated the inclusion of the antipodes in conceptions of a 'new' British history. Over the last decade many Australianists have begun to listen. Without drowning Australian history in an ocean of overseas influence (to borrow the words of Ann Curthoys and Marilyn Lake) much outstanding work has now been completed, particularly using the lens of transnational and inter-colonial and trans-oceanic biography (individual and collective).[47] Among 'labour' historians, however, this shift continues to be robustly contested in some places: we believe our study provides a wealth of evidence to suggest that the edifice of what one of the present authors has called 'Australian exceptionalism' as it applies to radicals and reformers is crumbling.[48] Moreover, the extent to which the historical actors insouciantly ignored the bounds of the Empire (physically, culturally and intellectually) may well suggest that the term 'British world' itself is tottering on the brink of becoming an oxymoron. Indeed, mindful of the possibility that 'British world' has outlived its usefulness as a reference, we have opted instead for 'Anglophone world'. Admittedly, this term is capacious and extends beyond the geographical limitations we have imposed, but it is at least an unambiguous descriptor of our vast dramatis personae. Here, we pick up the point made by Fedorowich and Thompson who noted that the contours of the Empire (and beyond) were 'strikingly illustrated through the dissemination of the English language'.[49] As such, we have resisted the call for a global framework for this project, not because we do not see merit in this approach but because our subjects and their culture, and the conceptual language we use to discuss them are not only Eurocentric, they are Anglocentric.[50]

It almost goes without saying, therefore, that by definition those who fall under our gaze were overwhelmingly white Anglophones. Our book is thus written within an understanding of a British imperium defined by 'whiteness' or what Marilyn Lake and Henry Reynolds have called the 'global colour line'. In their influential book of the same title Lake and Reynolds trace the 'transnational circulation of emotions and ideas, people and publications, racial knowledge and technologies that animated white men's countries'. They do not mention music but they easily might have. The fact that we have limited our focus to the colonies of settlement further homogenises this transnational and inter-colonial 'imagined community of white men'. Lake and Reynolds go on to make the point that the potency of transnational whiteness provided a template for some of those on the 'other side of the colour line' to establish forms of resistance.[51] We offer a few – all too few – glimpses of indigenous agency, appropriation, adaptation and resistance by those who used the musical culture of the white colonisers. Our actors – women and men – are therefore overwhelmingly white, and spoke (and sang in) English.

We have added to 'Anglophone World' the words 'reform' and 'radicalism' as part of our title and the framework within which the book is written. Joanna Innes and Arthur Burns have led an extended and revealing attempt to define 'reform' in numerous contexts and as it evolved and mutated. Their edited volume of essays offers a wide range of areas from medicine, slavery and domesticity to the law, the theatre and, notably, opera and 'high culture', which together highlight the innate complexity of the term the instant it passed the lips of those using it.[52] Innes's chapter tells us much about the 'lexical field' of 'reform', by which she means the extensive 'range of ways in which the word "reform" was used'. By the late eighteenth century, she tells us, the word and related vocabulary was 'increasingly bandied about, and put to new uses'. The noun form, she notes, led to 'snappy coinages' attached to an ever-increasing and complex raft of causes – institutional, political, religious, social, moral.[53]

The noun form 'radical' and related words used here are deserving of a similar forensic analysis. Although it was not included in Charles Pigott's notorious *Political Dictionary* published in 1795, by the early nineteenth century 'radical' had become widely used both as a 'term of very bad odour' – denoting a 'set of blackguards' – and, at the opposite end of the spectrum, for a class of political activist 'who glory in their designation'.[54] Our canvas is equally broad but here we have used 'reformers' and 'radicals' and related vocabulary as plural nouns of convenience. In our pages 'reform' and 'radical' are also employed as roomy adjectives and, in the case of 'reform', also as a verb. Our dramatis personae we denote as 'radicals' and 'reformers'; their creeds, causes and activities we crudely refer to as 'reform' and 'radicalism' and variations thereof. We do so in the full knowledge that while all radicals were reformers in an abstract sense, and many embraced the term 'radical-reformer', some radicals regarded reformers as milk-and-water dissemblers to be treated with suspicion or contempt.[55] Similarly, many reformers would have bitterly resisted the appellation 'radical' as an indelible mark of extremism. Their repertoires of action overlapped substantially and diverged dramatically. Some radicals and reformers collected petitions or campaigned for political office (together and against one another). For some radicals and reformers, with dog-eared songbooks stuffed in one pocket and careworn bibles in the other, their *raison d'etre* was the pursuit of moral uplift; for others the quest for a new moral world was underpinned by a shared doubt or disbelief. Some threw bombs, others campaigned for access to the land; some smashed machines or hatched plans to wrest control of the means of production from the bourgeoisie while others were self-consciously bourgeois. Some had 'horny hands and unshorn chins', others wore delicate gloves or dog collars. We will argue that many of those who engaged with indigenous peoples – even patronisingly – are equally entitled to be called reformers or radicals as those who embraced these designations proudly despite their virulent racism. Some radicals and reformers erected picket lines during bitter strikes and lockouts; others rioted, marched, starved themselves or cached arms. Indeed, there is room in our usage of the words for George Orwell's cocksure Marx-quoting types, book-trained socialists, Labour Party backstairs crawlers, fruit-juice drinkers, nudists, sandal-wearers, sex-maniacs, Quakers, 'Nature Cure' quacks, pacifists and feminists.[56]

Of course, we might have almost endlessly added nouns – trade unionists, suffragists, Chartists, communists, teetotallers, repealers, democrats, secularists and so on – and we do use these terms throughout. Our title, however, promises encounters with those we have simply called reformers and radicals. Our justification for herding one and all under this rubric will please few but for us the defining characteristic of the multifarious women and men we have featured was a dissatisfaction with the world as they lived in it and a commitment to forging a better one. There was no unifying vision of the future – not only were radicals and reformers often divided against one another but the ranks of reform and radicalism were themselves routinely factionalised and fissiparous. But they all had a vision. And they all made music.

If we have eschewed the British world as a framework, the idea of 'Britishness' remains, particularly during the long nineteenth century, salient conceptually and as a heuristic. At one level we simply endorse Lester and Lambert's distinction between physical relocation and an enduring 'affective personal and emotional affiliation with a British "home"'.[57] Overwhelmingly, the radicals and reformers who migrated permanently – including those with their teeth clenched in fury that they had been forced to give up the struggle for change at home, as well as those fervently hoping to find a better Britain – still regarded themselves as British. And so did their progeny, well beyond the chronology of this book. We are looking then at a species of Britishness and its transmission throughout an Anglophone world without feeling that we are contradicting ourselves.

Beyond Lambert and Lester's emotional register, the tug of the heartstrings, we have examined Britishness as a cultural formation and explored the culturally informed and interconnected means of its transmission: an indexical baseline for culture and a shared repertoire of political action and cultural practices. Having said that, a consensus about what constitutes Britishness has proven elusive and illusive. There have been many attempts to define it. As Ian Donaldson has noted, the OED's etymology suggests that the word was first coined in the seventeenth century with a meaning akin to 'Brutishness': a way to describe those with a proclivity for getting about without the 'habiliment of a Shirt'.[58] Notably, for our purposes, some attempts to define the term have used the lens of shared political culture: from the declaration by Britain's former prime minister Gordon Brown that the 'golden thread' running through the history of the Sceptred Isle is a 'passion for liberty anchored in a sense of duty and an intrinsic commitment to tolerance and fair play' to his successor David Cameron's remarkably similar 'muscular' defence of 'British values' such as 'freedom, tolerance of others, accepting of personal and social responsibility, and respecting and upholding the rule of law'. When pressed, Cameron insisted that, 'Our freedom doesn't come from thin air. It is rooted in our parliamentary democracy and free press.'[59] For the student of radicalism and reform in the Anglophone world this early twenty-first century bipartisan construction can be seen as part of a continuum that is very helpful when seeking to understand the ground rules of British politics during the long nineteenth century. The overwhelming majority of the radicals and reformers we will meet in the pages to follow would have agreed that 'thin air' had little to do with their cherished discourse about their rights. Indeed, for most the so-called 'Rights of the Freeborn Briton' were sanctioned by a shared understanding of a distant past and they travelled with Britons over time and distance. As we shall see, this trope was imprinted on much of their music.

But Britishness for our subjects was inherently more than a cluster of political ideas. On the contrary, it was cultural in a broader sense. We can glimpse evidence of this at every turn: in the Protestantism and enmity to the French identified by Linda Colley; in George Orwell's ritualised instructions for making a 'nice cup of tea' ('one should take the teapot to the kettle and not the other way about'); and in T. S. Eliot's extended litany of 'all the characteristic activities and interests of the people': 'Derby Day, Henley Regatta, Cowes, the twelfth of August, a Cup Final, the dog races, the pin table, the dart board, Wensleydale cheese, boiled cabbage cut into sections, beetroot in vinegar, nineteenth-century Gothic churches and the music of Elgar'.[60] Eliot went on to invite the reader to 'make his own list' but there is little to be gained here by continuing a quest for iconic qualities identifiable with Britons. On the contrary, the fact that Eliot tacked Edward Elgar onto the end of his inventory is a useful place for us to stop doing so. The first of Elgar's 'Pomp and Circumstance Marches' (a title drawn from *Othello*) was premiered in 1901. As is well known, it included the melody used for *Land of Hope and Glory*, a song pressed into service for the coronation ode for Edward VII the following year. By any measure this bombastic anthem – soon to be a staple of populist promenade concerts down to our own day – deserves a more prominent place as a signifier of British culture than boiled cabbage. But Eliot's facile treatment of music as an afterthought is not uncommon in studies of Britishness as something that is graspable – 'experience-near' in the anthropological sense – and thus both transmittable and a transmitter. From the exhaustive literature review offered by Fedorowich and Thompson, for example, it is clear that the role of music and music-making in the circulation and preservation of Britishness has not been explored in any depth and is often overlooked. Lambert and Lester, for example, point to the importance of '[f]ormal and informal communicative networks' facilitated by the development of the postal service, imperial news services and the 'circulation of newspapers, publications and correspondence' as key drivers of 'knowledge exchange' in the British world but do not mention the significance of music (or the creative arts in general).[61]

Students of radicalism and reform have not treated music and music-making well either. As we have noted elsewhere in relation to Chartism, references to the presence of music in the social culture of the movement – when they are present at all – are almost invariably offered in passing. Too often music and music-making have been by implication treated as marginal, decorative, frivolous even. A glance at extant anthologies of Chartist literature (and reformist, radical and popular literature more generally) include many *songs* that are treated as poetry.[62] Even when Chartist verses have been recognised as songs and contextualised, as Timothy Randall did some years ago, it is the lyrics that attract interest.[63] The 'songs of democracy', Watson tells us, were primarily 'ideology expressed in aesthetic terms'. The historian, he continued, should focus on 'what songs *say*'.[64] Pouring over contrafacta – forensically dissecting, historicising and contextualising – is central to our task and occupies many of the pages to follow but it is only part of our purpose. We will argue that melody was not only mnemonic in a general sense but also that melodic choices were often taken with great deliberation to evoke particular pasts; to connect the causes of the present to the struggles of the past.

As we will show, tunes offered layers of associative meanings which were utilised to great effect to reinforce a current political message by a process of accretion. A glance at the genealogy of a recent song, well beyond the chronology of our study, provides an illustration of the approach we take. The lyrics to *English Civil War*, a song by British punk band The Clash, were self-evidently a contribution to the bitter campaign against racism underway at the end of the 1970s. As the title suggests, the song contained several references linking the fascistic National Front to Cromwell's New Model Army; it also referenced the spectre of a police state in Orwell's *Animal Farm*. But some listeners would have recognised the significance of the fact that the song's composer, Joe Strummer, had appropriated the melody from a famous American Civil War song, *When Johnny Comes Marching Home*, which in turn was a contrafactum of an Irish anti-war song from the 1790s. 'War is just round the corner,' Strummer told the *Record Mirror*, 'Johnny hasn't got far to march'.[65] Thus, not only do we interrogate the words chosen by radicals and reformers during the long nineteenth century, we also ask what radicalism and reform sounded like. What were the sounds of liberty?[66] To borrow the wonderfully mixed metaphor penned by musicologist John Caldwell, our aim always is to ensure that the 'soundscape' is 'painted in'.[67] Moreover, as noted above, the choices that informed music and music-making carry the student of radicalism and reform beyond the horizon of the nation to the ends of an Anglophone world where the sounds of liberty – similar, different, hybrid, syncretic and identical – can be heard loud and clear. It is thus unsurprising that The Clash's *English Civil War* could be found on the shelves of record stores in Australia, New Zealand and Canada (and elsewhere): it travelled a well-worn route.[68]

By taking this approach we are, in part, responding to Leon Botstein's call in 2005 to draw 'music out of the margins' and position it as a

'central component to life'.[69] Arguing for the quintessential importance of music is, of course, not new. Thumbing through a desktop
calendar one will almost inevitably find among the daily quotations
Longfellow's trite homogenising aphorism, penned in the 1830s, that
music is a universal language. In the 1880s Friedrich Nietzsche, to
take an example unlikely to appear in a calendar, observed famously
in his philosophical manifesto, *Twilight of the Idols*, that 'Without
music life would be a mistake'. 'Music as we understand it today', he
continued, 'is also a total area – excitation and – discharge (*Gesammt-
Erregung – und – Entladung*) of the emotions'. Nietzsche's text continues 'but...'. Without pursuing the implications of the qualification – as
Gary Tomlinson has done – it is safe to conclude that his overall point
stands: for Nietzsche music mattered at a visceral level.[70]

Paradoxically, however, for all that the Victorian world was (to
borrow Ruth Solie's words) saturated with music, traces of its significance are comparatively few. As the eminent musicologist Leo Treitler
has put it, music's 'very centrality is marked by its absence'.[71] In
Clifford Geertz's terms, music and musical behaviour were 'experience-
near' – spontaneous, un-self-conscious and colloquial.[72] Elsewhere
Geertz observed that the creative arts, such as jazz and painting, are
profoundly difficult to talk about, possibly even 'beyond the reach
of discourse'; but he insisted that '[s]omething that meaningful to us
cannot be left just to sit there bathed in pure significance': 'The surface
bootlessness of talking about art seems matched by a depth of necessity to talk about it endlessly.'[73] Similarly, not only did Botstein insist
that music be 'treated as a species of fundamental social action', ignoring the challenges and the silences, he demanded that it be used as a
'primary source' to 'test and perhaps even profoundly revise our sense
of the past'.[74]

While bemoaning its neglect by historians of radicalism and reform,
nowhere do we suggest that music was the most important method
utilised by radicals and reformers for the expression, performance
and transmission of their politics. Indeed, by centring music here our
aim is, at one level, simply to understand better the part it played
in the world as reformers and radicals lived it and thereby to learn
about the culture within which it was composed, performed and
consumed. Having said that, we demonstrate that from one end of
the Anglophone world to the other, music and music-making were
an essential element of the lived experience of nineteenth-century
oppositional politics. As the American anarchist Emma Goldman once
reputedly quipped, 'a revolution without dancing is a revolution not
worth having'.[75] Although not seeking to hide behind his ample skirts,
it is worth enlisting Edward Said on this point: 'To think of music and

politics during the seventeenth and twentieth centuries (Monteverdi, Schoenberg, jazz, and rock culture)', he argued, is 'to map an ensemble of political and social involvements, affiliations, transgressions, none of which is easily reducible either to a simple apartness or to a reflection of coarse reality.'[76] Notably, Said left out the nineteenth century, characterising the relationship between music and society in the mid to late nineteenth century as 'cultural exoticism'. Here, we humbly demur. The sounds of liberty during the long nineteenth century offer much for the student of popular politics across an inter-colonial and transnational world.

Having said that, we will argue that music and music-making are undoubtedly a highly effective lens for investigating the inter-colonial and transnational history of radicalism and reform between 1790 and 1914, not only because of their consistency across Anglophone societies but also because of the differences they highlight. As noted, musical practices and repertoires were mutable, readily adapted to new environments, easily appropriated to new causes and, at the same time, they provided a connective tissue that crossed vast expanses of time and terrain, revealing the outlines of a culture that otherwise is at risk of being overlooked within constricting geographical and chronological parameters. Below we show inter alia that music and music-making offer an important way of calibrating culture; we show that music was dialogic – mediating the relationship between leader and led; we reveal the ways that song moved in and out of daily exchange with ease, at times spontaneously while at others with aforethought; we demonstrate the way it was often pressed into service as a highly efficient form of ideological precis and one that, in situations that frequently involved clashes with the full force of state power, was hard to police. We offer examples of the way it encouraged, unified, attacked, divided, consoled, reminded and constructed. We show that attention to music and music-making is particularly perspicacious when seeking to understand the affective register of political life. As we have observed elsewhere, listening to Engels sing the *Vicar of Bray* and watching Marx dance the mazurka provides a lens to fundamentally change the way we understand their political lives. A radical's hymnal or a reformer's songbook were not just words on printed pages, they were also something meant to be sung and heard. This fundamentally alters our sense of its significance as an object of paper and ink.[77]

So, returning to Botstein's challenge, how do we use music to 'profoundly revise our sense of the past' or in our case to better understand radicalism and reform in the Anglophone world during the long nineteenth century? Our methodology is both inter- and multi-disciplinary. In 2005, in a book entitled *Music and History: Bridging the Disciplines*,

Jeffrey Jackson and Stanley Pelkey asked rhetorically, 'Why haven't historians and musicologists been talking to one another?'[78] Our book was conceived with such a conversation in mind. One of the present authors is a musicologist, the other a historian; our starting point is to draw upon the disciplines of musicology and history. Like our friends at the *Musical Times* in the 1930s, vigilantly policing the borders of ineffable 'music', until the 1980s many musicologists still clung to a focus on the 'work': for them the composer died before the author. Writing in 1991, Edward Said joined a rising chorus from within the ranks of musicology that fervently rejected this 'police regime': 'music can be more, and not less, interesting if we situate music as taking place, so to speak, in a social and cultural setting'. The 'role played by music in Western society', he continued, 'are extraordinarily varied, and far exceed the antiseptic, cloistered, academic, professional aloofness it seems to have been accorded.'[79] Said went on to lament the fact that musicologists had failed to develop a methodology for the task of situating music in the world.[80]

Nearly three decades on this judgement is simply wrong. His comment was made in the midst of a transformative revolt against positivist musicology. In subsequent decades musicology burst its bounds in ways that are beyond Said's wildest expectations, engaging with and absorbing, inter alia, cultural studies, literature and literary theory, philosophy, sociology, feminist studies, film studies, anthropology, race, political studies and history. If the academic world for those in the humanities and the arts today comprises a series of 'turns' then musicologists have been around most of them, including most recently a turn to the archives. A glance at the programme of the 2015 American Musicological Conference, held in Louisville, Kentucky, gives some idea of the profusion of diverse offerings from musicology. Among the fifty or more papers given on the first full day of the conference were: '"Double Masked" Minstrelsy in the Metropolitan Opera's 1929 Production of Ernst Krenek's *Jonny spielt auf*'; 'Musical Encoding in Metadiegetic Space in Ingmar Bergman's *From the Life of the Marionettes*'; 'Gender, Nature, and Religiosity in Liszt's Musical Landscapes'; 'The Political Context of Schütz's *Saul, was verfolgst du mich*'; 'Richard Wagner as Ecocritic: Wagnerian Climate Theory and the Anthropocene'; 'Selling Difference: Sonic Hipness and Racial Tension in Contemporary Advertising'; and 'The "Social Mobility" of Johnny Rotten's T-Shirt: Countering Class Narratives of Punk'.[81] Little wonder that two years earlier Phyllis Weliver and Katharine Ellis felt compelled to invoke Ruth Sollie's 1999 quip: 'at last report it seemed that there is not a living soul anywhere who claims to comprehend exactly what musicologists do'. 'Perhaps this is understand-

[20]

able', Solie continued, 'given our nature as a yeasty and sometimes indigestible mix of historian, critic, paleographer, and musician'.[82] Has the demise of the composer presaged the death of the musicologist? Notwithstanding their long demise, our composers, appropriators, performers, peddlers and listeners are all alive.

To the extent that we can legitimately regard the Louisville conference as a barometer of the state of the discipline, two points are important here. First, notwithstanding Johnny's t-shirt, the papers overwhelmingly dealt with so-called art music. As indicated, except in cases when it mattered to those composing, playing or singing, we are more interested in the music of the people not destined for the canon. Second, notwithstanding the diversity, the overwhelming preponderance of the Louisville papers focussed on the composer, artist, the musical work, genre or the instrument as the unit of analysis. The first section of our book also uses music as its core focus. We have chosen to examine three songs in considerable detail: the *Marseillaise*, *John Anderson my Jo* and *Song of the 'Lower Classes'*. Obviously, these are but three of many hundreds of songs that might have been preferred. Many of the other candidates are discussed in this section and elsewhere in the book. Some aren't.

Undoubtedly, many readers will find reason to question our choices. Our justification for the selection comes in two parts. On the one hand, we feel that these songs are representative of important genres. The *Marseillaise* is arguably the most iconic song in the repertoire of radicalism and reform. Composed during the French Revolution, the French quickly lost control of it; indeed, it soon became a song that belonged to the world. *John Anderson my Jo* is a traditional folk song that was co-opted into political discourse in complex ways. *Song of the 'Lower Classes'* will be unfamiliar today to virtually everyone save specialists and aficionados of radicalism and reform, but during the long nineteenth century it travelled far and wide and is an ideal song for us to follow. Moreover, its status as an 'original' composition was complex and multifaceted and provides an important opportunity to explore questions of class and cultural self-reliance. For these songs we believe that we can make a case for typicality or at least we suggest that substituting other songs might simply have provided another way to make the same points. In addition to the songs chosen as representative, hymns appear often. Hymn-singing was an intrinsic part of life in Victorian Britain and her colonies and, as Sanders has shown, those hymns are often associated with conservatism, if not reaction. Here, we join him in highlighting the genre of radical and reform hymns.[83] These hymns resonated in radical chapels, connecting the faithful with what we would nowadays call liberation theology, as well as secularist gatherings where social justice was demanded without any reference to higher powers.

In discussing music we have used the conventional musicological tools where necessary and we have drawn inspiration and insight from the proliferating musicological turns but our book is, first and foremost, offered as a work of history. For all the richness of their contributions we seek to do something intrinsically different from musicologists. Whereas 'musicologists look at the past to better understand musical works or practices', as Jackson and Pelkey have put it, historians look at music 'to better understand the past'.[84] In short then, this is not a book about music, the social-historical context of music or the place of history in music; it is a book that examines the role of music *in* history. Thus, while the tools of musicology are often utilised, our methodology is grounded in the discipline of history. We take a granular approach in the belief that by telling small stories we can unpack broader narratives. In stories are arguments, which, in turn, contain explanations. We do this with respect for those whose stories we seek to tell. People do not speak (or sing) in parenthesis waiting to be quoted glibly or dragged into 'apt anecdotal illustration' (Eric Hobsbawm's expression).[85] We surely need to listen to what the social actors had to say – or at least strive to find ways to listen as best we can – to what they said. And sang. And played. In taking a granular approach to storytelling we draw upon the methodological stricture advocated and pioneered in the teeth of a polemic within Marxist historiography by Edward Thompson. Fifty years on, Thompson's injunction to get inside episodes in order to better understand history writ large still has much to offer.[86] Again, Geertz is helpful for us to elaborate this aspect of our project, describing his anthropological-cum-ethnographic methodology as 'hopping back and forth between the whole conceived through the parts that actualise it and the parts conceived through the whole that motivates them'. This 'intellectual perpetual motion', as he puts it, seeks to turn whole and parts into 'explications of one another'.[87]

For the student of a cultural formation across significant expanses of space and time this approach is not simply about scalability – asserting that episodes can carry the burden of generalisation – it is also a claim for the importance of repetition. Greg Urban has argued that 'what falls under the rubric of culture is touched by replication'.[88] Through a saturation of examples drawn from different settings and different times we have used music and music-making as way of illustrating a culture replicating itself. Like those on stage with Paul Robeson – singing, bowing and blowing – our historical actors constantly re-enacted their history and their aspirations. Having said that, as we have noted, we do not use music and music-making to obfuscate difference and change. For all that we sketch the outline of what we postulate was effectively a shared radical and reformist culture throughout an essentially white Anglophone world, nowhere do we suggest that it was monolithic, canonical or fixed. On the contrary, it was mutable, organic and mutually constitutive. What it provided over time was the basis for a 'conversation-through-music' (to borrow Inga Clendinnen's words); a register that allowed people to recognise in the sound of each other's voices a common cause, be they in Sydney, Sheffield or Saskatchewan.[89] The musical conversations we listen to are similar – often significantly so – to those held in other places and at other times but never exactly the same. Our research suggests that Bernard Shaw was correct when he quipped that the so-called universal language of music was spoken with many accents – detectable even between London and Manchester.[90]

Our approach is thus based on an understanding that history happens in real time. Here, again, we are returning to the work of Thompson and Geertz as our starting point. Although it is unwise to elide the contributions of a Marxist historian and a (non-Marxist) anthropologist-cum-ethnographer, both Thompson and Geertz were primarily interested in social action. To make a case for 'thick description' (an approach which continues to resonate throughout the humanities and social sciences) Geertz argued, 'Behaviours must be attended to, and with some exactness, because it is through the flow of behaviour – or, more precisely, social action – that cultural forms find articulation.'[91] In the preface to his seminal *The Making of the English Working Class*, Thompson famously declared that class was 'something which in fact happens (and can be shown to have happened) in human relationships'.[92] As one of the present authors has noted elsewhere,[93] this aspect of Thompson's praxis is under-theorised and while here is not the place to re-join that discussion it is important to ponder briefly the implications if we substitute 'music' for 'class'. If 'class happens' diachronically – in real time – then surely a song is only meaningful when it is sung and simultaneously heard. Of course, among radicals and reformers culture was embodied in a plethora of objects. Many of them, from battered euphoniums to tattered songbooks, were connected to music, but, as Geertz has noted, artefacts 'draw their meaning from the role they play ... in an ongoing pattern of life'.[94] This is a book about the dynamic operation of music as a form of cultural production. It matters if music is read, played, sung or passively listened to – it has a different affective register – but it is never inert. Songbooks feature extensively in the pages to follow but for us they are meaningless unless we catch them in the moment they are

[23]

printed, transported, advertised, sold, given away, read, sung, played, disavowed, lost, stolen or thrown away.

Pondering this intrinsic dynamism of music, Christopher Small revived an archaic verb-noun: 'musicking'. 'The act of musicking', he wrote in an influential book published in the late 1990s, 'establishes in the place where it is happening a set of relationships and it is in those relationships that the meaning of the act lies. They are to be found not only between those organised sounds which are conventionally thought of as being the stuff of musical meaning but also between the people who are taking part, in whatever capacity, in the performance'.[95] We have foresworn the grating word, opting instead for a clumsy conjunction of music (the object) and music-making (the activity). Songs should not be unsung; trumpets should not be silent.

It goes without saying that the essential precondition for a granular approach based on repetition is the availability of sources. Here, we are mindful of Greg Dening's stricture: before choosing which 'beach crossings' to interrogate it is necessary to read every document about crossing beaches.[96] We have not done so here but, as we hope we will more than adequately demonstrate, we have consulted many. Not only does the book draw upon extensive use of the increasingly rich digital archives for historians working on transnational projects, we also conducted extensive research across the terrain covered by the book and beyond: Canberra, Melbourne, Sydney, Adelaide, Brisbane, London, Manchester, Salford, Edinburgh, Glasgow, Los Angeles, San Marino, Chicago, New York, Toronto, Hamilton, Ottawa, Montreal, Vancouver, Wellington, Dunedin and Amsterdam. We have, in R. H. Tawney's sense, got plenty of mud on stout boots.[97] Our sources are both musical and non-musical, public and private: slip ballads, song sheets, songbooks, songsters, hymnbooks, printed and manuscript scores, newspapers, pamphlets, handbills, programmes, posters, books, memoirs, diaries, letters. We use images but, despite the fact that the technology existed during the final decades of our period, recordings of radicalism and reform have evaded our grasp.

The basic structure of the book to follow is based on four units of analysis discussed across three sections. As noted, the first section examines songs; the second looks at the place of music in the public sphere wherein people (individually and collectively) made music as part of processing, electioneering and celebrating, as well as striking, rioting and rebelling. In the third section we examine the role of music and music-making within the walls of a range of associations and institutions. Moving from close scrutiny of two progressive religious organisations we look more generally at how music operated in reform and humanitarian movements, including an examination of the difficult and often destructive role music played in European interaction with indigenous people in the cross-cultural environment of the mission, a colonial context that is characterised, as Fiona Paisley and Kirsty Reid have reminded us, by 'asymmetries of power'.[98] We will see both a weapon of oppression and deculturation, as well as, crucially, the opportunities music and music-making provided for resistance. Of course, between the public and private spheres we see many synergies: defiance and solidarity are different sides of the same coin. Nevertheless, there is much to be learned by treating each separately.

Our fourth unit of analysis – to persist with the social science construction – is those women and men we have herded together under the rubric of reformers and radicals. They are the heroes and villains of the pages to follow. When focussing on the sounds of struggle, from moral reform to violent revolution, we never turn our gaze from the people striving to effect change in different places and at different times. We will repaint their portraits in the hope of seeing things for the first time the second time around. We will meet Jack Cade and Ernest Jones again; we will get to know Tom Mann and his equally important partner, Elsie Harker, among a dramatis personae of hundreds. We will again visit South Place along with dozens of other niches in a capacious inter-colonial, transnational, trans-historical world. We will sit on many platforms listening to stentorian oratory without ignoring the humble pianist to the side and march in numerous parades shoulder to shoulder with those pounding drums and sounding trumpets. We will sing arms locked with those on the picket line, as we contemplate revolution and sharpen pikes. We will tell old stories in music, we will celebrate those who suffer for the cause and we will mourn the dead. We will warble along with a plethora of hymns and popular songs – old and new. We will strive to decode songs like *Cutty Wren* and we will contemplate original words and music, such as Jones and Lowry's *Song of the 'Lower Classes'*, and many more besides. We will attempt to hear history as it happened.

Notes

1 *Festival of Music for the People* (London, n.p., 1939), p. 11.
2 Hazel V. Carby, *Race Men* (Cambridge, MA: Harvard University Press, 1998), p. 3. See also Jordan Goodman, *Paul Robeson: A Watched Man* (London: Verso, 2013).
3 See *Manchester Guardian* (25 June 1937). This process culminated in 1938 when Robeson accepted an invitation from the well-known Marxist J. B. S. Haldane to visit Spain in support of the volunteers of the International Brigade laying down their lives there.
4 See Richard Stoker, 'Alan Bush (1900–1995)', *Oxford Dictionary of National Biography* (Oxford: Oxford University Press, 2004), online edn, September 2013, available at www.oxforddnb.com.virtual.anu.edu.au/view/article/60406 (accessed 6 September 2016).
5 See Andy Croft, 'Randall Swingler (1909–1967)', *Oxford Dictionary of National*

Biography (Oxford: Oxford University Press, 2004), online edn, September 2013, available at www.oxforddnb.com.virtual.anu.edu.au/view/article/62375 (accessed 6 September 2016). It is not clear if Swingler wrote the programme notes.

6   Kate Bowan has work in progress on a collective study of these composers.

7   An addendum notes that the tune to only one of the Levellers's songs was extant. See also: E. A. White, 'The Diggers' Song', *Journal of the English Folk Dance and Song Society*, 4:1 (1940), pp. 22–30.

8   'Notes and News', *Musical Times*, 80:1155 (1939), p. 373.

9   'Ad Libitum', *Musical Times*, 83:1195 (1942), p. 276.

10   *Ibid.*, p. 277.

11   'Notes and News', *Musical Times*, 80:1155 (1939), p. 373.

12   Capell cited in 'Notes and News', *Musical Times*, 80:1155 (1939), p. 373.

13   *The Times* (3 April 1939).

14   See Lisa Whitaker, 'Adorno interview about Joan Baez singing Oh Freedom', *Contextual Studies*, 13 January 2012, available at http://l-whitaker1013-cts.blogspot.com.au/2012/01/adorno-interview-about-joan-baez.html (accessed 31 May 2016). The excerpt from the interview can also be found at www.youtube.com/watch?v=Xd7Fhaji8ow (accessed 31 May 2016).

15   Nicholas Mathew, *Political Beethoven* (Cambridge: Cambridge University Press, 2013).

16   See, for example, the journal *Music and Politics* published by University of Michigan and Ian Biddle, Mark Carroll, Paul A. Merkley and Ian Peddie (eds), *The Library of Essays on Music, Politics and Society* – a four-volume series published by Ashgate in 2012. See John Street, Seth Hague and Heather Savigny, 'Playing to the Crowd: The Role of Music and Musicians in Political Participation', *British Journal of Politics and International Relations* (2007), pp. 1–17 (accessed 14 May 2016), doi: 10.1111/j.1467-856x.2007.00299.x.

17   See, for example, Dave Russell, *Popular Music in England 1840–1914*, 2nd edn (Manchester; New York: Manchester University Press, 1997); Michael Pickering, 'The Study of Vernacular Song', *Jahrbuch für Volksliedforschung*, 33 (1988), pp. 95–104; Vic Gammon, 'Not appreciated in Worthington? Class Expression and Popular Song Texts in Mid-nineteenth-Century Britain', *Popular Music*, 4 (1981), pp. 5–24.

18   Chris Waters, *British Socialists and the Politics of Popular Culture 1884–1914* (Stanford: Stanford University Press, 1990); Eileen Yeo, 'Christianity in Chartist Struggle', *Past and Present*, 91 (1981), pp. 109–39; Michael Davis, '"An evening of pleasure rather than business": Songs, Subversion and Radical Sub-Culture in the 1790s', *Journal for the Study of British Culture*, 12:2 (2005), pp. 115–26.

19   See Waters, 'Music and the Construction of Socialist Culture', chap. 4 in *British Socialists*, pp. 97–130. Similarly, Robert E. Weir's *Beyond Labor's Veil: The Culture of the Knights of Labor* dedicates a chapter to the importance of song in the working-class associational culture of the American labour organisation, the Knights of Labor. See 'Storm the Fort: The Knights of Labor in Song', chap. 3 in Robert E. Weir, *Beyond Labor's Veil: The Culture of the Knights of Labor* (Pennsylvania: Penn State Press, 1996), pp. 103–44.

20   Duncan Hall, *'A Pleasant Change From Politics': Music and the British Labour Movement Between the Wars* (Cheltenham: New Clarion Press, 2001).

21   Michael Sanders, *The Poetry of Chartism* (Cambridge: Cambridge University Press, 2009); Michael Sanders, 'Poetic Agency: Metonymy and Metaphor in Chartist Poetry 1838–1852', *Victorian Poetry*, 39:2 (2001), pp. 111–35; Anne Janowitz, *Lyric and Labour in the Romantic Tradition* (Cambridge: Cambridge University Press, 1998); Solveig Robinson, 'Of "Haymakers" and "City Artisans": The Chartist Poetics of Eliza Cook's Songs of Labor', *Victorian Poetry*, 39:2 (2001), pp. 229–53. See also Ruth Livesey, 'Socialism and Victorian Poetry', *Literature Compass*, 1:1 (2004), pp. 1–6; Matthew Rowlinson, 'Lyric', chap. 3 in Richard Cronin, Alison Chapman and Antony H. Harrison (eds), *A Companion to Victorian Poetry* (Oxford: Blackwell, 2002), pp. 59–80. The field of word-music studies is expanding rapidly.

See, for example, Phyllis Weliver (ed.), *The Figure of Music in Nineteenth-Century British Poetry* (Aldershot: Ashgate, 2005); Phyllis Weliver and Katharine Ellis (eds), *Words and Notes in the Long Nineteenth Century* (Woodbridge: Boydell & Brewer, 2013).

22 See Laura Mason, *Singing the French Revolution: Popular Culture and Politics, 1787–1799* (Cornell: Cornell University Press, 1996); Ralph P. Locke, *Music, Musicians, and the Saint-Simonians* (Chicago: University of Chicago Press, 1986).

23 See, for example, Roy Palmer, *A Touch on the Times: Song and Social Change 1770 to 1914* (Harmondsworth: Penguin, 1974); Vera Brodsky Laurence, *Music for Patriots, Politicians and Presidents* (New York: Macmillan, 1979); Gerald Porter, *The English Occupational Song* (Umeå: University of Umeå, 1992); Philip Foner, *American Labor Songs of the Nineteenth Century* (Urbana: University of Illinois, 1975); John Greenway, *American Folksongs of Protest* (Philadelphia: University of Philadelphia, 1953); Rona Bailey and Herbert Roth (eds), *Shanties by the way: A Selection of New Zealand Popular Songs and Ballads* (Christchurch: Whitcombe and Tombs, 1967); Edith Fowke and Joe Glazer, *Songs of Work and Protest* (New York: Dover Publications, 1973); Edith Fowke and Richard Johnston, *Folk Songs of Canada* (Waterloo, Ontario: Waterloo Music, 1954); Hugh Anderson, *Colonial Ballads* (Melbourne: Cheshire, 1962); Hugh Anderson, *The Story of Australian Folksong* (Melbourne: Hill of Content, 1970); John Meredith, Patricia Brown and Roger Covell, *Folk Songs of Australia and the Men and Women who Sang Them*, 2 vols (Sydney: New South Wales University Press, 1985–1987); Douglas Stewart and Nancy Keesing (eds), *Australian Bush Ballads* (Sydney: Angus and Robertson, [1968]); Warren Fahey, *Ratbags & Rabblerousers* (Sydney: Currency Press, 2000).

24 Ron Eyerman and Andrew Jamison, *Music and Social Movements: Mobilizing Traditions in the Twentieth Century* (Cambridge: Cambridge University Press, 1998), p. 9.

25 Ian Watson, *Song and Democratic Culture in Britain* (London: Croom Helm, 1983).

26 Clark D. Halker, *For Democracy, Workers and God: Labor Song-Poems and Labour Protest 1865–95* (Urbana: University of Illinois Press, 1991).

27 Halker, *Democracy, Workers and God*, p. 4.

28 See, inter alia, Jens Eder, 'Transmediality and the Problems of Adaption: Concepts, Forms and Strategies', chap. 5 in Dan Hassler-Forest and Pascal Nicklas (eds), *The Politics of Adaption* (Basingstoke: Palgrave Macmillan, 2015), pp. 66–81 and Maureen N. McLane, 'Mediating Antiquarians in Britain, 1760 – 1830: The Invention of Oral Tradition; Or, Close Reading Before Coleridge', in Clifford Siskin and William Warner (eds), *This is Enlightenment* (Chicago: University of Chicago Press, 2010), pp. 247–64.

29 Halker, *Democracy, Workers and God*, p. 2.

30 Pickering, 'Vernacular Song', p. 96.

31 See Michael Pickering and Emma Robertson, *Rhythms of Labour: The History of Music at Work in Britain* (Cambridge: Cambridge University Press, 2012).

32 Thomas Turino, *Music as Social Life: The Politics of Participation* (Chicago: University of Chicago Press, 2008), esp. 'Music and Political Movements', chap. 7, pp. 189–224.

33 William Weber, *Music and the Middle Class: The Social Structure of Concert Life in London, Paris, and Vienna* (London: Croom Helm, 1975); William Weber, *The Great Transformation of Musical Taste: Concert Programming from Haydn to Brahms* (New York: Cambridge University Press, 2008); Derek B. Scott, *Sounds of the Metropolis: The Nineteenth-Century Popular Music Revolution in London, New York, Paris and Vienna* (Oxford: Oxford University Press, 2008).

34 Ian Peddie, *The Resisting Muse: Popular Music and Social Protest* (Aldershot: Ashgate, 2006).

35 Annie J. Randall, *Music, Power, and Politics* (New York: Routledge, 2005).

36 Jeffrey Richards, *Imperialism and Music: Britain 1876–1953* (Manchester: Manchester University Press, 2001), p. viii.

37 Richards does examine a Dominions tour of 1911 and looks in some detail at the careers of selected colonial singers.

38 'Old Marxist Still Sorting Global Fact from Fiction', *Times Higher Education Supplement* (12 July 2002), available at www.timeshighereducation.com/170348. article (accessed 24 March 2016).

39 Kent Fedorowich and Andrew S. Thompson (eds), *Empire, Migration and Identity in the British World* (Manchester: Manchester University Press, 2013), p. 2.

40 David Lambert and Alan Lester (eds), 'Introduction: Imperial Spaces, Imperial Subjects' in *Colonial Lives: Across the British Empire: Imperial Careering in the Long Nineteenth Century* (Cambridge: Cambridge University Press, 2006), pp. 6–7.

41 Paul Pickering, 'Why We Should Tell Stories of the British World: An Afterthought', *Humanities Research*, 8:1 (2006), pp. 85–90. See also Fedorowich and Thompson, *Empire, Migration and Identity*, p. 18.

42 See Paul Pickering, 'The Highway to Comfort and Independence: A Case Study of Radicalism in the British World', *History Australia*, 5:1 (2008), pp. 06.1–06.14; D. W. A. Baker, 'Lang, John Dunmore (1799–1878)', *Australian Dictionary of Biography*, Australian National University, available at http://adb.anu.edu.au/biography/lang-john-dunmore-2326/text2953 (accessed 23 March 2016).

43 Herbert Roth, 'Atkinson, Harry Albert', *Dictionary of New Zealand Biography. Te Ara – the Encyclopedia of New Zealand*, available at www.TeAra.govt.nz/en/biographies/2a16/atkinson-harry-albert (accessed 2 April 2016).

44 Judith Allen, 'Montefiore, Dorothy Frances (Dora) (1851–1933)', *Australian Dictionary of Biography*, Australian National University, available at http://adb.anu.edu.au/biography/montefiore-dorothy-frances-dora-7626/text13329 (accessed 3 April 2016).

45 Janice N. Brownfoot, 'Goldstein, Vida Jane (1869–1949)', *Australian Dictionary of Biography*, Australian National University, available at http://adb.anu.edu.au/biography/goldstein-vida-jane-6418/text10975 (accessed 3 April 2016).

46 See, inter alia, Ian Tyrrell, 'American Exceptionalism in an Age of International History', *The American Historical Review*, 96:4 (1991), pp. 1031–55; 'The Myth(s) That Will Not Die: American National Exceptionalism', in Gérard Bouchard (ed.), *Constructed Pasts, Contested Presents* (New York: Routledge, 2013), pp. 46–64. These articles bookend Tyrrell's contribution. See also Alex Tyrrell, 'Making the Millennium: The Mid-Nineteenth Century Peace Movement', *Historical Journal*, 20:1 (1978), pp. 75–95.

47 J. G. A. Pocock, 'British History: A Plea for a New Subject', *Journal of Modern History*, 47:4 (1975), pp. 601–21; 'Ann Curthoys and Marilyn Lake (eds), *Connected Worlds: History in Transnational Perspective* (Canberra: ANU E Press, 2006), pp. 12–13. See also, inter alia: Neville Kirk, *Comrades and Cousins: Globalization, Workers and Labour Movements in Britain, the USA and Australia from the 1880s to 1914* (London: Merlin, 2003); Lambert and Lester (eds), *Colonial Lives*; Desley Deacon, Penny Russell and Angela Woollacott (eds), *Transnational Ties: Australian Lives in the World* (Canberra: ANU E Press, 2008).

48 See Terry Irving, 'Pickering Un-Picked', *Labour History Review*, 79:2 (2014), pp. 227–37; Paul Pickering, 'Those Damnable Radicals: A Case Of Australian Exceptionalism?', *Labour History Review*, 79 (2014), pp. 228–35. See also, inter alia, Marcel van der Linden, *Transnational Labour History: Explorations* (Aldershot: Ashgate, 2003) and Neville Kirk, *Labour and the Politics of Empire: Britain and Australia 1900* (Manchester, Manchester University Press, 2014).

49 Fedorowich and Thompson, *Empire, Migration and Identity*, p. 18.

50 See Marcel van der Linden, 'Labour History Beyond Borders', in Joan Allen, Alan Campbell and John McIlroy (eds), *Histories of Labour: National and International Perspectives* (London: Merlin, 2010), pp. 353–83. See also Paul Pickering, review of *Histories of Labour: National and International Perspectives* (review no. 1041), available at www.history.ac.uk/reviews/review/1041 (accessed 8 September 2016).

51 Marilyn Lake and Henry Reynolds, *Drawing the Global Colour Line: White*

Men's Countries and the International Challenge of Racial Equality (Cambridge: Cambridge University Press, 2008), pp. 4–5.

52 Arthur Burns and Joanna Innes (eds), *Rethinking the Age of Reform: Britain 1780–1850* (Cambridge: Cambridge University Press, 2003). See also Joanna Innes and Mark Philp (eds), *Re-imagining Democracy in the Age of Revolutions* (Oxford: Oxford University Press, 2013).

53 Joanna Innes, '"Reform" in English Public Life: The Fortunes of a Word', in Burns and Innes (eds), *Age of Reform*, pp. 63, 83, 85, 93 and *passim*.

54 Charles Pigott, *A Political Dictionary: Explaining the Meaning of Words* (London: n.p., 1795). The usages dating from 1802 and 1842, respectively, are in the longer *Oxford English Dictionary* (OED).

55 See Innes, '"Reform" in English Public Life', pp. 94–6.

56 George Orwell, *The Road to Wigan Pier* (London: Victor Gollancz, 1937), pp. 206, 216–17, 248.

57 Esme Cleall, review of *Empire, Migration and Identity in the British World* (review no. 1597), doi: 10.14296/RiH/2014/1597 (accessed 8 September 2016).

58 Ian Donaldson, 'Opening Address', paper presented at the 'Britishness and Otherness' symposium, Humanities Research Centre, Australian National University (July 2004).

59 G. Brown, 'The Golden Thread That Runs through Our History', *Guardian* (8 July 2004); David Cameron quoted in *Royal Oxford Academy* (2 July 2014).

60 Linda Colley, *Britons: Forging the Nation* (New Haven: Yale University Press, 1992); George Orwell, 'A Nice Cup of Tea', *Evening Standard* (2 January 1946); T. S. Eliot, *Notes Towards the Definition of Culture* (London: Faber and Faber, 1948), p. 31. Notably, Orwell argued that his code was equally applicable for Eire, Australia and New Zealand where the passion for tea was shared.

61 Lambert and Lester, 'Imperial Spaces, Imperial Subjects', p. 28.

62 Y. Kovalev (ed.), *An Anthology of Chartist Literature* (Moscow: Izdatel'stvo Literatury na Inostrannykh Iazykakh, 1956); Peter Scheckner (ed.), *An Anthology of Chartist Poetry* (Cranbury: Associated University Press, 1989). This conflation can also be found in Mary Ashraf (ed.), *Political Verse and Song from Britain and Ireland* (London: Lawrence and Wishart, 1975); Ann Janowitz, *Lyric and Labour in the Romantic Tradition* (Cambridge: Cambridge University Press, 1998); Brian Maidment (ed.), *The Poorhouse Fugitives* (Manchester: Manchester University Press, 1987); Ulrike Schwab, *The Poetry of the Chartist Movement* (Dordrecht; Boston: Kluwer Academic, 1993); Martha Vicinus, *The Industrial Muse* (London: Croom Helm, 1974). One of the present authors has also previously conflated poetry and song. See Paul Pickering, 'Glimpses of Eternal Truth: Chartism, Poetry and the Young H. R. Nicholls', *Labour History* (Australia), 70 (1996), pp. 53–70.

63 Timothy Randall, 'Chartist Poetry and Song' in Owen Ashton, Robert Fyson and Stephen Roberts (eds), *The Chartist Legacy* (London: Merlin, 1999), pp. 171–95. On the social role of poetry (songs) see Ian Haywood, *The Literature of Struggle: An Anthology of Chartist Fiction* (Aldershot: Ashgate, 1995), p. 3. See also Frank O'Gorman, 'Campaign Rituals and Ceremonies: The Social Meaning of Elections in England 1780–1860', *Past and Present*, 135 (1992), pp. 79–115.

64 Watson, *Song and Democratic Culture*, p. 6 (original emphasis). Watson does recognise, however, that melody and performance were intermediate stages between text and song. Writing about Ireland in the same period Georges-Denis Zimmermann has argued that 'ballads are … one of the few means at our disposal to know the popular mind'. See *Irish Political Street Ballads and Rebel Songs 1780–1900* (Genève: Imprimerie La Sirène, 1966), p. 10.

65 The Clash, 'English Civil War', CBS, 7082, released February 1979; available at www.songfacts.com/detail.php?id=30543 (accessed 9 September 2016).

66 An exception is the laudable attempt to recreate a Chartist choir. An eighty-strong Chartist choir was formed for a one-off performance in Yorkshire in 2006. Fortunately, an invaluable CD recording was made of the event: J. Russell, *Chartist*

Songs. As Sung by the Yorkshire Chartist Choir, [privately produced], 2006. We are grateful to Malcolm Chase for providing us with a copy of this CD, the production of which undoubtedly benefitted from his unequalled knowledge of Chartism. In 1998 the English group Chumbawumba included the 'Chartist Anthem' in their collection, *English Rebel Songs 1381–1984*, EMI 8769, 1998, track 5.

67 John Caldwell, *The Oxford History of English Music*, vol. 2 (Oxford: Oxford University Press, 1999), p. 536.

68 http://australian-charts.com or http://australian-charts.com/showitem.asp?interpret=The+Clash&titel=English+Civil+War&cat=s

69 Jeffrey H. Jackson and Stanley C. Pelkey (eds), 'Introduction', in *Music and History: Bridging the Disciplines* (Jackson: University Press of Mississippi, 2005), p. xiii.

70 Friedrich Nietzsche, *Twilight of the Idols or How to Philosophize with a Hammer* (New York: Macmillan, [1889] 1911), p. 6; Gary Tomlinson, *Metaphysical Song: An Essay on Opera* (Princeton, NJ: Princeton University Press, 1999), p. 11–19.

71 Quoted in Ruth A. Solie, *Music in Other Words: Victorian Conversations* (Berkeley: University of California Press, 2004), pp. 1–2.

72 Clifford Geertz, '"From the Native's Point of View": on the Nature of Anthropological Understanding', reprinted in *Local Knowledge* (New York: Basic Books, 1993), p. 58.

73 Clifford Geertz, 'Art as a Cultural System', reprinted in *Local Knowledge*, pp. 94–5.

74 Jackson and Pelkey (eds), 'Introduction', in *Music and History*, p. xiii.

75 The quotation is actually paraphrased from her autobiography. See Emma Goldman, *Living My Life*, vol. 1 (New York: Courier, [1931] 1970), p. 56.

76 Edward Said, 'On the Transgressive Elements in Music', in *Musical Elaborations* (New York: Columbia University Press, 1991), p. 71. We are grateful to Ian Donaldson for this reference.

77 See Kate Bowan and Paul Pickering, 'Bridging Music and Politics: Radicalism in Mid-Victorian London' (unpublished paper, Musicological Society of Australia Annual Conference, University of Newcastle, September 2009); 'Marx and the Mazurka: Music and Politics in Mid-Victorian London' (unpublished paper, St Andrews University, June 2010); 'Songs of the Millions: Chartist Music and Popular Aural Tradition', *Labour History Review*, 74:1 (2009), pp. 44–63.

78 Jackson and Pelkey (eds), 'Introduction', in *Music and History*, p. vii.

79 Said, *Musical Elaborations*, pp. xvi, 56.

80 *Ibid.*, pp. xvi–xvii. He does nominate a group of promising emergent studies.

81 *Program and Abstracts of Papers Read at the American Musicological Society Eighty-first Annual Meeting* (Louisville, Kentucky, 12–15 November 2015).

82 Weliver and Ellis (eds), *Words and Notes*, p. 4.

83 Michael Sanders, '"God is our Guide! Our Cause is Just!": The National Chartist Hymn Book and Victorian Hymnody', *Victorian Studies*, 54:4 (2012), pp. 679–705.

84 Jackson and Pelkey (eds), 'Introduction', in *Music and History*, p. vii.

85 Eric Hobsbawn, 'From Social History to the History of Society', *Daedalus*, 100:1 (1971), p. 27.

86 E. P. Thompson, 'The Peculiarities of the English' (1965), reprinted in *The Poverty of Theory and Other Essays* (London: Merlin, 1979), p. 65.

87 Geertz, 'Nature of Anthropological Understanding', p. 69.

88 Greg Urban, *Metaphysical Community: The Interplay of the Senses and the Intellect* (Austin: University of Texas Press, 1996), pp. 241–2.

89 Inga Clendinnen, *Dancing With Strangers* (Edinburgh: Canongate, 2005), p. 10.

90 George Bernard Shaw, *Music in London: 1890–94*, vol. 1 (New York: Constable & Co., 1932), pp. 91–2. The original reference to music as a universal language is from H. W. Longfellow, *Outre-Mer: A Pilgrimage Beyond the Sea*, vol. 2 (New York: Harper & Brothers, 1835), p. 4.

91 Clifford Geertz, 'Thick Description: Towards an Interpretive Theory of Culture', in *The Interpretation of Cultures* (New York: Basic Books, 1973), p. 17.

92 E. P. Thompson, *The Making of the English Working Class* (Harmondsworth: Penguin, [1963] 1978), p. 8.

93 Paul Pickering, 'Edward Thompson: Does Class Happen?' (unpublished paper,

British Society for the Study of Labour History, Conference to Commemorate to 50th Anniversary of the publication of the *Making of the English Working Class*, Halifax, November 2013).

94 Geertz, 'Thick Description', p. 17.

95 Christopher Small, *Musicking: The Meanings of Performing and Listening* (Middletown, CT: Wesleyan University Press, 1998), p. 13.

96 A personal conversation between Greg Dening and Paul Pickering.

97 See Ross Terrill, *R. H. Tawney and His Times* (Cambridge, MA: Harvard University Press, 1973), p. 7.

98 Fiona Paisley and Kirsty Reid (eds), 'Introduction', in *Critical Perspectives on Colonialism: Writing the Empire from Below* (New York: Routledge, 2014), p. 6. ProQuest Ebook Central (accessed 8 September 2016).

CHAPTER ONE

Songs of the world

When Fabian socialist and pioneering social scientist Beatrice Webb described her research into the history of the Co-operative Movement, she used the metaphor of securing a 'bunch of keys'. Going on to elaborate what in essence was her methodology, Webb identified the individual components of the bunch as 'key events, key societies, key technical terms and key personalities'.[1] Drawing from Webb's metaphor, which implies an approach very similar to our own, this chapter will take for its key the song. More exactly, as noted in our introduction, we have selected three songs from a vast array of possibilities to examine in close detail: Rouget de Lisle's war hymn the *Marseillaise*, Robert Burns's Scots ballad *John Anderson my Jo* and Chartist leader Ernest Jones's labour song *Song of the 'Lower Classes'*. In certain ways they can be understood as representative of different song types, with very different relationships between words and music, orality and notation.

The *Marseillaise* was written literally overnight at a crucial moment in the French revolutionary wars. Although it began its life as a fully notated, patriotic war song, it was soon to become unambiguously synonymous with liberty and, for a century at least, was taken up by almost every imaginable freedom cause. The music of this ubiquitous radical anthem remained unchanged and, notwithstanding its many adaptations, so did the sentiments of the original text. Indeed, its place in popular culture was effectively sealed. As such, the *Marseillaise* was – both in print and performance – the perfect example of a song serving as a form of ideological shorthand. For some the stirring melody evoked revolution and freedom, while for others it portended danger. No one was in any doubt what it meant. Of course, our interest is in its history beyond the borders of France, both its place in radical Anglophone culture and its presence in the mainstream press where it was a metonym for revolution. This requires no apology. As we shall see, for much of the long nineteenth century the *Marseillaise* was not simply or even primarily a French song; it was a song of the world. Burns's *John Anderson my Jo*, with its many pre-existing variant forms, is an archetypal example of what Matthew Gelbart has identified as the 'emerging category of folk music' of the late eighteenth century.[2] A sentimental favourite, it was both part of a long-standing oral tradition and a popular inclusion in the late eighteenth-century ballad collections in notated form. It became a staple not only of Burns commemorations but also of celebrity singers and thereby found a place in the nineteenth-century Victorian parlour song repertoire. Ostensibly, the choice of this humble ballad over Burns's more overtly political songs such as *Scots Wha Hae* and *A Man's a Man for a' That*, both of which figured prominently in radical song culture (and are noted many times throughout our book), may seem odd. However, numerous political parodies of the ballad appeared throughout the long nineteenth century. This process was both a common and complex one, and as such *John Anderson my Jo* serves as an example that allows us to examine it. Jones's labour song, *Song of the 'Lower Classes'*, never attained the anthem status of, for example, *The Red Flag*. It nonetheless found a deep-rooted place in working-class political culture, appearing across the world in predominantly labour publications. Written in the mid-nineteenth century – a key period of transition for both radical political and musical culture – the song assumed a central role in a lecture series given by Jones in London in 1856. Both the series and song were shaped by questions of class and respectability. We will argue that these questions had a direct effect on the different forms that the song assumed, which can be understood as an important attempt to bridge oral and print traditions. This chapter explores the genesis, history and travels of these three songs, charting their movements across the radical Anglophone world and considering their functions and meanings in different local settings.

The origin of the *Marseillaise* is well known. One evening in April 1792 after a lively dinner involving much champagne, French army captain and amateur poet and musician Claude-Joseph Rouget de Lisle accepted a challenge from his host, the Mayor of Strasbourg, to compose an inspirational song. By the next morning he had produced *Chant de guerre de l'armée du Rhin*. With the music and words both penned by a single author the song is unusually formal in that, unlike the other two case studies, it exists as a 'single definitive version that was fixed in print'.[3] For all that de Lisle was reputed to be a royalist – he later barely escaped the guillotine during the Terror – his war song was designed to protect the gains of the revolution (then still a constitutional monarchy) by carrying the French to victory against their Austrian enemies. Moreover, de Lisle's words and music were sufficiently general that they could be taken up by republicans, most notably by the *fédérés* of Marseilles. As described vividly in Lamartine's *History of the Girondists*, it was the *fédérés'* awe-inspiring renditions as they marched into Paris and on to the Tuileries on 10 August 1792, signalling the end of the monarchy, which transformed it into the hymn not only of the French revolution but the French republic.[4] Napoleon established it as the national anthem in 1795 only to ban it a decade later during the Empire; the proscription was continued by Louis XVIII during the Second Restoration. Rehabilitated in 1830, it was later banned by Napoleon III and so it remained until 1879 when it was once more declared the French national anthem.

The Scottish ballad *John Anderson my Jo* is a far cry from the bellicose French march. Burns's song, the best known of the extant versions, is a testament to enduring love. It has also played its part in shaping Scottish cultural identity.[5] It was published in 1790, two years before the *Marseillaise*, as one of Burns's more than 200 contributions to James Johnson's substantial collection, the *Scots Musical Museum* (1787–1803). Taking his place alongside notable figures such as Thomas Percy and Joseph Ritson, Johnson was an important figure in the rise of literary antiquarianism and what has been called the 'eighteenth-century British ballad revival'.[6] Multiple versions and variants of *John Anderson my Jo* in both textual and musical forms are found in ballad collections from this period. Burns's version as it appears in Johnson's collection is as follows:

> John Anderson my Jo, John,
> When we were first acquent,
> Your locks were like the raven,
> Your bony brow was brent;
> But now your brow is belt, John,
> Your locks are like the snaw,
> But blessings on your frosty pow,
> John Anderson my Jo.
>
> John Anderson my Jo, John,
> We clamb the hill thegither,
> And mony a canty day, John,
> We've had wi ane anither;
> Now we maun totter down, John,
> But hand in hand we'll go,
> And sleep thegither at the foot,
> John Anderson my Jo.[7]

Like many of Burns's poems, it is a polite adaption of a far older and bawdier text, the second stanza of which is given below. Only the first line is common to both versions.

John Anderson my Jo, John,
When first that ye began,
Ye had as good a tail-tree,
As ony ither man; but now it's waxen wan, John,
And wrinkles to and fro;
I've twa gae-ups for ae gae-down,
John Anderson my Jo.[8]

John Anderson my Jo is at once a tune and a poem. The origins of the gentle, lilting tune are, as is usual with oral tradition, equally unclear as the text. It appeared, for example, with this title as early as 1630 in the *Skene MS*; in 1731 it accompanied the Scottish poet Allan Ramsay's words in John Watt's *Musical Miscellany* and was used twice in Ramsay's own *Tea-Table Miscellany*; it was printed again in James Oswald's *Caledonian Pocket Companion* of 1752, and in James Aird's *Selection of Scotch, English, Irish and Foreign Airs* in 1782.[9] Scholars from the nineteenth century on, however, have noted its similarity to other tunes, in particular two English melodies, *Paul's Steeple* and *I am the Duke of Norfolk*.[10] One recent commentator has identified it as a Scottish fiddle song, surmising correctly that it 'probably derived from a bawdy song'.[11] The multiple variants of both tune and text that are all *John Anderson my Jo* in the oral tradition exemplify the complexities of popular song provenance and remind us of Foucault's insight into the fruitful but ultimately doomed pursuit of origins in his work on history and genealogy.[12]

Song of the 'Lower Classes' was written between 1848 and 1850 while Jones was in Newgate Prison, serving a sentence for conspiracy and sedition. Trained as a lawyer, Jones was the last leader of Britain's first nationwide working-class movement, Chartism. On one level, the Chartist agenda appears innocuous to modern eyes; an unexceptional programme of democratic reform. But Jones was what was known as 'a Chartist and something more' – a man prepared to contemplate the use of political power, once gained, to change the world. In the late 1840s and early 1850s the mention of his name would have been sufficient to send a frisson of alarm through polite society and there was a collective sigh of relief when he was imprisoned in 1848. He also enjoyed a reputation as a minor poet, and succeeded another notorious Chartist leader, Thomas Cooper, as the poet laureate of Chartism. For Jones, his poetry was inseparable from his politics. He had first come to the attention of the radical public in the mid-1840s for verse suffused with political commentary. Following his release in 1850 he often recounted the story of how he had kept up the stream of ideological invective in iambic pentameter from his cell on pages torn from a prayer book with a nib dipped in his own blood.[13]

Although *Song of the 'Lower Classes'* was to come to wider public
notice during Jones's 'Evenings with the People', a set of six political
soirees held in 1856, it had already appeared as *Song of the Low* in
the poetry column of Jones's *Notes to the People* in April 1852 and
three months later in his *People's Paper* under the grand heading of
'Truth Set to Music'. While the poem was preceded by the subtitle
'Democratic Songs to Popular Airs', no tune was given. Early the following year it appeared on the programme for the *People's Paper* soiree
held at the Eclectic Institute in Denmark Street, Soho, London.[14] In
1856 at St Martin's Hall it assumed a more significant place in radical
song culture. On this occasion it was set to original music by Jones's
coadjutor, the composer John Lowry. Jones's lyrics clearly set up the
division between the non-productive and productive classes and the
use of quotation marks around 'Lower Classes' in the title suggests a
clear ironic inversion:

> We're low – we're low – we're very very low,
> As low as low can be;
> The rich are high – for we make them so –
> And a miserable lot are we!
> And a miserable lot are we! are we!
> A miserable lot are we!
>
> We plough and sow – we're so very very low,
> That we delve in the dirty clay,
> Till we bless the plain with the golden grain,
> And the vale with the fragrant hay.
> Our place we know – we're so very low,
> 'Tis down at the landlords' feet:
> We're not too low – the bread to grow,
> But too low the bread to eat.
>
> Down, down we go – we're so very very low,
> To the hell of the deep sunk mines.
> But we gather the proudest gems that glow,
> When the crown of a despot shines;
> And whenever he lacks – upon our backs
> Fresh loads he deigns to lay,
> We're far too low to vote the tax.
> But not too low to pay.
>
> We're low, we're low – mere rabble, we know,
> But at our plastic power,
> The mould at the lordling's feet will grow
> Into palace and church and tower –
> Then prostrate fall – in the rich man's hall,
> And cringe at the rich man's door,

We're not too low to build the wall,
But too low to tread the floor.

We're low, we're low – we're very very low,
Yet from our fingers glide
The silken flow – and the robes that glow,
Round the limbs of the sons of pride.
And what we get – and what we give,
We know – and we know our share.
We're not too low the cloth to weave –
But too low the cloth to wear.

We're low, we're low – we're very very low,
And yet when the trumpets ring,
The thrust of a poor man's arm will go
Through the heart of the proudest king!
We're low, we're low – our place we know,
We're only the rank and file,
We're not too low – to kill the foe,
But too low to touch the spoil.[15]

Notwithstanding Jones's melodramatic flourish about the circumstances of its composition – bloody nibs, etc. – the song was actually
an appropriation of sorts. As F. B. Smith has noted, the key line of *Song
of the 'Lower Classes'* was clearly inspired by Pierre-Jean de Béranger's
Le Vilain:

Je suis vilain, et trés-vilain,
Je suis vilain,
vilain, vilain.[16]

Le Vilain had been first published in English in 1837 but a translation
by Chartist W. J. Linton appeared in the *Northern Star* in July 1851 (as
well as in his own journal, *The English Republic*) with the title 'The
Low Born'. Linton's translation read:

I am low-born, and very low, –
I'm very low
Low, Low.

Jones, however, had turned Béranger's self-obsession about proving his
humble roots – 'I'm very low' – into an inclusive 'We're low'. Indeed,
the poem's engagement with different kinds of labour – farming,
mining, weaving, building and military service – contributed to a
larger ongoing discourse around the notion of 'the People'. Set in the
inclusive first-person plural, the song speaks as the collective labouring class and centres on the contest over the control of the means of
production.[17] As we will see, this is unsurprising.

[37]

The different functions of these three songs in radical culture were produced in part by the different balance between words and music. Jones's song could be set to a range of pre-existing popular tunes in addition to Lowry's original music; it is, therefore, not defined by its melody but by its text. Its flexibility lay in the fact that musically it was never a fixed and stable work. For *John Anderson my Jo*, however, the opposite is true; its use lay in the attractiveness of its melody and the character and semantic function of its opening two lines which rendered it an obvious candidate for parody. As noted, the existence of a single authoritative version, both in musical and textual terms, distinguishes the *Marseillaise* from most popular songs and from the other two case studies. However, such definition resulted in a diminished capacity for flexibility and nuance. It, and its many appropriations, could not escape its potent symbolic meaning. The 'politics of binary opposition', to borrow Laura Mason's words, expressed in the original lyrics made it a prime candidate for dissent, contest and provocation.[18] In political circles, it functioned as part of ritual and ceremony. It served as a call to arms – it could gather crowds, break up meetings, show allegiance and perpetuate protest. *John Anderson my Jo* was more malleable. Its association with radicalism did not define it; its value lay more in that it was very much part of popular song culture. *Song of the 'Lower Classes'* is different again, and stands as one of many songs written specifically for the labour movement that helped to construct and sustain a distinct radical working-class identity.

The nineteenth century saw the continued and rapid proliferation of print culture. Nonetheless, the relationship between printed forms of song and the oral tradition remained dynamic. As Maureen McLane reminds us, books of ballads are 'print objects that ceaselessly point beyond print and to other modes of communication – singing, reciting, speaking, saying, writing'.[19] Of course, it is not only ballad books that did this: newspapers, journals, pamphlets and other ephemeral printed formats both disseminated and mediated oral song culture. Evoking music in print had its place, but it was a static and silent form of communication. Music realises its full affective potential in performance; it is a somatic experience wherein meaning is made or altered by vocal tone and physical gesture. Singing was a highly efficient form of communication and it quickly became a central component of radicalism's rituals and commemoration. But performance and print worked powerfully together; as Carla Hesse has explained, the 'mixing of media – image, words, and music – could extend the reach of revolutionary print media further still, even to the illiterate and to the young'.[20]

Setting new words to pre-existing tunes was nothing new: it had long been axiomatic in popular song culture and continued throughout the nineteenth century and beyond. As noted, the *Marseillaise* and *John Anderson my Jo* provide quite different examples of how appropriation and parody have functioned. A central theme of Mason's study of popular song and the French Revolution is the genre's 'highly improvisational' quality and its rich potential for 'reshaping', often to mock or distort the original meaning in different performance contexts or to give local relevance.[21] As we will show many times in the pages to follow, appropriations served a range of functions: not only did they pay homage to the original and seek to enlist its meaning for their own agenda, they could also take the form of parody (in the generally understood sense of that term), ridicule, satire or attack. Parody is thus a practice that lies within the broader category of appropriation. It provided a critical distance, allowing questioning and dissent, which in turn created a space for ironic inversion. New texts born of local contexts interacted with a song's older meanings. The new text's relationship to the original was varied and often complex, and the new meanings were reliant on a shared knowledge of the original text and melody. Intertextuality was then at the centre of this fluid cultural practice, and was often signalled by the use of music.

In his well-known eponymous newspaper, Douglas Jerrold described ballads as 'narrow strips of history'.[22] For us, however, this metaphor does not go far enough: it neither takes into account the vast terrain nor the considerable chronological periods they traversed. These songs act as threads with which to weave together histories and historical processes that would otherwise remain discrete. The songs themselves are at once agents and vessels of history, both shaping it and containing it. Our case studies open up multiple lines of inquiry into the role of song and singing practices in the spread of radical and reformist political culture across the British world.

First key: the Marseillaise

> It was the song of the world, the Marseillaise, the song that rises in every land when the oppressed rise against the oppressor, the song that breathes of wrongs to be revenged and of liberty to be won, of flying foes in front and a free people marching, and of blood shed like water for the idea that makes all nations kin.
>
> William Lane, *The Workingman's Paradise* (1892)

It would be difficult to find anyone more enthralled by the affective power of the iconic French revolutionary hymn than Australian socialist William Lane. Born in Bristol, Lane arrived in Queensland via Canada and the United States. He is perhaps best known as the

[39]

architect of the ill-fated New Australia Colony, a utopian settlement scheme in Paraguay, but he was also a journalist of some repute – he was founding editor of the Brisbane-based weekly socialist newspaper, the *Worker* – and a would-be novelist.[23] His passionate account of the qualities of the *Marseillaise* appeared in his novel *The Workingman's Paradise*, published in 1892. Referring to a rendition of the *Marseillaise* on the piano, he employed prose stuck somewhere between gushing and the baroque: 'The hand of a master struck the keys and brought the notes out, clear and rhythmic, full strong notes that made the blood boil and the senses swim,' he wrote. 'A volume of sound rose, of clashing notes in fierce, swinging movement, a thrilling clamour of soul-stirring melody, at once short and sharp and long-drawn, at once soft as a mother's lullaby and savage as a hungry tiger's roar.' As the novel's protagonist, Ned, overcome by the injustice of his society succumbs to a 'mist of unquenchable tears', he demands to know why 'this mighty music' was not 'borne wherever a man was to be found who had a wrong to right and a long account to square?':

> Ah! How they would all leap at it! How they would swell its victorious chanting and gather in their thousands and their hundreds of thousands to march on, march on, tramping time to its majestic notes![24]

Lane's rhapsodic flourish allows us to make several interconnected points germane to the discussion to follow. First, although it is instantly recognisable today as the French national anthem, it is clear that for much of the long nineteenth century the *Marseillaise* was not a French song. By 1845 the principal Chartist newspaper, the *Northern Star*, was already pointing to its 'world-wide fame'.[25] Indeed, it would come to be embraced by advocates of almost every imaginable cause – political, nationalist, social and humanitarian – who identified their cause with freedom. It is not difficult to find copies of the *Workers' Marseillaise*, the *Labor Marseillaise*, the *Temperance Marseillaise*, the *Women's Marseillaise*, the *English Marseillaise*, the *Scotch Marseillaise* and the *British Marseillaise*. Both sides of America's fratricidal conflict had their own version. Beyond the limits of the Anglophone world, there was an *Italian Marseillaise*, a *German Marseillaise*, a *Greek Marseillaise*, a *Polish Marseillaise*, an *Indian Marseillaise*, a *Chinese Marseillaise* and even the *World's Marseillaise*. In this sense, the French had undoubtedly lost control over their song.

At the same time, the *Marseillaise* never lost its fundamental connection with the idea of liberty. Indeed, understood simultaneously as a patriotic hymn, in the sense of being a secular song of praise, and a bellicose song denoting the struggle for freedom, its meaning was not malleable and thus the overwhelming majority of its appropriations drew upon a shared understanding of the ideals of the French Revolution as expressed in the sound of its unmistakable tune. It was the performance of the melody – its sound – that provided the unshakable link to the core idea of liberty. Parodies were few and far between. Moreover, despite (or because of) its ban in France for most of the nineteenth century, the song played an important and highly visible role in the French struggles of 1830, 1848 and 1871.[26] This, in turn, further contributed to the stability of its core meaning. In addition, notwithstanding George Bernard Shaw's characteristic irreverence – the 'incurable vulgarity of that air is a disgrace to the red flag', he opined in 1889[27] – the *Marseillaise* is both an infectious and inspiriting melody. It's still moving to sing as part of a crowd. As part of a repertoire of political action, it was an affective and effective choice of melody and, unsurprisingly, it features consistently in accounts of demotic politics. This continued replication again served to reinforce the original meaning and associations. Perhaps the French never lost control of it after all.

As we have noted, almost before the ink was dry on de Lisle's parchment he lost control of his composition to the Marseille *fédérés*; within a year British radicals and supporters of the French Revolution had reached across the Channel and enthusiastically appropriated it for their own ends. The ideas of the French Revolution were profoundly influential on the development of British radicalism and reform and, unsurprisingly therefore, the *Marseillaise* was foremost among a clutch of French revolutionary songs pressed into service by late eighteenth-century British radicals. It is difficult to underestimate the extent to which it caught on: it soon could be heard on the streets as a broadside ballad, at political meetings both indoor and outdoor, and during marches and protests; it was advertised as sheet music and sung at all kinds of concerts reported insouciantly in the columns of the press. By 1850 even a 'miserable Italian organ grinder' had the audacity to strike up the *Marseillaise* under Thomas Carlyle's window. [28]

For the authorities and many commentators in the mainstream press the *Marseillaise* was not a patriotic paean to freedom but rather the 'hymn of terror'.[29] The British government were aware of the tremendous fillip it had given to the cause of reform and sought to proscribe its use. They regarded the song as a powerful semiotic device; the title alone served as a metonym to communicate danger, insurgency, even treason. The potential to incite rebellion and revolution was something to be feared; at least this is how it was most often characterised in mainstream reportage of both the revolutionary upheavals in France and political tensions closer to home. A committee of the House of Commons, John Barrell tells us, took special note of a 'studied selection of the tunes which have been most in use in France since the revolution' among the various forms of radical propaganda that they uncovered during their raids of 1794 (raids that resulted in the well-known treason trials later in that year).[30] By 1817, when three men were being tried for their involvement in the Pentrich Rising in Derbyshire, the *Marseillaise* had been accepted as a touchstone in popular parlance. On learning that one of the accused had composed revolutionary poetry, the Attorney General pronounced that if 'those lines were set to music they were likely to do as much mischief in this country, as Ça Ira and the Marsellois hymn had done in France'.[31] The Attorney General was clearly less concerned about the poems than their potential transformation into song: it was the rendering of text as singable that made it far more formidable. Even as late as the final decade of the nineteenth century, journalist, organist and composer J. Cuthbert Hadden was still alerting his readers to the 'element of danger' in the *Marseillaise*.[32] It was, he noted in dramatic terms, 'kept in constant thraldom'. To buttress his point Hadden invoked the characterisation given by music educator and political radical Joseph Mainzer. Writing in 1848, Mainzer had declared that the song was 'always feared, always watched, like a lion ready to break forth from its den and spread a second time desolation and carnage over half the nations of Europe'.[33]

Reports such as this appeared not only in Britain but also in the vast body of print which circulated around the British Empire. It is important to remember that print culture was in no way geographically bounded at this time: no sooner were printing presses in the colonies of settlement operating than a proliferation of newspapers were publishing extensive extracts from the British press. In this way, from the late eighteenth century onwards, accounts of the singing of the *Marseillaise* on both sides of the English Channel were soon echoing throughout the Anglophone world. For example, marine officer Watkin Tench (one of the company of the First Fleet sent to colonise New South Wales) recalled in a collection of letters published in 1796 how French officers and men had 'with united voice sang the *Marseilles Hymn*, with a fervour and enthusiasm which astonished me'.[34]

Given we have stressed the relationship between music and music-making, it is not surprising that in a flagrantly confrontational challenge to their Francophobic government, radicals and reformers adopted the National Assembly's ritual of closing their meetings with a mass rendition of the song. In other words, not only were the ideas of their French confrères hugely influential, so too were the ways they shaped the performance of politics. As well as the *Marseillaise*, *Ça ira* and *La Carmagnole* were taken up with enthusiasm by those active within a rapidly emerging culture of extra-parliamentary associational life. The role of revolutionary songs in this process has not escaped the notice of scholars of the period.[35] According to Iain McCalman, for example, songs became useful weapons in the armoury of what he called the 'British Jacobin cultural resistance'.[36] It is important to remember, however, that this group of French political songs took their place within an extant native popular song culture present from at least the sixteenth century.[37] For example, the charismatic radical leader Thomas Spence, who was found guilty of sedition in 1794, whiled away the hours in his cell producing satirical songs and verse that subsequently appeared in his journal, *Pigs' Meat, or Lessons for the Swinish Multitude,* as well as being published in separate collections.[38] Spence's lyrics were also referenced in a taxonomical song book, *A Humorous Catalogue of Spence's Songs,* compiled by Thomas Evans, a fellow Spencean. The songs became staples in the ritual performance of politics. According to Evans, to take one example, they were sung at the 'Free and Easy Meetings' at The Fleece every Tuesday evening throughout 1807. Subsequently, they played an important role at meetings of the Society of Spencean Philanthropists, formed after his death in 1814.[39]

What is perhaps the first British publication of the *Marseillaise* appeared on 10 November 1792, a mere six months after its composition.[40] The radical publicist and pamphleteer William Holland and his young engraver Richard Newton, both well known in the fast-emerging counter-public sphere (famously characterised by McCalman as the 'radical underworld') produced the *Marche des Marseillois,* replete with musical notation and the complete six stanzas of verse in French (see figure 1.1).[41] Unsurprisingly, it was Spence, in his *Pigs' Meat,* who published the first English translation of the *Marseillaise* in 1793.

Initially, opponents of the revolution used song in the battle for control of the public imagination, but in this case their purpose was not inspiration but abuse. Indeed, Francophobia found full voice in a series of *Anti-Gallican Songsters,* beginning in February 1792, two months before the *Marseillaise* was published. Thomas Paine, author of the iconic treatise *The Rights of Man,* was singled out for a dose of splenetic wit. Notably, these barbs were set to determinedly English patriotic airs such as *Derry Down, Hearts of Oak, O, the Golden Days of Good Queen Bess* and, of course, *Rule, Britannia.*[42] In *A Word or Two of Truth,* which was addressed to 'all Loving Englishmen', Paine was described as a 'vip'rous' foe in league with the French:

> He talks of our rights, of our freedom, and good
> But his aims be assur'd are in this understood,

1.1 *Marche de Marseillois, chantée sur diferans theatres,* possibly the first version to be published in London by William Holland and engraved by Richard Newton, 10 November 1792.

For he only would set us together a wrangling,
That his friends o'er the water may seize us while jangling.[43]

A New Song, sung to *O, the Golden Days of Good Queen Bess*, attacked radicals suspected of encouraging an invasion by the French. Iconic national symbols were invoked to increase alarm at the prospect:

What a dinner they'd provide for their friends the mounsieurs,
Good beef, and good pudding, with plenty of strong beer
How they'd sing *Ça ira* as they march'd up to London
With the thoughts of good cheer, and the hopes of good plund'ring.[44]

The dire warnings against those who would force Britons to become French citizens again invoked Paine: 'Or we'll cut all your throats to enforce the Rights of Man'. Ironically, Spence produced his own homage to Paine entitled *The Rights of Man*, set not to a seditious French melody but to that most English of tunes, *Chevy Chase*.[45] In fact, it is notable that, with the exception of *Ça ira*, opponents of the revolution and Spence drew upon an identical corpus of songs for their tunes.[46]

In one of the rare instances where the *Marseillaise* was parodied, its meaning was inverted firstly by reference to British patriotism. A slip ballad, entitled *The Genius of Britain*, opened with the lines:

Ye British Sons awake to glory
Hark! Hark! What myriads round you rise?

Significantly, however, this was not published until 1803 – at the height of the Terror – and its target was not primarily the *san culottes* or the members of the Jacobin club, but the enemy of liberty personified:

Shall BONAPARTE mischief breeding
With hirelings hosts a ruffian band
Affright and desolate our land
Our peace and liberty lie bleeding,
By a Savage Tyrant's hand?[47]

By this time, the *Marseillaise* was continuing to strengthen its hold over the British radical imagination: from those described by the idiosyncratic Tory-radical scribe William Cobbett as the 'rabble', to moderate radicals such as Sir Francis Burdett. Following the success of his election as MP for Middlesex in 1802, Burdett's victorious supporters celebrated their triumph at London's Crown and Anchor where the band of music played patriotic airs such as *God Save the King* and *Rule, Britannia*, as well as *Ça ira* and the *Marseillois Hymn*.[48] As we shall see, this broad-spectrum appeal was a pattern evident among future generations agitating for political reform.

Among British politicians and commentators the July Revolution of 1830 in France was celebrated or abhorred with equal passion. For the Whiggish *Morning Post* it epitomised the worst of human nature: 'The tri-coloured flag and cockade, the emblem of everything that was atrocious and sanguinary in the worst areas of the Republic, have been restored.' The *Marsellois Hymn* was denounced as 'murderous' as it provided accompaniment for the 'savage rabble' that 'marched to scenes of unexampled slaughter'.[49] Less conservative commentators were jubilant. The London *Standard*, for example, reported on a dinner held at Freemason's Tavern that celebrated the 'triumph of liberty in France'. It closely echoed festivities held almost three decades earlier. None other than Francis Burdett took the chair and around 300 'respectably dressed individuals' filled the hall, 'many of whom wore tri-coloured cockades and rosettes'.[50] Similar enthusiasm was evident in the provincial press. The *Bury and Norwich Post*, for example, included a letter from an English expatriate living in Paris who fondly remembered the triumph of the blue and white cockade over forty years before, and declared that France 'will be a better country than ever to live in'.[51] Not surprisingly, there were references to the *Marseillaise* in both reports. The *Hull Packet and Humber Mercury* reported on celebrations as far afield as New York, where the *Marseillaise*'s chorus was sung 'with one voice, and in the full fervour of exultation'.[52] Accounts of the use of the *Marseillaise* peppered reports of the ferment occurring in Germany and Poland after 1830.[53] As the political landscape shifted, so did the role of the song. Whereas Louis Philippe was initially toasted and celebrated with performances of the *Marseillaise*, such as by the almost 4,000 people who attended a dinner of the Birmingham Political Union, the song was later used to condemn his treachery.[54]

The events in Paris in February 1848 were followed with great interest by the British press; the radical response was immediate and dynamic. Delegations rushed to Paris. One was headed by Mazzini and prominent radical-republican W. J. Linton, and another was led by Ernest Jones and the leader of the Fraternal Democrats, the self-styled *L'ami du peuple*, George Julian Harney. The fact that there were two sets of emissaries who failed to acknowledge each other tells us something about the fissiparous nature of London radicalism as opposed to anything about significant ideological fissures. Indeed, the fact that the *Marseillaise* features in their separate accounts suggests otherwise. Linton remembered witnessing from the balcony of the Café du Grand Balcon the 'strange and strangely impressive' funeral procession 'for those who had fallen in the Three Days'. Representatives from the Provisional Government attended on foot 'as chief mourners' and among 'every regimental or other band taking part, one [played] the "Marseillaise" and the next the song of the unlucky Girondins, – "Mourir pour la patrie"'.[55]

Jones, Harney and Philip McGrath (a lieutenant of the pre-eminent Chartist leader Feargus O'Connor) met with the Provisional Government at the Hotel de Ville the day after Mazzini and Linton had paid their respects.[56] Addressing the members of the Executive Committee – Garnier-Pagès, Ledru-Rollin and Marrast – in fluent French, Jones described his small group as 'a deputation of the oppressed to the free', who had come 'in the name of England and the world'.[57] At a large meeting the same evening, the *Northern Star* reported, the *Marseillaise* 'was sung with a thrilling effect, and the assembled thousands greeted the appearance of the Chartist guest with rapturous cheering'.[58] It is important to note that the *Marseillaise* captured not only the fervid mood of the meeting but it also served as a highly effective precis of the ostensibly awkward binary between the national and the international contained in Jones's remarks.

The aftermath of the 1848 February Revolution continued to hold the attention of the radical press, as seen by the constant reports to unfolding events and their reception in publications, which made much of the use of the use of *Marseillaise* and *Mourir pour le Patrie*.[59] These songs were often joined by other local musical tributes. *The Men of 'Forty-Eight'*, penned by Chartist poet and freethinker Gerald Massey, was one such song, but other offerings were made, such as *The Hopes of '48*, an anonymous ode published in the *People's Paper* in 1854.[60] The enduring place that the failed revolutions of 1848 had in radical consciousness was such that well into the twentieth century socialists were still celebrating it and the persistence of *The Men of 'Forty-Eight'* exemplifies this. Like the *Marseillaise*, the song travelled great distances as well as over time, appearing, for example, in the New Zealand Socialist Party's songbook in 1908 and *Socialist Songs* published in Melbourne the previous year.[61]

The decision to once again take to the barricades in Paris in 1871 marked another moment of inspiration for British radicals but also an opportunity for conservative commentators to attack socialists and reformers with the *Marseillaise* as a point of entry. The *Derby Mercury*, for example, denigrated the Communards in no uncertain terms, using the *Marseillaise* as a symbol for communism, bemoaning the appearance of republican clubs and declaring the members of the International Democratic League to be of 'contemptible character' – 'the lowest of the low'.[62] The French revolutionaries' subsequent defeat saw another wave of political refugees seek safe haven in London and the Commune became, as Anne Janowitz has noted, 'an image that was claimed almost exclusively by the Socialist movement in the 1880s and 1890s'.[63] As the 'Commune anthem', the *Marseillaise* was played at almost every key socialist event, convivial and strategic alike. For example, William Morris's Socialist League continued the practice of closing meetings and events with it long after it had once again become France's national anthem.[64] Morris's comrade David Nicolls produced *A New Marseillaise* that was first published in *Commonweal* and quickly became a staple of socialist songbooks across the world.[65]

As noted, during the nineteenth century Britain became a refuge for political exiles from continental Europe: at one point London was known as Little Germany. But this description is misleading: the political haunts of the imperial metropolis were quintessentially cosmopolitan.[66] Flashpoints – such as the failed uprisings of 1830, 1848 and 1871 – gave rise to new waves of refugees. The *Marseillaise* assumed a special kind of significance in this hotbed of international radicalism, which traversed a range of languages and cultures, by providing a symbol of shared recognition of similarity within diversity. Indeed, the performance of songs characterised the emerging internationalism and attendant cosmopolitanism in Britain from the 1840s onwards. It helped the British see themselves as part of a broader international movement, of which London for a period was perhaps the most important centre. For example, the leading lights of the so-called 'Young Europe' were 'not unfairly represented' at the French Democratic Society's commemoration of Bastille Day in 1846. In attendance were English (Jones and Harney), Scottish, Irish, French, German, Swiss, Spanish, Polish and Italian democrats (including Mazzini), not to mention representatives from Hungary and Turkey. Joseph Moll sang the *Marseillaise* 'with great effect, and excited thunders of applause'. Later in the evening a Turkish democrat sang 'several patriotic songs in different languages' and a number of Italian patriots sang their national hymn in answer to the *Marseillaise*.[67] This was typical of just one of a growing number of events in honour of the Europeans. The Chartist John James Bezer gave a series of lectures following his release from Newgate Prison in 1850, at the commencement of which, so the advertisement claimed, 'a talented Company' would sing the *Marseillaise* in English, German and Polish.[68] This European cosmopolitanism through polyglot performance was taken even further when the Fraternal Democrats, again in 1850, met to develop a 'correct response' to the barbarities of the Austrian General Haynau, or in their parlance 'Hyena', during which a Hungarian sang the 'Italian *Marseillaise*, followed by the French *Marseillaise* sung by a Polish refugee in which the entire meeting joined in the chorus in English'. How it sounded was not reported.[69]

Performances of the *Marseillaise* in these multifarious forms were overt demonstrations of solidarity with the refugees. They were sometimes joined with more practical avenues of support; for example, O'Connor gave a lecture for the benefit of Polish and Hungarian refugees. Again solidarity was shown through music-making: 'the songs of their country' were sung but only after the '*Marseillaise* Hymn'.[70] The mélange of language and culture on show at these events reveals a supra-national and supra-cultural outlook that coalesced around a consistent theme of liberty. At another level it simultaneously provided separate nationalist struggles a sense of unity and in so doing revealed a significant paradox: as a national patriotic song the *Marseillaise* catered for a broad internationalism. It is important, however, not to over-emphasise this apparent contradiction. After all, for much of the nineteenth century, liberty and nationalism were causes of the Left.

A key function of the *Marseillaise* was the part it played in celebrating and commemorating an array of local events. Given the theme of liberty, it was often heard at the release of radicals from prison. Throughout the long nineteenth century across the Anglophone world – from the celebration of the release of Henry Hunt, the hero of Peterloo, in 1819 in London and Thomas Wooler, editor of the *Black Dwarf*, in Birmingham in 1822, to trade union leaders in Brisbane in 1893 and waterside workers in Wellington in 1913 – these events followed a familiar template.[71] The song also featured in the commemoration and celebration of rites of passage, including the birthdays of Paine, Cobbett, Robert Owen, Daniel O'Connell and 'the hero of two worlds', Giuseppe Garibaldi.[72] The Fraternal Democrats, led by Harney, radical poet John Arnot and a 'select company of ultra-democrats', evinced a surprising extremism even for them when in 1849 they chose to celebrate the birthday of Robespierre; a provocative choice beyond the pale for many more moderate radicals.[73] From 1792 onwards there were attempts to fuse the song with events in Britain's past. Indeed, a week before it was first published in English it was sung with great enthusiasm by the influential radical association the London Revolution Society at a celebration of the Glorious Revolution of 1688.[74] The French foreign minister had supplied copies of the song. Half a century later, to take another example, the London-based journal the *English Republic* printed a contrafactum entitled *Cromwell's Sword* set to the *Marseillaise*:

> Awake, thou Sword of England's glory!
> The day of strife dawns on thy grave:
> Gleam again as in our old story!
> Let thy flash light the brow of the slave![75]

Writing in 1906 one commentator in Brisbane's *Worker* predicted that, 'Some day the historian will write the part of the Marseillaise has played in the progress of civilization.'[76] Long before this, however, the prominent place of the song in demotic politics had led to several attempts to explore its provenance, notably among radicals and reformers. *Cobbett's Magazine* had published one as early as 1833.[77] Before the smell of cordite had dissipated in 1848, J. D. Collett produced the *History of the Marseillais, and the origin of the Marseillaise Hymn from Lamartine's History of Girondists – Also, the Chaunt of the Girondins, with the music, and prose translations of the Hymns.*[78] In 1852 Gerald Massey contributed a lengthy tribute to Rouget de Lisle, replete with his own translation of the song, to Harney's newspaper, *Friend of the People*. Massey made clear his belief in the song's innate power: 'The sound of the *Marseillaise* is more dreaded in the camp of Tyranny, than a thousand parks of artillery, it makes the Tyrants tremble even in their triumphant car. It is the Soul of Revolution rendered to us Rhythmically.'[79] Another Chartist bard, John Bedford Leno, prefaced his *Reformer's Book of Songs and Recitations* from the mid-1860s with an intimate and detailed history of the song.[80] Late Victorian socialists also contributed to this form of commemoration. At least two detailed histories of the song appeared in 1887 in William Morris's *Commonweal*. In the same month a history was published in an ephemeral radical periodical, *Common Sense for People with Brains and Hearts.*[81] This practice endured well into the twentieth century, seeing a resurgence in the lead-up to the First World War. Queensland's *Worker*, for example, reprinted the song itself several times between 1892 and 1942. [82] The common theme running through the articles published over several decades was that – even after it had been well and truly restored as France's national anthem – the *Marseillaise* belonged not only to France but also to the international labour movement.

The epicentre of the heady internationalism of British radicalism from the late 1840s was, as noted, undoubtedly the metropolis, but we should not lose sight of the intense interest shown in the *Marseillaise* beyond its bounds geographically, politically and in popular culture. A glance at the columns of the press in the self-governing colonies, for example, makes clear the many functions the anthem fulfilled across the Anglophone world. Indeed, as we have seen, the story of the *Marseillaise* was from the outset an inter-colonial and transnational one. Newspapers in New Zealand, like their British counterparts, seized upon the song's popular appeal and included accounts of its use in such far-flung places as Spain and Russia while at the same time revealing the range of causes to which it was enlisted. In 1911, for example, the *Poverty Bay Herald*, published on the east coast of New Zealand's North Island, reported that the Czech violinist Jan Kubelik had been banned by the Russian authorities 'on the ground that the last time the famous musician appeared in Russia he played the "Marseillaise"'.[83] Six months earlier the same newspaper told of a violent street encounter between Carlists and Republicans in Barcelona: 'The trouble arose because a barrel-organ played "The Marseillaise" outside a Carlist club. Shots were exchanged, and one man was badly wounded.'[84] The electric telegraph drastically cut the time it took a story about Irish nationalist Willie Redmond's address at an 1895 convention to reach New Zealand's *Evening Post* from London. Redmond declared that 'if freedom were withheld from Ireland, in the event of war the Irish would march to the sound of the "Marseillaise", not of the British National Anthem.'[85] Of course, this was not the first (or last) time the *Marseillaise* had been recruited to the Irish cause. Allen Davenport's *Ireland in Chains* set to the tune of the 'Marseillaise Hymn' had appeared in the *Northern Star* in 1846, almost fifty years earlier.[86]

Reporting accounts of disruptive performances of the song provided good copy. The events surrounding the sensational trial of the suffragist Adela Pankhurst (discussed in a later chapter) were covered in detail in New Zealand where female suffrage had been achieved years earlier. Reports of rousing performances of the *Marseillaise* by women smashing windows at Holloway Prison were colourful to say the least.[87] As we shall see, when a large number of 'Mrs Pankhurst's women sympathisers ... marched from the court singing the suffragette war song to the tune of the *"Marseillaise"* in a demonstration of solidarity', they were, inter alia, making an important point about the relationship of radicalism and reform to the apparatus of the State.[88] The well-known Australian radical poet Henry Lawson was in Wellington when New Zealand women won the vote in 1893. He invoked the *Marseillaise* immediately in a congratulatory poem:

> In the morning of New Zealand we should sing a Marseillaise!
> We should sing a hymn of triumph, we should sing a song of praise!
> For our women are enobled! The narrow days are o'er.[89]

Again we see how the word 'Marseillaise' on the printed page functioned as a kind of synecdoche carrying enormous symbolic power, a power that was extensively exploited by print journalism.

In addition to providing excitement and colour to mainstream journalism and poetry, the song played an active role in the culture of New Zealand's labour movement. In various forms, either de Lisle's original version or as *A New Marseillaise* or *The Workers' Marseillaise*, it appeared in the song columns of the *Maoriland Worker* and leading

New Zealand socialist Robert Hogg's *Commonweal* alongside such socialist staples as Morris's *The March of the Workers* (set to *John Brown's Body*) and fellow socialist John Glasse's *Onwards Friends of Freedom* (to Arthur Sullivan's *Onward Christian Soldiers*). [90] Newspaper accounts of its performance during meetings reveal that it fulfilled the same ritual functions as it did in Europe.[91]

Across the Tasman, Australian radicals put the song to use from the mid-nineteenth century onwards. The strains of the *Marseillaise* rose and fell over the Victorian goldfields throughout the agitation leading up to the Eureka Stockade. The former Chartist George Black, a central figure in the agitation, helped raise emotions to fever pitch by perambulating around Ballarat in a cart brandishing a sword and singing the *Marseillaise*. On another occasion a band led two thousand 'diggers' – a term that itself had a distinct historical resonance – who raised their voices in song as they marched with another leader of the uprising, Thomas Kennedy.[92] A few years later in 1858, a procession demanding the eight-hour working day, again organised by ex-Chartists, wound its way to the Victorian Parliament accompanied by six bands playing the *Marseillaise*. The increasingly conservative *Argus* condemned this as 'gross' and 'un-British'.[93] During the same period Daniel Deniehy, a radical politician and publicist as well as a disciple of Australia's first republican, John Dunmore Lang, sang the *Marseillaise* along with *God Save the Queen* at a Saint Patrick's Day dinner in Sydney.[94]

As is well documented, there was a marked upsurge in Australian labour activism during the last decade of the nineteenth century. Lawson again drew upon the French song for his *The Australian Marseillaise*. Subtitled *Or, A Song for the Sydney Poor*, his political sympathies were immediately evident:

> Sing the strong, proud song of Labour,
> Toss the ringing music high;
> Liberty's a nearer neighbour
> Than she was in day's gone by.
> Workmen's weary wives and daughters
> Sing the songs of liberty;
> Men hail men across the waters,
> Men reply across the sea.[95]

Likewise the ideals of liberty, equality and fraternity permeate the Melbourne anarchist J. A. Andrews's contrafactum *For Wealth and Liberty*, which appeared alongside the original in his own *Labour Song Book*:

> On! on in unity,
> For wealth and liberty,

From servile woe, in might we go,
To build a nation free.

The local context appears in the final lines:

Of fair Victoria's brotherhood
Whose labour shall be each man's pleasure.[96]

From the local to the global, the utopian vision of Elizabeth Johnson – an otherwise unremarkable member of the rank and file – was enunciated in her *World's Marseillaise*, published by the *Worker* in 1890.[97]

The use of the anthem became more flagrantly provocative in the last decades of the century as the socialist and anarchist movements grew in volubility (if not always numerical strength). Larry Petrie, a one-armed anarchist with what was reputed to be a fine baritone voice, sang the *Marseillaise* to 'gather a good crowd around him', taking the opportunity of his own physical misfortune to inject an element of humour into his performance by raising his only arm when he sang 'to arms, my citizens'. He was remembered for his peripatetic movements through the streets and parks of Sydney, passionately calling on the workers 'to take up arms and man the barricades' and, at the 'slightest provocation', would burst into the *Marseillaise*, 'his eyes flashing, and his black moustache bristling'.[98] Not surprisingly, a report of Petrie's escapades appeared in the British socialist press.[99]

To the extent that we have drawn upon examples from 'advanced radicals', Chartists and late Victorian socialists, we in no way wish to imply that the *Marseillaise* became increasingly narrow in its popularity or use. On the contrary, what is abundantly clear is the broader appeal of the song among radicals and reformers – and within popular culture writ large – from one corner of the Anglophone world to the other. For example, it was no accident that among the 100 bands involved in the massive trade union parade to London's Hyde Park to advocate for the eight-hour day in 1892, the *Marseillaise* was the tune played most often.[100] Nor should we be surprised that when the Reform League – the nationwide movement based on a broad alliance between middle-class liberals and reformers and former Chartists to demand an extension of the franchise – gathered after an extensive public meeting (also in Hyde Park) in 1866, the *Marseillaise* featured in the proceedings. According to the conservative London *Standard*, the tune was beyond the capacity of the band, making the air 'hideous'; some present stumbled over the French but play and sing they did.[101] Although the meeting had been proscribed this was no hotbed of extremism: in the chair was the national president of the League, Edmond Beales, a respectable barrister. Also present were P. A. Taylor, the Liberal MP for Leicester, and John Stuart Mill, already famous as the oracle of liberty.[102] Similarly, it was not at all unexpected that it rang out at a temperance meeting in Alnwick, Northumberland, in 1870 or on the hustings in Brisbane in support of the Labour candidate:

> To the Polls! to the Polls! ye braves,
> Each man with his neighbour.
> March on! March on! each man resolved.
> To straight out for Labour.[103]

The association of the *Marseillaise* with mainstream reformist politics was also evident in 1844 when one of the best-known contrafacta was penned for the Anti-Corn Law League by a moderate radical: the famous 'Corn Law Rhymer', Ebenezer Elliott. Notwithstanding the gothic hysteria of the imagery, Elliott's *British Marseillaise*, subtitled *A Hymn for Masters and Men*, is a measured plea for a fair dispersal of food in the face of aristocratic avarice:

> Shall brutal things, in human form,
> Feed on your souls, like rat and worm?
> Say to your wives, 'Ye shall not eat?'
> Bid son with sire for graves compete?
> And mothers kill their babes, in flight from law and life,
> 'Till lawless law become th' assassin's match and knife?[104]

Unsurprisingly, a variety of popularised versions of the song notated for a range of instrumentations, such as *Favourite Airs of La Parisienne, la Marseillaise, for Harp, Piano and Guitar*, became readily available.[105] The degree to which the song had become lodged in popular culture can be appreciated by a brief glance at the career of long-forgotten music-hall performer Pauline Vaneri. For nearly twenty years Vaneri toured the music halls of Britain and Ireland, and the kernel of her act was the *Marseillaise*. Reports of Vaneri's performances from the late 1850s to the end of the 1870s almost invariably drew attention to her stirring renditions of the anthem. Her performance of the *Marseillaise* 'in the original', enthused one correspondent, 'was given with such power and dramatic effect as to give an idea of the influence it must have had in past days'. Vaneri's act was especially effective in Scotland where she performed it in combination with Scottish songs. 'For her singing of the "Marseillaise" in French she had to respond to an encore,' a reviewer from Dundee wrote, 'while her rendering of "Scots wha ha'e" must have caused the blood of even the most sluggish Scot present to course more rapidly though his veins.'[106] During her 1865 season in Glasgow, Vaneri was 'equally successful in the rendering of tender and plaintive airs as in those spirit-stirring strains which breathe forth love of country or hatred of oppression'. Back in Glasgow in 1869 and 1871 she 'took the house by storm' when she sung the *Marseillaise*.[107]

What these examples have in common is a belief on the part of the appropriators that their cause was underpinned by the original meaning of the anthem: the struggle of freedom and liberty. The same was true across the Atlantic, with the abolition of slavery the obvious cause. As early as 1848 William Brown, a fugitive slave, published the *Anti-Slavery Harp*, a volume that was reputed to be the first publication by an African American designed specifically for abolitionist meetings. Among a collection of popular tunes was Brown's appropriation of the *Marseillaise*, *Ye Sons of Freemen*, which echoed the metre and the sentiment of famous lyrics with an exhortation: 'Pray on, pray on, all hearts resolved – these captives shall be free'.[108] The *Marseillaise* thereafter went on to feature as the basis for appropriations in Union songbooks. The *Stars and Stripes Songster*, published in 1861 as the first shots were fired, for example, contained the *Union Marseillaise* (alongside iconic American songs including *John Brown, Tramp! Tramp! Tramp!* and *Red, White and Blue*). The song wove together liberty, nation and historical authority:

> AROUSE, ye men who love your Nation!
> Your starry standard boldly raise!
> March on! March on! All hearts as one!
> 'REMEMBER WASHINGTON!'[109]

It is important to recall that the trope of liberty was claimed by both sides of the fratricidal conflict and thus the *Marseillaise* is also found in the pages of songsters produced by the Confederacy. The *Jack Morgan Songster*, compiled by a captain in General Lee's army, included the *Southern Marseillaise* by A. E. Blackmar. As discordant as it might sound in our own day, the text would not have given pause to supporters of the rebels, including a number of former radicals, Chartists and Irish nationalists who took up arms to defend the right to secede.[110]

Decades before they were torn apart by internecine struggle, some Americans had looked over the border to offer their support to the Canadians in their fight for independence from Britain. Notably, at a large meeting in Buffalo, New York, at the height of the Upper and Lower Rebellions in Canada at the end of 1837, a performance of the *Marseillaise* set the tone for the proceedings, which included 'prayers for the freedom of Canada', delivered by a veteran of the American revolutionary wars, and 'Three cheers for Papineau and the patriots'.[111] Here, too, the association with rebellion, as opposed to liberty, can be misleading. One of the prominent campaign songs in support of Edward Blake, the Liberal candidate for prime minister in 1882, was a contrafactum based on the familiar air:

To arms! Swift vengeance take!
Your votes can powers unmake
March on! march on! all hearts resolved
For Canada and Blake![112]

Decades later, in 1909, the *Marseillaise* was taken up as a battle song by the Canadian women's movement and featured at the International Congress for Women held in Toronto.[113] The *Women's Marseillaise*, with words by Florence Macaulay, a well-known peripatetic agitator, was at that time the official anthem of Britain's Women's Social and Political Union (WSPU). The week before the Toronto meeting, Flora Denison, secretary of the Canadian Suffrage Association (CSA), had printed the text in full in her column 'Under the Pines', where she gave an account of its recent performance at Carnegie Hall.[114] Despite Denison's efforts the Toronto audience had obviously not learnt the words and the attempt went off with a whimper rather than the desired bang. The *Toronto Star* generously noted its fine qualities as a revolutionary song but admitted that 'it suffered somewhat on Saturday night because nobody knew it very well'.[115] The journalist for the *Toronto Saturday Night* was more forthright: 'I feared the effect of this terrible appeal to the passions. But it was really quite mild. This may have been due to the fact that the words of the songs were absolutely indistinguishable. I recognised snatches of the familiar tune, but it was shorn of its war-like character.'[116] During the congress Denison invoked, on behalf of 'sixteen million organised women', a conciliatory ballad in a plea to 'the men of the world'. She entreated Canadian men 'to let them climb the ladder together', clarifying her poetic allusion with a full stanza of *John Anderson my Jo*.

John Anderson my Joe [*sic*] John
We'll climb the hill together
And mony a cantie day, John
We'll hae wee ain an either,
And then we'll totter down, John
But hand in hand we'll go,
And sleep together at the foot
John Anderson my Joe.[117]

Second key: John Anderson my Jo[118]

Unlike the *Marseillaise*, *John Anderson my Jo* is not obviously radical in its origins or consistently so in its appropriations. As such it had a greater flexibility of use and provided an interface between popular culture at large and radicalism and reform. The new settings had to fit the template of the original in terms of syllabic count, metric rhythm and stanza length; they also often utilised the affective qualities of the music. Whereas de Lisle's music inspired consistently defiant lyrical themes that suited its militaristic march-like musical qualities, the lamenting quality of *John Anderson my Jo*'s tender minor mode inflections provoked various kinds of complaint (see figure 1.2). The utmost seriousness of the *Marseillaise* contrasts with the irreverence and frequent bawdiness of *John Anderson my Jo*. Humour and earnestness alike could serve a cause. For example, both tunes were enlisted to the temperance movement in quite different ways. The parody *John Alcohol, my Jo* appeared in New Zealand and American newspapers,[119] whereas a more high-minded appropriation of the *Marseillaise* appeared in Melbourne's *Victorian Band of Hope Union Hymn Book* of 1860 addressed to 'Ye friends of Temperance, self- denying'. [120]

The song had appeared as a tune for new texts from the mid-eighteenth century before Burns had produced his own poem. Parodies continued to appear throughout the next century, covering a range of topics from poverty to local government and city parks.[121] Among these parodies are examples not only of intertextual play with the poetic text but also a kind of play in which the titles of the tune are in conversation with the original. In some instances these changes in the title of the tune served to intensify the sense of loss expressed in the new text. For example, the song *The Departed* in Joseph Barker's *Democratic Hymns and Songs* (1849) is set to the tune of *John Anderson's Gone*, and a street ballad called *In the Days When I was Hard Up*, which centred on the individual experience of privation and difficulty, takes it one decisive step further with the tune given as *John Anderson's Dead*.[122]

Sometimes *John Anderson my Jo* appeared in the political world in its original form, but more often than not it was used by radicals and reformers as the basis for contrafacta, either as expressions of fidelity and affection (in keeping with Burns's poem) or as rebuke and derision. An example of the former was when it was featured prominently during the liberation tour of Scotland by the so-called Chartist Martyrs, John Collins and Peter Murray McDouall, in 1840. Far from being objects of satire, these Chartists were celebrated as returning heroes. Collins and McDouall had spent the previous year imprisoned for sedition, both victims of the government crackdown in the aftermath of the presentation of the Chartist's National Petition in 1839. Scottish songs dominated the celebrations. The liberated patriots were heralded by performances of many of Burns's best loved and politicised songs, notably *Scots Wha Hae* and *A Man's a Man for a' That*, as they travelled across Scotland. The working people paid their respects, particularly to John Collins, through various performances of *John*

[57]

1.2 'John Anderson my Jo', James Johnson, *The Scots Musical Museum*, vol. 3 [1790], p. 269.

Anderson my Jo. Unsurprisingly, in this context, ironic inversion is absent in their appropriation of *John Anderson my Jo* in which they retained and celebrated the powerful sense of affection that permeates Burns's version. The connection between song and individual was made explicitly at Glasgow's Grand Soiree, during which a Mr McCrea from Kilbarchan was called upon to sing his own version of *John Anderson* in a tribute to the Chartist leader in which the last line of every verse was changed to 'John Collins, oh my Jo'.[123] At the post-procession dinner the following week in Edinburgh, Collins was introduced by both the chairman and the 'excellent instrumental band' that heralded him with a performance of his namesake.[124]

The ballad played a more everyday role in a shared popular culture that spread rapidly over the British Empire with the onset of mass emigration. In his account of the voyage to Australia aboard an immigrant ship, John Hood described an evening 'when, to the great delight of us Scots, a Blairgowrie man and two other Highlanders struck up, in admirable style, a whistling trio – "Scots wha hae wi' Wallace bled," and "John Anderson my Jo." The effect was electric: the airs of Scotia on the wild strange sea sounded more touchingly to us than they ever did before.'[125] This collective expression of Scottish identity in the face of an uncertain and unknown world captures the emigrant experience. Emigration – with the prospect-cum-hope of a better life for the working classes in the colonies of settlement – was a regular if controversial subject of discussion among reformers of different stripes. This account also provides a vivid and immediate explanation of how Burns and his political sentiments, which had been shaped by the French Revolution and a Scottish radical heritage, made their way with the Scottish diaspora to the far reaches of the Empire. Scottish and Caledonian concerts became a regular popular entertainment, while Burns Clubs and Caledonian Societies proliferated from Cape Town to Melbourne and from Halifax to Dunedin.

Although the ballad lacked the political power of some of Burns's other songs, it nonetheless retained its capacity to carry political resonance in these new environments. Satirical parody, although absent in Collins's liberation tour of Scotland, was an integral part of the political culture of opposition and subversion, taking its place in what E. P. Thompson has identified as the plebeian tradition of counter-theatre.[126] Like many ballads, *John Anderson my Jo* gives itself up easily to ironic inversion in which the gently humorous but still loving reference to the encroachment of old age is turned on its head to become a mocking reproach for betrayal and disappointment. Many of the surviving printed parodies are satirical addresses to politicians and they can be found throughout the British world.

In stark contrast to the celebration for the Chartist Martyrs, for example, there was no trace of affection in the parody of *John Anderson my Jo* that appeared in Sydney almost a decade later in the *People's Advocate*, a radical newspaper edited by Edward Hawksley, a former Chartist and poet.[127] Hawksley's target was Lord John Russell. As is well known, Russell had been active in the Whig campaign that resulted in the passage of the Great Reform Act of 1832, a cause that gave rise to widespread optimism among reformers generally. Radicals, who had vociferously supported the campaign, had been given the impression by the Whigs that the passage of the Act would be the first instalment in a process of incremental reform. In government, the Whigs had proven a great disappointment and popular hopes for further democratic reform had been dashed when Russell explicitly ruled it out in 1837, earning him the sobriquet 'Finality Jack'. *John Anderson my Jo* lent itself to parody in part because it is an address to an individual. In almost all parodies, specific individuals are taken to task for acts of political betrayal. In this parody Russell is censured for his betrayal of fundamental democratic ideals. The dynamism inherent in the print-oral nexus is brought into play as the tune comes to mind despite the resolute silence of the printed medium.

> John Minister, my Jo, John, when we were first acquaint,
> Ye were a bold Reformer, on liberal measures bent;
> But now ye're growing cold, John, ye're getting slack and slow;
> I wonder what has come to ye, John Minister, my Jo.

Betrayal and disappointment suffuse the poem, as the singer protests, 'Ah! Ye're not what ye used to be, John Minister, my Jo' and then goes on to accuse him of being 'tamed'. The lyricist suggests that if Russell were to have a change of heart and 'resume the path of progress' he would find forgiveness. Ultimately, however, the final stanza condemns Russell as irredeemable, and the image of the couple sleeping 'thegither at the foot' after facing life's challenges is destroyed:

> John Minister, my Jo, John, we've clamb the hill together,
> And both have had to struggle with very stormy weather;
> And I have kept ahead, John, but you have crept below,
> And now are sleeping at the foot, John Minister, my Jo.

The song's renewed relevance for Sydney radicals and reformers in 1849 was the fact that by this time Russell was the prime minister of a government bent on reintroducing the transportation of convicts to New South Wales. Opposition to transportation generated Australia's first nationwide political movement and quickly became a capsule statement for the campaign for self-government.[128] The publication of the song in a radical Sydney newspaper at this moment was no coincidence, and this new dimension of dissent would not have been lost on its readership.

Russell was again the target for a parody of the song in 1863. This time his attackers came from the other side of the Pacific. He was now Earl Russell and was serving as foreign minister in Palmerston's government. The change in title was noted in the stinging rebuke, *Uncle Samuel Singeth Unto Earl Russell to the Air of John Anderson my Jo*, which appeared in the Union publication, *The Continental Songster*. The premise invoked is hard to fathom given that Russell had been prime minister and was now simply a member of the cabinet, albeit a powerful one:

> Lord John Russell, my Jo, John,
> When we were first acquent,
> Your voice warn't much to speak of, Jo,
> In Britain's Parliament;
> But now that you're an Earl, John
> 'Tis marvel how you crow!
> 'Little, but loud,' like Sambo's fowl,
> Lord John Russell, my Jo!

The demand to desist from siding with the South in a later verse is clear:

> And don't go back on Uncle Sam,
> Lord John Russell, my Jo! [129]

This was not the only instance when protagonists in the American Civil War enlisted Burns's song in relation to the British. A number of songbooks contain parodies of the song, which refer to the generic John Bull, published at a time when it seemed inevitable that Palmerston's government would intervene in the Civil War on the side of the South. In *Jonathan to John*, the lyricist used the song as a vehicle to take the British to task for threatening intervention in the form of a mock conversation between John Bull and Uncle Sam:

> It don't seem hardly right, John
> When both my hands was full,
> To stump me to a fight, John –
> Your cousin, tu [*sic*], John Bull!
> Ole Uncle S. sez he: 'I guess
> We know it now,' sez he:
> 'The lion's paw is all the law,
> According to J. B.'[130]

Confederates also used the familiar cultural symbol of Britishness; this time it was expressed as a personal address to the British fleet lying in wait off shore, ready to come to their aid. The headnote suggested that this fraught situation 'gave rise to the following imitation of an old song'. The final verse makes clear the alliance between the South and Britain:

> O, Johnny Bull, my Jo John, let's take the field together,
> And hunt the Yankee Doodles home, in spite of wind and weather,
> And ere a twelvemonth roll around, to Boston we will go,
> And eat our Christmas dinner there, O Johnny Bull, my Jo![131]

Note here how the quatrain turns on the use of the word 'you'. *John Anderson my Jo* lent itself to parody in part because it is an address to an individual in a conversational tone (if their name was John or Jo so much the better, but it was not required). The same is also true of the positive contrafacta. Indeed, the song's political utility stemmed from its capacity to create an intimacy, a personal exchange among friends, former friends and foes. In summary, the song facilitated a personification of politics. As we have seen (and will see further) this was accomplished by the use of terms for a face-to-face engagement in the lyrics – you, ye, we, we're, us and so on – but it is also embedded in the title: 'my Jo'.

John Russell was by no means the only major British politician to be subjected to derision through parodies of *John Anderson my Jo*. Benjamin Disraeli came under attack in the British broadside ballad *Ben Dizzy*, one made even more confronting by its anti-Semitism:

> Ben Disraeli ye Jew Ben
> When ye politics began
> Ye were a thorough Radical
> Perhaps an honest man
> But soon ye turned your [coat] Ben
> And turned a Tory [?]
> For parties all were all the same
> For Ben the crafty Jew.[132]

As we have seen, the song resonated throughout the Anglophone world. Although *John Anderson my Jo*'s most frequent appearance in New Zealand was in advertisements for an eponymous pub (once again demonstrating its place in the everyday), it was also brought into the political arena. A resident of Toko – a rural settlement on New Zealand's North Island – was not impressed with his Member of Parliament and on behalf of the 'simple-minded Toko folk' took him to task:

> John Anderson my Jo, John,
> When first we were acquaint,
> Ye were a smooth-tongued canty chiel –
> A beauty without paint.
> But you're now an MHR, John,

> And I should like to know
> If ye have gathered any sense
> John Anderson my Jo.[133]

A correspondent to Canterbury's *Star* in 1899 revealed his thought processes in a way that highlights how some traditional songs existed as a sort of available stockpile: 'Sir,' he wrote to the editor, 'As I sat the other night contemplating the conduct of the junior member for Christchurch, the old air of "John Anderson my Jo" came into my head.' The point is that not only was the song available to spring to mind, he knew the context to which it could be put:

> Taylor, T. E., of Christchurch
> When we were first acquent,
> I thought you were a Radical
> And what you said you meant ...
>
> 'T. E.', you're now a different man,
> A Tory, not a 'Rad',
> And everything seems very good
> You once thought very bad.[134]

Flora Denison's evocation of Burns's ballad was by no means the first time a Canadian had used it to advance their political cause. In Montreal, in the early decades of the nineteenth century, the song was put to specific local use. *Another New Song to Another Old Tune* was an election ballad addressed to the Irish-Canadian politician John Donellan. The mock exasperation and wry knowingness expressed in the title's use of the word 'another' suggests the lyricist's broader awareness that many 'new' songs were often not new. The opening stanza essays the familiar trope:

> John Donellan, my Jo, John,
> When we first acquaint,
> Your politics were good, John,
> On Freedom you were bent.
> But now you're getting old, John,
> You've forgotten long ago
> And you've turned Tory on our hands
> John Donellan, my Jo.

There is a wealth of historical detail in the ballad's six octaves: Donellan's career over an extended period is raked over. The ballad is peppered with the names of key individuals and historical references: 1832, Tracey, the Ninety-Two Resolves (Resolutions), O'Connell, Auldjo, Tom Begley, Papineau, Nelson. Although no publication details or authorship have survived, these details identify it as an election ballad that formed part of the arsenal of the reformist Patriote campaign led by Louis-Joseph Papineau and Robert Nelson against the conservative Irishman John Donellan and William Walker for Montreal West in the strife-torn election of late 1834. Even though the ballad can be seen as reflective of the events leading up to the 1837 rebellion it ends by warning Donellan of his impending defeat at the ballot box:

> John Donellan, my Jo, John
> The day is coming fast
> When you will be defeated John –
> When you'll have polled your last.
> And then you'll toddle home, John.[135]

The ballad played into what Mary Finnegan has termed a 'climate of sympathy' between the Irish and French in Canada.[136] As well as being co-religionists, the two ethnic groups shared a common experience of British oppression. It was at this time that Daniel O'Connell was agitating on behalf of the French Canadians in the British Parliament, who embraced him as their 'Liberator' – the title he earned for championing Irish Catholic Emancipation – holding him up as a 'symbol of hope' and drawing favourable comparisons between him and their own Papineau.[137] O'Connell's activities were not only reported in the radical Irish newspaper *The Vindicator*, edited by Daniel Tracey, who worked closely with the Patriotes, but also in the radical French broadsheet *La Minerve*. Notably, the song reveals a fact not taken account of in current scholarship of this period:[138] although Donellan and Daniel Tracey had previously worked together (in 1828 they convened the first meeting of the Society of the Friends of Ireland, and both had held office as president and vice president, respectively, of the Hibernian Benevolent Fund), by the 1834 by-election Donellan had turned against Tracey, a particular instance demonstrating wider Irish unrest. It is notable that this song comes from within the Irish ranks and surely played a role in the noisy meetings of Irish electors of the West Ward prior to the election. The election of 1834 was not the first time Papineau and Nelson had run together. They had won the riding of Montreal West earlier in 1827. But in 1834 Nelson was important to the Patriotes. Despite not being Irish and coming from one of the Patriotes' most radical factions, he had Irish support. This was due in part to the many cholera victims among the recent Irish population he had treated as a doctor. The French Canadians had to be careful not to let their opposition to Donellan be seen as an attack on the Irish. Indeed, in this election song we can hear both the disunity that had arisen among the Irish population from 1832 and the death knell of the brief period of Irish–French Canadian solidarity in Lower Canada during the Patriote-led campaign for constitutional reform.

Another New Song to Another Old Tune captures and preserves a key moment in early nineteenth-century Canadian history and as such is an important example of the potency of election ballads – and political ballads more generally – to act as what Leslie Shepard has called a 'kind of musical journalism'. As we shall see in a subsequent chapter, the more recognisable form of the election ballad dates from the eighteenth century – possibly earlier – and continued well beyond the emergence of cheap mass-circulation newspapers.[139] The significance of *John Anderson my Jo*, as an example of the engagement between popular politics and a popular oral tradition, goes further. Firstly, its title lent itself to use in connection with well-known public figures with the first name John – a common name – and with the broader figure of John Bull, an unmistakeable symbol of Britishness. It had an easy convenience for pundits. Secondly, by personifying politics it created an illusion of intimacy – the basis for a conversation between equals – that, in turn, opened up the possibility for praise or censure. A consistent theme in many of the appropriations discussed here is betrayal. Inverting the meaning of Burns's lyrics creates this semantic space: fidelity and devotion are replaced by derision and reproach. A similar intimacy, however, is at the core of positive contrafacta of the song; it facilitates a renewal of personal fidelity and loyalty consistent with the original. The haunting, melancholy tune sustains both iterations. For those making and listening to the music, the key to appreciating the ironic use of *John Anderson my Jo* – to rebuke Lord John Russell or John Bull writ large or to welcome John Collins – is to know the original, not because it was a political song but because it provided for a face-to-face encounter. In this way the song mediated the relationship between the individual and the collective. It made sense.

Third key: Song of the 'Lower Classes'

The age has passed when nations can be sung into liberty.
                    Ernest Jones in the *Northern Star*, 3 August 1850.

Democracy has hitherto not had songs of its own – music has not yet been wedded to the people's cause, and poetry made the servitor of the working classes. An attempt is now made to remedy this remarkable deficiency. At the Saint Martin's Hall Soirees, a series of Democratic songs, by Ernest Jones, will be given, partly to popular and well-known airs, partly to original music. They are for the people – friends! make them of the people!
                    'Grand Political Soiree in Saint Martin's Hall', *People's Paper*,
                    11 October 1856.

[65]

The Festival of Music for the People in South Place in 1939 was not the first time Ernest Jones's *Song of the 'Lower Classes'* had enjoyed a moment of celebrity. Midway through the previous century, it had been performed on another public stage, sung by Jones's friend John Lowry. As composer and performer, Lowry never came close to attaining the international recognition of Paul Robeson, either as musician or as political radical. Nonetheless, the story of *Song of the 'Lower Classes'* at St Martin's Hall in 1856 marks an important point for a number of reasons, which shall be explored in this section.

Early in October 1856 Jones's *People's Paper* featured an advertisement for 'A Grand Political Soiree and Address to be given in Saint Martin's Hall, Long Acre'.[140] Although events of this kind were in no way new, Jones's own sense of what was to be a set of six soirees, called collectively 'Evenings with the People', was that in terms of intent, form and content, they were unprecedented. Indeed, with more than a soupçon of hyperbole, he claimed for them a special place in political history. The combination of politics and music was, he boasted, 'the first attempt of the kind ever made'. He did not wish politics to be 'a dry, repulsive study', he insisted, and thus 'song and music' were enlisted 'to the service of political truth'.[141] The notice was explicit: both 'instruction and amusement' were to be provided to the public. Music, and particularly *Song of the 'Lower Classes'*, was to play a part in this. A closer reading of the initial notice reveals some important issues that deserve further attention. For example, it signalled that Jones was to demonstrate how easily '*Harmony*' could be 'established between *ALL CLASSES*'. At the same time 'A selection of the choicest music' was to be provided by 'AN EFFICIENT CHORUS of first-rate *professional* talent ... under the direction of Mr. John Lowry' and 'THREE *ORIGINAL* ODES' by Jones were to be 'sung *for the first time*' and '*copies* given away [emphasis added]'.[142] The mid-nineteenth century signalled an important shift both for Jones in terms of his political aspirations and for musical culture more generally. By the mid-1850s Jones was looking for a rapprochement with the middle classes and at the same time musical culture was also experiencing new forms of commercialisation, production and professionalisation. The advertisement in the *People's Paper* reflected both these new directions.

The content of Jones's speeches at St Martin's Hall was unsurprising if not a little more intemperate than he intended. His first words set the tone for much of what followed over the next six months. 'I invite your solemn consideration of a subject the importance of which no tongue can overstate,' he told the audience before it had scarcely had time to catch its breath from singing. 'On it the safety of property, the protection of life, the duration of the empire depend.' His subject that autumn night was 'the relation of rich to poor, of man to man, of capital to labour'.[143] Over the coming months he discoursed on the condition of British workmen, the evils of hereditary aristocracy and the state church, the British Constitution – 'one of the vilest shams and greatest legislative curses ever inflicted on a people' – and the environmental spoliation of British cities.[144] These speeches were interspersed by a range of musical performances. The structure was highly formal; Jones warned the audience at the outset that encores might not be called for 'so as not to interfere with the time allotted to each part of the evening's proceedings'.[145] The newspapers responded in kind to Jones's renewed commitment to cultural performance. Their reports pay close attention to the many musical offerings: the performers were identified by name, and their renditions subjected to some critical scrutiny; even the piano was identified as a Collard.[146]

The heavy downpour that coincided with the inaugural soiree did not apparently stop a 'great concourse of people' assembling in the handsomely decorated St Martin's Hall, replete with the 'new tricoloured union jack, the colours being red, white and green'.[147] Surrounded by seven or eight musicians, Jones laid out the shape his 'novel experiment' would take before beginning his address on the relation of labour to capital.[148] The *Daily News* gave a detailed account of the musical performances, which included solo songs, glees and madrigals as well as instrumental numbers. It singled out the *Song of the 'Lower Classes'* for special praise, which it deemed 'cleverly written, simple to the very utmost in its language ... yet rhythmical, well balanced and full of points, and being sung to a popular air, it was exceedingly affective'. Jones's other ode performed that evening, *A Song of the Time of Cromwell*, did not fare so well and was dismissed as 'pretentious'.[149] The *People's Paper* stressed the 'professional talent' on stage and effused about the 'excellence' of the musical arrangements and direction. Like the *Daily News*, it commented favourably on *Song of the 'Lower Classes'* and hoped that it would 'be made "household"' among the people'. The full text of the song was provided, noting that the music was by John Lowry but could also be sung to the *The Brave Old Oak* among other popular melodies.[150] Such was the favourable response of the audience that Jones's proscription of encores was ignored and many were had, particularly of Lowry's performances of Jones's songs that were 'rapturously received'.[151]

Of course, Jones's claim that 'Democracy has hitherto not had songs of its own', that 'music has not yet been wedded to the people's cause, and poetry made the servitor of the working classes' was simply untrue.[152] As we have seen, from the Spenceans to Burdett's Whigs and before, music and music-making had been an integral part of the performance of politics. Why then did Jones make such a strong claim for novelty, and which aspects of his soirees were new? Although music had long been at the service of popular radicalism, his claim was based upon the fact that previously its expression had been typically communal, spontaneous and unstructured. In his opening remarks Jones explicitly connected music to politics by seeking to formalise what had previously been informal. The evenings were divided into four discrete sections: performance; lecture; performance; conclusion of lecture. The music was divided into two categories of amusement: innocent and intellectual. The 'intellectual' amusement was in fact Jones's poems set to music, the content of which often prefigured the theme of the evening lecture. His announcement that his poetry would be given to 'original music' in addition to the usual mode of transmission, popular and well-known airs, was of great importance to him and gives some substance to his claims for novelty.[153] Thereby a pattern was set: musical performances preceded, punctuated and followed the bi-partite lecture. Jones produced new odes for each soiree; some were set to original music by Lowry or assigned popular airs, or both. It was left to the *Daily News* and the *Morning Chronicle* to detail the musical performances, performers and repertoire presented. It is in their reviews that we learn of the glees, the madrigals, the concertina playing and the 'fine singing'.[154] Jones's own *People's Paper* chose instead to focus on the *original* compositions of 'the musical director', John Lowry.[155]

The second soiree on 'Hereditary Aristocracy' saw an 'immense audience' that contained, the *People's Paper* took care to note, a 'mixture of all classes' (including 'a goodly sprinkle of the aristocracy') who were privy not only to Jones's opinions but also two more of his songs: *Song of the 'Day Labourers'*, set to music by Lowry, as well as *A Song of the Resurrection*, performed by a full chorus.[156] *Song of the 'Lower Classes'* was repeated. The third soiree saw an audience almost double the size of the first. Again the music received comment. Although the *Morning Chronicle* complained of a 'somewhat noisy brass band' that played 'some not very well-selected airs' (which included a Hungarian march, perhaps in honour of Kossuth, who was touring Britain at the time); Lowry's voice was praised and his performances deemed tasteful.[157] His renditions of Jones's new odes, *The Marriage Feast* and *Song of the Factory Slave*, were encored. In response he again sang *Song of the 'Lower Classes'*. After this the *People's Paper* promised that a 'music department' would respond to the positive reception in the press by adding 'new features of interest' to make the concerts 'of the choicest character'.[158]

The final soiree differed fundamentally from the first five. Whereas previously the array of solo performances had been augmented by choirs and brass bands, the announcement of the sixth soiree on Home Affairs made it abundantly clear that, as it was being combined with the International Committee's anniversary of the French Revolution, there was to be 'NO music'.[159] This event had much in common with the celebrations of internationalism described in the first section of this chapter: the always sumptuous decorations now included French, Polish and German banners. Unsurprisingly, although the ban on music was largely adhered to, the 'great audience' (which included Karl Marx), concluded the anniversary by singing the *Marseillaise* 'with the utmost fervour'.[160]

The International Committee had used St Martin's Hall on previous occasions. Almost exactly two years before, it had met there to assert 'publicly, for the first time, its existence'.[161] But, importantly, Jones and the International Committee took their place among a number of organisations from across the spectrum of radical and reformist politics, which were tenants of the hall. These included the National Sunday League, the National Temperance Society and the association for promoting the repeal of the taxes on knowledge supported by such radical luminaries as Richard Cobden and George Holyoake as well as the well-known music publisher Vincent Novello and his son Joseph Alfred Novello. The hall also hosted trade union meetings, benefit concerts in support of émigrés fleeing oppressive regimes on the continent. Located on Long Acre in Covent Garden in the heart of London's West End, St Martin's Hall was opened in 1850 with a capacity of 3,000. For the best part of two decades it served as a hotbed of politics in the imperial metropolis, bringing together many of those who were known as 'advanced radicals' in philosophy and religion – socialists, republicans, atheists, internationalists – as well as liberals better known as advocates of more moderate reform in education, economics and religion. Perhaps the apogee of the hall's political notoriety occurred in 1864 when the International Workingmen's Association (later known as the first Communist International) was formed there. 'Citizen' Jones was there; so too was Marx, then busily finishing the first volume of *Das Kapital* (published in 1867). Marx was back in attendance the following year for the Communist International's Anniversary Soiree that combined politics, music and dance.

St Martin's Hall was the venue for a range of political and social activities and on one level that fact helped to define it. Of course, for all that they often rubbed shoulders in its commodious spaces, those we have grouped loosely under the rubric of radicalism and reform were not always in agreement. St Martin's Hall, however, was primarily a centre for music-making – its full title was St Martin's Music Hall – and this in turn helped to define its multifarious tenants. The hall was a place of culture and hosted a wide range of entertainments, including pantomimes, ballets, music hall shows, orchestral and piano concerts, readings by authors including Charles Dickens and even performances by 'Mr Howard's unrivalled minstrels from Australia'.[162] Indeed, it had been built by subscription for the use of music educator John Pyke Hullah.

By any measure Hullah was a key figure in popular music education: the 'sight singing mania' that swept England from the 1840s and taught literally thousands to sing.[163] In 1839 he had travelled to Paris to study the Wilhelm singing method, which was used primarily to teach the working classes musical literacy by using an alternative form of notation. Hullah adapted and translated this method and became, along with Joseph Mainzer and John Curwen, a major force in the sight singing movement. His long association with liberal politician and educationalist Dr James Kay-Shuttleworth saw him become government inspector for schools in 1872. He ran his singing classes in St Martin's Hall and conducted countless concerts including the monthly series 'Ancient and Modern Music', which showcased a wide-ranging repertoire from Purcell and Handel to Beethoven and Spohr, as well as major nineteenth-century composers Mendelssohn, Weber and Gounod and contemporary English composer Sterndale-Bennett.[164]

But it is important to note that Hullah's tireless commitment to music education was part of a broader commitment to reform. Some explanation of his openness to a wide range of radical thought can be found in the two formative influences of his father and his teacher. From these men the young Hullah imbibed the ideas of the French Revolution. In particular, he later recalled, he was exposed to the extreme theory of radical egalitarianism outlined by the French philosopher Claude Adrien Helvétius, whose *De L'Esprit* was famously burned in public by the Paris Executioner in 1759. Helvétius's suggestion that all men were equal, their abilities determined by their education, influenced Hullah greatly. As he admitted later in life, 'I am not sure that some of it does not hang about me still'.[165] His circle comprised like-minded individuals including literary figures such as Charles Dickens, important Christian Socialists and social commentators as well as many prominent musicians, including Vincent Novello. They were part of a cultural field permeated with ideas of progressivism and reform. Like many middle-class reformers Hullah was no radical – he had served as a special constable during the Chartist crisis of 1848 – but his hall was a place where a wide spectrum of reformist thought was expressed, including at its most extreme end an appearance by Feargus O'Connor, who was regarded by many as the most dangerous man in England.[166]

Until St Martin's Hall was gutted in 1867, thousands of people from all social classes passed through its doors, not only to learn Hullah's singing method but also to listen to concerts of music ranging from Mendelssohn to Lowry to minstrel songs, and to learn of the latest developments in scientific, secularist and political thought. St Martin's Hall was a space where all these different things coalesced, united by a general reformist impulse and a commitment to education. It would be a mistake to assume that the audiences for this cornucopia of offerings were discrete. It was a site where popular and high culture mingled, aristocrats rubbed shoulders with the middling and lower classes, where the whole gamut of progressive thought was expressed, but it was, above all, a place of music, and here music, much as it did in Jones's 'Evenings with the People', asserted its own centrality in mid-Victorian culture and its power to effect change. Jones could not have chosen a better venue for his novel approach of political reform through music (see figure 1.3).

Through his modes of performance and work as a composer and publisher, Lowry assumed a modest place in a new kind of music world. This period saw the staging of highly popular ballad concert series and cheap performances such as those put on by August Mann at Crystal Palace in 1855. Series, including the London Ballad Concerts, became intertwined with sheet music marketing through ballad catalogues promoted by a growing number of music publishers such as Boosey, Novello, Davidson, Hopwood and Crew, and Charles Sheard. It was an increasingly egalitarian undertaking catering to all classes. It was also the time when cheap pianos were making their way not only into the middle-class parlour but increasingly into the front rooms of the aspirational working class. As the new comprehensive collection of popular music, *Davidson's Universal Melodist* (itself an example of the explosion of the commercial popular music industry), asserted in its preface: 'there is hardly in England at this time a respectable house which does not count a Piano-forte in its inventory of furniture.'[167] The desire for cheap pianos was accompanied by an increasingly voracious appetite for the simple drawing room song with piano accompaniment suitable for the amateur musician.[168]

From the outset Jones and Lowry made a concerted effort to commodify their venture. The lectures were published as individual pamphlets and collectively as *Evenings for the People*. The song lyrics were offered for sale as nine separate sheets entitled together as *Songs of Democracy*.[169] In keeping with much traditional popular song publishing, the texts did not all give suggestions for tunes. Both lectures and

1.3   The interior of St Martin's Hall on Long Acre, in Covent Garden,
London. The hall seated 3,000. In the engraving of the opening in February
1850 the owner and well-known music teacher, John Hullah, can be seen
conducting an orchestra and extensive choir. Image: 'Opening of St Martin's
Hall'; *Illustrated London News* (16 February 1850), p. 116.

song sheets were on sale at the soirees and through radical booksellers.
In addition to these, Lowry published his own original compositions
as fully notated sheet music appropriate for the drawing room. He
named this series *Songs for the People* to make clear the connection to
Jones's lecture series. Given that a stated objective was to take *Song of
the 'Lower Classes'* into the home, itself an acknowledgement of the
growing market for domestic music, the conversion into parlour music
was an obvious development.[170] The determination on the part of
Lowry to produce original sheet music for *Song of the 'Lower Classes'*
and other songs for the soirees points to the moral and intellectual
objectives as well as the social aspirations represented by drawing
room music.[171]

   In terms of their appearance, Lowry's publications assumed many
of the features of popular sheet music typography.[172] As other publishers were doing, he sought to promote his publications by establishing

himself up as a celebrity singer – along the lines of popular performers such as Henry Russell, Madams Vestris and Vaneri – and many advertisements stressed his talent as a vocalist. The importance of his performances as a selling point was evident at the top of the page: *Songs for the People*, potential customers were advised, had been '[c]omposed expressly for and enthusiastically received at the Political Soirees, St Martin's Hall, London'. It is clear from other aspects of the appearance of Lowry's scores that he had given careful thought to a marketing strategy. Whereas his sentimental ballad *Stars of the Night* follows the typical format of a popular ballad with a highly coloured pictorial front page and a catalogue of his compositions accompanied by newspaper reviews on the back, the two surviving *Songs for the People* are more sober and serious in appearance. Here, Lowry judiciously eschewed visual extravagance for a simple black-and-white font with no illustrations (see figure 1.4). As Derek B. Scott reminds us, the lack of colour was considered less vulgar; the decorative rather than pictorial title page was intended to communicate the high-minded seriousness of what lay between the cover pages.[173] The parlour room song was a capacious genre that included a wide range of types from Scottish folk songs to 'blackface' minstrel hits.[174] Despite their modest musical attributes, Lowry's *Songs of the People* stand apart as an example of where what one of the present authors has called the 'trade of agitation' was brought into direct contact with a music culture undergoing profound and rapid transformation through a new kind of professionalisation and commercialisation.[175]

Why did Jones, who had spoken so dismissively of music's role in political change in 1850, change his opinion so radically? Why was he so convinced of music's power to 'introduce and engraft' political truths 'onto the minds of the people' just six years later? The elevated and central position that music assumed in mid-nineteenth-century Britain may be a partial answer. There was a renewed recognition of music's capacity to elicit sympathy, of its 'intimate relationship to the soul'.[176] For the artists and intellectuals who embraced art for art's sake, the condition of music became, as the Victorian aesthete and critic Walter Pater so famously put it, that to which all art aspired.[177] It was not only artists who were seduced by the 'language of the emotions'; the working-class poet J. B. Leno, a comrade of Jones and Lowry, well understood music's usefulness, noting in less extravagant prose than Pater that, 'Utility and amusement do not always walk hand in hand, but in the highways and byways of a song, their separation can never be of long duration.'[178] Music had at once an enormous symbolic power as an artistic ideal and a utilitarian capacity to improve. For middle-class reformers, music became the key vehicle in the rational

SONGS FOR THE PEOPLE.

Composed expressly for and enthusiastically received at the Political Soirees, St. Martin's Hall, London.

THE SONG

OF THE

"LOWER" CLASSES.

THE POEM BY

ERNEST JONES,

THE MUSIC COMPOSED & SUNG BY

JOHN LOWRY.

PRICE THREEPENCE.

LONDON: John Lowry, 115a, Old Street, Finsbury, and of all Book and Music Sellers.

1.4 Title cover of John Lowry's setting of Ernest Jones's *Song of the 'Lower Classes'*. The poem first appeared as *Song of the Low* in Jones's *Notes to the People* in April 1852 and later in the same year in his next newspaper publishing venture, the *People's Paper*. In 1856 it was set to original music by Lowry. In this form it was published and sold (by Lowry) as sheet music.

recreation movement that sought to control and provide social and moral improvement for the lower classes.[179]

The concept of originality was already an unquestioned aesthetic doctrine in art music and it was one Jones wished to buy into to assert his status as a creative artist as well as a respectable politician.[180] Music, as Cyril Ehrlich reminds us, had become 'a highly respectablising activity',[181] and one of the driving forces behind Jones's 'novel experiment' was a desire to attain this very Victorian of aspirations. Appropriate music provided a way to improve the reputation of politics, which had been, according to the once shamelessly unrespectable Chartist, 'too much confined to the tavern and the pothouse'. It was, Jones continued, 'the object of the soirees to introduce them on a more appropriate stage and to accompany them with musical and social recreation'.[182] In five years he had come a long way from his declaration that nations could no longer be 'sung into liberty'.[183] In this new and rapidly changing political and cultural terrain he sought to advance his own shifting political career by connecting politics to appropriate forms of musical recreation.[184] By making formal what was previously informal, Jones sought to move from the sphere of what Scott has termed 'unofficial culture' to a more formal political framework.[185] Lowry's decision to compose original scores for Jones's similarly original odes was bound up with the status accorded to these emerging aesthetic categories. Given the openly polarising and unrespectable character of Song of the 'Lower Classes', it is ironic that it occupied such an important position in Jones's new shift to the centre, which depended on attracting a new middle-class audience and attaining an increased respectability (see figure 1.5). Lowry's score reveals his compositional talents to be at best meagre (further support for the amusing but ungenerous observation that 'Victorians, it seemed, could do anything with music – except compose it').[186] If it were not for the political circumstances that produced these modest compositions, they would perhaps take their place in what Lowry's better-known contemporary Eliza Cook dismissed in her eponymous Journal as the 'heap of Polka and Song' that 'we really must condemn to the tender mercies of the waste-paper basket'.[187]

As we have seen, the initial advertising for the lectures clearly stated that 'a series of Democratic songs, by Ernest Jones, will be given, *partly to popular and well-known airs, partly to original music* [emphasis added]'.[188] The musical hybridity and flexibility found in the different forms of song production of Songs of Democracy and Songs for the People was then present from the very outset. It is important to remember here too that the People's Paper provides accounts of public performances of Song of the 'Lower Classes' as early as 1852,[189] well

1.5 Opening page of John Lowry's setting of *Song of the 'Lower Classes'*. The 1856 version has been hand-corrected to rectify an obvious mistake in the original published in 1852. In the seventh line of the first verse 'bread to grow' has been changed to 'grain to grow'.

before Lowry put pen to paper. *Song of the 'Lower Classes'* went on to feature throughout the soirees in different musical guises. At times Lowry sang his original setting; at others it was sung to popular airs. The *Morning Chronicle* noted that it could be sung to the *Monks of Old*, whereas the *People's Paper* suggested *The Brave Old Oak*. In later collections *The Lass of Richmond Hill* and *My Old Friend John* were nominated. Popular airs – staples of the broadside ballad repertoire – allowed for participatory singing, whereas the original fixed work could find a place in the domestic setting of the parlour.[190] It would seem in this case that Jones and Lowry, driven by pragmatism, took advantage of the full range of available publishing and performing options.

The relationship between Lowry's version and these other possible settings using pre-existing tunes reveals important aspects of the musical and political culture of this period. *Song of the 'Lower Classes'* has already received attention by two important scholars of popular music, Derek B. Scott and Richard Middleton.[191] Neither of them, however, noted that the song was written and performed to popular airs. Instead their discussion focuses entirely on Lowry's original score of 1856. Scott uses Lowry's setting to argue that the working class recognised the 'strength of the dominant culture' and so appropriated the genre and musical style of 'bourgeois domestic music' to give their protest 'greater dignity or status'.[192] It is interesting to view this interpretation against Vic Gammon's earlier claim that, given the fluidity of Victorian culture, song type could not easily be equated with class.[193] Middleton has offered a comparison between *Song of the 'Lower Classes'* and the *Marseillaise*, making much of their shared martial character and their openings both marked by an initial interval of a rising fourth. This is, however, not only a standard opening device for tonal music, as it clearly establishes the key of the piece, but also, perhaps more significantly, an opening feature of all the popular tunes that have been used for *Song of the 'Lower Classes'*, including the ones used later in the century.

In terms of rhythmic motives and overall character, Lowry's version has much in common with *The Brave Old Oak*, which also shares the simple metre and major mode of Lowry's song. The British song is also warlike in character; its influence is apparent in Lowry's indication of *marcato* (marked) at the start of the work. One could argue that Lowry may have had this popular air in mind when he composed his own music and was drawing upon its recognisability (see figure 1.6). The other common setting, the *Monks of Old*, is an anomaly in important ways. Most notably, it is in compound time; the more jovial rolling character created by this metre renders it more bucolic than bellicose. In fact, it is almost the antithesis of a martial anthem and thereby in

Song of the 'Lower Classes'

Brave Old Oak

1.6 Comparison of the openings of Lowry's setting of *Song of the 'Lower Classes'*, bars 5–8 and *The Brave Old Oak*, bars 9–12. *The Brave Old Oak* was written by Edward Loder (with lyrics by Henry Chorley) and first appeared in 1834.

a gentle way musically supports the heavy irony of the parentheses around 'Lower Classes' in the title (see figure 1.6).

The co-existence of both pre-existing tunes and Lowry's original music begs attention. The flexibility of musical choice and the different modes of music-making maximised the range of dissemination. The audience was given a choice: to embrace the original contribution as a staged professional performance (or subsequent amateur performance in the parlour), or to have the familiar inclusive experience of participatory singing in a public venue. Jones was negotiating the efflorescence of print culture, including the production of cheap printed music, the changing forms of popular entertainment and the professionalisation of music with the expectations of his audiences, which were increasingly drawn from a range of social classes. He was attempting to straddle different worlds and audiences: one that privileged fixed works of originality and those that offered a more familiar shared experience of the popular oral tradition. Obviously,

1.7 Opening of *Monks of Old*, bars 1–8. *Monks of Old* was composed by Stephen Glover (with lyrics by William Jones) and published in 1842.

Jones did not want to lose his predominantly working-class audience; after all, his poetry dealt with their everyday existence. He therefore needed to retain the mode of communication that spoke directly to, and involved, his audience. He did not want to ventriloquise for the working class. This was their song: they should be able to sing it. But he also wanted to legitimise his own position as politician and poet. In effect he was bridging print and oral culture, collective and staged entertainment, the working and middle classes and taking account of shifts in working-class culture. Rather than a 'collision between bourgeois and working-class musical practice' (to borrow Scott's words), or a surrender to hegemonic cultural pressures, this venture seems to have been carefully conceived and strategically implemented.[194]

In its various forms, *Song of the 'Lower Classes'* was a response to a musical and political world in transition: designed to take full advantage of possible audiences and modes of consumption. The case of Leno, a prominent late Chartist, is also illuminating here. One of his better-known lyrics, *Song of the Spade*, was also set to music by Lowry. In his memoir, however, Leno boasted that not only had it been published in many European languages but had also been set to 'at least, *four different tunes,* in England and America [emphasis added]'.[195] That the use of multiple possible tunes was for Leno a sign of success captures this moment of transition. The idea of a popular song was mutable. This musical flexibility, which as far as Leno was concerned in no way affected its state as a single 'song' or the importance of Lowry's role, reminds us that the ontological conception of a song at this time was fundamentally different to current understanding. At the same time, Leno's experience demonstrates the evolving modes of cultural production. Writing in 1892, Leno claimed that he was 'never desirous' of hearing his songs 'sung in the streets'. The 'surest way to kill a good song', he opined, was 'to over popularise it'. Although he went on to confess to a sneaking pride when he heard one of his tunes 'pass from the lips of a street singer' he suggested he would have been even more pleased 'if the singer had learned them from copies [he] had sanctioned'.[196]

Lowry's role in the soirees was recognised beyond his singing and compositional achievements. His direction over the musical segments of the evenings was unanimously praised in the press. We know too that he shared Jones's commitment to radical reform, an association that continued well into the 1870s. Who then was he? If Jones was notorious, Lowry was not. We know that at some point in the mid-1850s, he converted his modest tobacconist in Old Street in the unfashionable London district of St Luke's into a music-selling business. As newspapers such as the *Era* and the *People's Paper* tell us, Lowry had been actively promoting himself as a musical director and singer for several years before the soirees.[197] He had combined musical activity with political interests from at least the early 1850s and was to continue this long after his collaborative venture with Jones. It is clear from his presence in Jones's paper that by 1856 their relationship was already well established.

An examination of Lowry's activities opens up a window onto a network of writers and musicians with similar interests in music, poetry and radical politics. Indeed, if we use Jones and Lowry's network of relationships as a point of entry we can glimpse an expansive landscape of reform underpinned by a shared involvement in making music and popular cultural production. Eliza Cook, to take the first example, was a talented poet, feminist and radical thinker who hailed from a working-class background. By dint of her own brow and tenacity she succeeded in the highly competitive world of popular print culture, her journal attracting an extensive audience.[198] Although Cook became internationally famous for thoroughly apolitical hits, such as the sentimental *The Old Armchair*, she believed strongly in democratic ideas and wrote poems with overtly political and radical themes, which found a receptive audience in radical newspapers, including the *Northern Star* and Jones's *People's Paper*. G. W. M. Reynolds, Jones's rival for the hearts and minds of the later Chartists and radical liberals, published Cook's verse in his prodigiously successful newspaper, referring to her as the 'poetess of the people'.[199] Her verse was set to music by many composers including Lowry, who wrote the music for her mawkish poem *The Blind Boy's Been At Play, Mother*.

The popularity of Cook's *The Old Armchair* was due in part to the fact that Henry Russell set it to music. Russell was a very popular composer and singer who enjoyed celebrity on both sides of the Atlantic. In addition to his panoply of apolitical hits Russell produced a handful of songs concerned with social issues. As well as setting many of Cook's poems to music, he worked closely with the popular poet, journalist and writer Charles Mackay. A Scot, Mackay was also committed to social reform and was known, for example, for his support of the Anti-Corn Law League. Two of his most famous songs, *Cheer Boys Cheer* and *There's a Good Time Coming* (set to music by Russell), are examples of a bold optimism in the face of hardship. Both songs became enduring hits around the Anglophone world and quickly became staples in the political canon, appearing in countless political songbooks and as song sheets. Mackay and Russell's shared belief in the importance of political reform is also seen in a lesser-known song, *Gather Ye Nations, Gather; or The Festival of Labour*, which they 'respectfully dedicated' to Richard Cobden, the pre-eminent leader of the League and one of the most important radical liberals of the day.

As we have seen, Leno was also part of the Lowry–Jones network. He first came to notice as the founder and editor of a radical newspaper, the Uxbridge *Spirit of Freedom*. Having moved to London in 1851, Leno immersed himself in radical activities; he founded an organisation known as the Propagandists and became deeply involved in the Reform League. Composing poetry was part of his political life, as he remarked, 'If I was not on the platform, I was engaged in council or scribbling an article or a song with a political purpose.'[200] His journalistic career was given a fillip when he replaced Cook as contributor to the *Weekly Dispatch*. He also had his poetry published, advertised and reviewed in radical newspapers including the *Workingman's Advocate*, the *Commonwealth* and the *People's Paper*. The latter regularly featured his poems and also reported on both his singing as well as his politicking, often both occurring at the same event.[201] Leno married his radical activism with his literary and musical talent with such success that he was dubbed as both a 'poetic Radical' and 'the Burns of Labour'.[202] Jones's own review of a volume of Leno's poetry declared the *Song of the Spade* to be 'equal to the lyrics of Mackay'.[203] The article also noted that Lowry set many of his poems to music. As we have seen, this included *Song of the Spade* as well as his other well-known piece,

Judge Not a Man. As with *Song of the 'Lower Classes'*, Lowry published *Judge Not a Man* separately as sheet music.[204] The association between Leno and Lowry continued well into the 1860s. Charles Watts and Austin Holyoake's *Secularist's Manual of Songs and Ceremonies* (1871) included several of Leno's songs with the indication that they were set to music by Lowry (this will be discussed in a later chapter).[205] In addition to his contributions to the *Secularist's Manual of Songs and Ceremonies*, Lowry wrote election songs for Charles Bradlaugh's campaigns and lectured alongside G. J. Holyoake and other important radical figures such as Harriet Law.[206]

Thus, by joining the crowd at the remarkable *Evenings for the People* held in Hullah's St Martin's Hall and pursuing the partnership between Ernest Jones and John Lowry we learn much about the cultural life of radical London in the middle years of Queen Victoria's reign. It provides us with a way of meeting a broader group of intellectuals, reformers, radicals, poets and musicians whose music-making was inextricably linked to their campaign for a better world; it provides a way to glimpse a vast, seething cultural system of music publishing, performance, composition and consumption.

It is not at the heart of the imperial metropolis where the story of *Song of the 'Lower Classes'* ends. Although Lowry's original setting was never to find the abiding place in the household he desired, *Song of the 'Lower Classes'* travelled the Anglophone world as part of a shared radical and reformist culture. Lowry's music didn't make the journey but Jones's lyrics did not travel unaccompanied as poetry. On the contrary, an array of popular tunes could and did make the trip. The spontaneous expression of an oral culture demanded immediacy; and thus the title of the tune had to provide for extemporaneous performances of participatory music. Leno, it will be recalled, boasted that his *Song of the Spade* had been sung to at least four tunes. As we have seen, in addition to Lowry's musical scribbling, *Song of the 'Lower Classes'* also attracted four tunes: *The Brave Old Oak* and *Monks of Old* gave way over time to James Hook's *Lass of Richmond Hill* and the broadside ballad *My Old Friend John*.[207] The latter two melodies are markedly similar in terms of melodic shape, metre and rhythmic patterns to the previous settings, including Lowry's.

The trajectory of *Song of the 'Lower Classes'* across space and time is worth lingering over. Indeed, the vicissitudes of the humble song provide eloquent testimony to the existence of a radical and reformist culture that criss-crossed the Anglophone world. Even before it appeared in Leno's *Reformer's Book of Songs and Recitations* in 1867 and the secularist manual four years later, it had appeared in radical publications in Boston, Chardon (Ohio) and Sydney. In August 1865

the *Boston Daily Evening Voice*, a publication of the labour movement, reprinted the entire song unaltered (apart from the title which
was changed to *Song of the Unenfranchised*).[208] A month later it
featured – with the same new title – on the front page of Chardon's
Jeffersonian Democrat, a newspaper 'devoted to dissemination of
Republican principles, education, temperance, literature [and] agriculture'. Although he did not credit Jones, the paper's owner and editor
Julius Orrin Converse, a pugnacious Republican Party stalwart, was
entirely familiar with the original context of the song's production (and
the fact that it was sung). 'The following song', he noted, 'is being sung
in England by several millions of the unenfranchised working men, to
the disgust of the snobs and aristocrats.'[209] Three years later, in mid-
1868, Jones's song appeared in Sydney's *Freeman's Journal* (this time
with the original title).[210] In 1878, it surfaced again in north-eastern
United States, this time in the radical *Labor Standard*, the organ of the
newly established International Labor Union, which comprised dis-
enchanted Marxists and former members of the Workingmen's Party
of the United States who had elected not to stay in the now renamed
Socialist Labor Party. Whether or not these apparatchiks knew of
Jones's personal connection to Marx, they nonetheless acknowledged
Jones as 'our deceased friend'.[211]

Around the turn of the century the song was published in Melbourne
democratic monthly *The Beacon*.[212] In 1893 Henry Taylor quoted lines
from the song during a lecture he gave in the small South Australian
town of Burra. The lecture focused on poverty and the failures of the
agricultural industry and the taxation system to adequately remunerate
the worker.[213] At the time Taylor was secretary of the South Australian
Single Tax League (inspired by Henry George's nostrums) and was
soon to embark on the first boat full of Christian Socialists heading
to Paraguay to found Lane's New Australia Colony. Jones's lyrics certainly sat well with George's ideas (even in a South Australian dust-
bowl); whether they made it to Paraguay is not known. The song also
appeared in Sydney's *Mail and New South Wales Advertiser* (1878),
the Launceston *Cornwall Chronicle* (1879) and the *Euroa Advertiser* in
Victoria (1894).[214] Of course, the song continued to appear sporadically
in Britain. In 1867 an account of a meeting of the Holborn chapter of
the Reform League on Clerkenwell Green, for example, indicated that
it had been among the evening's extensive repertoire. Fifteen years
later, in 1881, the *Cooperative News*, based in the north of England,
published the song (under the title *Song of the Unenfranchised*) 'by
request' following its performance at Co-operative Society's annual tea
meeting held at the Mechanic's Institute in the village of Windy Nook
in Tyne and Wear.[215] Other British radical newspapers that included

Jones's song among their cultural offerings in the final decades of the century included the *Voice of the People*, the *Eastern Weekly Leader* and the *Gadfly*.[216]

Song of the 'Lower Classes' continued to feature intermittently in radical and labour newspapers around the Anglophone world from the turn of the nineteenth century into the early decades of the twentieth. Brisbane's *Worker*, for example, featured the song on several occasions between 1898 and 1930.[217] Another Australian newspaper with the title *Worker* (published in the small town of Wagga Wagga in rural New South Wales) published the song in 1889 in connection with a discussion of 'Work and Wages'. The decision to publish emphasised the ongoing transnational links within the labour movement: the source was identified as Morris's *Commonweal*. The editor chose to print it again eight months later to support an article on the close relationship between the Australian and British labour movements at a time when what were relatively massive amounts of money were flowing back and forth in support of strikers.[218] In 1907 Sydney's *People*, the official organ of the Australian Socialist League, underscored even further what it perceived to be the song's relevance to debates about wages and arbitration by the inclusion of a caption: 'A chattel-slave was a slave, and he never voted for it; a serf was a serf, and he never voted for it. But a Wage Slave is a slave, and he votes for it.'[219] Jones would have approved. It appeared again in Sydney's *International Socialist* in 1910.[220] But this was not just a bilateral relationship. At about the same time the song appeared in Manitoba's labour newspaper, the *Voice*.[221] Its publication in 1893 in New Zealand's *Auckland Star* highlights the web of transnational and inter-colonial connections aided by syndication: identical accounts of the lyric's genesis by way of headnote appeared in the *Wrexham Advertiser* and the *Hampshire Telegraph and Sussex Chronicle* within weeks of one another.[222] It also attracted hostile comment in the land of the long white cloud. Writing in 1896, a correspondent to the Nelson *Colonist* described it tautologically as 'flapdoodle rubbish': 'spicy and racy, and high sounding without much meaning'.[223] Wellington's socialist newspaper the *Commonweal*, by contrast, published it enthusiastically in 1908. In 1913 R. S. Ross, in a thumbnail sketch of Jones ('The Poet of the Chartists') published in his *Maoriland Worker*, described it as an 'evergreen' song.[224] These sporadic appearances invite questions about the role played by the movement of individuals and the cultural baggage they chose to take with them. How it ended up in Chardon, Boston, Wellington, Auckland, Manitoba, Melbourne, Sydney, Burra, Euroa, Wagga Wagga or Windy Nook are questions for which, in many cases, we have no definitive answers. Whose suitcase contained a copy of a radical newspaper? Who had committed it to memory unaffected by time and distance? Although we should not give up the search for answers to these specific questions, what we can clearly see here are the tendrils of a transnational and inter-colonial cultural formation linking radicals and reformers geographically and diachronically.

The array of examples given above clearly indicate that *Song of the 'Lower Classes'* spoke to a particular audience among radicals and reformers and, for a relatively minor composition, enjoyed a wide audience among the faithful as well as a surprising longevity. Its appearance in mainstream collections would have brought the song to the attention of many beyond the ranks of radicalism and reform. For example, the inclusion of Jones in Alfred Miles's multi-volume omnibus *The Poets and the Poetry of the Nineteenth Century* in 1892 was a mark of recognition if not success. Miles included a short biography and eight of Jones's musings, including *Song of the 'Lower Classes'*. Had he lived, Jones would have no doubt felt damned by faint praise: his verse, Miles concluded, had a 'simple directness' suitable for 'popular use'.[225] This was a more generous appraisal than the one the song received in John Ashton's well-known *Modern Street Ballads*, published four years earlier in 1888. Ashton included *Song of the 'Lower Classes'* as a representative political ballad and he made no pretence at impartiality in his introductory paragraph, dismissing it as the 'sort of stuff that was disseminated among the people at the time of the agitation for "the Charter"'. He sought, apocryphally, to connect the song to the 'convulsion of 1848, which shook Europe to its centre' and retrospectively congratulated the lower classes for their 'good sense ... that they were not stirred up to acts of violence by such inflammatory rubbish'.[226] The cruellest blow, however, awaited Jones with the publication of Henry Coppeé's *The Classic and the Beautiful from the Literature of Three Thousand Years* in Philadelphia in 1900. The collection included *Song of the Unenfranchised* but listed its author as Anon.[227]

The big loser in the process of transmission and the effluxion of time was John Lowry. For the performance of *Song of the 'Lower Classes'* in the Festival of Music for the People in 1939, British modernist composer Elizabeth Maconchy arranged Lowry's original composition rather than any of the popular airs associated with it. But this is very much the exception which proves the rule. Indeed, Ashton was one of the few after the 1860s to nominate Lowry's music (and the earlier *Monks of Old*). There is an irony in the failure of Lowry's original music to take hold, as it was increasingly a desire of late Victorian socialists to seek new forms of artistic expression, a desire presaged in Jones and Lowry's endeavour decades earlier. They keenly felt the tension between building on accustomed cultural practices and

[85]

providing a new culture for a new age.[228] Unlike other Chartist songs such as Thomas Cooper's *Truth is Growing*, Jones's song never became a staple of late nineteenth-century socialist songbook literature. By way of explanation, Chris Waters suggests that its overtly revolutionary content precluded its inclusion in key socialist song collections produced by the more moderate form of socialism espoused by socialist movements such as the Fabians and the Labour Church. The Socialist Democratic Front (SDF) and Socialist League had no such reservations and *Song of the 'Lower Classes'* appeared in their songbooks along with a handful of earlier radical songs.[229] This tendency was felt as far away as Sydney, where the Social Democratic League included it in their *Socialist Songs* as *We're So Very Low* with *My Old Friend John* as the suggested tune. The Aberdeen branch of the Socialist League offered as the tune either *Lass of Richmond Hill* or *My Old Friend John*.[230] James Leatham, organiser of the branch and loyal supporter of William Morris, included it again in his reprint of the *Songs for Socialists* the following year in 1890. The Aberdonians were closely connected to the SDF and the songbooks included advertisements for the SDF's journal, *Justice*, as well as freethinker William Stewart Ross's *Agnostic Journal*. The advertisements themselves point to a close network of likeminded groups. Ross published his own collection of socialist songs (under his publisher's name W. Stewart & Co.) around the same time with the two tunes identified grudgingly with the prefatory explanation that the '[s]ongs [were] not selected because they were the best' but because they 'had managed to secure well-known tunes for them'.[231]

Another Scottish socialist, John Bruce Glasier, put forward a similar case. His own uncertainty about using pre-existing music comes through in the preface to his collection where he explained his decision not to set tunes to many of the songs:

> To the most of these, tunes might have easily been assigned, but I did not think it wise (now that a fair number set to tunes are available) to be in haste to fix down songs breathing the spirit of a new social life to airs of the past, many of which are instinct with feeling or reminiscences of an anti-Socialist character, and many of which however suitable otherwise, could only be parted with merciless violence from the words to which they have long been wedded.[232]

Despite these misgivings, *Song of the 'Lower Classes'* appeared in Glasier's volume with *Lass of Richmond Hill* offered as the tune.[233]

The inclusion of *Song of the 'Lower Classes'* in Fabian socialist William Reeves's *Songbook for Socialists* stands as an exception to Waters's claim. Reeves arrived in Britain from New Zealand with his suffragist wife in 1889 and produced *Songbook for Socialists* soon after. He continued his involvement in radical publishing and quickly became involved in Fabian circles, making friends with Sidney and Beatrice Webb among others. Perhaps his passionate interest in taxation and wage arbitration goes some way to account for the inclusion of Jones's song in his collection.[234]

British social reformer, socialist, central figure in the Humanitarian League and author of another staple of socialist song literature, *Hark! The Battle Cry is Ringing*, H. S. Salt generously acknowledged the earlier generations of minor radical poets in his substantial volume *Songs of Freedom*.[235] Jones took his place among other Chartist poets in Salt's collection, characterised as: 'Men of less genius, but truer social instincts'. Salt concluded, somewhat patronisingly, that 'to these lesser men will be the greater honour'. *Song of the 'Lower Classes'* won special mention as an example of a poem of 'genuine passion', which was therefore 'more deserving of immortality, than many of the productions of misinformed, or indifferent, or purely "academic" genius'.[236]

Despite the obvious enthusiasm the more extreme socialist factions had for the song, its enduring place in socialist song literature was due also to Edward Carpenter, whose bohemian lifestyle and middle-class disposition perhaps set him apart from the more extreme political Left (although his *England Arise* became a popular labour anthem). Carpenter included *Song of the 'Lower Classes'* in his iconic collection *Chants of Labour*.[237] The influence of this seminal volume spread far across the Anglophone world and played a key role in the creation of a socialist song canon in which *Song of the 'Lower Classes'* occupied a modest position. A review of *Chants of Labour* in the *Commonweal* isolated a moment in the song's development. The reviewer rebuked Carpenter for his failure to always use 'fitting tunes' and used Jones's song as an example where the song had been 'torn away from its own air, the one written for it, and to which it was published and quite unnecessarily given another, hitherto unconnected with it'.[238] The melodic interloper that supplanted Lowry was *My Old Friend John*, which quickly became the tune that dominated subsequent socialist publications. The rapid uptake of the new melody once again demonstrates the enormous adaptability of popular political song culture.

Chants of Labour's influence is also felt in the songbooks of the American labour movement, for example in the collections produced by labour leaders such as Thomas Phillips Thompson. Phillips Thompson was a thoroughly transnational figure. Born in Newcastle upon Tyne, he emigrated as a child with his family to Canada in 1857 and went on to spend a formative period of his professional life working as a journalist in Boston before returning to Canada. In political terms his adult years were marked by an inexorable shift to the left. His increasing concern for the working classes took him into the labour movement both as an activist and journalist and resulted in his active membership in the Knights of Labor, one of the most powerful labour organisations in North America at the time. By the mid-1880s Phillips Thompson was a regular writer for the *Palladium of Labor*, the main journal of the Knights. For our purposes it is important to note that a significant contribution to the organisation was his *Labor Reform Songster*, published by the Knights in 1892. *Song of the 'Lower Classes'* is the final song in his collection, accompanied by the notated melody of *My Old Friend John*.[239]

A 'bunch of keys'

In different ways the three case studies explored in the preceding pages contribute to an understanding of the importance of song and singing in nineteenth-century demotic politics and the role of print and the oral tradition – separately and together – in transmitting and sustaining a radical and reformist culture. Retracing some of the myriad journeys of these three songs across time and place throws up a rich diversity of events, individuals and material objects to ponder. They reveal important differences and idiosyncrasies in the lived experience of politics produced by diverse contexts, but they also reveal shared dispositions and a collective repertoire of cultural practices. They remind us of the centrality of music in everyday political life during the long nineteenth century.

We have also seen how distinctive songs operated in different ways. The *Marseillaise* was a song of the world; it became so because it was *the* sound of liberty. When a humble district secretary of the Australian Workers Association in Far North Queensland came across a gang of German cane workers who spoke no English he knew they were onside because, he reported, they could sing the *Marseillaise*.[240] Nothing had changed since the *fédérés* of Marseilles marched into Paris. Unsurprisingly, the melody attracted contrafacta – too numerous to catalogue – with one thing in common: the idea that their cause was a struggle for liberty. *John Anderson my Jo* was not a political song as such but it was part of a known and shared reservoir of culture that provided the basis for an intimate conversation between the collective and an individual political figure, albeit to express fidelity or point a finger of rebuke. *Song of the 'Lower Classes'* was a political song in every sense. Its sporadic appearances far and wide – published and performed – meant that it too was in some senses a song of the world. Unlike the *Marseillaise*, however, the text remained remarkably unchanged across space and time. The music was a different matter. Although it attracted an original composition it could and was sung to several others. This apparent insouciance in respect of the music does not diminish its import. On the contrary, it highlights the myriad ways that radicalism and reform drew upon a broader cultural formation. Sometimes the melody meant everything; at others any old tune would do so long as it fitted the words. Thinking again of songs as keys – not strictly in Webb's sense of the word, but as a device to help unlock meaning – has proved to be enormously useful as a starting point. They have also led us to events, objects and individuals worthy of investigation. In both instances, the sounds of liberty – often faint, sometimes deafening – draw us in search of more.

Notes

1 Beatrice Webb, *My Apprenticeship*, vol. 2 (Harmondsworth: Penguin Books, 1938), pp. 404–5.

2 Matthew Gelbart, *The Invention of 'Folk Music' and 'Art Music': Emerging Categories from Ossian to Wagner* (Cambridge: Cambridge University Press, 2011).

3 Laura Mason, *Singing the French Revolution: Popular Culture and Politics, 1787–1799* (Ithaca: Cornell University Press, 1996), p. 99. Although it has long been assumed that de Lisle composed the music as well as the text, there has recently been some debate led by the violinist Guido Rimonda as to whether de Lisle borrowed the theme from the *Theme and Variations in C major* written over a decade earlier in 1781 by the Italian composer Giovanni Battista Viotti (1755–1824). An appropriation of Viotti's music would account for the song's comparatively sophisticated musical language. Rimonda, a recognised Viotti specialist, has recorded the work with the Orchestra Camerata Ducale. Although this discovery has not yet received scholarly attention, Rimonda and the Orchestra Camerata Ducala have publicised this claim. See, for example, the Ricardo Lenzi, 'La Marsilgeliese? E' di un italiano', *l'Espresso*, 9 May 2013, available at http://espresso.repubblica.it/visioni/cultura/2013/05/09/news/la-marsigliese-e-di-un-italiano-1.54308?refresh_ce (accessed 1 December 2015); 'Progetto Viotti', Orchestra Camerata Ducale official website available at www.camerataducale.it/_dynapage/index_Home.asp?pageId=79&lingua=l2 (accessed 1 December 2015).

4 Alphonse de Lamartine, *History of the Girondists, or Personal Memoirs of the Patriots of the French Revolution. From Unpublished Sources*, 3 vols (London: Henry G. Bohn, 1848).

5 See James Johnson, *The Scots Musical Museum* (London; Edinburgh, 1787–1803). There is another somewhat anomalous version in Percy's *Reliques of Ancient English Poetry* (1765), which bears little resemblance to other versions. In a lengthy headnote Percy claimed that it was a 'burlesque sonnet' set to 'solemn church music' written during the reformation as an attack against the Catholic Church. According to Percy the original was held 'in an ancient MS. Collection of Scottish poems in the Pepysian library'. John Anderson himself was a town piper from Kelso sometime in the 1600s. See Thomas Percy, *Reliques of Ancient English Poetry*, vol. 2 (London: Dodsley, 1765), pp. 110–11. This is repeated in the notes found in the *Scots Musical Museum* index. For further details on its provenance see Norman Cazden, Herbert Haufrecht and Norman Studer, *Folk Songs of the Catskills* (Albany, NY: SUNY Press, 1982), pp. 368–9.

6 For a detailed account of the emergence of these collections, see Maureen N.

McLane, 'Mediating Antiquarians in Britain, 1760–1830: The Invention of Oral Tradition; Or, Close Reading Before Coleridge', in Clifford Siskin and William Warner (eds), *This is Enlightenment* (Chicago: University of Chicago Press, 2010), pp. 247–64.

7   Burns's poem appears in several broadside ballads with two additional stanzas.

8   The bawdy versions appear in *Philomel* (London, 1744) and *The Masque* (London, 1768) and appeared later in 1800 in Burns's own collection of bawdy and erotic verse, *The Merry Muses of Caledonia*. There is another obscure version in Percy's *Reliques of Ancient English Poetry* (1765) which bears no resemblance to either.

9   See John Watts, *The Musical Miscellany*, vol. 6, no. 202 (London: John Watts, 1731); Allan Ramsay (ed.), *The Tea-Table Miscellany: A Collection of Choice Songs, Scots and English*, 4 vols (Edinburgh: Thomas Ruddiman, 1723–37); James Oswald, *The Caledonian Pocket Companion*, vol. 4 (London: Printed for J. Simpson, 1745), p. 22; James Aird, *Selection of Scotch, English, Irish and Foreign Airs*, vol. 2, no. 167 (Glasgow: n.p., 1782).

10 See, for example, William Chappell, *Popular Music of the Olden Time: A Collection of Ancient Songs, Ballads, and Dance Tunes, Illustrative of the National Music of England* (London: Cramer, Beale and Chappell, 1859), pp. 117, 770.

11 Gelbart, *Invention of 'Folk Music' and 'Art Music'*, p. 1.

12 See Michel Foucault, 'Nietzsche, Genealogy, History' (1971), in Paul Rabinow (ed.), *The Foucault Reader* (New York: Pantheon, 1984), pp. 76–100.

13 'The Song of the "Lower Classes"', *Hampshire Telegraph and Sussex Chronicle* (3 June 1893). See also Alfred H. Miles (ed.), *The Poets and the Poetry of the Century* (London: Hutchinson, 1892), pp. 547–62. According to Miles, the ink was hidden in the soap and the pen fashioned from rooks' feathers gathered in the prison yard.

14 *Notes to the People*, vol. 2 (April 1852), p. 953; 'Poetry. "Truth Set to Music". Democratic Songs to Popular Airs. The Song of the Low', *People's Paper* (26 June 1852); 'Notices to Correspondents. Soiree for the "People's Paper"', *People's Paper* (15 January 1853).

15 This text is taken from the poem as it first appears in Jones's *Notes for the People* entitled 'Song of the Low'. There are many subsequent variants of title and text. See *Notes for the People* (April 1852), p. 953.

16 F. B. Smith, *William James Linton: Radical Artizan* (Manchester: Manchester University Press, 1974), pp. 123–4; *Oeuvres complètes de P.-J. de Béranger*, vol. 1 (Paris: Perrotin, 1847), pp. 185–6. See also Joseph Phelan, 'The British Reception of Pierre-Jean de Béranger', *Revue de littérature compare*, 1:313 (2005), pp. 5–20.

17 Richard Middleton gives an extended account of this song in which the social and political context is analysed in some detail. See Richard Middleton, *Voicing the Popular: On the Subjects of Popular Music* (London: Routledge, 2006), pp. 1–6.

18 Mason, *Singing the French Revolution*, p. 99.

19 McLane, 'Mediating Antiquarians in Britain', p. 256.

20 Carla Hesse, 'Print Culture in the Enlightenment', in Martin Fitzpatrick, Peter Jones, Christa Knellwolf and Iain McCalman (eds), *The Enlightenment World* (New York: Routledge, 2004), p. 379.

21 Mason, *Singing the French Revolution*, p. 2.

22 Quoted in Hugh Anderson, *Colonial Ballads* (Melbourne; Canberra; Sydney: F. W. Cheshire, 1955), p. 2.

23 See Gavin Souter, 'Lane, William (1861–1917)', *Australian Dictionary of Biography*, Australian National University, available at http://adb.anu.edu.au/biography/lane-william-7024/text12217 (accessed 8 September 2016); Gavin Souter, *A Peculiar People: The Australians in Paraguay* (Sydney: Sydney University Press, 1968).

24 William Lane, *The Workingman's Paradise: An Australian Labour Novel* (Sydney; Brisbane; London: Edwards. Dunlop & Co, 1892), pp. 61–2.

25 *Northern Star* (5 July 1845).

26 See Mason, *Singing the French Revolution*, p. 219.

27 [George Bernard Shaw], *London Music in 1889* (London: Constable & Co., 1950), p. 115.

28 Derek B. Scott repeats an earlier claim that along with the ban on performance by military bands, 'all public performances' of the *Marseillaise* were 'long proscribed'. J. C. Hadden, 'Our Patriotic Songs', in *British Minstrelsie*, vol. 5 (London: Blackwood, Le Bas, c.1890), p. iv, quoted in Derek Scott, *The Singing Bourgeois: Songs of the Victorian Drawing Room and Parlour* (Maidenhead: Open University Press, 1989), pp. 179–80. For Carlyle, see: 'Letter from Thomas Carlyle to Ralph Waldo Emerson, Chelsea, 14 November 1850', in *The Collected Letters*, vol. 25, pp. 279–281, *The Carlyle Letters Online: A Victorian Cultural Reference*, available at http://carlyleletters.dukejournals.org/ (accessed 9 September 2016).

29 Bishopsgate Institute, George Howell Collection, Howell Pamphlet, 103.32 782.4; J. D. Collett, *History of the Marseillais, and the Origin of the Marseillais Hymn from Lamartine's History of the Girondists – Also the Chaunt of the Girondins, with the Music, and Prose Translations of the Hymns* (London: J. Watson, 1848), p. 8 .

30 *Parliamentary History*, 31:708, quoted in John Barrell, 'Radicalism, Visual Culture, and Spectacle in the 1790s', *Romanticism on the Net*, 46 (May 2007), available at www.erudit.org/revue/ron/2007/v/n46/016131ar.html (accessed 8 September 2016).

31 'State Trials at Derby', *Morning Chronicle* (28 October 1817).

32 Hadden, 'Our Patriotic Songs', p. v. Scott discusses this passage in *Singing Bourgeois*, pp. 179–80.

33 Hadden, 'Our Patriotic Songs', p. iv. The unacknowledged quotation comes from Joseph Mainzer. See Joseph Mainzer, *Music and Education* (London: Longman, Brown, Green, and Longmans, 1848; republished by Cambridge University Press, 2013), p. 31.

34 Watkin Tench, *Letters Written in France to a Friend in London* (London: J. Johnson, 1796), p. 13.

35 See, for example, Michael Davis, '"An evening of pleasure rather than business": Songs, Subversion and Radical Sub-Culture in the 1790s', *Journal for the Study of British Culture*, 12:2 (2005), pp. 115–26. Davis notes the speed with which French revolutionary song was assimilated and shaped to the needs of British radicalism (see p. 120).

36 Iain McCalman, 'Newgate in Revolution: Radical Enthusiasm and Romantic Counterculture', *Eighteenth-Century Life*, 22:1 (1998), pp. 95–110.

37 For a detailed account of the importance of street literature including broadside ballads and popular song, see Leslie Shepard, *The History of Street Literature* (Devon: David & Charles, 1973).

38 See also *Spence's Songs* (1811). This collection also includes many songs by other Spenceans such as Evans and radical ballad singer William Tilly.

39 Allen Davenport, *Life, Writings and Principles of Thomas Spence* (London: n.p., 1836), p. 4; See also *A Humorous Catalogue of Spence's Songs by Mr. Evans* (England: n.p., 1807).

40 English translation of the Marseillaise, in *Pigs' Meat, Or Lessons for the Swinish Multitude*, 2nd edn (London: n.p., 1793), pp. 71–2.

41 In the provenance statement given by Christies auction house, Rouget de Lisle, Claude Joseph, [La Marseillaise]. 'Marche des Marseillois. Chantée sur diferans theatres. Chez Frere Passage du Saumon' (London: William Holland, 10 November 1792), is identified as 'the earliest edition known to have been printed in England'; Iain McCalman, *Radical Underworld: Prophets, Revolutionaries, and Pornographers in London, 1795–1840* (Cambridge: Cambridge University Press, 1988). McCalman also discussed Newton's engravings in 'Newgate in Revolution', pp. 95–110.

42 See *Anti-Gallican Songster* (London: J. Downes, 1793). John Halliwell has written on the appropriation of radical satire in a government publication, the loyalist *Anti-Jacobin*, designed to counteract the emerging counter-public sphere. See John

Halliwell, 'Loyalist Satire, Parody and *The Anti-Jacobin*', in Simon Hull (ed.), *The British Periodical Text, 1797–1835: A Collection of Essays* (Tirril: Humanities-EBooks, 2008), pp. 35–67.

43 'A Word or Two of Truth', *Anti-Gallican Songster*, vol. 1, p. 15.

44 'A New Song', *Anti-Gallican Songster*, vol. 1, p. 12.

45 Cambridge University Library, Madden Ballad Collection (hereafter Madden), vol. 15, no. 8, Thomas Spence *The Rights of Man* (London: T. Spence, 1783).

46 Other songs written and/or printed by Spence include *The Complaint of the Emerald Swine* set to *Ally Croaker*; *Address to the Swinish Multitude: Hair Powder Tax* set to *Down Derry*; *A New Song Dedicated to Liberty* set to *The Hardy Tar*; *A New Song* set to *Bow, Bow, Bow*; *Common Sense* set to *Maggie Lauder*; *Sergeant Kite's Invitation to the Swinish Multitude* set to *Old Sir Simon the King*; *Wholesome Advice to the Swinish Multitude* set to *Mind Huffey What You Do*. See Madden, vol. 15.

47 Madden, vol. 15, no. 61, *The Genius of Britain to the Tune of The Marseilles Hymn* (London: J. Asperne, 1803).

48 *Bury and Norwich Post* (4 August 1802).

49 *Morning Post* (13 August 1830).

50 'French Revolution', *Standard* (19 August 1830).

51 *Bury and Norwich Post* (18 August 1830).

52 *Hull Packet and Humber Mercury* (12 October 1830).

53 See *Freeman's Journal* (27 December 1830); 'Poland', *Morning Post* (8 January 1831); *Sheffield Independent* (5 May 1832).

54 'Important Dinner at Birmingham', *Belfast News* (19 October 1830). This was only one of several instances where broadside ballads were used to vilify Louis Philippe for his betrayal. See, for example, Madden, vol. 12, no. 313, *The Subjects of the Times, or the Scenes of 1848* (Seven Dials 10 & 39 St. Andrews St.: Thomas Birt).

55 W. J. Linton, *Threescore and Ten Years 1820 to 1890* (New York: Charles Scribner's Sons, 1894), p. 105.

56 See Smith, *William James Linton*, pp. 73–4.

57 'Report of the Delegation to Paris', *Northern Star* (11 March 1848).

58 *Ibid.*; 'Great Meeting in the Salle de Valentino, Rue St Honore', *Northern Star* (11 March 1848).

59 See also *People's Paper* (31 December 1853).

60 'The Hopes of '48', *People's Paper* (11 February 1854).

61 See *Socialist Songs* (Wellington: New Zealand Socialist Party, 1908), no. 26 and *Socialist Songs* (Melbourne: Socialist Party Press, 1907), no. 26.

62 *Derby Mercury* (26 April 1871).

63 Anne Janowitz, *Lyric and Labour in the Romantic Tradition* (Cambridge: Cambridge University Press, 1998), p. 230.

64 For handbills, cards, programmes and song sheets produced for these events, see International Institute of Social History, Amsterdam, Socialist League (UK) Archives, Items SL 3453, 3455–3458.

65 David Nicoll, 'A New Marseillaise', *Commonweal* (July 1885), p. 11. It appeared in Brisbane's *Worker* on 2 December 1893.

66 See Rosemary Ashton, *Little Germany: Exile and Asylum in Victorian England* (Oxford; New York: Oxford University Press, 1986).

67 'Commemoration of the Glorious Lesson to Tyrants, The Destruction of the French Bastille By the Brave Parisians. July 14, 1789', *Northern Star* (18 July 1846).

68 'Vile Doings in Newgate', *Northern Star* (22 June 1850).

69 'Meeting of Fraternal Democrats', *Northern Star* (14 September 1850).

70 'Poland and Hungary!', *Northern Star* (19 October 1850). See also 'Sympathy with Hungary and Poland', *Northern Star* (26 October 1850) and 'Poland, Hungary and England', *Northern Star* (21 December 1850).

71 *Morning Post* (14 September 1819); *Black Dwarf* (7 August 1822); *Worker* (25 November 1893); *Maoriland Worker* (10 December 1913).

72   See *Brighton Patriot* (19 March 1839); *Douglas Jerrold's Weekly* (20 May 1848); *Northern Star* (15 February 1851); *Dundee Courier* (10 August 1875).
73   *Northern Star* (14 April 1849).
74   The Revolution Society and its regional counterparts (particularly those in Norwich, Sheffield and Nottingham) had enthusiastically supported the French Revolution from the outset .The year before in 1791, *Ça ira* had been sung. On that occasion the special guest was the newly elected Mayor of Paris, Jérome Pétion.
75   *English Republic* (1855), p. 8.
76   *Worker* (20 January 1906).
77   See 'Origin of the Marseillaise Hymn', *Cobbett's Magazine* (1 March 1833).
78   Collett, *History of the Marseillaise*.
79   Gerald Massey, 'Memoir of Rouget de Lisle: "Author of the Marseillaise."', *Friend of the People* (24 April 1852).
80   John Bedford Leno, *Reformer's Book of Songs and Recitations* (London: Commonwealth Office, n.d.).
81   See, for example, *Commonweal* (15 June 1887; 31 December 1887); *Common Sense* (15 June 1887).
82   See, for example, 'How the Marseillaise Was Written', *Worker* (22 October 1892); 'The Marseillaise!: Freedom's Hymn', *Worker* (20 January 1906); 'The World's Song of Revolt: Dramatic Birth of "The Marseillaise"', *Worker* (22 August 1918); 'Marseillaise, Anthem of International Labour', *Worker* (28 January 1926); 'Birth of "The Marseillaise": Story of a Famous Anthem', *Worker* (29 June 1942).
83   'Kubelik's Mistake', *Poverty Bay Herald* [NZ] (8 December 1911).
84   'Riot in Barcelona', *Poverty Bay Herald* (12 July 1911).
85   'A Redmond Threat. Received from London October 9', *Evening Post* [NZ] (9 October 1895).
86   *Northern Star* (25 April 1846).
87   'Wild Women: Suffragettes at Holloway Gaol', *Evening Post* [NZ] (5 March 1912).
88   'The Pankhurst Trial', *Otautau Standard and Wallace County Chronicle* (10 June 1913).
89   Quoted in Rosemarie Smith (ed.), *Suffrage Song Book: Songs and Poems about the Women's Franchise* (Wellington: Women's Studies, Victoria University, 1993), p. 10.
90   *Maoriland Worker* (3 January 1913); *Commonweal* [NZ] (1 November 1909).
91   It was sung at a mass workers' rally in 1913. See *Maoriland Worker* (7 March 1913).
92   See National Library of Australia, Papers of Harry Hastings Pearce (1897–1984), MS 2765, Series 7/7, Folder 4, 'Eureka Stockade (Part One)' by Harry H. Pearce [typewritten manuscript], Eureka Stockade Inaugural Lecture founded by the Ballarat Labor Party Federal Electoral Assembly delivered by Harry H. Pearce, 26 November 1979, p. 14.
93   *Argus* (22 April 1858).
94   *Sydney Morning Herald* (20 March 1860).
95   Henry Lawson, 'The Australian Marseillaise. Or, A Song for the Sydney Poor (1890)', available at www.ironbarkresources.com/henrylawson/AustralianMarseillaise. html (accessed 12 September 2016).
96   J. A. Andrews, 'For Wealth and Liberty', *Labour Song Book* (Melbourne: Tocsin Print, n.d., pp. 30–1.
97   Elizabeth Johnson, 'The World's Marseillaise', *Worker* (7 August 1890).
98   E. H. Lane ('Jack Cade'), *Dawn to Dusk: Reminiscences of a Rebel* (Brisbane: William Brooks, 1939) p. 44.
99   See 'News from Australia', *Commonweal* [UK], 12 December 1891.
100 *Worker* (16 July 1892).
101 *Standard* (31 July 1866).
102 See *Blackburn Standard* (1 August 1866).
103 *Alnwick Mercury* (15 October 1870); *Worker* (29 December 1900).
104 Ebenezer Elliott, 'A British Marseillaise', *Sheffield and Rotherham Independent*

(21 December 1844), available at www.judandk.force9.co.uk/NewPoems1.html#
Marseillaise (accessed 12 September 2016).

105 *Morning Post* (28 October 1830); *Morning Post* (20 February 1841).

106 *Southern Reporter* (9 March 1871); *Dundee Courier* (31 January 1877). According
to Per G. L. Ahlander, Vaneri was an Anglo-Scots-French-Italian Revolutionary.
See Per G. L. Ahlander, 'Madame Pauline Vaneri Filippi – An Anglo-Scottish-
French-Italian revolutionary?' (unpublished paper, University of Edinburgh, n.d.).

107 *Glasgow Herald* (31 January 1865); *Glasgow Herald* (9 November 1869); *Glasgow
Herald* (21 February 1871).

108 William W. Brown, *Anti-Slavery Harp: A Collection of Songs for Anti-Slavery
Meetings* (Boston: Bela Marsh, 1848).

109 *Stars and Stripes Songster: Original Patriotic Songs and Marching Choruses,
Written to Popular Operatic Airs and Well-Known Melodies* (New York: R. M. De
Witt, c.1861). It also appears in *The Campfire Songster: A Collection of Popular,
Patriotic, National, Pathetic and Jolly Songs, suited for the Camp or March* (New
York: Dick and Fitzgerald, n.d.), p. 32.

110 *Jack Morgan Songster* (Raleigh, NC: Branson & Farrar, 1864). For British radical
support for the Confederacy see, inter alia, Roy Boston, *British Chartists in
America* (Manchester: Manchester University Press, 1971).

111 *Weekly True Sun* (7 January 1838).

112 University of Toronto, Thomas Fisher Rare Book Library (hereafter Fisher),
Ballad Collection, *Campaign Song No. 4* (as sung by E. W. Schuch at the Liberal
Ratification Meeting, Grand Opera House, Toronto).

113 Fisher, Flora MacDonald Denison Papers 1898–1921, Man Coll 51 (hereafter
Denison Papers), Box 8A, Folder 12, Collection of newspaper clippings relating to
women's suffrage 1890–1919, International Council of Women Congress, Toronto
Meeting 1909, *Mail and Empire* (17 June 1909).

114 Fisher, Denison Papers, Box 7, Mfm Dup. 77, Scrapbooks, 'Under the Pines, What
Women are Doing for the Advancement of Civilization – Suffrage News', *Toronto
Sunday World* (13 November 1909). For Denison see Ramsay Cook and Michèle
Lacombe, 'Merrill, Flora MacDonald (Denison)', in *Dictionary of Canadian
Biography*, vol. 15 (Toronto: University of Toronto/Quebec: Université Laval,
2003), available at www.biographi.ca/en/bio/merrill_flora_macdonald_15E.html
(accessed 11 September 2016).

115 Fisher, Denison Papers, Box 8A, Folder 12, Collection of newspaper clippings relating to women's suffrage 1890–1919, *Toronto Star* (22 November 1909).

116 Fisher, Denison Papers, Box 8A, Folder 12, 'Concerning Boots and Brickbats',
Toronto Saturday Night (27 November 1909).

117 Fisher, Denison Papers, Box 7, Mfm Dup. 77, 'Under the Pines. What Women are
Doing for the Advancement of Civilization – Suffrage News', *Toronto Sunday
World* (7 November 1909).

118 Parts of this section appear in Kate Bowan, 'The Travels of John Anderson my
Jo', *Humanities Research*, 19:3 (2013), available at http://press-files.anu.edu.au/
downloads/press/p245301/html/ch05.xhtml?referer=1299&page=9 (accessed 11
September 2016). Reprinted with permission of the editor.

119 For temperance parodies of John Anderson my Jo in New Zealand see *Ashburton
Guardian* [NZ] (24 April 1891); 'Parody on "John Anderson my Jo"', *Auckland
Star* (22 September 1883); 'The Praises of King Alcohol', *Wanganui Chronicle* (7
April 1891); for the United States see 'John Alcohol. A Temperance Parody', *Daily
Sanduskian* [Sandusky, Ohio] (6 August 1849); *Columbia Washingtonian* (25
August 1842); *Californian Farmer and Journal of Useful Sciences* (25 March 1875).

120 'Friends of Temperance', in Edwin Wilson (ed.), *Victorian Band of Hope Union
Hymn Book* (Melbourne: W. H. Willliams, 1860), p. 89.

121 See, for example, Oxford University, Bodleian Library, Broadside Ballads Online
(hereafter Bodleian Ballads), '"Airn John", To the tune of: "John Anderson my Joe"'
[sic] (Glasgow: n.p., 1858), available at http://ballads.bodleian.ox.ac.uk/static/
images/sheets/15000/12790.gif (accessed 6 May 2015).

122 J. Barker, *Democratic Hymns and Songs* (Wortley: n.p., 1849), p. 23; Bodleian Ballads, 'In the days when I was hard up' (London: Ryle and Co, n.d.), available at http://ballads.bodleian.ox.ac.uk/static/images/sheets/20000/16908.gif (accessed 6 May 2015). For broadside ballads about poverty, see James G. Hepburn, *A Book of Scattered Leaves: Poetry of Poverty in Broadside Ballads of Nineteenth-Century England*, 2 vols (Lewisburg, PA: Bucknell University Press, 2000–2).

123 *Northern Star* (26 September 1840). Expressions of solidarity through banners, clothing, toasts, recitations and singing were central to 'the culture of popular protest'. James Epstein has explored how many of these became 'radical dining rituals'. For an extended discussion of such symbolic practices see James Epstein, 'Radical Dining, Toasting and Symbolic Expression in Early Nineteenth-Century Lancashire: Rituals of Solidarity', *Albion*, 20:2 (1988), pp. 271–91.

124 *Northern Star* (3 October 1840).

125 John Hood, *Australia and the East Being a Journal Narrative of a Voyage to New South Wales in an Emigrant Ship with A Residence of Some Months in Sydney and the Bush and the Route Home by Way of India and Egypt in the Years 1841 and 1842* (London: John Murray, 1848), p. 1.

126 See, particularly, E. P. Thompson, 'Patrician Society, Plebeian Culture', *Journal of Social History*, 7:4 (1974), pp. 382–405.

127 *People's Advocate* (29 September 1849). It was reprinted from the British magazine *Punch*.

128 For the campaign against transportation see P. A. Pickering, 'Loyalty and Rebellion in Colonial Politics: The Case Against Convict Transportation in Australia', in P. Buckner and R. D. Francis (eds), *Rediscovering the British World* (Calgary: University of Calgary Press, 2005), pp. 87–107.

129 *The Continental Songster: A Collection of New, Spirited Patriotic Songs for the Times* (Philadelphia: Winch, 1863), pp. 54–5.

130 'Jonathan to Jo', *The Campfire Songster: A Collection of Popular, Patriotic, National, Pathetic, and Jolly Songs Suited for the Camp or March* (New York: Dick and Fitzgerald, 1862), pp. 36–7.

131 'O Johnny Bull, my Jo John', *Rebel Rhymes and Rhapsodies collected and edited by Frank Moore* (New York: Putnam 1864), p. 150.

132 'Ben Dizzy' (n.p.), available at http://ballads.bodleian.ox.ac.uk/static/images/sheets/25000/22202.gif (accessed 11 March 2015).

133 *Bruce Herald* (3 July 1888).

134 W. H. D., 'Correspondence: the junior member for Christchurch', *The Star* (19 August 1899).

135 Metropolitan Toronto Library, CIHM, No. 51821, 'Another new song to another old tune air, "John Anderson my Jo"' (no publication details).

136 Mary Finnegan, 'Irish-French Relations in Lower Canada', *CCHA Historical Studies*, 52 (1985), p. 35.

137 James Jackson, 'The Radicalization of the Montreal Irish: The Role of "The Vindicator"', *Canadian Journal of Irish Studies*, 31:1 (2005), p. 92.

138 *Ibid.*, pp. 90–7.

139 See Shepard, *Street Literature*, p. 21 and chap. 3.

140 'Instruction and Amusement for the Public', *People's Paper* (4 October 1856).

141 'Grand Political Soiree in Saint Martin's Hall', *People's Paper* (11 October, 1856).

142 'Instruction and Amusement for the Public', *People's Paper* (4 October 1856).

143 'Grand Political Soiree in Saint Martin's Hall', *People's Paper* (11 October 1856).

144 See *People's Paper* (8 November 1856); *People's Paper* (29 November 1856); *People's Paper* (31 January 1857).

145 'Grand Political Soiree in Saint Martin's Hall', *People's Paper* (11 October 1856).

146 In addition to the *People's Paper* reports cited above, see *Morning Chronicle* (8 October 1856); *Morning Chronicle* (26 November 1856); *Daily News* (8 October 1856); *Daily News* (5 November 1856).

147 *People's Paper* (11 October 1856).

148 'Mr. Ernest Jones. A Political Soiree', *Daily News* (8 October 1856).

149   *Ibid.*
150   *The Brave Old Oak* was written in 1834. The art and music critic H. F. Chorley provided the words and Edward Loder the music.
151   'Songs of Democracy', *People's Paper* (11 October, 1856).
152   *Ibid.*
153   *Ibid.*
154   *Morning Chronicle* (26 November 1856).
155   'Songs of Democracy', *People's Paper* (11 October 1856).
156   *People's Paper* (8 November 1856).
157   *Morning Chronicle* (26 November 1856).
158   *People's Paper* (3 January 1857).
159   'Important Notice: Sixth Political Soiree and International Demonstration', *People's Paper* (14 February 1857).
160   *People's Paper* (28 February 1857).
161   *People's Paper* (3 May 1856).
162   'Howard's Unrivalled Minstrels from Australia', *Daily News* (25 April 1854). For reviews and reports on activities at St Martin's Hall see also 'Meeting on Taxes on Knowledge', *Daily News* (6 March 1851); 'Meeting of Trades on Engineers' Strikes', *Morning Chronicle* (25 March 1852); 'Educational Exhibition of the Society for the Arrangement of Arts, Manufacturers and Commerce', *Daily News* (1 August 1854); 'National Sunday League Meeting', *Reynolds' Weekly Newspaper* (28 September 1856); *Morning Chronicle* (30 April 1858); 'Sunday Evenings for the People', *Daily News* (8 January 1866); *People's Paper* (21 December 1854); *People's Paper* (24 November 1855); *People's Paper* (8 March 1856).
163   Dave Russell, *Popular Music in England, 1840–1914: A Social History*, 2nd edn (Manchester; New York: Manchester University Press, 1997), p. 28.
164   See *Morning Chronicle* (14 January 1851); 'Mendelssohn's Elijah at St. Martin's Hall', *Morning Chronicle* (16 April 1855); *Daily News* (22 February 1850); *Daily News* (4 March 1850); *Daily News* (13 March 1850); *Daily News* (22 March 1850); *Daily News* (14 January 1851); *People's Paper* (8 April 1854); *People's Paper* (11 March 1854).
165   Frances Rosser Hullah, *Life of John Hullah LL.D. by His Wife* (London: Longmans, Green and Co., 1886), pp. 5–6.
166   See Paul A. Pickering, *Feargus O'Connor: A Political Life* (London: Merlin, 2008).
167   *Davidson's Universal Melodist consisting of the music and words of popular, standard, and original songs, & arranged so as to be equally adapted for THE SIGHT-SINGER, THE PERFORMER ON THE FLUTE, CORNOPEAN, ACCORDION, VIOLIN, OR OTHER TREBLE INSTRUMENT*, vol. 1 (London: G. H. Davidson, 19, Peter's Hill, Doctor's Commons, 1853), 'Preface'.
168   For more on nineteenth-century British publishing history and the rise of domestic music see, particularly, 'Promoters, Publishers, and Professional Performers', chap. 6 in Scott, *Singing Bourgeois*, pp. 120–34.
169   There is an extant copy held in the British Library. No publication details are given on it.
170   Ernest Jones, *Evenings for the People* (London, 1856); Ernest Jones and John Lowry, *Songs of Democracy*; John Lowry, *Song of the 'Lower Classes'* (London: Williams, [1856]).
171   Scott, *Singing Bourgeois*, p. 188.
172   Scott has outlined the important typographical strategies used by publishers of ballads. See Scott, *Singing Bourgeois*, p. 127.
173   *Ibid.*, p. 54.
174   *Ibid.*, p. viii.
175   For detailed historical accounts of this musicosociological shift see Derek B. Scott, 'Music and Social Class in Victorian London', *Urban History*, 29:1(2002), pp. 60–73; Derek B. Scott, *Sounds of the Metropolis: The 19th-Century Popular Music Revolutions in London, New York, Paris, and Vienna* (New York: Oxford University Press, 2008); William Weber, *Music and the Middle Class: The Social*

Structure of Concert Life in London, Paris and Vienna (New York: Holmes and Meier, 1975); William Weber, *The Great Transformation of Musical Taste: Concert Programming from Haydn to Brahms* (Cambridge: Cambridge University Press, 2009). See also Paul Pickering, 'Chartism and the 'Trade of Agitation' in Early Victorian Britain', *History*, 76:247 (1991), pp. 221–37; Ruth A. Solie, '"Music their larger soul": George Eliot's "The Legend of Jubal" and Victorian Musicality' in Phyllis Weliver (ed.), *The Figure of Music in Nineteenth-Century British Poetry* (Aldershot: Ashgate, 2005), pp. 107–31.

176   Solie, '"Music their larger soul"', p. 120.
177   Walter Pater's famous statement, 'All art constantly aspires towards the condition of music', appeared in his essay, 'The School of Giorgione'. See Walter Pater, *The Renaissance: Studies in Art and Poetry* (London, 1873), p. 135.
178   John Bedford Leno, *Herne's Oak and other Miscellaneous Poems* (London: W. Freeman, 1853), p. v.
179   For a comprehensive account of the radical recreation movement in Britain see Russell, *Popular Music in England*.
180   For the nineteenth-century doctrine of originality see Carl Dahlhaus, *Between Romanticism and Modernism: Four Studies in the Music of the Later Nineteenth Century*, trans. Mary Whittall (Berkeley: University of California Press, 1980), p. 42.
181   Cyril Ehrlich, *The Music Profession in Britain Since the Eighteenth Century* (Oxford: Clarendon Press, 1985), p. 67.
182   'Mr Ernest Jones' Political Soirees', *Daily News* (5 November 1856).
183   *Ibid.*
184   Anne Janowitz, Miles Taylor, and, much earlier, A. B. Wakefield, have noted Jones's shift towards middle-class Liberalism during the mid-1850s. See Janowitz, *Lyric and Labour*, p. 190; Miles Taylor, *Ernest Jones, Chartism, and the Romance of Politics 1819–1869* (Oxford University Press, 2003); and A. B. Wakefield, *Ernest Jones, The People's Friend* (Halifax: Womersley, Exchange Printing Works, 1891), p. 11.
185   Scott, *Singing Bourgeois*, p. 188.
186   K. Theodore Hoppen, *The Mid-Victorian Generation (1846–1886)* (Oxford: Clarendon Press, 1998), p. 394. Quoted in Solie, *Music in Other Words*, p. 44.
187   'Our Musical Corner', *Eliza Cook's Journal* (21 August 1852).
188   *People's Paper* (11 October 1856).
189   *People's Paper* (26 June 1852); *People's Paper* (15 January 1853).
190   As Scott again reminds us, it was common for popular drawing room songs to be published as broadsides. See Scott, *Singing Bourgeois*, p. 183.
191   See Scott, *Singing Bourgeois*, p. 192; Middleton, *Voicing the Popular: On the Subjects of Popular Music*, pp. 1–6.
192   Scott, *Singing Bourgeois*, p. 192.
193   Vic Gammon, '"Not appreciated in Worthington?" Class Expression and Popular Song Texts in Mid-Nineteenth-Century Britain', *Popular Music*, 4 (1984), p. 5.
194   See Scott, *Singing Bourgeois*, p. 187.
195   John Bedford Leno, *The Aftermath With Autobiography of the Author* (London: Reeves and Turner, 1892), pp. 90–1.
196   *Ibid.*
197   The *Era* mentions Lowry's musical activities at various music and concert halls and advertised his entertainment business and publications between 1849 and 1872. See *Era* (30 December 1849); *Era* (29 October 1854); *Era* (5 August 1855); *Era* (4 May 1856); *Era* (1 June 1856); *Era* (13 May 1859); *Era* (31 March 1872). Likewise the *People's Paper* followed his musical achievements from 1853. See *People's Paper* (17 December 1853). The following year he performed as part of the *People's Paper*'s Second Anniversary Soiree. See *People's Paper* (22 April 1854).
198   For Cook's radical ideas see Solveig Robinson's 'Of "Haymakers" and "City Artisans"': The Chartist Poetics of Eliza Cook's Songs of Labor', *Victorian Poetry*, 39:2 (2001), pp. 229–53.

199 *Reynolds' Newspaper* (27 November 1864).
200 Leno, *Aftermath*, p. 49.
201 The *People's Paper* gives an account of Leno's contributions to the opening soiree of the Chartist Political and Literary Institution. See 'Meetings of the Week', *People's Paper* (14 April 1855).
202 Leno, *Aftermath*, pp. 90–1.
203 See 'Mr. John Bedford Leno', *Commonwealth* (6 October 1866).
204 John Lowry, 'Judge Not a Man', 3rd edn (London: B. Williams, 11, Paternoster Row, n.d.).
205 These included *The Future is Ours, Hurrah; Let All Your Songs by Angel-Songs; Judge Not a Man*. See Austin Holyoake and Charles Watts (eds), *Secularist's Manual of Songs and Ceremonies* (London: Austin, 1871), pp. 65–6. Lowry's music for *Song of the 'Lower Classes'* was included by Annie Besant in a songbook produced for the National Secular Society in 1876. See Annie Besant, *Secular Song and Hymnbook* (London: Watts, 1876), pp. 117–18.
206 See, for example, Bishopsgate Institute, London, George Jacob Holyoake Archive (hereafter Holyoake Archive), 'Bradlaugh for Northhampton by John Lowry'; Holyoake Archive, 'A Course of Popular Controversial Lectures, for April 1869'.
207 Hook wrote the *Lass of Richmond Hill* in 1789. It was popularised by the celebrity singer, James Incledon.
208 *Daily Evening Voice* (18 August 1865).
209 *Jeffersonian Democrat* (1 September 1865). For Converse see *New York Times* (28 June 1889).
210 *Freeman's Journal* [Sydney] (21 July 1868).
211 See Philip S. Foner, *American Labor Songs of the Nineteenth Century* (Urbana: University of Illinois Press, 1975), p. 104.
212 'Song of the "Lower Classes"', *Beacon*, 1:9 (1894), p. 139.
213 *Burra Record* (9 August 1893).
214 *Sydney Mail and New South Wales Advertiser* (28 December 1878); *Cornwall Chronicle* (3 April 1879); *Euroa Advertiser* (5 January 1894).
215 *John Bull* (4 May 1867); *Co-operative News* (17 September 1881).
216 *Voice of the People* (13 October 1883); *Eastern Weekly Leader* (27 April 1895); *Gadfly* (July 1897).
217 See 'The Song of the "Lower Classes"', *Worker* (8 January 1898); 'The Letters of Lionel Lynx. The Chartist Movement and Ernest Jones', *Worker* (21 August 1919); 'The Song of the "Lower Classes"', *Worker* (28 April 1930). In 1919 an extended article on Jones was published, which included lengthy quotations from *Song of the 'Lower Classes'*, and in 1930 it appeared in full with 'Jones, Chartist Leader' given as the author.
218 'Work and Wages. Song of the "Lower Classes"', *Worker* [Wagga Wagga, NSW] (25 March, 1909); 'Song of the "Lower Classes"', *Worker* [Wagga Wagga, NSW] (25 November 1909). The second time Jones was again identified as a Chartist.
219 'Song of the "Lower Classes"', *People* (30 March 1907). It also appeared in Adelaide's *Daily Herald*, which maintained close links with the South Australian Labor party. See *Daily Herald* (9 August 1913).
220 'Song of the "Lower Classes"', *International Socialist* (13 August 1910).
221 'Song of the "Lower Classes"', *Voice* (14 May 1909).
222 *Wrexham Advertiser* (3 June 1893); *Auckland Star* (15 July 1893); *Hampshire Telegraph and Sussex Chronicle* (3 June 1893).
223 *Colonist* (30 June 1896).
224 'Song of the Low', *Commonweal* [NZ] (1 October 1908).
225 Miles (ed.), *Poets and Poetry*, pp. 547–62. See also Mike Sanders, *The Poetry of Chartism* (Cambridge: Cambridge University Press, 2009), p. 39.
226 John Ashton, *Modern Street Ballads* (London: Chatto and Windus, 1888), p. 338.
227 Henry Coppeé (ed.), *The Classic and the Beautiful from the Literature of Three Thousand Years* (Philadelphia: Carson and Simpson, 1900), p. 36.
228 For a discussion of this problem see Chris Waters, *British Socialists and the*

Politics of Popular Culture 1884–1914 (Stanford: Stanford University Press, 1990), p. 118. Ulrike Schwab and Solveig Robinson have drawn similar conclusions about Chartist poetry, pointing out that oral tradition and the popular song provided a familiar and fertile ground in which to plant new ideas. See Schwab quoted in Robinson, 'Of "Haymakers" and "City Artisans"', p. 231.

229 See, for example, *Socialist Songs* (Aberdeen: The Committee of the Aberdeen Branch Socialist League, 1889), p. 16; *SDF Songbook* (London: Twentieth Century Press, 1898), p. 18.

230 *Socialist Songs*, p. 16; James Leatham (ed.), *Songs for Socialists*, 2nd ed. (Aberdeen: James Leatham, 1890), p. 18.

231 *Socialist Songs* (London: Stewart & Co, n.d.), p. 16.

232 John Bruce Glasier, 'Preface', *Socialist Songs* (Glasgow: Labour Literature Society, 1895).

233 *Ibid.*, p. 33.

234 *A Songbook for Socialists* (London: William Reeves, [1890]), p. 39.

235 Henry S. Salt, *Songs of Freedom* (London: Walter Scott Publishing Co., [1893]).

236 *Ibid.*, pp. xxi–xxii.

237 Edward Carpenter (ed.), *Chants of Labour: A Song Book of the People with Music* (London: Swann Sonnenschein, 1888), pp. 38–9.

238 'Chants of Labour', *Commonweal* (26 May 1888).

239 Thomas Phillips Thompson, *The Labor Reform Songster* (Philadelphia: Journal of the Knights of Labor, 1892), p. 33. The song makes another appearance much later in 1935 in the *Rebel Song Book* produced by the Rand School, which was itself an institution established by the Socialist Party of America in 1906. This songbook provides another rare example of where Jones's song has again been set to original music, this time by Agnes Cunningham. See *Rebel Song Book* (New York: Rand School Press, 1935), p. 87.

240 *Worker* (19 August 1911).

CHAPTER TWO

The sound of marching feet

On 1 October 1900 the citizens of Cobar in the far west of New South Wales gathered to march in celebration of Labour Day, which in New South Wales falls in October.[1] The day commemorates the granting of the eight-hour working day in the Australian colonies from the late 1850s. 'Cobar' is an anglicised Aboriginal word meaning 'red ochre'. The choice of name was thus both prosaic and appropriate: it was a town built upon red earth. It was a harsh and desolate place. As one commentator put it, 'a solitude, vast and depressing, pervades the landscape'. Nevertheless, when approaching the town by rail, he continued, the skyline is punctuated by evidence of 'the presence of man and his handiwork': 'like masts of distant vessels, the tops the stacks and poppet-heads of the Cobar mines appear'.[2]

The area was settled by white Australian colonists following the discovery of copper in 1870 and by 1891 it could boast approximately 1,200 souls, the majority of them engaged in mining conducted by eleven principal companies.[3] The copper mines were badly affected by a great depression that afflicted the Australian colonies during the 1890s and undoubtedly the years before this march occurred would have been especially difficult. Nevertheless, there was a vibrant community in the Cobar region sustained by a cluster of organisations that included a branch of the miners' trade union, the Amalgamated Miners' Association (AMA), and the Cobar Town Band. A rare photograph of the 1900 parade is extant, which depicts the AMA and the band readying themselves for action on this morning at the turn of the century (see figure 2.1). The photograph is rich with suggestive detail; we can see bicycles, boaters, people wearing their Sunday best, a large banner, numerous vehicles (including at least two floats, one carrying a model of a poppet-head – the winching frame at the top of a mine shaft) and the brass band. The dramatis personae are women, men and children. We know more than the photograph tells us about those prepar-

2.1 The 8 Hour Day procession assembles on the outskirts of Cobar in 1900, headed by the AMA band followed by floats and a banner. Image: 8 Hour Day procession at Wrightville – Cobar area, NSW, 1 October 1900, W.S. Bundren, Wrightville. Call number: BCP0536.

ing to march behind their banner as well as those about to make music amidst the dust and flies. The moment is frozen in time, but were we to restart the camera we could reconstruct something of what we would see; we also know something of what we would hear. In other words, we can use this episode to glimpse a culture in the making.

Commemorative parades, such as those on Labour Day and May Day, were but one site of musical behaviour among many in the public sphere. Music was also made on street corners, in the fields, on hastily erected platforms, in cavernous halls, on the hustings, during funerals and even behind barricades. In this chapter and the next we examine the making of music that was unambiguously intended for the full gaze of public scrutiny. The first examines parades using Labour Day as the focus for a broader discussion of the sound of marching feet. The second considers the place of music in the formal political world of electioneering. Our point of entry into the public sphere of music-making by radicals and reformers is to rejoin the parade about to set off down Marshall Street under the burning sun in Cobar.

The photograph of Cobar gives a sense of the structure of a parade and the role of music-making within it. A procession, large or small, usually culminating in a public meeting, became the staple template for public protest in demotic politics early in the nineteenth century and remained so until at least the First World War. This was as true in Winnipeg as it was in Wellington. Indeed, a hostile reporter for a London weekly in 1856 concluded that there was little point in comparing political parades; it was always 'bands of music and idle addresses'.[4] An observer of the Labour Day activities in Sydney in 1886 agreed, although he singled out the bands to emphasise both similarity and difference: 'As a rule processions are not that interesting,' he quipped. 'There is a sameness about them which is only diversified by the discordance of the bands.'[5] Nonetheless, music-making played several important roles in this mode of collective action that are worthy of more detailed attention. For the larger parades that coursed the streets of the massive conurbations of the nineteenth century Anglophone world, the importance of these roles increased manifold.

First, bands served a Pied Piper-like function by, to borrow the words of one bemused commentator in Glasgow, 'perambulating the city rousing the laggarts from their couches' and summoning them to their posts.[6] When the Chartists in London gathered for a meeting in January 1841, to take another example, the band's rallying cry took the form of a song with words obviously adapted from a popular pro-Jacobite ballad, *The Landing of Royal Charlie*. According to a journalist from the leading radical journal of the day, 'At length the well-known sound of "Come o'er the heather, Come a' the gather, Come both late and early" was heard issuing from the direction of Ray-street, played in a masterly manner, by a capital band.' This proved to be highly effective. Within 'a few minutes more', continued the report, 'the Marylebone and Kensington men had joined their brother Chartists on the Green'.[7]

The obverse of rallying was heralding. In Cobar, as we can see, the band was set to lead the procession, ready to announce its progress both physically and sonically. Similarly, during a parade in 1907 in Ipswich, a small town in south-eastern Queensland, the 'throb of drum and tuneful blare of brass bespoke the Excelsior Band'.[8] The same was true for larger parades when music fuelled anticipation. Standing on Hyde Park Corner in London in May 1893, one enthusiastic commentator noted, 'I listened. A faint, distant, vibrating boom, boom, at regular intervals … Yes. It was the band. Slowly, louder, nearer. On, on, on. Numbers, noise, glitter, dust.'[9] The sense of anticipation worked as well on foe as it did on friend. In Toronto in 1901, for example, the Plumbers' Union used their banner to recognise the role of music: 'Strike up the band, here come the plumbers'.[10]

Together with the emblematic banners and, in many cases, floats and other vehicles, bands also played an important part in providing a structure for a procession by delineating its components. A correspondent for the *Manchester Guardian* in 1892 employed a military metaphor to make this point: 'The bands, formed into a square, aided in breaking up the mass into companies.'[11] Uniquely, however, marching music *ipso facto* set the tempo that regulated the pace of a procession and drove it forward. In Brisbane in 1899, for example, 'when the bands struck up lively and inspiriting music ... everyone previously waiting with impatience for the signal stepped out resolutely in time'.[12] For *Reynolds' News* the 'beating drums, the shrill fifes, and the solid intervals of brass' during the massive Labour Day parade through the streets of London in 1892 suggested 'a military side of the great show – the marching of the Army of Labour'.[13]

The importance of these roles could also be highlighted if things went wrong. For example, at the Labour Day parade in Sydney in the same year, when the 'Army of Labour' trooped its way to its own Hyde Park there were simply too many bands that ended up marching too close together 'playing different airs' to the consternation of marcher and spectator alike.[14] Like the legendary Pied Piper of Hamelin, a band could also lead a crowd astray, accidently or otherwise. In the middle of the speeches that followed the parade in Toronto in 1872, for instance, 'one of the bands struck up a lively air, and started down town, followed by about three-fourths of those who had marched in the procession'.[15] In Wellington in 1890, the problem was silence: when the bandleader entrusted with the music failed to arrive, noted a bemused reporter, the parade could not start.[16]

When things went according to plan, as they almost invariably did, music-making not only played a central role in executing the parade, it also 'enlivened' it with 'thrilling tunes' and 'spirited airs' and lessened the 'toil' of a long march. According to a correspondent to the *Barrier Truth*, a radical newspaper published not far from Cobar in Broken Hill, the 'value of a band as an inspiriting factor cannot be overestimated'. 'Most men's hearts and pulses beat quicker', he continued, 'at the sound of a quick march step.'[17] And, collective singing, often itself a key component of the meeting at the culmination of the parade was, as we shall see, a unifying experience based around familiar songs or facilitated by printed song sheets. As with the 'exuberance of drum and a carillon of bells' (to borrow the effusive words of a witness to the parade in Hobart in 1894)[18] generated by an inspiriting band, the effect of communal singing could be extraordinary. At the massed meeting of branches of the Political Union on Newhall Hill in Birmingham in 1832, the proceedings opened with 200,000 people singing. 'There were nine stanzas containing fifty-four lines in all,' recalled one witness. 'Never did [a] political meeting so large sing a song so long, before or since in this world.'[19] In Carmarthen in Wales a few years later the local Chartists were certain that their singing would have 'electrified the two houses of aristocrats to have heard it'.[20]

The idea that a parade could be heard when it could not be seen is a powerful one. As the Queensland *Worker* noted in 1898, the 'boom of the bands in procession' could be caught in workshops where employers had prevented workers from joining the parade.[21] Benjamin Franklin famously attempted to calculate how many people at a rally could hear the speakers, a problem that led many popular radicals to supplement their message by adopting a uniform for public performance.[22] The musical components of processions and public meetings – communal singing as well as instrumental playing – were far less problematic as a condensed form of communication. The language used in reports of parades was typically that bands 'boomed' or 'blared'.[23] In Toronto in 1894 two rival bands 'made the willow leaves quiver', [24] while in a procession in London two years earlier, recalled one participant, 'there was almost an earthquake of drums'.[25]

The composition of marches and parades offers important evidence about identity within reformist movements, large and small. At its most rudimentary level a procession comprised relatively small groups defined either geographically – villages, towns, suburbs, neighbourhoods – or by association, such as factory, trade union, congregation, political branch and so on. By bringing these units together into one space, parades and the mass meetings that followed constituted a broader identity. To take one example, the 1899 procession in London, Ontario, involved contingents from Paris, Woodstock, Ingersoll, Stratford and St Thomas.[26] Sometimes parades were the crucible for initiating shared identity. In Saskatchewan, for example, the participation of trade unionists from Regina and Moose Jaw in a joint Labour Day parade in 1907 opened a new chapter in regional co-operation.[27] The involvement of delegates from other Australian colonies in a Labour Day parade through the streets of Sydney in 1885 invoked the putative nation fifteen years before federation.

At the same time as it fostered regional and even national solidarity, music could also buttress a sense of inter-colonial and transnational identity through the act of performance. After calling a roll of 'delegates from all over the world' at a Women's Christian Temperance conference in Edinburgh in 1900, for example, the participants sang an apposite hymn, *We All Belong*.[28] Nor was physical proximity a perquisite; on the contrary, an ethereal sense of common cause was a powerful force and exploring its musical expression exposes the contours of a capacious transnational and inter-colonial world. Under the headline 'Song of the Suffragettes', a report from Ottawa published in a New Zealand newspaper told readers of women's suffrage demonstrations in the United States: 'Banners were flying, bands playing, and thousands singing, when the suffragettes in every quarter of the United States demonstrated.' In Lafayette Park in the heart of Washington, the report continued, 'Every American state was represented by a chorus of a 1,000 women robed in white, who sang "The March of the Women" composed by Dr Ethel Smyth, England.'[29] Unsurprisingly, reports of the demonstration, including prominent mentions of Smyth's song, were published in every Australian state capital city as well as in dozens of provincial towns such as Broken Hill, where it would have undoubtedly made it to miners' kitchen tables in Cobar.[30] As we shall see throughout subsequent discussion, oceans of ink were devoted to churning out musical literature of various kinds, defining a canon that was transported in countless suitcases throughout the Anglophone world. It is no accident that numerous copies of Smyth's score are held in many libraries in Australia, Canada, New Zealand, the United States and throughout the British Isles. The fate of Smyth's score was not exceptional. Every songbook or slip ballad produced by a plethora of printing presses is compelling evidence of the role of music in communication within and beyond cartographical boundaries.[31]

It is not stretching the point too far to suggest that those marching and making music in Cobar were thus part of a community of millions of others around the globe doing likewise. In 1899 at a similar type of gathering 12,000 miles away in the imperial capital, Ben Tillett, a trade union leader famous for his role in protracted industrial action around the Anglophone world, made this very case using a musical metaphor. 'From the slums, hills, valleys and mountains of every European country' and 'in America, Canada, Australia and even Japan', he told the crowd in London, 'was being sung to-day the song of nations made one – the song of the rights of the common peoples.'[32] In Cobar, as in a multitude of places, Labour Day revellers sang the song both metaphorically and literally.

Commenting on the 1892 marches, the Toronto *Globe* took this point even further by highlighting the potential of a parade to promote solidarity and a shared identity not only over space but also over time. 'In a thousand towns and cities of North America yesterday from the Gulf of Mexico to the most northerly fringe of civilisation the organized workmen of the continent marched in procession', the editorial ran, 'just as they marched in the motherland centuries ago in the days of the old trade guilds'.[33] The template for celebrating Labour Day owed its place in the repertoire of demotic politics to more than appeals to the distant past; on the contrary, it was sustained by flesh and blood. The first Labour Day procession in the Anglophone world, held in Melbourne in 1856, included two bands and a piper interspersed between union branches marching with their banners. It was no accident that it should take this form. The chair at the public meeting which concluded the Melbourne march was Thomas Vine. He had been born in the 1790s and was a veteran of radicalism in the period following the Napoleonic War, the Reform Bill crisis and Chartism before migrating to Victoria.[34] Indeed, many of the leaders of the eight-hour day campaign in Melbourne (and the organisers of the parade) were Chartist émigrés. These corporeal links to the past survived well into the century. A report of the procession in Toronto in 1883, for example, noted that an 'old man, bent with age and toil, felt himself young again' by 'telling with glee his faint recollections of the Chartist agitation, and the bloody field of Peterloo'.[35] He surely had stories to tell; he would have undoubtedly done his share of singing and he might have played an instrument as part of countless parades and public meetings. Had he been among the estimated 300,000 Chartists that marched to Manchester's Kersal Moor in September 1838, for example, he would have followed two trumpeters and several bands; had he been among the thousands of Chartists who trudged through the fetid streets of Manchester, the 'Shock City' of the industrial revolution in 1840, he might have been a member of one of three bands.[36] And, as we shall see in a later chapter, the field at Peterloo in the same city was awash with blood and littered with fragments of slashed banners and shattered musical instruments.

Consideration of the place of music and music-making in public parades provides other opportunities to examine collective identity, the place of music within popular culture and, in turn, of radical and reform movements in the different societies that comprised the Anglophone world during the long nineteenth century. It also highlights sharp and significant differences within the Anglophone world. The fact that the hardy citizens of Cobar had a band, its members bedecked in tailored uniforms, is a testament to their tenacity and the depth of their commitment. In fact, the large number of bands engaged in parades per se is truly impressive. In Adelaide in 1892, for example, the procession comprised thirty organisations and eight bands; in Winnipeg in 1894 the procession consisted of three bands and a piper interspersed among a dozen or more union branches and factory-based contingents of workers; in Wellington in 1891 thirty trades organisations as well as 'unskilled labour organisations' marched with five bands.[37] In a truly striking showing, the Sydney parade in 1889 comprised twenty-three organisations and twenty-one bands.[38] In terms of raw figures the May Day parade in favour of an eight-hour day that culminated in London's Hyde Park in 1892 was possibly unsurpassed. Taking up to four hours to pass any given spot the march included 110 bands, one for every three banners carried (see figure 2.2).[39]

When pondering the composition of parades the eye of the historian is perhaps drawn to the list of trades and unions as a means of assessing the movement and to explore questions of consciousness and identity. We can delve deeper into the story of the unions and their members that participated. We know, for example, that most of the men marching in Cobar were members of a militant branch of the AMA that was involved in a succession of bitter disputes for more than a decade. To help gauge the strength of the organised labour movement we could also compare a list of trades that marched with a socio-economic profile of the locale. But to stop at this point would result in a partial and somewhat distorted representation. Indeed, a richer picture emerges if the trades are considered together with the bands that marched in step with them. A detailed example is illuminating here.

At the same time as the citizens of Cobar were beginning their march in 1900, across the Tasman in Christchurch in the Canterbury region of New Zealand's South Island another Labour Day parade was taking place. Reports in the Canterbury newspapers included a detailed list of nearly fifty bodies in the local march. Of these, fifteen are explicitly identified as formal trade unions, associations or societies; a further fifteen are listed by trade or occupation (a number of these would have also been union branches). Of the formal associations one is identified by gender (the Tailoresses and Pressers Union). Four of the occupational groups are associated with a location (three with Canterbury and one with a specific factory). The final cluster of organisations identified in the reports comprised twelve bands of music which can be teased apart. Five bands are described as brass bands and one as a bagpipe band; the others were either brass or military-style bands (the latter defined by the inclusion of woodwind among the instrumentation). Six of the bands are identified with a geographic location, one with a reformatory school and two by reference to military functions (the Engineers and Garrison bands). The latter did not include the Lyttelton Marine Band, which owed its name to the fact that Lyttelton is a port town (not strictly a suburb of Christchurch). Two bands were explicitly identified with varieties of social reform (the Linwood Temperance Band and the Salvation Army Band) and one band had chosen to designate itself 'Elite'.[40]

The reasons why these bands were there on Labour Day are not self-evident. A weekly column – 'Band News' – in the Canterbury *Star* allows us to go beyond the superficial categories in search of answers.

2.2 The caption for the engraving in the *Graphic* identifies these bandsmen and standard-bearers as being part of the contingent of 'agitators' from London's East End. It goes on to note that 'the banners, the bands, and the rosettes appeal to the heart of the East-Ender'. Image: 'May Day in London: on the way to Hyde Park. Drawn from life by Paul Renouard', *Graphic* (9 May 1896).

Obviously, some of the Christchurch bands were paid to participate. This is not surprising; after all, by the end of the nineteenth century the professional musician was a long-recognised vocation that was, in many cases, unionised. A staple of the Labour Day parades in Toronto during the early 1900s, for instance, was the band of the Musical Protective Association and the band of the Musicians' Union was often at the head of the processions in Melbourne and Sydney.[41] Even vaudeville artists were unionised and, according to the 'Official Bulletin' published during the general strike in Brisbane in 1912, vaudeville performers in both Britain and the US were supporting their Queensland comrades.[42] One of the best-known (at the time as opposed to now) performers who combined professional singing and socialism was Harry Starr. Known as 'Carl the Clockmaker', Starr was much loved on the music-hall scene in Britain between 1890 and the First World War for his comedic acting, singing and dancing, performing his own silly and sentimental songs. In marked contrast to the orthodox view of music hall as a bastion of Tory jingoism, Starr was well known as a socialist who contributed trenchantly to public debate in the columns of the press and served as secretary of the Blackpool branch of the British Socialist Party.[43]

We know that the Christchurch bands sometimes tendered to play but, like the Cobar players, overwhelmingly they were not professional musicians. On the contrary, most bandsmen were volunteers and their avocation was, to borrow the words of a member of the Engineers Band, 'a hobby'. Moreover, as one correspondent pointed out, Christchurch bands 'have at all times shown a willingness to play for any charitable purposes, and have many times given their services gratis'.[44] The Elite Band and the Woolston Band, for example, played at a benefit rally for unemployed workers.[45] This was a familiar pattern. In Cobar, the Town Band, together with members of the AMA, played a key role in raising funds for a local hospital.[46] In London over forty years earlier the 'good and true men of Kentish Town' hired the local assembly room to conduct a 'ball and concert' in aid of the 'democratic refugees' from Poland and Hungary living in the capital.[47] No student of radical politics in the nineteenth century will fail to recognise these rituals of mutuality.

In cases where bands did accept payment it was almost invariably to cover costs, to raise funds for a new set of instruments (worth £400 in New Zealand in 1904) or to travel to contests that were often the highpoint of a band's year.[48] Instruments were expensive; so too were the military/naval-style uniforms that were de rigueur for brass and military band performances. Quality instruments were not only important sonically but they (and the uniforms) were also a source of pride (see

2.3 A procession in December 1908 from Holloway Prison in London following the release of Christabel and Emmeline Pankhurst. The standard-bearer is Daisy Dugdale, wearing the new 'uniform' of the Women's Social and Political Union. The band is not identified in contemporary reports. Image: Suffragette procession, London, 1908.

figure 2.3.). In 1908 a correspondent revelled in the fact that on Labour Day in Broken Hill the AMA band was 'resplendent in its striking uniform with brass instruments polished to mirror like luminesce'.[49] Commenting on the Wellington Waterside Workers' Union band in 1913, one correspondent suggested that when 'Our Band ... get the new set of silver-plated instruments there will be something doing'. 'Every wowser band in Wellington has silver-plated instruments,' she or he continued, 'why not the Watersiders?'[50] For one commentator, however, the naval uniform was a problem because it reminded him of a 'short and stormy time I spent in the Navy'.[51]

The cause of the disgruntled former sailor's 'stormy time', whether personal or ideological, is not clear, but it provides an opportunity to clarify the relationship with the armed forces that is implied by the musical style, the military nomenclature and the martial raiment. As noted, in musical terms the difference between a brass band and a military band was the instrumentation used. The concept of a band that could march while they played was obviously borne of a venerable military tradition and official forces' bands provided a template. Some bands were formed around local militia and volunteer corps, but by and large the typical band discussed here had no formal connection with the armed forces.[52] It is true enough that many bands had members who were former (or serving) soldiers or sailors. For example, in 1899 the Lyttelton Marine Band numbered two veterans among its approximately thirty members.[53] Bandsmen had often learned to play while serving in the armed forces and, as a consequence, numerous bandleaders in particular were often retired military men. In Toronto, for example, one of the Labour Day bands was known as the Army and Navy Veterans' Association Band.[54] But the typical bandsman who marched in Labour Day parades was not a soldier or sailor. The Lytteltonians even went to the trouble of writing to the local press to clarify the fact that they had nothing to do with the Lyttelton Volunteers.[55] For many men who reached middle age before the First World War a band uniform would be the only uniform they would ever have to put on.

The fact that each of the Christchurch bands has a detailed story to tell is a reminder of the rich complexity of collective experience at street level. The Burnham Industrial School Band, for example, came from a reformatory school for 300 delinquent children aged sixteen and below. Male inmates undertook work on a 1,000-acre farm and were subject to a strict disciplinary regime, religious instruction and education.[56] Music was clearly part of the syllabus. The Lyttelton Marine Band, on the other hand, was formed in 1898 as a result of a dispute within the ranks of a local Oddfellows' Friendly Society Band over an unspecified question of 'independence'. By the time of the 1901 Labour Day parade the new band was held in high regard by the local community and civic authorities alike, and it marched at the head of the parade with a new set of instruments obtained the previous April thanks to public support.[57] The Elite Band too was 'born in adversity'; in this case the result of a schism within the Linwood Temperance Band. According to local commentators, despite its rocky beginning, the Elite Band lived up to its grand appellation. The details of the dispute are unclear but it surely concerned alcohol. The band would later become embroiled in controversy when it lent its support to the campaign of a local independent liberal candidate by performing at a function where drink flowed freely.[58] For decades New Zealand politics was riven by the issue of drink. Between 1894 and 1914 every general election was accompanied by a referendum on liquor licensing which allowed citizens to declare their region 'dry'. The temperance movement in New Zealand (and elsewhere) had a vibrant musical culture and music-making was often at the forefront of their campaigns.[59] The experience of the Elite Band is a reminder that, even among reformers, temperance was a contested issue. The Elite bandsmen obviously liked a drink. Others did not. In Ipswich, Queensland, for example, a regular feature of Labour Day parades was the Excelsior Brass Band, comprising members of the Excelsior Band of Hope Temperance Lodge.[60]

It would be possible to explore further the life of the Christchurch bands but the threads that we have pulled thus far are sufficient to raise two very important points. First, it is clear that by following the bands home from their duty on Labour Day we can see the extent to which the labour movement expressed in these important public rituals was embedded within a community, actual as well as imagined. The same point would undoubtedly emerge were we to retrace the footsteps of anyone who marched, whether they carried an instrument or not, but the point is the music-makers are an excellent unit of analysis to guide our eye. In fact, the lists of bands encourage us to think of parades as indexical: a register of the segment of society from which they emerged. The view is partial and shaded at the edges but by using music-making as an entry point we start to glimpse a community rather than a cause. The results are often surprising and inevitably thought-provoking. In 1883, for example, a 'Grand Demonstration' of trades and labour societies in Hamilton, 'the hub of industry in Canada', commenced with a procession which occupied more than a mile in length. The organisers did not claim that the whole community was involved; on the contrary, they recognised that 'there are many in the city who may be designated Workingmen who did not join in the parade. To have secured everybody's approbation and presence was not hoped for.'[61]

The procession was headed by the thirty-five-strong 'Independent Band' followed by flag-bearers 'blending in one breeze the Union Jack, the Stars and Stripes and the flag of our own Dominion, emblematic of the international fraternity of Labor'. Next in line a place of honour was given to various visitors from branches of the Knights of Labor in other towns – Brantford, Burlington, Oshawa and Guelph. The main body of the parade comprised large contingents from numerous trade unions associated with the Knights. Notable among these was the 'pretty feature of the "procesh", a representative body of the female operatives in the shoe and other factories of the city' marching behind a 'rattling good fife and drum band'.[62] The gendered language grates to the modern ear, but this should not distract us from its importance. Among the women marching was undoubtedly Katie McVicar, a Hamilton shoe factory operative, who gained national attention as the organiser of the first all-female branch of the Knights of Labor. At the time of the parade she was engaged in secret negotiations with the local leadership of the Knights that culminated in the formation of the branch the following year. As one historian has put it, this development reflected the Knights' vision of unionising workers regardless of gender, race or skill.[63] At the conclusion of the parade was an extensive programme of sports followed by a dinner and concert. It is worth noting that the centrepiece of the latter was a singing competition of explicitly 'Labour' songs (*Ninety Years Ago, The Nobleman and Laborer, The Poor Man's Family* and *The Thoughts of a Laboring Man*) all since lost to the passage of time.

One significant element of the Hamilton parade has been passed over, however. Marching close to the front of the parade, between the visitors and the main body, was a 'Band of Indian Musicians' and 'their dusky comrades in feathers and paint'.[64] The phrase is eye-catching. We know that the 'comrades in feathers and paint' were members of the Cayuga (people of the Great Swamp) and Tuscarora, two of the groups that comprised the Six Nations whose lands traversed the US–Canada border. We know that later in the day they made a boisterous contribution to a lacrosse match.[65] It could argued that they were included in the procession as an exotic novelty – and surely that is how they were regarded by some spectators – but the inclusive vision of the Knights suggests that this was not the intention of the organisers. The use of the noun 'comrades' suggests that this was not how they appeared in the reporter's eyes either.

When exploring this story, inflected as it is by issues of identity, gender and race, it is also important to give due attention to the participation of the 'Indian Band of Musicians'. From the mid-1860s dozens of First Nations brass bands were established in Canada. The movement was particularly strong in British Columbia, extending as far north as Kitamaat near the Alaskan border.[66] Music-making in Kitamaat was a ubiquitous feature in the life of the community. Reporting on a series of social meetings, for example, the local newspaper commented: 'a cup of tea and "a good sing" goes a long way with the Indian to give a good heart'.[67] Again, the language grates but the point is an important one. The local band (formed in 1899), casually noted another correspondent, had shown a marked improvement thanks to 'very fine new instruments'.[68] The 'Band of Indian Musicians' that marched in Hamilton on that day in 1883 is evidence of a less well-known parallel phenomenon at the opposite side of the Dominion from British Columbia. It was not short-lived. The following year – 1884 – the band marched again headed by their 'Chief', described this time as the 'Tuscarora Band of Brantford'.[69] On both occasions the Hamilton bandsmen almost certainly included men who would later form the Victoria Brass Band of the Six Nations in Brantford, west of Hamilton.

The movement was not confined to Canada. There was a native brass band movement in New Zealand, which, according to historians, was extremely popular, although (as David Hebert has noted) it is yet to attract the systematic study it deserves.[70] Nevertheless, a significant example of Māori music-making at a Labour Day parade raises some important issues similar to those evident in a consideration of the phenomenon in Canada. The Labour Day procession in Wellington in 1900 was headed by a carriage containing the dignitaries of the local labour movement and a representative of the Māori 'King' Mahutu, followed by two Māori bands. It was not the first time that Māori bands had participated in the Wellington parade. As with Hamilton, there was undoubtedly an element of exoticism for some of the Pākehā (non-Māori people) who witnessed the event. The report in the *Evening Post* noted, 'The band, with the Waikato chief Parakau as drum-major, was the centre of attraction, the grotesque dancings of the chief caused great amusement.'[71] This was not surprising; in fact, it was often complemented by other expressions of obscene racism. In Wellington three years previously, for example, the parade was led by a 'nigger on horseback, clothed in a suit of sacking and armed with a bladder on a string'. The rudimentary instrument described – an ancient, burlesque bladder fiddle (or bumbass) consisting of a string stretched on a pole over a bladder and bowed with a notched stick – is a reminder of the persistence of a long-standing tradition of charivari or 'rough music' (discussed below), as well as the much later emergence of the practice of 'blackface' minstrelsy.[72]

During the 1900 Labour Day festivities, however, insouciant expressions of racism were not characteristic of the day as a whole. Much as in Hamilton, the Māori contingent later participated in the sports programme (they won the tug of war) but, on this occasion, Māori singing was also a prominent part of the concert which took place later in the evening. The singers – Hone Heke Ngapuha, Apirana Ngata and James Carroll – were important individuals; in fact, with the possible exception of Sir James Ward, the Liberal prime minister who hosted the concert, they were arguably the most important to be involved in the evening's events. All three men were Liberal politicians. The eponymous nephew of Hone Heke, the revered leader of a Māori rebellion and war in the 1840s, Hone Heke Ngapuha had been elected to Parliament in 1893. His most significant contribution as a politician was the introduction of a Native Rights Bill which formed the basis of legislation passed in 1900. Apirana Turupa Ngata was a lawyer renowned for his tireless efforts to protect Māori culture and language. He entered Parliament in 1905 and is regarded by many to be the most important Māori politician to have ever served in it. Carroll might have also claimed this mantle. He was of Māori-Irish descent and worked as an interpreter and land agent before becoming a Liberal

Member of Parliament in 1887. He was Colonial Secretary from 1895, being the first Māori to hold the cabinet office of Minister of Native Affairs, a post he occupied as he sang on that night.[73]

The reports of the day's proceedings do not indicate what the band played as they marched and nor do they indicate what was sung over dinner. We know that about this time Ngata and Heke had commenced working on a volume of translations of popular English songs, including *Te Kaianga Tupu* (*Home, Sweet Home*), *He Pua Puawai* (*There is a Flower that Bloometh*) and *E Nita!* (*Juanita*), but there is no evidence that they drew from it to entertain the revellers in Wellington.[74] Whether they did or not, it is likely that their contribution to the musical programme was, ostensibly at least, apolitical. At first glance, the sentiments encapsulated in the lyrics of the songs they were translating had no political significance and there is no apparent common theme to their selection other than the popularity of the original. But this misses the point. Firstly, it should be noted that their booklet was written as a souvenir for the Māori Congress of 1908; a quintessentially political event. Moreover, Hone Heke and Ngata claimed that their translations 'catch the spirit of the original very well whilst maintaining the purity of our mother language and its poetical qualities'.[75] This statement of the terms on which the translation was undertaken was innately political. In this way, it did not matter if they sang Māori songs or translations of popular English ditties; it was done so on their terms.[76] Finally, it should be remembered that Hone Heke, Ngata and Carroll were leading political figures and, irrespective of what they sang, their standing as liberal reformers and advocates of Māori rights would have provided a clear political context for their performance.

The music also raises questions of power relations, transculturation, hybridity, authenticity and appropriation. The importance of repertoire among the settler-colonisers (and in the Pax Britannica, for that matter) will be considered below; the point here is that the question of what was performed and the form in which it was performed are fundamentally different issues when examined in a cross-cultural context. Hebert has shown that by the time the Māori bands were marching down the streets in Wellington, what he calls 'mainstream' bands were already playing pieces based on Māori melodies.[77] Indeed, he offers the Māori band formed in Ratana Pa (close to Wanganui on New Zealand's North Island) in the early 1920s as a case study of transculturation by which music changes both sonically and socially as it crosses cultural boundaries. Without sufficient evidence it is only possible to speculate, but, given who was making music during the Labour Day festivities in Wellington, it is likely that the authenticity of both Māori and European music was destabilised during the performances, creating what might be called a hybrid musical identity. As a social process that happened, the musical identity that was created was a fleeting moment in a shifting cultural exchange mediated by a fluctuating power relationship. The point is that the study of music and music-making affords us this glimpse.

Having said that, it is important to recognise that there was common ground where inter-cultural exchange was only one factor and, in some cases, perhaps not the most important. The First Nations bandsmen at Kitamaat, for example, lived and worked in an area where the economy was dominated by a fish cannery. Inevitably, many would have worked there. For them, as for their European co-workers, the struggle for improved pay and conditions was likely to have been conducted, at least in part, through the lens of class.[78] To that extent it was reflected both in their music and their musical behaviour. It is not clear where the First Nations musicians in Hamilton worked, but in Ontario's industrial heartland it is likely that they were courted by the Knights of Labor precisely because they were fellow workers who were potentially 'comrades'. The fact that the Indian Band of Musicians and the 'comrades in feathers and paint' participated in a Labour Day parade is significant in and of itself. Admittedly, in New Zealand, Māori were sometimes used to break strikes, but this was by no means universally true. During the bitter waterside workers' strike in Wellington in 1913 (discussed in detail in a later chapter), for example, Tureiti Te Heuheu Tukino, chief of the Taupo tribe (Ngāti Tūwharetoa iwi) and later a prominent parliamentarian, gave an explicit guarantee that Māori would not break the strike by signing on as 'special police' and they were welcomed on the picket lines at the docks as fellow workers.[79]

The willingness of both the First Nations and Māori bandsmen to sport the uniforms that symbolised the martial power of the coloniser is, on one level, a clear example of cultural imperialism. In addition, there is evidence that in some cases First Nations bandsmen were prevented from wearing their traditional clothing. [80] Nevertheless, the files of the Department of Indian Affairs are full of enthusiastic requests from Indian band members seeking funds to purchase uniforms, suggesting that the jackets and hats were not simply the outward manifestation of the imposition of imperial will.[81] On the contrary, their embrace suggests a form of translation and adaption and certainly agency. Moreover, it is important to remember that the fascination with military raiment was entrenched in the band movement generally. As with subjugated indigenous peoples, bandsmen across the political spectrum (including some reformers, radicals, trade unionists and socialists)[82] adopted uniforms ordinarily worn by the apparatus of the State, which represented the threat (real or imagined) of repression, a fact that introduces broader questions of independence, class, cultural authority and social control. Space prevents a detailed consideration of this complex paradox here. What we can say is that in relation to the issue of the presentation of self in the public sphere there are few grounds to separate out the members of indigenous bands for special consideration. Nevertheless, it could be argued that instances where indigenous peoples combined traditional clothing with the uniform of the coloniser suggest a greater – or at least pointed – degree of agency than simple appropriation.

If the participation of indigenous bands in public events (radical or otherwise) was innately political, the same is not true of bands more generally. Indeed, the Christchurch Elite Band's dispute over a pint or two while lending their arm to the local Liberal candidate raises again the issue of the extent to which bands that were involved in Labour Day parades were politically motivated. As we have seen, most parades counted at least one official band linked directly to a trade or political organisation among their number. Moreover, it is clear is that many bands across the Anglophone world donated their services to Labour Day parades (and to the political marches in general). As one historian noted, however, the relationship was a complicated one,[83] and certainly was not always harmonious. In the aftermath of the procession in Broken Hill in 1908, for example, it emerged that in fact only the official union band had been 'paid' by having its expenses covered, much to the chagrin of the other bands involved.[84] In Sydney and Melbourne there is evidence of bitter disputes between the peak union bodies and the organisers of the parades on the one hand and the Professional Musicians' Unions on the other, the latter accusing the organisers of employing amateur bands at the expense of their members.[85]

In some cases the ready willingness to participate might well have been an instance of a community-based band simply taking any opportunity to perform. Having said that, it is clear that in many circumstances participation in Labour Day was not taken lightly and could even be contentious within the band. Among the Broken Hill bands, for example, some members of the Alma Band refused to participate in an eight-hour day event and resigned when the majority went ahead, effectively 'killing' the band.[86] The potentially fissiparous nexus between bandsmen and politics (as well as official union structures) was brought into stark relief by a bitter exchange in Wellington in 1913. Ostensibly, the dispute was provoked when the question arose in the press of whether union bands would take part in contests where bands containing 'scabs' were also to participate.

Underlying this was a deep-seated ambiguity over what constituted

[117]

a union band. Effectively, some correspondents insisted that only bands officially affiliated with a union could be considered as such; others insisted that many bands comprised union members and were entitled to be acknowledged for their place in the labour movement. Undoubtedly, at a time when union membership was high, many bands contained a large number of union members; in 1902 the Toronto Musicians' Union estimated that 'most' of the members of the bands that 'enlivened the march' could be numbered among their ranks. Significantly, however, none of the bands identified in the report were designated as official union bands.[87] In Wellington a bitter dispute between the official Waterside Workers' Band and other Wellington bands also, somewhat ironically, underscores this point. The flashpoint occurred when a correspondent to the *Maoriland Worker* accused the official band of participating in a music contest with bands containing 'scabs', the worst form of abuse in the unionists' lexicon. The details of the dispute are not important; the point is that among the acrimonious exchange members of other bands insisted that their members were unionists and some were even supporters of the communist Industrial Workers of the World (IWW).[88]

The tension over political motivation and what constituted an official band was, in turn, symptomatic of a growing consternation within the labour movement about the observation of the anniversary. For some commentators, the conduct of a successful celebration was an unequivocal paean of triumph. In Ontario the 'fine procession attested to the strength of Toronto unionism'; in Sydney the parade was the 'outward sign of a great and peaceful victory'.[89] In 1891 Robert Stout, veteran freethinker and former Liberal premier of New Zealand, opined somewhat prosaically: 'The object in having an anniversary day was to let our children, and others who came after them, know something that had been gained.'[90] At Broken Hill in 1908, Arthur Griffith, a local Labour Member of Parliament, put the case with greater eloquence: 'The celebration meant a great deal more than that they believed in the Eight Hours Principle. It was a recognition that Labor had won the right to demand what hours and under what conditions it should work.'[91] For others the glow of victory was accompanied by a flicker of unease. In Winnipeg the editor of the labour newspaper, the *Voice*, made this point, arguing that the 'extraordinary growth' of Labour Day as a 'world institution' by 1909 'must bring joy to the stalwart pioneers of earlier days, who had to fight police and mobs in order to secure the liberty of demonstrating the magnitude of labor's cause, and the right of all, even common people, to live'. At the same time he was concerned that the celebration was losing its meaning. It 'too often happens', he wrote, 'that the details get out of balance with the result that the original intention is lost sight of and the general public view the affair as an ordinary entertainment.'[92]

He was not alone. Numerous critics within the movement were also perturbed by the festive elements that they believed diluted the central focus on politics. By 1883, for example, T. V. Powderly, the national leader of the Knights of Labor in the US, stated emphatically that he would no longer speak at these events. 'Men and women go there for fun and lager not for *wind*,' he grumbled.[93] In the same year in Toronto the committee was undoubtedly piqued when they had to abandon the speeches as 'it was found inadvisable to endeavor to suspend the amusements'.[94] Of course, these earnest advocates would have known that a combination the festive and the political was not new. From the outset, Labour Day parades in the second half of the nineteenth century, like the post-Napoleonic War radical processions upon which they were modelled, took place within a cultural tradition that had deep roots in the ancient conduct of British politics. During the eighteenth century, excesses of licentiousness and debauchery, sustained by strong drink, emblemised political events and resistance to authority was often expressed through irreverent mockery and ribald humour. Charivari or 'rough music', including bawdy and profane songs, was an essential part of this cultural tradition, which was still alive well into the 1830s and beyond as we have seen in Wellington.[95] When, for example, the leader of the rebellion in Lower Canada, Louis-Joseph Papineau, and Sir John Colborne, commander-in-chief of the government forces in Canada, both separately visited Saint-Hyacinthe in Quebec in November 1837, they each received a markedly different reception. According to a report reprinted in a Chartist newspaper, the *Northern Liberator*, when Papineau arrived 'all the inhabitants of the village assembled in an instant and, accompanied by music, went to Mr. Papineau's residence to salute him'. Expecting a similar reception, the report continued, Sir John 'threw open his windows' but 'the crowd commenced immediately huzzaring for Papineau!! and crying "Down with Colborne and Gosford!!!"' In the evening, Colborne was 'treated to a tremendous Charivari (un charivari affreux)'. Translating this as a 'concert of marrow bones and cleavers', the reporter concluded, 'in consequence of which' Sir John 'and his suit beat a retreat at daybreak the next morning'.[96] The fact that marrowbones and cleavers is an old synonym for discord and the literal translation of *affreux* is 'hideous' gives a better sense of the cocktail of cacophonous music and intimidation that Sir John 'and his suit' endured in the dark of night.

Notwithstanding efforts to sanitise the raucous plebeian culture of eighteenth-century politics, Labour Day parades around the radical

Anglophone world almost invariably culminated in a combination of picnic, excursion, sporting events, dinner, musical concert and dance. A glance at innumerable reports reveals throngs of people enjoying a cornucopia of fun that included skipping rope contests; wrestling tents; roulette wheels and 'other forms of speculation'; tugs of war and running races for a huge variety of classes (from professional sprints to egg-and-spoon races and even a gentle handicap for elderly members of the organising committees) witnessed by crowds 'ten and twenty deep at the railings'; jugglers and acrobats; and even a snake charmer defying death. A plethora of food and refreshment booths – often supplying alcohol – 'doing a roaring trade' sustained these activities. In Tyrone in British Columbia, a handbill announced that the highlight of the Festival of Labour would be a chicken pie dinner.[97] In the photograph of the Cobar parade we can see hawkers and vendors plying their trade and children riding bicycles, playing and having fun. Their laughter echoes across a vast expanse of space and time. So too does the music made by the Cobar Town Band.

We should not lose sight of the fact that music was integral at both ends of the affective spectrum – from pomp and circumstance to gleeful conviviality – that suffused much popular politics in the public sphere. The reports in the press invariably recount singing, dancing and musical performances as a feature of the carnivals. Music was everywhere: from ballad-singers and lone pipers to dance bands and choirs. As we have suggested, it would be a mistake to dismiss the festal as frivolous filigree inimical to the serious business of the day. On the contrary, separating the political from the festal establishes a false binary; what we can see from Moose Jaw to Melbourne is the echo of older cultural forms continuing to resonate within new parameters of respectability and social control.[98] In this way it is easier to understand why one commentator in Sydney in 1886, for example, felt that it was important to stress that 'the honest working man, whilst bent on displaying the deepest devotion to his cause, seemed equally determined to secure a good day's enjoyment'.[99] Likewise, a correspondent in Toronto noted that 'labor' had set apart the holiday 'for its especial leisure and enjoyment and the celebration of the progress which the industrial army has made on this continent'.[100] Another Sydneysider emphatically made the point that the speeches being given amidst the crowds by 'professors of political logic' were less important than the fun that stemmed from the success of the eight-hour system.[101]

By this time, however, some socialist commentators had even begun to deride the significance of the victory in the first place. In Melbourne, the home of the eight-hour day, the editor of the *Socialist* adopted a tone dripping with cynicism:

Bands of music galore, belching in brazen glamour the sweets of victory; beauteous banners braving the breeze – a kaleidoscope of rainbows ... All – ALL – for what??? To celebrate the subservience of Labour.[102]

In Sydney another socialist journalist lamented the prominence of what he called an 'empty jubilee'.[103] Critics, doubters and naysayers alike were perturbed by two developments. First was the fact that the parade was increasingly a tableau of the community as a whole and, apparently unrelated to the vicissitudes of the local economy, a proclamation of a consensus between labour and capital. In Toronto a headline in the *Globe* made the point that the 1892 parade was 'thoroughly representative'. 'The demonstration', the report ran, 'to the intelligent observer, was much more than an exhibition of the strength of trades unionism in Toronto; it was unanswerable proof of the prosperity of the city.'[104] Nearly a decade later the *Globe* characterised it even more pointedly as an exhibition of 'Organized Labor and a large representation of Organized capital'.[105] Similarly, in Hamilton, Ontario, one commentator noted (with perhaps less overt enthusiasm) that the parade was 'highly representative of the city's trades *and* business [emphasis added]'.[106]

What surely rankled with many radicals was the increasing presence of advertising floats interspersed among the union contingents. In 1897 the *Sydney Morning Herald* noted that the remark, 'The procession is not what it used to be', 'was frequently heard in the streets yesterday':

> The eight-hours procession has come to be not so much the great display of the workers' genius and strength, nor the outcome of their enthusiasm at the achievement of a great principle, but rather the display of their employers' wares, merchandise, and products in a way most likely to attract the purchaser's attention.[107]

A report from Wellington at about the same time made the point succinctly: 'the parade is getting every year more into the hands of the enterprising business man, and out of the jurisdiction of the unionist'.[108] Hand in hand with creeping commercialism was official recognition. Labour Day become an official public holiday in Victoria in 1879, in New South Wales in 1885, in Canada and the US in 1894 and in New Zealand in 1900. By this time a gaggle of conservative politicians and the representatives of the Crown often graced the celebrations. In 1903 one of the bands in the Brisbane parade even played a request from the Governor.[109]

Nevertheless, it can be argued that the fact that the celebration had become more consensual and embedded in the community, even to the point of accommodating the Governor's musical preferences, is in and of itself evidence of the success of the labour movement.

[121]

There are some sharp contrasts evident on this point between Britain and the colonies of settlement (and the US). In many parts of the Anglophone world the eight-hour day was won relatively quickly across large sections of the economy and well before a more piece-meal reduction of working hours in Britain. The celebration of an annual day devoted to the victorious campaign became institution-alised outside Britain during the third quarter of the nineteenth century, whereas it was not proclaimed as an official public holiday in Britain until 1978.

In some respects 1 May was an ideal date for British radicals and reformers to proclaim their cause. By the middle of the nineteenth century the celebration of the ancient rite of spring on May Day had been reduced to a formulaic 'annual breakfast for chimney sweeps' (to borrow the words of one critic), but its political significance was still well known in popular politics. Admittedly, for some Chartists the limitations seemed more important. According to the editor of the *Northern Star*, May Day was 'a short saturnalia in which Labour forgot its penalty of Poverty, and rank condensed into a temporary equality (a satire upon class distinction)'.[110] But for others it offered a motif of fecundity, renewal and liberty – perhaps also libertinism – for song that was irresistible. Thus, the author of a song entitled *The Chartist Gay Day* connected the presentation of a massive Chartist petition to parliament on 2 May 1842 to a distant past:

> It was nature's gay day
> Bright smiling May Day,
> Each heart yearning our country to be free;
> The banners were bringing,
> The people were singing
> Of the days of their fathers and sweet liberty.[111]

Ernest Jones was also lured by this trope in his *A Song for May*:

> Every bud is filled to bursting
> With its future fruit and flower;
> Hearts of men! are ye thirsting
> For the fruits of Freedom's hour?[112]

An annual celebration of Labour Day in May did commence in Britain in 1890 and the impetus for the early celebrations was primarily the campaign for an eight-hour day, itself sustained for some radicals and reformers (both in Britain and elsewhere) by reference to the benevo-lent regime of Alfred the Great.[113] The link to the original May Day held powerful sway. William Morris penned a well-known poem; another commentator in the socialist press was equally enthused if not as talented. 'The vivifying sap, welling up in the trees', he wrote, 'is a counterpart of the new red blood of Socialism coursing through our veins.'[114]

By any measure, the initial Labour Day parades in Britain proved to be spectacularly successful but in the longer term the trajectory was notably different. Commenting on the third annual eight-hour demonstration in London, a journalist for London's leading populist newspaper, *Reynolds' News*, could barely contain his enthusiasm: '1890 was a magnificent send-off for the movement; 1891 was almost as good; but 1892 has swallowed all the others'.[115] Even the hostile press had to concede that the 1890 demonstration was, 'as far as demonstrations go, a very big thing indeed'.[116]

For the student of the politics of the street these demonstrations displayed numerous recognisable features: from a monster procession comprising a congeries of organisations defined by a range of criteria such as occupation, political conviction or locality to a grand public meeting suffused with the festal. The success of the London events was replicated across the United Kingdom and Ireland: in Dublin, Edinburgh, Aberdeen, Glasgow, Liverpool, Kingston upon Hull, Manchester, Wolverhampton, Bradford and 'other provincial centres'.[117] Moreover, the celebrations generated a familiar discourse. Ever vigilant, 'Gracchus' noted in his regular column to *Reynolds' News* the same debate about the balance between the festive and the political that had occurred elsewhere in the Anglophone world. 'Some people may urge that the workers will forget to proclaim their grievances and their social demands if Labour Day becomes an occasion for merry-making,' he noted, although he did not share the view: 'Whether eating or drinking or making merry', he continued optimistically, 'these men will always remember that an industrial tyranny exists around them ... A loud-voiced demand for better social will always be raised on Labour Day.'[118]

Having said that, even at the obvious highpoint in the early 1890s there is little evidence that Labour Day parades had become embedded in the community at large. According to Frederick Engels, writing for *Arbeiter Zeitung*, the processors in the inaugural Labour Day parade in 1890 were collectively the 'English proletariat'.[119] Although he agreed with Engels on little else, the irascible Robert Blatchford wrote effusively in the *Clarion* of the potential of the Labour Day parade in Manchester in 1892 to bring together the 'sturdy miner, the skilful engineer, the broad-handed navvy, the white-fingered artist, the lusty farmer, the fragile seamstress, the outcasts of the streets, the despised denizen of the slums, the sweater's slave, the hearty sailor'.[120] Likewise, in Glasgow in 1894 it was estimated that the crowd of 10,000–12,000 was mainly working class in composition; the 'few capitalists' present were seen as something of an oddity given that 'one of the chief objects of the movement' was to bring their existence to a 'speedy end'.[121] Even where the word 'representative' was used, as it was in connection with the massive parade in London in 1892, the intention was to describe the involvement of a cross section of those designated as the working classes and little else. The several reports – both in the labour and radical press as well as the mainstream journals – enumerate the bands involved but do not provide the names to allow us to follow the musicians home as we have done with those in Christchurch. In Blatchford's *Clarion*, for example, we are given a detailed list of organisations that were to march in Manchester in 1892 accompanied by the bald statement: 'at least twelve Bands'.[122] We do know that the question of what constituted a band could arise. 'G. F.' from the Battersea Socialist Band, for example, wrote to *Justice* to plead for new members to join their band: 'We have been able to keep the band together for the last two years', he wrote, 'but owing to a lack of enthusiasm on the part of our members we seem to be depending on strangers, who are not Socialists.' The consequence was that 'we cannot turn out for the cause as often as we should like'.[123] The noun 'strangers' is a weighty one. The contrast to Wellington, where non-official bands were clamouring in the pages of the labour press to be recognised as part of the cause, is stark.

By the end of the decade the halcyon days of the London parades were gone; in 1898 the London demonstration was described as a 'dismal outing', the 'smallest since the inception of Labour Day'. The weather undoubtedly added to the miserable showing. 'Even the brave vigour of the half drowned bandsmen', quipped the reporter from the *Daily News*, 'failed to impart much life to the procession as it slouched its way through the rain and the muddy streets.' The biggest losers, he continued, were the hawkers and vendors that had 'speculated heavily' on a tidy profit from beer and sherbet, nuts and oranges and other consumables only to be left with soggy biscuits and buns.[124] The following year the London procession numbered 500–600; the meeting itself about 6,000. Commentators agreed that by this time the annual event in London had become disconnected from the mainstream trade union movement (let alone the wider community) and was the property of a socialist rump whose tenacity reflected the fact that the Second International had proclaimed May Day as an occasion to celebrate the international solidarity of labour.[125]

What this meant in reality was that Labour Day in Britain could be a grim affair that was reflected not only in the composition of the parade but also, and indeed most obviously, in the music. In Bangor in Wales in 1897, for example, the meeting opened with the Welsh hymn *Beth sydd I mi yn y byd* ('What is there for me in the world') set to *Aberystwyth*, composed by Joseph Parry (ironically becoming the tune for the South African National Anthem in the same year).[126] The lyrics were written in the eighteenth century by Morgan Rhys and tell a bleak tale of a miserable life before salvation:

> What does the world hold for me?
> Trials and Tribulations continually
> Enemy upon enemy maim me day and night...[127]

The procession comprised groups of miners from every district in North Wales accompanied by several brass bands and culminated in a public meeting addressed by prominent politicians including Lloyd George, the future prime minister. The occasion was far from festive, a tone that was reflected in the speeches, which were uniformly combative. John Burns, a celebrated veteran of the London Dock Strike and a socialist who sat in the House of Commons alongside Keir Hardie as an Independent Labour MP, summarised the mood of the meeting with a warning that cultural imperialism went hand in hand with capitalist exploitation: 'In this part of industrial Britain', he told the crowd, 'the men's religious sentiments, their imaginative characteristics, their poetry and their peaceful disposition are all being exploited'. Their enemies, he continued, 'would not be satisfied until Wales was Anglicised, which meant Wales commercialised and its working classes disorganised and ultimately brutalised'.[128] The meeting concluded with the mass singing of *Men of Harlech*, a lyric written in the 1790s and published with music around 1830. Given that its lyrics refer to the seven-year-long siege of Harlech Castle by a future king of England in the fifteenth century, the selection was appropriate and arguably one of the highpoints of the day, sonically and ideologically:

> Men of Harlech, march to glory,
> Victory is hov'ring o'er ye,
> Bright-eyed freedom stands before ye,
> Hear ye not her call?

Despite this reference to a victory shrouded in the mists of time, Labour Day events in the British Isles were not built upon a celebration of success. The dominant motif was combative and beleaguered, drawing upon the fierce independence and abrasive class-consciousness of the Chartists of previous generations. As Engels reported in relation to a parade he witnessed in London: 'The grandchildren of the old Chartists are stepping into the line of battle'.[129] But, as he well knew, some of the old Chartists had contemplated taking up pikes and rifles as well as trumpets and drumsticks and sometimes instead of them.

By contrast, the sustained success of Labour Day festivities outside of Britain was, at least for some commentators, a capsule statement of the achievements of the movement in socio-economic conditions often seen as amounting to a workingman's paradise. From the Antipodean vantage point of a desk in Christchurch the contrast between Britain and her colonies of settlement was obvious to the editor of one newspaper in 1900: 'The workers of the colony yesterday celebrated Labour Day in the customary manner and, in this city, under favourable auspices,' he wrote. 'It had long been recognised that in the colonies of the British Empire labour conditions generally are superior to those existing in older countries, and, in New Zealand in particular, the lot of the worker is usually one that leaves very little room for grumbling.'[130] Having witnessed the Labour Day parade in 1889, the editor of Sydney's leading daily newspaper was even more cocksure: 'The Trades Union, which has come down to us as the natural descendant of the British Guilds, has found, perhaps, a more congenial home in Australia than in any other part of the world and no one who witnessed yesterday's procession, with its bands, its banners, and its thousands of well-dressed and happy workmen, could doubt this assertion.'[131]

As noted, the music itself tells this story. Our use of the term 'appropriate' in connection with the rousing rendition of *Men of Harlech* in Bangor is intended here to carry significant weight. Indeed, it is hard to overestimate the value of the term in connection with repertoire both as a measure of 'the political' and as a bellwether of an episode about to unfold. In other words, understanding what was considered by the historical actors to be an appropriate repertoire provides the historian with a sage guide as to the level of tension and putative conflict and, again, is a perspicacious way to consider differences across the radical Anglophone world. Unfortunately, the details of a repertoire are often frustratingly elusive, cloaked in countless reports behind a host of adjectives such as stirring, thrilling, exhilarating, inspiriting and, in some instances, appropriate. Where there is evidence, however, it is almost inevitably revealing. In some cases the choice of repertoire was a clear attempt to excite controversy by sounding a note of discord. When, for example, the Invercargill Volunteers paraded the streets of their town on the southernmost tip of New Zealand's South Island in August 1864 'with rifle, bayonet, belt etc., shining in the moonlight' they were caterwauling *Old John Brown*. At least one angry resident objected to the fact that they had adopted 'a revolutionary Yankee song as their martial music!' and suggested that more funds be invested in the Provincial Brass Band to rival them.[132] Coming a fortnight after Admiral David Farragut of the Union navy issued his famous order to 'Damn the torpedoes' and attack the Confederate fleet (with outstanding success as it transpired) the exchange was surely even more pointed. Similarly, when a senior official arrived in Nelson in the far north of New Zealand in 1859 to lay the foundation stone of a government building, the local newspaper was horrified to report that 'a band … commenced their proceedings playing a French air, the "Partant Pour La Syrie"'. It got worse: 'And if this was not sufficient, they attempted the Marseillaise'.[133] No further details about the miscreant band are provided in the report of the incident but they identified themselves by their selection of tunes. Undoubtedly, everyone, including the hapless superintendent, took their point.

The selection of music could just as easily be used to frame an oppositional public meeting within a broader protestation of loyalty. Opponents of the reintroduction of transportation in south-eastern Australia in the late 1840s, for example, almost invariably bookended their meetings with a rousing rendition of *God Save the Queen* and three cheers for Her Majesty so as to emphasise that their grievance was with the Queen's ministers and that they did not seek to overturn the constitutional framework that she headed. In Hobart protesters even burned an effigy of the colonial governor to the strains of the national anthem.[134] The venerable anthem (and other iconic selections, such as *Rule, Britannia*, which proclaimed similar sentiments) was often performed insouciantly as part of the repertoire of the music-makers involved in Labour Day events. This was just as true in Ontario in 1883 as it was in New South Wales in 1886.[135] In some cases, however, the performance of the tune was tinged with ambiguity, and recognised as such. At the mass parade on the twelfth anniversary of the eight-hour day in Melbourne, for example, all four bands played the anthem in succession as they passed the Treasury Building. One commentator noted: 'To some of the onlookers, this proceeding seemed to possess a political significance, but it was simply an observance of the practice invariably adopted in these celebrations.'[136] Reading this evidence against the grain, it is worth noting the reference to the invariable practice of anthem-playing, suggesting that despite the reporter's certitude the episode had a political significance either way. Of course, in the nineteenth century Anglophone world the fingerprints of radicals were to be found on the words and music of several national anthems. This was a time when nationalism was primarily a cause of the Left and even many hard-line radicals understood their cause as one underpinned by a higher loyalty to the traditional values of an imagined nation. For many, however, the music denoted a deep ambivalence. In the pages of the Victorian *Socialist*, for example, Tom Mann insisted that there were two Englands: the England of the oppressor and the imperialist, and 'our England, the Merrie England of our love; the England of song, that is almost invariably on the side of the oppressed, of deep-seated and long continued revolt against the arrogance of kings, barons, landlords, manufacturers, sweaters and military marionettes.'[137]

Ambivalence slipped easily into outright hostility. In an issue a few short weeks after Mann's editorial the newspaper published a contrafactum set of words penned by socialist and poet Marie Elizabeth Pitt that gave vent to a melange of sarcasm and outrage:

> 'God save the King!' they pray,
> Keep him from dark dismay
> Or evil thing!
> Loud swells the mocking chant
> Up from this world of 'cant,'
> Drowning the moans of want –
> 'God save the King!'[138]

Among a plethora of subversive if not hostile appropriations was another published the *Maoriland Worker* in 1911:

> Hail! Sacred Comradeship,
> Praised be with heart and lip
> All the world o'er!
> Through the victorious,
> Happy and glorious
> Days are in store for us,
> All the world o'er.[139]

Similarly, in Queensland in 1912 'Anti-Scab' composed *An Australian Anthem* appropriating the all too familiar tune:

> God speed you one and all
> That answered the Union's call
> For Liberty.[140]

These latter-day appropriations were part of a tradition that extended back into the eighteenth century to the time when *God Save the Queen* itself was first popularised. For example, a version republished by the Chartists in the 1840s had been written in the 1790s by Thomas Spence.[141] Yet another contrafactum, *Lord! Free Us All*, was published in the eponymous newspaper of William Lyon Mackenzie, leader of the popular rebellion in Upper Canada in 1837–38:

> Lord! o'er our own loved land
> Spread the protecting hand!
> Help! ere we fall!
> Free us from Monarchy-
> Free us from Hierarchy,

Sabres and Squirearchy-
Lord free us all.

O, men of England! rise!
Arm for thy precious prize,
Your birthright, all!
With firm heart, with iron-hand
As One let Millions stand,
A true and steadfast band-
Triumph, or fall! [142]

It is also true that *God Save the Queen* could be appropriated with great subtlety. In Kitamaat, in far-north British Columbia, for example, May Day concluded with a nuanced inversion in which music and performance were used to emphasise local identity and authority among the First Nations people. The May Day Picnic revolved around the crowning of the May Day Queen, replete with a version of the familiar ceremonial genuflection afforded to royalty. 'As the sun sank low over the sea', the report concluded, 'we sang "God save our Queen" and after firing the cannon and three cheers for her Majesty, we wended our way back through the woodlands to our village homes feeling that the day had been pleasantly and profitably spent.'[143] The ambiguity of 'our' in this episode is worthy of note.

In some cases the performance of British anthems could highlight division within the movement (or perhaps, more accurately, serve to remind us that the rubric 'labour movement' is a capacious one). Witnessing the Melbourne parade in 1903, the correspondent for the *Tocsin*, for example, took exception to the fact that a band played *Rule, Britannia* as striking miners passed Parliament.[144] The disgruntled reporter suggested that nobody seemed to know why the band had chosen that selection. Presumably, the bandsmen knew the reason and saw nothing wrong with it. During the Hyde Park meeting in 1900, to take another example, one speaker was interrupted by a band playing the *Marseillaise* and he quipped that at least the *Marseillaise* was 'better suited for them than "God save the Queen"'. Significantly, however, his remark was greeted with both 'cheers and hisses'.[145]

In more general terms there is evidence that repertoire mattered. Reports of parades and concerts contain many instances when special attention was drawn to the performance of 'labour songs' just as there are numerous references to songs titles that clearly mused upon relevant themes, such the *Battle of Eureka* and *God Bless Our Trade Unions*.[146] For some participants, repertoire was particularly important as a means of supporting a sense of shared identity, pride and defiance. The example of the Sydney wharf labourers at the turn of the century is particularly illuminating. In the same year that the Cobar miners marched, a contingent of 1,500 'wharfies' dominated the parade in Sydney. Headed by the union's secretary, William Morris Hughes, a future prime minister and leader of Australia during the First World War, the unionists marched along singing shanties 'with which wharf labourers are want to accompany their work on shipboard'. The context for this ostensibly innocuous act of music-making was crucial. As the reporter for the *Herald* noted, the anniversary was 'specially jubilant' because the dockers had only lately won the eight-hour day across their occupation. Moreover, the union itself had relatively recently enjoyed a renaissance under Hughes's stewardship, a decade after a crushing defeat at the hands of employers during the dock strikes of the early 1890s.[147] A decade later the wharf workers were still contributing to the musical life of Labour Day in Sydney. Again headed by the obdurate Hughes, by this time Federal Attorney General in the Fisher Labor government, the Wharf Labourers Band played *Sons of the Sea* and 'the populace sang the refrain'.[148] There were several versions of the song lyrics that were popular at this time. One was a 'national' song published in 1900 with the Boer War in mind:

> Sons of the sea, all British born,
> Sailing ev'ry ocean, laughing foes to scorn.
> They may build their ships, my lads, and think they know the game,
> But they can't build boys of the bull-dog breed,
> Who made old England's name.[149]

A second version – of unknown provenance – essayed piracy on the Spanish Main inflected with national martial pride and constructed around a repeating phrase that (as a children's nursery rhyme) invites movement:

> Sons of the sea, bobbing up and down like this,
> Sailing the ocean, bobbing up and down like this.
> They may build their ships, my lads, bobbing up and down like this
> But they can't beat the boys of the Old Brigade,
> Bobbing up and down like this.
>
> Pirates so free, bobbing up and down like this,
> Searching the ocean, bobbing up and down like this.
> They care naught for wind and rain, bobbing up and down like this
> For they rob the gold on the Spanish Main,
> Bobbing up and down like this.

A third version, similar to the second and also tinctured with a patriotic reference to the British bulldog, had an accumulative lyric:

Sons of the sea,
Climbing up the ropes and rowing the boats and swabbing the decks and
  hitching up your pants and bobbing up and down like this.
Sailing the ocean,
Climbing up the ropes and rowing the boats and swabbing the decks and
  hitching up your pants and bobbing up and down like this.
Well you can build a ship my lad,
Climbing up the ropes and rowing the boats and swabbing the decks and
  hitching up your pants and bobbing up and down like this.
But you can't beat the boys in the bulldog ring,
Climbing up the ropes and rowing the boats and swabbing the decks and
  hitching up your pants and bobbing up and down like this.

The last two versions would have been widely familiar to the participating 'populace', although whether they bobbed while they sang
is not recorded. However, the wharfies, if not all those in the crowd,
would have been aware of a contrafactum written by the Melbourne-
based anarchist J. A. Andrews around the turn of the century that
also invoked a nationalist vision, but, in this case, an Australian one.
Andrews had spent time in Sydney editing the *Australian Worker*
before returning to Melbourne to edit the *Tocsin*. His *Sons of the South*
was a passionate encomium that was published in the *Bulletin* and
later featured in socialist songbooks in New South Wales and Victoria:

Our native land, free we'll enjoy,
Our own wealth we'll work for, in our own employ;
All shall be the worker's share – we'll mock the fleecer's claim
For the Sons of the South will have their own, and make Australia's name!

... Soon shall beam in welcome to the brave
The ruddy dawn of Freedom's joyous day.
But we want plenty yet, plenty yet, plenty yet,
And what we want we'll get, yes, we'll get, yes, we'll get![150]

Sons of the Sea and other sea shanties were appropriate songs for the
wharfies to sing to affirm their identity, celebrate their victories, and
remind themselves of and proclaim their collective power, but they
were also good fun (especially if the 'populace' were 'bobbing up and
down like this'). This is a reminder not to lose sight of the festive
atmosphere that shaped these rituals. A very popular song in Australia
during the 1890s, *I've Worked Eight Hours This Day*, also makes this
point well. Given the title – and the sentiment – the song understandably featured in Labour Day festivities (and it was included in numerous
other concert programmes besides). Written in 1899, the song was not
a serious anthem; it was a comedic burlesque that satirised the eight-
hour principle as much as it celebrated it. The story tells of individuals

inconvenienced by the strict application of the eight-hour rule. In one verse, for example, a man is undergoing a shave when the clock strikes six and the barber downs his razor, leaving the customer with whiskers on half his face:

> Keep your whiskers on
> Till the morning, John
> I won't work half a minute longer
> For I've worked eight hours this day
> And I think I've earned my pay.

In another verse a woman refuses to get up to let her drunken husband into their locked house:

> You can stop out there in the rain and swear
> I won't work half a minute longer
> For I've worked eight hours this day
> And I think I've earned my pay.[151]

Equally revealing are the many examples where repertoire did *not* seem to matter. Let us return to the day Hughes and the dockworkers marched along entertaining the Sydney 'populace' with the strains of *Sons of the Sea*. In the evening an eight-hour demonstration concert took place in the Town Hall. Part of the proceedings was devoted to the award of prizes for the best display of the day (the Waterside Workers won second prize behind the Furniture Makers). Obviously, most of the evening was occupied by music-making. The selection was thoroughly eclectic: a 'dainty "Gavotte"'; an 'exhilarating military march "Off to the Cape"'; 'a classical element' in the form of '"Marc Antony's Oration"'; a 'semi-comedic "relief"', '"Only a Woman's Way"' and '"In the Pale Moonlight"'; a 'sympathetic' rendition of 'Sullivan's "The Lost Chord"'; and '"Angus Macdonald," the score to which was "Killarney"'.[152] The *Herald*'s reporter understood what was going on: the committee, he commented, had 'arranged a miscellaneous programme of a varied and comprehensive character'. 'The whole,' he continued, 'though of somewhat unwieldy dimensions, formed just the kind of popular entertainment expected on such an occasion.'[153] The reference to expectation in relation to repertoire is telling; the organisers clearly did not feel that it was necessary always to use music to buttress the cause of the working man. Of course, the fact that the programme was apparently dictated by popular taste did not mean that it was not political. Moreover, the fact that the audience included Governor Earl Beauchamp is further testimony to the success of the labour movement. Apparently, on this occasion, the Earl was not given the opportunity to make a request but it surely would not have mattered to the trade unionists sitting in the hall if he had. In circumstances where the eight-hour day had been won – from Hobart to Hamilton – eclectic musical programmes at Labour Day marches and concerts were, in fact, the norm. In some instances overt political songs were missing from the evening's entertainment altogether. In Komata, on the North Island of New Zealand, the Labour Day revellers enjoyed *Waves of the Ocean, Queen of the Earth, The King's Own, Killarney, Any Old Thing Will Do, Take Me Back to Bendigo, The Laughing Song, The Last Milestone*, a sailor's hornpipe and a highland fling.[154]

Again, a contrast to Britain is evident. The evidence of musical repertoire that can be gleaned from the reports of British May Day (Labour Day) parades between 1890 and 1900 suggests that it became more stridently and determinedly political as the parades themselves became increasingly partisan. In 1892, for example, the programme was described as 'miscellaneous', ranging from the *Marseillaise* and *Faithful till Death* – 'a familiar air during the London dock strike' – to *The Minstrel Boy* and 'the inevitable "Ta-ra-ra-boom-de-ay"'.[155] By the end of the decade even the May Day children's choir was given no latitude. In 1897 the choir was allocated their own platform by organisers from which they would sing songs within the narrow compass of a well-known socialist canon: *All for the Cause, England Arise, No Master, What Ho, My Lads!, When the Revolution Comes* and the *Marseillaise*.[156] As we shall see in a chapter to follow, the appropriateness of the repertoire is inter alia an excellent barometer of conflict as well as success.

Not long after the publication of Andrews's *Sons of the South*, it was appropriated by 'Mr M. O'Hair' of Quorn, a small town tucked in the Flinders Ranges in South Australia, as the title for a 'franchise ditty'. Unfortunately, Mr O'Hair's musings have, as far as we have been able to ascertain, passed unrecorded into history, but we know his version of *Sons of the South* formed part of the programme sung by a 'company of young men' at a meeting under the auspices of the United Labor Party in 1906.[157] The structure of the episode, including the role of music and its performance, shared many characteristics with Labour Day festivities in the radical Anglophone world that we have examined in detail. Switching our attention to the public interface with the world of formal politics, however, means we can also see significant differences in the way that demotic culture happened. To do so we must narrow our field of vision and join the crowd in front of the hustings.

Notes

1   In New South Wales this day falls in October, which is different from Victoria where it is celebrated in March. In Queensland and Western Australia the day falls in May; whereas in South Australia it is in September. In Canada and the United States it is also celebrated in September and in New Zealand in October.
2   *Town and Country Journal* (4 May 1904).
3   *Ibid.*
4   *Political Examiner* (20 September 1856).
5   *Northern Star* [Lismore, New South Wales] (13 October 1886).
6   *Northern Star* (26 September 1840).
7   *Northern Star* (9 January 1841). *The Landing of Royal Charlie* was published by Thomas Birt in Seven Dials *c.*1830. It is unknown if it related to an earlier song. See http://digital.nls.uk/broadsides/broadside.cfm/id/16615 (accessed 13 September).
8   *Brisbane Courier* (7 May 1907).
9   *Justice* (13 May 1893). See also *Scotsman* (2 May 1892).
10 *Westralian Worker* (19 October 1900); *Open Court* (11 August 1892); *Globe* (3 September 1901).
11 *Manchester Guardian* (2 May 1892).
12 *Brisbane Courier* (2 May 1899). In some cases collective singing served this purpose. *Song of the Reformers* by 'Jay Gee', for example, was published for pianoforte and as a part song 'specifically adapted for the singing of bodies of men marching in procession'. See *Commonwealth* (23 March 1867).
13 *Reynolds' News* (8 May 1892).
14 *Sydney Morning Herald* (4 October 1892).
15 *Globe* (16 April 1872).
16 *Evening Post* (29 September 1890).
17 *Barrier Truth* (27 January 1909).
18 *Hobart Mercury* (8 March 1894).
19 George Holyoake, *Sixty Years of An Agitator's Life* (London: T. F. Unwin, 1906), p. 30. This episode is discussed in subsequent chapters.
20 *Northern Star* (21 April 1838).
21 *Worker* (7 May 1898).
22 Benjamin Franklin, *Autobiography* (London: Dent, 1968), p. 179; Paul Pickering, 'Class Without Words: Symbolic Communication in the Chartist Movement', *Past and Present*, 112:1 (1986), pp. 144–62. Reprinted in *Past and Present: E. P. Thompson Special Issue* (2014).
23 *Socialist* (30 May 1909).
24 *Globe* (4 September 1894).
25 *Manchester Guardian* (2 May 1892). Nonetheless, the best-laid plans could come unstuck. At Manchester, a Labour Day parade comprising 60,000 souls culminated in a meeting on approximately thirty acres in Alexandra Park, Hulme. To serve the vast crowd six platforms had been erected several hundred yards apart from which speeches were to be given simultaneously. At one point an attempt was made to synchronise the passage of a set of resolutions with the aid of a cornet on 'Platform 1'. 'The cornet was brought into action', ran the report, 'but was scarcely audible to the platform from which it "trumpeted forth".'
26 *Industrial Banner* (September 1899).
27 *Labour's Realm* (13 September 1907). It could also throw divisions into sharp relief. In Hamilton, Ontario, rival branches of unions in the motor industry based, respectively, in Canada and the US ended up holding separate parades. See the collection of cuttings relating to a bitter dispute between metal workers in Canadian labour leader Ralph Ellis's scrapbooks. McMaster University, Hamilton, Archives & Research Collections, Ralph Ellis Fonds, RCO411, Book 2.
28 *White Ribbon* (September 1900), Hocken Library, University of Otago, NZ.

29 *Poverty Bay Herald* (1 August 1914).
30 See issues of the *Sydney Morning Herald, Argus, Brisbane Courier, West Australian, South Australian Register* and *Hobart Mercury* for 11 May 1914; *Barrier Truth* (12 May 1914).
31 See Kate Bowan and Paul Pickering, 'Singing for Socialism', in Laurajane Smith, Paul Shackel and Gary Campbell (eds), *Heritage, Labour and the Working Classes* (New York: Routledge, 2011), pp. 192–215.
32 *Reynolds' News* (10 May 1899).
33 *Globe* (7 September 1897). See also Craig Heron and Steve Penfold, *The Workers' Festival: A History of Labour Day in Canada* (Toronto: University of Toronto Press, 2005).
34 *Socialist* (21 April 1906); *Age* (9 November 1882); W. E. Murphy, *History of the Eight Hours' Movement* (Melbourne: Spectator Publishing, 1896), p. 38.
35 *Globe* (23 July 1883).
36 *Northern Star* (29 September 1838); *Northern Star* (22 August 1840).
37 State Library of South Australia, South Australiana Pamphlets, *Official Program of the 19th Anniversary of the Eight Hour Movement*, n.p., 1892, p. 8; *People's Voice* (8 September 1894); *Evening Post* (28 October 1891).
38 *Sydney Morning Herald* (8 October 1889).
39 *Reynolds' News* (8 May 1892).
40 *Star* (8 October 1900).
41 *Globe* (2 September 1902); *Socialist* (21 April 1906); *Sydney Morning Herald* (4 October 1910). See also Duncan Bythell, 'The Brass Band in the Antipodes: The Transplantation of British Popular Culture', in Trevor Herbert (ed.), *The British Band: A Musical and Social History* (Oxford: Oxford University Press, 2000), pp. 240–3.
42 State Library of Queensland, John Oxley Library, *Official Bulletin no. 9, issued by the Strike Committee, 9 February 1912* (Brisbane: William McCocker for the Combined Unions Strike Committee, 1912).
43 See Working Class Movement Library, Salford, Harry Starr Scrapbooks, 2 vols [uncatalogued].
44 *Canterbury Star* (30 April 1904); *Canterbury Star* (30 November 1889).
45 *Canterbury Star* (19 July 1909).
46 *Barrier Truth* (16 September 1899).
47 *Northern Star* (21 September 1850).
48 *Canterbury Star* (30 April 1904).
49 *Barrier Truth* (9 October 1908).
50 *Maoriland Worker* (29 October 1913).
51 *Maoriland Worker* (13 October 1913).
52 See S. P. Newcomb, *The Music of the People: the Story of the Brass Band Movement in New Zealand 1845–1963* (Christchurch: G. R. Mowatt, 1963).
53 *Canterbury Star* (24 June 1899).
54 *Globe* (6 September 1898).
55 *Canterbury Star* (28 July 1906).
56 *The Cyclopedia of New Zealand* (Christchurch: Cyclopedia Company, 1903); *Canterbury Star* (30 November 1889).
57 *Canterbury Star* (17 December 1898); *Canterbury Star* (16 November 1899); *Canterbury Star* (24 June 1899); *Canterbury Star* (30 April 1901); *Canterbury Star* (1 May 1901); *Canterbury Press* (5 October 1901).
58 *Canterbury Star* (25 April 1903); *Canterbury Star* (27 November 1905); *Canterbury Star* (2 December 1905). The candidate was a local clothing storeowner, Charles Gray, who was Mayor of Christchurch (1891, 1904–5) and MP for Christchurch North (1905–8). See J. O. Wilson, *The New Zealand Parliamentary Record 1840–1984* (Wellington: Government Printer, 1985).
59 See, inter alia, C. O. Davis, *Temperance Songs, in the Maori Language* (Auckland John Henry Field, 1873); Montreal Temperance Society, *Canadian Temperance Minstrel* (Montreal: Rollo Campbell, 1842); Arthur Toombes, Queensland

Prohibition League, *Community Song Book* (Brisbane: Read A. Flack, n.d.); United Kingdom Band of Hope Union, *Hymns & Songs for Bands of Hope* (London: Richard L. James, n.d.); Anna A. Gordon (ed.), *The White Ribbon Hymnal*, compiled for the National and World's Woman's Christian Temperance Unions (Chicago: Woman's Temperance Publishing, 1892).

60   *Brisbane Courier* (11 June 1872); *Brisbane Courier* (16 March 1886); *Brisbane Courier* (7 January 1898).

61   *The Palladium of Labor* (11 August 1883).

62   It is unclear if the band was also female.

63   Gregory S. Kealey, 'McVicar, Kate', in *Dictionary of Canadian Biography*, vol. 11 (Toronto: University of Toronto/Quebec: Université Laval, 2003), available at www.biographi.ca/en/bio/mcvicar_kate_11E.html (accessed 12 September 2016).

64   *The Palladium of Labor* (11 August 1883).

65   The following year a Six Nations team participated in a lacrosse match in Toronto. See *Globe* (5 August 1884).

66   Dale McIntosh, *History of Music in British Columbia 1850–1950* (Victoria: Sono Nis Press, 1989), pp. 43–9; David Mattison, 'On the March: Indian Brass Bands 1866–1916', *British Columbia Historical News*, 15:1 (1981), pp. 6–14; Leslie Drew, 'Indian Concert Bands', *Beaver*, Summer (1971), pp. 26–9.

67   *Na-Na-Kwa* (June 1898); *Na-Na-Kwa* (February 1899).

68   *Na-Na-Kwa* (October 1900).

69   *Globe* (5 August 1884).

70   See David Hebert, 'Music Transculturation and Identity in a Maori Brass Band Tradition', *Alta Musica*, 26 (2008), pp. 174–5.

71   *Evening Post* (10 October 1900). The band had also participated in the parade in 1891. See Alexander Turnbull Library, Wellington, NZ, Herbert Otto Roth Papers MS-Group-0314, Research Notes and Documents on the Eight-Hour Day Movement, 94–106–72/13. See also *Evening Post* (29 October 1892).

72   For charivari see Violet Alford, 'Rough Music or Charivari', *Folklore*, 70:4 (1959), pp. 505–18, and, more famously, E. P. Thompson, 'Rough Music', in *Customs and Common* (London: Merlin, 1991), pp. 467–553 (originally published in *Annales* in 1972). According to Derek Scott, T. D. Rice started performing as Jim Crow in 1832 and blackface started in the 1840s. See Derek B. Scott, 'Blackface Minstrels, Black Minstrels, and their Reception in England', in Rachel Cowgill and Julian Rushton (eds), *Europe, Empire and Spectacle in Nineteenth-Century British Music* (Aldershot: Ashgate, 2006), pp. 265–80.

73   For Carroll, see Alan Ward, 'Carroll, James', *Dictionary of New Zealand Biography*. *Te Ara – the Encyclopedia of New Zealand*, available at www.TeAra.govt.nz/en/biographies/2c10/carroll-james (accessed 13 September 2016).

74   Hone Heke and A. T. Ngata, *Souvenir of Maori Congress, July 1908, Scenes from the Past with Maori versions of Popular English Songs* (Wellington: Whitcombe & Tombs, 1908), prefatory note and pp. 16, 25, 27.

75   Heke and Ngata, *Scenes from the Past*, prefatory note.

76   At this time Ngata was also centrally involved in a cultural preservation project that produced four volumes of songs and chants known as *Nga Moteatea*. This is discussed in a later chapter.

77   Hebert, 'Music Transculturation', p. 182.

78   Some historians, notably Neville Kirk, have argued that, notwithstanding the virulent racism among white working-class trade unionists on the colonial frontier, in many instances class was more important than race in motivating their activities. See Neville Kirk, *Comrades and Cousins: Globalization, Workers and Labour Movements for the 1880s to 1914* (London: Merlin Press, 1983).

79   *Maoriland Worker* (10 December 1913).

80   See Susan Neylan, 'Here Comes the Band! Cultural Collaboration, Connective Traditions, and Aboriginal Brass Bands on British Columbia's North Coast, 1875–1964', *BC Studies*, 152 (2007), p. 139. There were exceptions; see the picture of the Nelson Band in Dale McIntosh, *History of Music in BC*, n.p.

81 See Library and Archives Canada, Ms. Indian Affairs RG, vol. 2235, file 45, 549.
82 See, for example, *Lloyd's London Weekly* (4 May 1890).
83 Bythell, 'Brass Band in the Antipodes', pp. 240–3.
84 *Barrier Truth* (11 November 1908).
85 Bythell, 'Brass Band in the Antipodes', pp. 241–2.
86 *Barrier Truth* (11 November 1908).
87 *Globe* (2 September 1892).
88 *Maoriland Worker* (19 September 1913); *Maoriland Worker* (3 October 1913); *Maoriland Worker* (15 October 1913).
89 *Globe* (3 September 1912); *Sydney Morning Herald* (5 October 1897).
90 *Evening Post* (28 October 1891).
91 *Barrier Truth* (9 October 1908).
92 *Voice* (7 September 1909).
93 *Journal of United Labor* (July 1883).
94 *Globe* (23 July 1883).
95 Bryan Palmer has argued that the tradition of charivari survived in Canada in some form well into the twentieth century. See Bryan Palmer, 'Discordant Music: Charivari and White Capping in Northern America', *Labor/Le Traveilleur*, 1 (1978), pp. 5–62. See also Pauline Greenhill, *Make the Night Hideous: Four English Canadian Charivaris 1881–1940* (Toronto: University of Toronto Press, 2010).
96 *Northern Liberator* (18 November 1837). The report originated in the *Vindicator*.
97 University of British Columbia, Vancouver, Rare Books and Special Colections, handbill, 'Labor Day at Tyrone!', 4 September 1898.
98 See E. P. Thompson's seminal review essay, 'On History, Sociology and Historical Relevance', *British Journal of Sociology*, 27:3 (1976), pp. 387–402.
99 *Sydney Morning Herald* (5 October 1886).
100 *Globe* (12 September 1892).
101 *Sydney Morning Herald* (4 October 1904).
102 *Socialist* (30 April 1909).
103 *People* (7 October 1905); *People* (9 May 1908).
104 *Globe* (12 September 1892).
105 *Globe* (3 September 1901).
106 *Ibid.*
107 *Sydney Morning Herald* (5 October 1897).
108 *Evening Post* (10 October 1900).
109 *Brisbane Courier* (6 May 1902).
110 *Northern Star* (24 April 1847).
111 *Northern Star* (4 June 1842).
112 *Northern Star* (8 May 1847).
113 See Paul Pickering, 'Confronting the Good Monarch: Searching for a Democratic Case for the Republic', in Benjamin Jones and Mark McKenna (eds), *Project Republic* (Melbourne: Black Inc., 2013), pp. 118–32.
114 *Justice* (30 April 1892).
115 *Reynolds' News* (8 May 1892).
116 *Morning Post* (5 May 1890).
117 *Pall Mall Gazette* (2 May 1892).
118 *Reynolds' News* (2 May 1897).
119 *Arbeiter Zeitung* (23 May 1890) in Karl Marx and Frederick Engels, *Articles on Britain* (Moscow: Progress Publishers, 1971).
120 *Clarion* (30 April 1892).
121 *Glasgow Herald* (1 May 1894). In the *Glasgow Reformer*, a temperance journal engaged with a parliamentary campaign in favour of local option in relation to drink and women's suffrage, the massive event in 1892 passed without a word.
122 *Clarion* (30 April 1892).
123 *Justice* (13 September 1890).
124 *Daily News* (2 May 1898).
125 *Ibid.* The International had also chosen the day to commemorate the Haymarket

'martyrs' executed after a bomb had been thrown during a strike meeting in favour of the eight-hour day in Chicago in 1886.

126 *North Wales Chronicle* (8 May 1897). See also John T. Koch, *Celtic Culture: A Historical Encyclopedia*, vol. 3 (Santa Barbara: ABC-Clio, 2006), p. 942.

127 We are grateful to Owen Ashton for arranging for this hymn to be translated from the Welsh by Margaret Davies of Caernarvon.

128 *North Wales Chronicle* (8 May 1897). The fact that Burns was a Londoner apparently did not matter.

129 *Arbeiter Zeitung* (23 May 1890) in Marx and Engels, *Articles on Britain*.

130 *Press* [Christchurch, NZ] (11 October 1900).

131 *Sydney Morning Herald* (8 October 1889).

132 *Evening Bulletin* (18 August 1864).

133 *Colonist* (30 August 1859).

134 See, for example, *People's Advocate* (21 September 1850). See also Paul Pickering, 'Loyalty and Rebellion in Colonial Politics: The Campaign Against Convict Transportation', in Philip Alfred Buckner and R. Douglas Francis (eds), *Rediscovering the British World* (Calgary, Alberta: University of Calgary Press, 2005), pp. 87–107.

135 *Palladium of Labor* (11 August 1883); *Sydney Morning Herald* (5 October 1886).

136 *Argus* (22 April 1868).

137 *Socialist* (6 October 1906).

138 *Socialist* (24 November 1906).

139 *Maoriland Worker* (11 June 1911).

140 State Library of Queensland, John Oxley Library, *Official Bulletin* (Brisbane: William McCocker for the Combined Unions Strike Committee, 1912).

141 *Northern Star*, (17 January 1846).

142 McGill University, Rare Books and Special Collections, Lende Collection of Canadiana, *Mackenzie's Gazette* (3 November 1838) in John S. Moir, *Rhymes of Rebellion* (Toronto Ryerson Press, 1965). Note his reference to England.

143 *Na-Na-Kwa* (July 1900).

144 *Tocsin* (30 April 1903).

145 *Standard* (5 May 1890).

146 *Sydney Morning Herald* (7 October 1890); *Worker* (1 March 1890). The origin of this song is unknown as are its melody and libretto. There are sporadic reports of its performance in regional Australia between 1890 and the 1920s. See *Clarence and Richmond Examiner* (5 September 1891); *Launceston Examiner* (27 December 1898); *Adelaide Advertiser* (19 June 1901); *Northwest Advocate* (20 August 1910); *Advocate* [Burnie, Tasmania] (11 October 1921).

147 *Sydney Morning Herald* (2 October 1900). For Hughes see L. F. Fitzhardinge, 'Hughes, William Morris (Billy) (1862–1952)', *Australian Dictionary of Biography*, available at http://adb.anu.edu.au/biography/hughes-william-morris-billy-6761/text11689 (accessed 13 September 2016).

148 *Sydney Morning Herald* (4 October 1910).

149 Felix McGlennon, *Sons of the Sea* (Melbourne: Allan & Co, c.1900).

150 *Barrier Socialist Songster* (Broken Hill: Truth Print, n.d.); *Labour Song Book* (Melbourne: Tocsin Print, n.d.).

151 Johns Hopkins University, Levy Sheet Music Collection, Box 047, Item 083, Felix McGlennon, 'I've Worked Eight Hours This Day' (Broadway: R.A. Saalfield, [1892]), https://jscholarship.library.jhu.edu/handle/1774.2/18823 (accessed 13 September 2016). See also *South Australian Register* (2 September 1899); *Argus* (9 December 1916); *Examiner and Times* (17 October 1906); *West Australian* (22 August 1892); *Queenslander* (10 October 1891). The Salvation Army used an appropriated version: 'I've had enough sin, and I won't serve the devil any longer'. See *West Australian* (8 June 1899).

152 *Sydney Morning Herald* (2 October 1900).

153 *Ibid.*

154 *Ohinemuri Gazette* (10 October 1910).

155 *Scotsman* (2 May 1892).
156 *Reynolds' News* (4 April 1897). For the student of the Socialist Sunday School movement that swept Britain during the 1890s this will come as no surprise. See Labour History and Archives Centre, Socialist Sunday School Collection (Ivy Tribe Collection), GB 394 SSS.
157 *Adelaide Advertiser* (1 December 1906).

CHAPTER THREE

Votes for a song

Oh, young Mrs. BRAND has gone down to the East!
To give the Electors a musical feast,
And save her fine treble she weapons has none;
Yet she means with that voice that the seat shall be won.
So good at a lay, at a ballad so grand,
There never was a dame like the young Mrs. BRAND!

Spell-bound stand the rustics; she's won the whole throng!
To the lady they've given their votes 'for a song.'
''Twill be ours, will the seat – 'tis the plot I have planned!
Oh, Music hath charms!' – exclaimed young Mrs. BRAND.

Punch (25 July 1891)

The streets of nineteenth-century cities were noisy places. In his landmark social investigations published in 1850, Henry Mayhew estimated that there were approximately 1,000 musicians and 250 ballad singers plying their trade on the streets of London.[1] By the mid-1860s parliament was being implored to strengthen the legislation to silence this 'lawless noise'. 'What is called the "Liberty of Englishmen"', one MP complained, ought to be 'widened so as to include the liberty of getting rest and sleep at the times nature intended'.[2] In many instances street performance was felt to be disrespectful, if not subversive: 'Some fellows, blacking their faces, go about, and are generally, very insolent, as well as noisy.'[3] Henry Vizetelly, a journalist well known for his contributions to the metropolitan press, captured this befuddling melange of political commentary and popular caterwauling in his memoirs: 'Our ears were incessantly assailed with such cries as "What a Shocking Bad Hat!" "There he goes with his eye out!" "How are you off for soap?"' as well as the obviously political '"Flare up and join the Union"'.[4] Similarly, Charles Manby Smith, a successful journalist and social commentator, recalled the 'gratuitous entertainment' provided by 'a chorus of ballad-singers … bawling the last new political ballad, with interlocutory explanation – or a lament for the Crimean army – or a dirge for Nicholas, from which we learn that the Czar lies "buried in" a hole in Sebastopol.'[5]

The link between the hubbub on the streets and the soundscape of more formal political rituals was a close one. Writing to a London newspaper in 1851 one commentator noted that music was an '*almost invariable* accompaniment of electioneering proceedings'.[6] Indeed, music and music-making enjoyed a multivalent place in the conduct of elections throughout the long nineteenth century: from the behaviour of those on the platform to that of the crowd; from the sounds of the street-level peregrinations of the faithful to the churn of the printing press; from the nomination of the candidates to the declaration of the poll. An examination of these roles provides an opportunity to explore aspects of the mechanics of cultural transmission and, more particularly, to focus on the continuities and changes of political rituals across time and distance. In this case the task is cross cut by the incremental professionalisation of political campaigning, principally through the more systematic use of election agents, and by the varied pace of structural political reform within the Anglophone world. The orthodoxy in relation to Britain is that the gradual expansion of the composition and structure of the political nation during the nineteenth century produced a corresponding decline in extra-parliamentary political action; it removed its *raison d'être*. The year 1867 is often regarded as the Rubicon between what has been called the politics of interest and the politics of electoral pressure.[7] In the Antipodes and in North America, however, fundamental changes to some of the rules of the game came far more quickly. By the end of the 1850s, for example, the hard-won constitutions of the largest Australian colonies included manhood suffrage and the ballot, reforms that eluded British radicals for another generation. For newly enfranchised activists the pace of reform altered the very object of campaigning: from demanding inclusion in the political nation to the quest for power within it.

Similarly, structural changes such as the abolition of the public nomination of candidates and voting by show of hands, around which much of the ritualised performance of electoral politics revolved, occurred along a different timeline. In the imperial centre the show of hands ended with the introduction of the ballot in 1872. This was later than in South Australia (1856), Tasmania (1858) and Victoria (1865) and in the same year as Queensland, but it was ahead of New Zealand (1890), Canada (1875), New South Wales (1893) and Western Australia (1895). As we shall see in the next chapter, a corollary of constitutional reform was attempted by the State to regulate the conduct of elections, in particular to stamp out violence. The point here is that within the differentiated and unfolding political structures and modernising regulatory frameworks some time-honoured political rituals persisted beyond what we would nowadays call a shelf life. In this respect music and patterns of musical behaviour both exemplified and underpinned resistance to cultural change. Their continuing relevance was also a testament to their lingering importance irrespective of the passing seasons of politics. A longitudinal examination of the vicissitudes of a single constituency – and the place of music within the unfolding of its history in real time – is an ideal starting point for a broader conversation. Both this examination and the subsequent explication of episodes in the present chapter, however, do not focus on 'black eyes and broken heads'.[8] Endemic electoral violence will be our point of entry into the discussion in the next chapter.

In 1891 the constituency of Wisbech in Cambridgeshire became the focus of national politics in Britain due to a by-election caused by the resignation of the incumbent Member. Wisbech was an ancient town fortified by a castle that had been built by William the Conqueror in 1086. Over its long history the town had only very occasionally been tinctured with a whiff of political controversy – two of the Gunpowder Plotters had been imprisoned there in the seventeenth century and over a century later, in the 1760s, it had been the birthplace of Thomas Clarkson, the anti-slavery campaigner, and William Godwin, the radical philosopher better known today as the husband of Mary Wollstonecraft.

The seat had been created as recently as 1885 as part of the package of reform that included the extension of the franchise. Over the next twenty years it became what is known nowadays as a swinging seat. Indeed, it was what psephologists call a litmus test seat because it changed hands in line with changes of government: in 1885 it was a Liberal seat; a year later, in 1886, it went to the Conservative Unionists. Thus there was keen attention on the outcome in 1891. For Gladstone's Liberals it was potentially a 'bright example of renewed allegiance to the Liberal cause'; for Salisbury's Conservatives, on the other hand, defeat would be interpreted as a heavy blow, a reflection of the 'very natural disgust of the electors after five years of Tory rule'.[9]

The Liberal candidate was Arthur Brand, third son of Viscount Hampden. Brand based his campaign on the idea that 'farmers and labourers are entitled to live and thrive from the expenditure of their skill, their capital and their labour'.[10] This stance earned Brand a stinging rebuke from the Tory premier who accused him of being a 'dishonest Radical'. The liberal Daily News found this all too much, suggesting that it was in fact the Conservative candidate, S. W. Duncan, who had 'out-Heroded Herod in his Radical principles'.[11] To support Brand's campaign Gladstone included Wisbech on the itinerary of one of his famous whistle-stop tours. Unfortunately, Gladstone was ill on the day and remained in his bed on the train. Mrs Gladstone passed on his best wishes to the crowd before re-boarding the train and, with her husband and his doctors, beating a hasty retreat. The press reported that the train had only remained at the station for three minutes.[12]

Despite the fact that the national political stakes were high, many agreed that the most noteworthy feature of the campaign was the contribution of Edith Brand, the wife of the Liberal candidate, who gained international notoriety for singing on the hustings. Reports of her electioneering activities were published around the Anglophone world: from Brisbane to New York.[13] The strategy earned her the plaudits of the crowd and the enmity of the defeated Tory candidate who sneered that at least she would be unable to assist her husband by singing in the House of Commons.[14] Brand, a woman with hitherto no place on the historical record, has a story that is worth lingering over precisely because it provides a way to open up a discussion of the place of music and music-making in electoral politics.

Brand's role in the 1891 campaign was repeated at three subsequent elections and it is significant that her contribution was regarded as decisive. When she died in 1903 *The Times* concluded that she had 'sung her husband into Parliament four times'.[15] The *Sheffield Independent*'s editor was even more emphatic; giving short shrift to Tory objections he concluded: 'the Tories sing and lose; Mrs. Brand sings and wins'.[16] Born in Lancashire in 1863, Edith Brand was aged twenty-eight when her husband contested the by-election in the Cambridge Fens. Described variously as striking, charming, captivating, plucky, accomplished, fine-looking and elegant with lively black eyes and dressed in the 'latest fashion', she was undoubtedly a powerful presence by her husband's side and, commentators across the political spectrum agreed, she became extremely popular among the communities in the seat of Wisbech. Her platform skills were well honed. 'I used to take part a good deal in private theatricals before I was married', she told one interviewer, 'and that, you see, accustomed me to speaking and singing before an audience.'[17] The candidate, on the other hand, was reputed to be a poor speaker and, according to his critics, often cut his remarks short to give his wife more time to put her powerful voice to good use. Brand's performances – singing with 'appropriate actions' as well as speaking – became an integral part of her husband's campaign. She performed day or night; in the open air or indoors; on riverbanks or at factory gates; on stages; from balconies and on the hustings. Sometimes a zither accompanied her singing or, where one was available, a piano was used, but she could just as easily perform a cappella. The Brands often attended several meetings in a day, keeping up a punishing programme of canvassing for over a year prior to the election.

If Brand's charisma and undoubted vocal talents made her an accomplished politician, clearly eclipsing her husband as a campaigner, it is also important to ask: what did she sing? From numerous reports we can reconstruct her repertoire, at least in part. Some of it was simply drawn from the popular songs of the day. For example, we know that she sang *Thady O'Flinn*, a comic song about infidelity written by W. S. Gilbert and James Molloy in 1868:

> You said when we should mar-ried be,
> You'd make me quite a la-dy,
> But now I find you've changed your mind,
> It's ug-ly No-rah Gra-dy.[18]

We know that another of her songs was *Off to Philadelphia*, based on an 'old Irish melody' and lyrics. Although the song is also comedic the text was tinged with sadness:

> But the tears will sure-ly blind me
> For the friends I have left be-hind me,
> When I start for Phil-a-del-phia in the morn-in.[19]

Perhaps the best-known comedic song in Brand's repertoire, however, was *Hot Codlings*, a street ballad about a toffee apple seller on the streets of London. Written in 1819 by Joseph Grimaldi, the most celebrated pantomime clown of his generation, the song relied upon audience participation, filling in an obvious rhyme left hanging by the performer and the end of the chorus:

> A little old woman, her living she got
> By selling hot codlings, hot, hot, hot.
> Now this little old woman as I have been told
> Tho' her codlings were hot, she was monstrously cold.
> So to keep herself warm, she thought it no sin
> For to go and take a small drop of ...

Here, the auditors yell 'gin', to which the clown responds, reproachfully, 'Oh! For Shame!'[20]

Brand also folded a comedic element into one of her more explicitly political songs, *Brand for Cambridgeshire*, sung to the tune of *When Johnny Comes Marching Home*. At the height of the general election campaign that followed quickly on the heels of the by-election, the hapless Tory candidate wrote to Arthur Brand to complain that Edith had been singing a song with the refrain, 'We'll put the Tories to the rout,/ And shove old Duncan up the spout'. Edith replied on her own behalf to correct the record: in numerous places and with 'great success', she told him, she had sung a song with the couplet: 'We've kept Surr William Duncan out, and put the Tories up the spout'.[21] The exchange attracted attention as far away as Otago in New Zealand where the local newspaper interpreted it through the lens of gender. 'The granting of votes to the ladies is usually defended on the ground that their influence will tend to purify, soften, and refine politics and the ways of politicians,' commented the editor, but here was an example which showed that 'electioneering ladies can throw themselves with a truly masculine zest into the exchange of the little courtesies and amenities of the warfare of the platform'.[22] He had a point: Edith Brand was no mere adjunct. On the contrary, she was, as one commentator put it, a 'go-ahead woman' and was a prominent figure in the Liberal Party in her own right, subsequently sharing the platform with leading national figures and receiving a testimonial from her coadjutors.[23]

Political songs were designed to be blunt instruments. As a contemporary collector of a folio of election ballads that had been used in the Democratic presidential campaign of 1880 noted, 'Unlike "the handle of the door", political songs are not improved by much "polishing".'[24] Having said that, they comprised many sub-genres. Of course, these inevitably overlapped, shading into one another, but it is important here to attempt to disaggregate them.

Brand for Cambridgeshire was clearly intended to be funny. In this respect it took its place in a venerable tradition of political ballads that combined humour, ridicule and sarcasm. Writing in 1837 about the years from the reign of King John to Edward II, Thomas Wright noted that, 'Few historical documents are more interesting and important than the contemporary songs in which the political partisan satirised his opponents and stirred up the courage of his friends'.[25] The more recognisable form of the political ballad dates from at least the eighteenth century and continued *well beyond* the emergence of cheap mass-circulation newspapers. An excellent example of this genre is the proliferation of broadside ballads generated by the Prince Regent (later George IV). George's waistline was as large as his renowned debts and his profligacy made him an ideal target for satirical excoriation. As early as 1797, for example, he was lampooned in *O' GEORGE, Great Prince of Whales* to the tune of *God Save the King*.[26] In 1820 when the hapless George sought to divorce his popular consort, Caroline of Brunswick, her cause became the focus of a radical campaign and an ideal subject for the splenetic wit of numerous balladeers. Published by John Catnach, one of the infamous printers and ballad-mongers in London's labyrinthine Seven Dials district, *The Merry Life and Adventures of the Pig of Pelly-mill* is typical:

> Near Pelly-mill (as many know full well),
> A fat, rampageous, monstrous Pig doth dwell,
> So very large, so overgrown and big,
> That some do stile him, 'King of Pigs'.[27]

The form was mutable but it generally travelled across space, time and even cultural boundaries in a recognisable configuration. Thus, in 1870 in the remote north-west of Canada, a Scottish-born former Chartist, John Fraser (known as 'Cousin Sandy'), penned stinging musical commentaries on the ignominious retreat of the first lieutenant governor, William McDougall, who had been repulsed by the forces of Louis Riel's self-proclaimed Red River Republic. Published in the *New Nation*, a bilingual newspaper strongly supportive of Riel, *The Political Death and Dying Words of Recreant Willie, A New Song to an Old Tune* and *The Masterly Retreat of Gov. W. Macdougall* (sung to *The King of the Continental Islands*) would have presumably amused Canadian, Canadien and Métis listeners alike:

> Willie Macdougall went out one day
> Out to the North-West, far away,
> A sacrifice for place and pay
> Poor hungry Willie Macdougall.
> Poor simple Willie thought, you see,
> An Indian nabob he would be ...
> But the Indians of Hudson's Bay
> Made Willie shrink with sad dismay,
> And the half-castes made a cast-away
> Of Hungry Willie Macdougall.[28]

During a Sydney by-election in 1854 opponents of the Conservative candidate, Charles Kemp, including the former Chartist and radical candidate, Henry Parkes, published a volume of election songs entitled *Kempiana: a Hand Book for the Hustings*. Kemp was owner of the city's leading daily newspaper and had twice unsuccessfully sought election to the Legislative Assembly. Like the Prince Regent, he was portly and the songs focused on his weight as much as his political opinions:

> To church he walks in his gloves of white,
> And seems, to Childhood's eyes,
> A Cherub with trunk and limbs stuck on,
> Cut out of an elephant size ...
>
> Pity the wants of a Stout Man,
> Who wheels his weight to your door;

Beaten twice in his dearest aim,
He tries his luck once more.[29]

In Ontario at the turn of the century, to take another example, opponents of Prime Minister George William Ross and his cabinet published
a collection of satirical election ballads. The booklet takes advantage
of the double meaning of 'band' (with Ross depicted as the conductor)
to offer a relentless spoof, mixing narrative, illustration and song.[30]

Of course, oppositional, satirical and comedic ballads were only one
sub-genre: other ballads published in connection with elections were
even less edifying. *Manchester Election, 1868*, for example, referred
to Disraeli's government as 'the same old Tory crew, led by Benjamin
the Jew'.[31] They could also be aggressive, scurrilous, misogynist and
racist in terms that make a modern listener wince. In this respect there
was probably nothing to rival the execrable election jingles produced
during the 1864 election campaign in the United States. The *Little Mac
Campaign Songster* published in aid of campaign of General George
McClellan, Abraham Lincoln's Democrat opponent, for example, was
littered with vile racist diatribes from *All for the Nigger* and *Abe's
Brother of Negro Descent* to *Abraham the Nigger King* and *Darkies,
Abe Says There is Room*.[32] It is important to pause briefly here to reflect
on the significance of these songs as a form of political discourse in the
public sphere. The balladeers and editors of McClellan's campaign songster opined that not only did they represent, at least in part, McClellan's
platform (and their estimation of his values), but also that they would
resonate with potential voters. McClellan lost the election comfortably
but he did garner approximately 45 per cent of the vote. Surely these
songs then tell us something about McClellan voters (or some of them).
The songs are a reminder that, as with parades, the musical repertoire
of electioneering provides potentially fruitful evidence of political discourse operating at the nexus of the leader and the led, the candidate
and his constituency. This is a point to which we will return.

There was a difference between songs of scurrility and overt racism
and those devoted simply to negativity and complaint (although these
too were often tinctured with humour). Take the collection *Liberal
Election Songs*, published in the lead-up to the British general election of April 1880, for example. Not unsurprisingly given the Tories
had occupied the opposition benches for a number of years, the lyrics
of the songs typically contained a litany of complaint. The book comprised twenty-one songs, each with familiar tunes from *Tramp! Tramp!
Tramp!* and *March of the Men of Harlech* to *Hearts of Oak* and *Fine
Old English Gentleman*.[33] Nine songs were accompanied by sheet
music. To take one example, the lyrics of *The Tories are Up, and the*

Wages are Down!, sung to *The Laird o' Cockpen* (or the Psalm tunes, *Selina* and *Eden*), are predictably grim, at least in the opening verses:

> There is woe in the land, as the grief-stricken face
> Of the worker in cotton, woollen and lace,
> Is haggard and wan, both in village and town,
> For the Tories are up, and their wages are down!

In the fourth verse, however, the writer is more playful:

> When Gladstone the helm of affairs had in hand,
> There was peace and prosperity over the land,
> But we bartered our Billy for Dizzy the clown,
> So the Tories went up, and our wages came down.

By the last stanza the composer has opted for gawky comedic sanguinity:

> There is BRIGHT-ness in store, there is GLAD-ness to come,
> When the DIZ-mal arch humbug is powerless and dumb;
> John Bright we'll remember, Will Gladstone we'll crown,
> When our wages are up, and the Tories are down.[34]

Election songs could also be exhortative, inspirational, defiant and portentous. Those contained within *Liberal Election Songs* are a case in point. The collection had more than enough space for exhortations brimming with unadulterated anticipation and optimism, none more so than the prosaic *There's a Good Time Coming*, penned by the well-known progressive liberal Charles Mackay in 1846:

> There's a good time coming, boys, a good time coming;
> We hope to live to see the day when earth will glisten in the ray
> There's a good time coming ...
>
> There's a good time coming, boys, a good time coming;
> We'll aid it all we can, my boys – each mother's son must help, my boys,
> In the good time coming.
>
> Smallest help, if rightly given, makes the impulse stronger;
> It will be strong enough one day – wait a little longer boys.
> There's a good time coming &c.[35]

For Jacob Bright, brother of the famous advocate of Corn Law repeal and the peace movement and a progressive reformer and parliamentary candidate in his own right, a volume of Liberal songs published in the run-up to the 1868 general election 'was calculated to strengthen the growing enthusiasm of the people in favour of the honest and intelligent Government which we believe to be near at hand'. He undoubtedly had in mind songs such as *The Liberal March* (set to *Men of Harlech*):

Shoulder press to shoulder!
Quicker march and bolder;
Triumph we shall surely see
Before the day's much older
'Peace, Reform and Liberation',
Be our triune aspiration
Till we win them for the nation,
And our land be free![36]

Bright had been a candidate in Manchester in 1865; so too had Abel Heywood, a former Chartist who had served time in prison for his role in opposing the tax on newspapers during the 1830s. His candidature brought forth a clear echo of Chartist defiance in a campaign song:

Up, up, with our flag, unconquer'd and free
I've a vote, I've a vote, ABEL HEYWOOD, for thee![37]

Defiance and exhortation were different sides of the same coin. Some of the latter flowed from the pen of talented individuals, including some well-known veterans. For example, Gerald Massey, one of the last prominent leaders of the Chartists, composed *Election Song of the Labourers*, to be sung to the tune of *John Brown's Body*:

Ours are the voices that for ages were unheard!
Ours are the voices of a Future long deferred!
Cry all together; we shall speak the final word.
Let the cause go marching on.
Glory! glory! Hallelujah!
Glory! glory! Hallelujah!
Glory! glory! Hallelujah!

Ours are the votes that give us weapons we can wield,
Ours are the votes that make our proud opponents yield.
Vote all together, and our charge shall clear the field,
And the cause goes marching on.[38]

For the parliamentary election in Manchester in 1868 *When Johnny Comes Marching Home* was pressed into service for a blunt injunction – *How We Must Vote* – in favour of the Liberal slate of candidates, including another of Chartism's best-known erstwhile leaders, Ernest Jones:

If Ernest Jones should head the poll
Hurrah! Hurrah!
A cheer along the streets will roll,
Hurrah! Hurrah!
The rich and poor must then unite,
And vote for Bazely and for Bright,

And we'll all feel gay when the three of them are returned.
And we'll all feel gay when the three of them are returned.[39]

Like songs in general, election songs were often the product of the imagination of anonymous and less talented members of the ranks, including some individuals who always teetered on the brink of editorial rejection. For example, the editor of *The Hummer*, a journal of the Australian Shearers Union published in Wagga Wagga in 1891–92, advised P. E. R. Barellan to make another attempt at his song, preserving only the last eight lines:

> Then when we're all united,
> All Unions hand in hand.
> We'll crush Australia's greatest curse,
> Monopoly of the land.
> We'll fight it at the ballot,
> Denounce it far and wide.
> And future generations
> Will Speak of us with pride.[40]

As suggested, some elections songs were optimistically portentous and predictive. During the campaign for the Falkirk district in the Scottish Lowlands in 1874 a number of poetasters in the service of the Liberal candidate, John Ramsay, were 'unusually busy' composing election ballads set to familiar tunes such as *Johnny Comes Marching Home*, *The Standard on the Braes of Mar*, *An Ancient Burgh* and *My Love She's But a Lassie*. One song in particular, set to another of George F. Root's popular Civil War ballads, *Just before the Battle Mother*, and aimed at the Tory candidate, Alexander Baird, caught the attention of the bemused reporter:

> Just before the Polling, Sandy,
> We are thinking least of you.
> For we'll *Vote for Ramsay*, Sandy!
> Do you think we'd vote for you?
> Farewell Sandy! you need never
> Try the Falkirk towns again
> And we'll soon forget you, Sandy
> When you're numbered with the slain.[41]

It would be a mistake to underestimate the volume of election songs in circulation during the long nineteenth century. In his collection of Clydesdale ballads, published in 1882, A. Nimmo recalled that during 1831 election campaign copies of a song, *The Operatives' March*, were 'thrown in great numbers' from the carriage of the reform candidate.[42] Priced at 1*d.*, the cover of *Liberal Election Songs* boasted that 200,000 copies of the book had been sold to date. The final page contains examples of ringing endorsements of the volume given by the 'Principal Liberal Statesmen and Members of Parliament' as well as an advertisement for single printed sheets for general distribution. Already, it claimed, 10,000 had been ordered by the Manchester Liberal Association; 10,000 from Sheffield as well as from 'Liverpool, Midlothian, Norwich, Newcastle, Preston, Birmingham &c'. We need not be sceptical of these claims. In 1913 former Chartist Howard Evans, for example, claimed sales of more than 120,000 for his *Labourer's Songbook*.[43] By the turn of the century election song sheets were being mass-produced: it has been estimated that during the campaign of 1906 the Liberals printed 1,000,000.[44]

It is important to remember, however, that the meaning and cultural significance of election music, songs and ballads fundamentally changed at the point that they were played or sung. Music-making in this context served many functions. Firstly, it had a time-honoured role in reporting and commenting on political news. In colonial Australia and New Zealand the most famous journalist-cum-chronicler through the medium of the ballad was Charles Thatcher.[45] Born in Bristol, Thatcher migrated to Victoria in 1852 and soon established himself as a popular entertainer on the goldfields. His repertoire – performed and published – was often comedic and canvassed a huge variety of subjects. Indeed, this is a reminder that political songs were little more than a fragment of the mountains of humble slip ballads that were ubiquitous in popular culture. It is no surprise, therefore, that of the nearly 200 broadside ballads in an inventory of the stock of Thomas Willey, a well-known Chartist printer in Cheltenham, to take one example, only a relatively small number might be considered political.[46] As a consequence of his extended repertoire, historians have tended to overlook Thatcher's role as a social critic and political crusader. When he arrived at Invercargill in New Zealand, for example, he used a ditty entitled *The Town Board* (air: *Kitty Jones*) to outline the role he intended to play:

> I've come to Invercargill to redress your various wrongs,
> And tell you what I think of you in these my local songs,
> I've got my eye upon the Government coves, also the traps,
> And some folks high in office here will get some awkward raps.[47]

Moreover, Thatcher's political ballads often had a hard edge and, although giving vent to virulent racist values all too common on the colonial frontier, there was a recurrent note of sympathy for unjustly treated and 'poor' white settlers. His wickedly sarcastic assault on the administration of the Victorian goldfields is a case in point. Singing in the guise of 'Captain Bumble', a Dickensian character dispatched by the hapless governor of Victoria, Sir Charles Hotham ('And where is there a better?'), to root out disloyalty on the goldfields, Thatcher reported:

> Our first attack was on two drays
> Which we saw in the distance
> But the enemy surrendered
> After just a slight resistance
> We were disappointed in our search
> Of these two wretched traitors
> For instead of seizing powder
> It was loaded with potatoes.[48]

Thatcher was also famous for his election ballads. Reports of his tour of New Zealand in 1862 make clear that immediacy was an essential ingredient of this genre of which he was a past master. 'Mr. Thatcher', one report noted, was 'as usual, very successful, particularly his election songs, in which he was vociferously applauded.'[49] Another report added further context: 'Having been seen on the hustings during the time of the nomination yesterday, it was *expected* that he would give his audience the benefit of his observations. This he did in a most humorous style, and the expectations were in no way disappointed [emphasis added].'[50] The pointed reference to the audience's expectations of instant gratification again underscores the importance of music-making as a form of political discourse in action. The same urgency was true of the printed ballad. As John Ashton noted in 1888, 'street ballads were produced within a very few hours of the publication of any event of the slightest public interest'.[51] Dickens also knew this well. Musing on the songs generated by the great Preston lockout in 1854, he noted: 'the ballads vary constantly to meet the exigencies of passing events'.[52]

As polling day approached, balladeers such as Thatcher were only one part of the contribution of music-making to the episode writ large. In many cases music was as much a prerequisite as having a candidate and it was almost invariably part of the proceedings, even when there was ultimately no contest. It was a means to rally supporters to the cause, to summon them to the town hall meeting, hustings nomination and the polling station. And, almost invariably, music accompanied the candidate on their peregrinations. In 1802 Sir Frances Burdett was conveyed to an election rally on a barge along the Thames replete with band and flags and accompanied by a flotilla of craft.[53] Eighty years later the ritual of musical accompaniment was a ubiquitous feature of Canadian politics, albeit adapted to innovations in the mode of transportation. During the federal campaigns of the 1870s, for example, countless candidates were escorted to and from railway stations by bands of music.[54] These could be significant affairs. A case in point occurred in Montreal in September 1878 when a reform candidate arrived to be met by a crowd, which had been waiting around a 'huge bonfire', entertained by the Silver City Band. 'Subsequently a monster procession was formed,' ran the report, 'and, led by the band, marched through the streets, cheering and stopping to serenade the Dominion and the Local members of Parliament and the Mayor.'[55] Similarly, in February 1887 at St Thomas in Ontario, the Liberal prime ministerial candidate, Edward Blake, was met at the train station and accompanied into the town by a torchlight procession extending two miles in length and headed by two bands.[56]

Similar occurrences have been documented in New Zealand. When the Liberal premier, Richard Seddon (as we shall see, a vocalist in his own right), arrived in Lyttelton in November 1896, he was 'received by a band and escorted to the drill shed where he addressed an immense audience'.[57] In New South Wales the robustness of ritualised behaviour within an inter-colonial and transnational cultural formation was evident to one commentator, who pointed out that many of those who were participating were native-born Australians and had never actually witnessed a British election.[58] In Argyle, for example, the 'currency lads', as native-born white Australians were known, marched behind a band when escorting the well-known radical Daniel Deniehy to the hustings in 1857.[59] The capacity to make music could be seen as an index of popularity commensurate with voter endorsement. In 1832 a 'more glorious triumph for the great cause of reform has not been witnessed in Scotland', enthused the reporter for the *Scotsman*, when supporters of the Reform candidate, Admiral Adam, converged on the hustings in Dollar in the newly created seat of Kinross and Clackmannan, each headed by a band of music. 'A little time afterwards', the report continued, 'Mr Bruce, the Tory candidate, made his appearance, with a single band of music and a small knot of his conservative friends.'[60]

Again, attention to the repertoire used in electioneering is important. Election songbooks and slip ballads often included airs and, as we have seen, the range was very extensive, which allows us gain a better understanding of the rich soundscape of electoral politics. Nevertheless, an assessment of a plethora of reports reveals a compelling consistency in the use of one piece of music across time and space, irrespective of divergent patterns of electoral reform: *See, the Conquering Hero Comes*. Countless examples spanning the long nineteenth century are at hand. In Kaiapoi it was sung by supporters of the 'liberal hearted' candidate as they carried him on their shoulders draped in 'his' unspecified tri-colour; halfpenny tin whistles performed the same task in Port Lincoln in 1865 (followed by a skeleton of a horse 'plastered over with electioneering posters' and a dirty man in a 'rickety old cart'); in Pudsey, West Yorkshire, in 1900 it was sung 'to organ accompaniment' to welcome the successful Liberal candidate to a celebratory dinner.[61]

Not surprisingly, the prosaic title meant that *See, the Conquering Hero Comes* was readily pressed into service by political enthusiasts of all stripes: it foretold of victory, served as a paean of triumph or, by its absence, a marker of defeat. As the Liberal candidate, G. A. Lloyd, told an 1885 election meeting in Newcastle on the north coast of New South Wales: 'He remembered the time when he addressed them on the hustings, and was received with great cordiality, and carried through the town with a band playing "See, the conquering hero comes." (Applause.) Then, again, he remembered the time when he had to go down the back stairs having been beaten by a better man than himself.'[62] In fact, the central couplet made it universally adaptable outside politics; it said it all, whether the 'hero' wielded a sword or a cricket bat:

> See, the conqu'ring hero comes!
> Sound the trumpets, beat the drums.[63]

Nevertheless, the political usage of *See, the Conquering Hero Comes* is worth further consideration. The music comes from Handel's 1745 oratorio, *Judas Maccabaeus*. The circumstances and intent of its composition were unambiguous: it was written to celebrate the Duke of Cumberland's victory over the Jacobites at Culloden. On the other hand, there was much in Thomas Morrell's libretto, which told the story of the persecution of the Israelites in 160 BC, for reformers and radicals to justify wrenching it from its original context, including a phrase in the recitative that resonated throughout the nineteenth century (and beyond):

> Then, faintly, with expiring breath,
> 'Resolve, my sons, on liberty, or death!'
> We come! Oh see, thy sons prepare
> The rough habiliments of war;
> With hearts intrepid, and revengeful hands,
> To execute, O sire, thy dread commands.[64]

In the aftermath of Peterloo in 1819, the Lord Chancellor agreed. The existence of crowds singing the 'old song', *Give us Death, or Liberty*, he argued, was ample justification for the implementation of repressive suite of legislation known as the Six Acts to be implemented.[65]

At the same time as it provided immediacy, music and song could be mnemonic, offering direct links to the past and, in the case of Edith Brand, an extremely potent ideological touchstone on the hustings. As we have noted, Wisbech swung wildly after 1885 and a number of commentators agreed that the issue that had convulsed it, like the nation at large, was Home Rule for Ireland. For some commentators the by-election was a referendum on the issue. Reflecting on the result, the *Daily Mail*, for example, argued that the division had 'reversed the hasty judgment of five years ago, and declared its faith in justice for Ireland'.[66] In fact, this context was directly related to Brand's choice of repertoire. In some cases we need to excavate more than one layer below the surface of her selection. Her composition *Brand for Cambridgeshire*, as we have noted, was sung to the tune of *When Johnny Comes Marching Home*. This song had first been published in 1863 and featured in songbooks published by both sides in the American Civil War.[67] This was undoubtedly a popular air: at least one report of Brand's performance noted her audience stamping their feet and humming the tune long after she had left the hall (much to the chagrin of the next speaker). But it is vital to keep probing: the song was itself based on the melody of an Irish anti-war song, *Johnny I Hardly Knew Ye*, published in the early 1820s.

By more than simply scratching the surface we can identify the Irish association embedded in *Brand for Cambridgeshire*, but two of the other songs she sang require no excavation. Musing on her 'triumph', Edith admitted, 'They liked the old songs'. Two in particular were undoubtedly chosen with great care for unambiguous effect. The first was Thomas Moore's *Let Erin Remember the Days of Old* (set to *The Red Fox*). Moore's own account of the composition of this lyric is revealing. In the introductory memoir to his collection of Irish songs, the renowned Irish poet recalled that sitting alongside him as he contemplated the lines was Robert Emmet, the leader of the United Irishmen who would later be executed for high treason for his part in the Irish uprising of 1803. '[S]tarting up as from a reverie when I had finished playing', Moore recalled, 'Emmet exclaimed "Oh that I were at the head of twenty thousand men, marching to that air!"'[68]

The centrepiece of Brand's repertoire was a far more famous Irish revolutionary song of the 1790s: *The Wearing of the Green*. It 'was a great favourite', she told a reporter, 'they were never tired of listening to it'.[69] There were several early iterations of the lyrics, but it is likely that Brand was singing the most recent version that had featured in Dion Boucicault's highly successful play, *Arragh na Pogue, or the Wicklow Wedding*, which premiered in Dublin in 1864 and London the following year.[70] The lyrics, sung furtively in the play, were unambiguous:

[155]

O Kitty dear, did you hear the news that's gone round?
The shamrock is by law forbid to grow on Irish ground;
No man Saint Patrick's Day shall keep, their colours dare not be seen
For there's a bloody law against the wearing of the Green.

I met with Napper Tandy, he took me by the hand
He asked me how old Ireland was, and how does it stand,
It's the most distressed country that ever were yet seen,
For they're hanging men & women for the wearing of the Green.[71]

Significantly, Arthur Brand hardly mentioned Ireland or Home Rule in his speeches from the platform. As a hostile commentator in the *Scotsman* quipped, 'almost the only thing Irish about the contest was the melodies [Edith Brand] sang to admiring bucolic audiences'. He was being disingenuous, as he admitted: what Arthur Brand 'wanted in speech his wife made up in song'.[72] This is the point: Arthur Brand did not need to say anything. To sing *The Wearing of the Green* (or *Let Erin Remember the Days of Old* or to invoke *Johnny I Hardly Know Ye*, for that matter) from the platform during an English by-election in 1891 was a declaration of principle that, in context, is difficult to misinterpret. Of course, *The Wearing of the Green* was associated with the Irish uprising of the 1790s and, as we shall see in a subsequent chapter, the revolutionary overtones of the song echoed unambiguously down the years in connection with riot, rebellion and revolution. But the song lyric itself was an imploration against injustice (as opposed to an exhortation in favour of a particular solution) and, as Brand showed, it could be effective as a way to tap into a vein of sympathy for Ireland in support of Gladstonian Home Rule. The song thus helped to shape and, more importantly, was in turn shaped by the context in which it was performed. Brand clearly thought that singing *The Wearing of the Green* was good politics – she regarded it a crowd favourite. The fact that she was vindicated focuses our attention on the way that music could play a pivotal role in turning around a sizable conservative majority and delivering victory to her husband.[73] Moreover, it shows us again that music can tell us something crucial not only about those who made it but also those it was made for.[74]

The same injunction is equally pertinent when considering the numerous contrafacta that the song spawned. At least one other British Liberal candidate felt that the song provided a sentiment worth invoking in a plea to electors. *Songs for the Electors: The Creed of the Labourers* was a simple exhortation against the alienation of common lands:

To win that right again
We'll strive with might and main,

And vote for none but Liberals,
To win that right again.[75]

In the year of Brand's triumph William Kidston was a middle-aged migrant living in Queensland. A moderate socialist, democrat and trade unionist (and future premier of Queensland), he composed one of the better-known election ballads of his day, *The Ballot's the Thing*, which was published in one of Australia's foremost radical journals, the *Worker*. Written during a bitter shearers' strike, Kidston chose to set the words to *The Wearing of the Green*. The original song's complaint of injustice provided an ideal motif for a struggle against large landholders:

We used to have the notion that in Queensland men were free,
That before the law, the Squatter was the same as you or me;
But the sturdy Bushman now, they say, down to his knees we'll bring.
With this old law that once was made when George the First was King.

But Kidston's version did not advocate violence; on the contrary, the ballad celebrated the possibility of an electoral victory:

Then keep your heads, I say, my boys; your comrades in the town
Will help you yet to win a vote, and put your tyrants down.
Throw your old guns aside, my boys; the ballot is the thing
They did not have to reckon with when George the First was King.[76]

Later renowned for his use of music on the platform, Kidston's success as a politician (as well as the popularity of his song) rebounds in the face of the historian. Here is evidence into the *mentalité* of many of those who read the pages of the *Worker*, stood before him on the hustings and who voted for him on election day. His song was popular for a reason.

Brand and Kidston were not only gifted campaigners, they were also astute judges of context – in other words, they were good politicians. It was easy, however, to misjudge the relationship between performer, music and audience. The potency of *The Wearing of the Green* was evident, for example, when Richard Seddon, the long-serving Liberal prime minister of New Zealand, was travelling to England to participate in the official celebrations of Queen Victoria's Diamond Jubilee in 1897. Seddon was an Anglo-Irish radical at heart; as he told Michael Davitt (an Irish revolutionary and Nationalist MP) in the same year: 'his first reforming sympathies were awakened by a Lancashire Chartist who hailed from the country of Feargus O'Connor'.[77] At a shipboard dinner Seddon contributed a rousing rendition of *The Wearing of the Green* to the convivial proceedings, an act that excited considerable controversy when it was reported in the press. For some commentators it was a 'reprehensible display of Fenianism' that gave 'great umbrage to some English passengers' as well as the revelation that Queen Victoria apparently held a 'special aversion' to the song. The incident found its way into newspapers in Britain, the United States, Australia and in Seddon's adopted home of New Zealand.[78] Seddon was flummoxed, insisting that it was a 'sing-song'; his defenders claimed that although he possessed 'a broad-minded sympathy with the "most distressful country" in her agrarian and political troubles', the Premier was 'as English as they make them'. Davitt's account of their meeting was not yet published.

By all accounts Seddon had a voice like a 'fog-horn' but he 'had only succeeded in mastering two songs' to use it with: the Irish anthem and an innocuous song, *Wait till the Clouds Roll By*. Consequently, estimated one commentator with tongue firmly planted in cheek, Seddon had sung *The Wearing of the Green* 'three thousand two hundred and eighty-one times'.[79] Admittedly (following the success of the melodrama *Arrah na Pogue*), by this time *The Wearing of the Green* could be heard on an almost nightly basis in countless popular repertory programmes across the Anglophone world: from Miss M. Knight's rendition at the Edinburgh Theatre in Wellington and Mr John Collins's in the Prince of Wales Opera House in Sydney (followed by an Irish jig) to Master Herbert's version at the Prince of Wales in Auckland ('as sung with great success in Melbourne') and Maggie Moore's performance (rendered with 'Power, Force, Pathos, and Dramatic Fervor') at the Crystal Theatre in Broken Hill. Nevertheless, the political message remained clear. The song is introduced in Boucicault's narrative as a request that causes a frisson of alarm:

> Shaun: Whist, boys, are ye mad; is it sing that song and the soldiers widin gunshot? Sure there's sudden death in every note of it.
> Oiny: Niver fear; we'll put a watch outside and sing it quiet.
> Shaun: It is the 'Twistin' of the rope' ye are axin' for.[80]

Dick Seddon's faux pas in choosing to sing a song 'with sudden death in every note of it' in the wrong context is testimony to the potential power of music in the public sphere, but he suffered no more than embarrassment. It did not prevent him from being appointed to the Privy Council.[81]

Nevertheless, the consequences of dissonance between music and political context could have a catastrophic impact on a candidate's chances of victory. Just as in Wisbech, the 1882 Canadian election occurred against a backdrop of the developing debate over Home Rule in Ireland, which was further complicated in Ontario by a rancorous dispute within the ranks of the local Irish community when a prominent politician among their number accepted a cabinet post in the government of the incumbent nationalist prime minister.[82] Despite these complications, Edward Blake, the leader of the opposition Reform Party, was optimistic about carrying the election based in part on support from Irish Catholics in Ontario and French Canadians in Quebec. A grand faux pas, at least from his perspective, however, turned on an ill-chosen ditty. At a large public rally in Toronto proceedings were opened with E. W. Schuch, a well-known baritone, singing *Ontario, Ontario* (to the tune of a well-known Civil War song, *Maryland, My Maryland*). The lyrics had been composed specifically for the campaign and it was obviously familiar to the audience, which enthusiastically joined in the refrain. The lyrics referred to French Canadian voters in terms that were inflammatory, to say the least:

> The traitor's hand is at thy throat,
> Ontario, Ontario.
> Then kill the tyrant with your vote,
> Ontario, Ontario.[83]

The song was 'sprung as a surprise' on Blake, who was appalled. According to one account, the candidate turned to the person sitting alongside him on the platform and whispered, 'Who is responsible for this damned rubbish?' As the song finished he lamented, 'Well, these smart gentlemen have cost us the province of Quebec'. Apparently, however, the local reformers were proud of their song, subsequently sending Schuch on a singing tour of Ontario to rouse the faithful. When the singer again crossed paths with Blake, the latter refused to give a speech while Schuch remained in the room.[84]

Although they did not have the obviously devastating impact of *Ontario, Ontario*, there were other well-known reformist songs that helped to establish the tone of the 1882 election, despite Blake's strategy and his speeches. One such was *Rouse Thee, Canada!* The song courted Irish voters but pointedly failed to include French Canadians in its exhortation:

> Erin's sons hold Freedom's standard;
> Scotia's children form the van;
> All the valiant sons of England
> Echo proudly, 'Blake's the man'.[85]

Even a song that essentially offered a familiar anti-Tory critique of corruption, privilege and inequality, which might have been heard elsewhere in the Anglophone world in 1798 as easily as in 1882, was tinctured by a whiff of anti-Gallicanism. Addressing the incumbent Prime Minister John A. MacDonald, its lyrics ran:

The Blues of Quebec you dare not check,
They'd choke you dead, you poor old sinner,
You'd lick their feet and think it's sweet
Like the master's dog would after dinner.[86]

It is clear that these songs offered a truncated and strident message, which provides an insight into the views of the led rather than their leaders. As we have noted previously, another Blake campaign song utilised the *Marseillaise* as its tune but it remains unclear if this made things better or worse:[87]

To arms! Swift vengeance take!
Your votes can powers unmake
March on! march on! all hearts resolved
For Canada and Blake!

Needless to say, Blake did not carry Quebec, or the election more generally.

Taken together it is clear that the words from the mouths of Brand and Schuch are examples of a form of ideological exchange that shaped and was shaped by context. As such it was a medium that was dialogic. Brand used song to offer her listeners a more pointed message than her husband's speeches. She spoke *from* the platform. But, as we have seen, the communication was not always one way. In an important respect *Ontario, Ontario* was the means by which Blake's supporters gave him a blunt message and they kept singing it whether he approved or not. They spoke *to* the platform. In this way music provided the medium for equitable exchange between platform and crowd. Spontaneous or contrived, unifying or divisive, for fun or to fight it was an assertion of power either way. Moreover, understanding the context for music-making is key to gauging the appropriateness (and importance) of repertoire – whether emanating from the platform, the floor or on the march – which, in turn, provides a significant guide to the broader circumstances in which it happened. In other words, if we listen to the music and watch it being made we have an opportunity, one of many, to witness politics and culture happen. The elections in Ontario and Wisbech in 1882 and 1891, respectively, are exceptional only in that they bring the role of communicative musicality in formal politics into sharp relief. They are a reminder that the sound of music issuing from the hustings and echoing from building walls in countless constituencies – large and small – during the long nineteenth century was merely the continuation of a time-honoured association of music-making with electoral politics. But they do not tell the whole story.

Much of the role of music and music-making occurred in the grey area where formal politics – electoral and more besides – shaded off into the demotic and it often did so in an atmosphere tainted by confrontation, intimidation and violence. In 1894, for example, the Wisbech Tories sought to silence Brand, first by claiming that her musical performances were a form of 'treating' in breach of the 1883 Corrupt Practices Act, which outlawed the provision of 'any meat, drink or *entertainment*' to induce electors to cast their vote in a particular way. Second, they resorted to practices as nefarious as treating itself: Brand was pelted with eggs and stones when she attempted to sing and, significantly, a report in *The Times* noted, the Tories engaged a 'band of minstrels who paraded the streets singing a parody on "Off to Philadelphia" one of the songs which Mrs. Brand has been accustomed to sing at her husband's meetings'.[88] This behaviour is better considered under the heading of conflict, to which we now turn.

Notes

1 *Morning Chronicle* (1 June 1850).
2 Michael T. Bass, *Street Music in the Metropolis: Correspondence and Observations on the Existing Law, and Proposed Amendment* (London: John Murray, 1864), p. 15.
3 *Ibid.*, p. 19.
4 Henry Vizetelly, *Glances Back Through Seventy Years: Autobiographical and Other Reminiscences*, vol. 1 (London: Kegan Paul & Co., 1893), p. 103.
5 Charles Manby Smith, *The Little World of London* (London Arthur Hall, 1857), pp. 8–9.
6 *Reynolds' News* (27 April 1851).
7 This view was first put forward by Moisei Ostrogoriski in 1902. For classic studies of Britain see, inter alia, David Hamer, *The Politics of Electoral Pressure: A Study in the History of Victorian Reform Agitations* (Hassocks: Harvester Press, 1977); H. J. Hanham, *Elections and Party Management: Politics in the time of Disraeli and Gladstone* (London: Longmans, 1959); Norman Gash, *Politics in the Age of Peel: A Study in the Technique of Parliamentary Representation* (London: Longmans, 1953); Brian Harrison, *The Transformation of British Politics 1860–1995* (Oxford: Oxford University Press, 1996).
8 *Queenslander* (29 April 1871).
9 *Sheffield Independent* (30 July 1891).
10 *Daily News* (17 July 1891).
11 *Ibid.*
12 *Ibid.*
13 *Brisbane Courier* (15 September 1891); *New York Times* (25 July 1891).
14 *Standard* (23 July 1891); *Manchester Guardian* (18 July 1891), *Manchester Guardian* (23 July 1891); *Scotsman* (28 July 1891); *Ipswich Journal* (18 July 1891); *Argus* (15 September 1891); *Argus* (26 September 1891).
15 *The Times* (10 April 1903).
16 *Sheffield Independent* (30 July 1891).
17 *Pall Mall Gazette* (27 July 1891).
18 University of Indiana, Harmony Sheet Music Collection, W. S. Gilbert (lyrics) and J. L. Molloy (music), 'Thady O'Flinn', *Popular Vocal Gems*, n.d., available at http://purl.dlib.indiana.edu/iudl/lilly/starr/LL-SSM-2-137-0065 (accessed 12 September 2016).
19 University of Indiana, Harmony Sheet Music Collection, Stephen Temple (words revised and edited) and Battison Haynes (adapted from an old Irish melody), 'Off to Philadelphia', *Latest Gems of English Song*, New York, c.1870–1890, available

at http://purl.dlib.indiana.edu/iudl/lilly/starr/LL-SSM-2-137-0054 (accessed 12 September 2016). The Wisbech Tories published a contrafactum parody of the song ridiculing Brand's singing. See *Adelaide Advertiser* (15 September 1891).

20   Oxford University, Bodleian Library, Broadside Ballads Online (hereafter Bodleian Ballads), Harding B 11(1276), Charles Dibdin, 'Hot Codlings' (London: Hodges, n.d.), http://ballads.bodleian.ox.ac.uk/view/sheet/15135 (accessed 14 September 2016); John Ashton, *Modern Street Ballads* (London: Chatto & Windus, 1888); Jane Moody, 'Grimaldi, Joseph (1178–1837)', *Oxford Dictionary of National Biography*, Oxford University Press, 2004; online edn, May 2014, available at www.oxforddnb.com/view/article/11630 (accessed 12 September 2016).

21   *Pall Mall Gazette* (29 December 1892); *Hampshire Observer* (24 February 1892); *Otago Witness* (5 May 1892).

22   *Otago Witness* (5 May 1892).

23   See *The Times* (24 July 1891); *The Times* (22 September 1891); *The Times* (27 March 1894); *New York Times* (25 July 1891); *Hampshire Advertiser* (31 March 1894); *Pall Mall Gazette* (29 December 1892).

24   Huntington Library, San Marino, California (hereafter Huntington), *The Hancock & English Democratic Campaign Song Book* (Cincinnati: W. R. Swan, 1880).

25   Thomas Wright, *The Political Songs of England From the Reign of King John to that of Edward II* (London: Camden Society, 1837), p. vii. See also *Leader* (23 May 1857).

26   Cambridge University Library, Madden Ballad Collection (hereafter Madden), vol. 15, fol. 15.

27   Bodleian Ballads, 'The Merry Life and Adventures of the Pig of Pelly-mill', available at http://ballads.bodleian.ox.ac.uk/view/edition/17671 (accessed 12 September). For Catnach see Charles Hindley, *The Life and Times of J. Catnach, Late of Seven Dials, Ballad Monger* (London: Hindley, 1878); Manby Smith, *London*, pp. 251–66.

28   *New Nation* (7 January 1870); *New Nation* (8 April 1870). See also *Northern Journal* [Montreal] (15 June 1872) (obituary and tribute 'sits with Burns'); *Northern Journal* (6 July 1872). The song is an adaption of the scurrilous *King of the Cannibal Islands*, written sometime after 1813 and published in London by James Catnach. See Bodleian Ballads, Harding B36(10), available at http://ballads.bodleian.ox.ac.uk/view/sheet/23163 (accessed 12 September).

29   State Library of New South Wales, Mitchell Library, *Kempiana: A Handbook for the Hustings* (Sydney: n.p., 1854).

30   University of Toronto, Thomas Fisher Rare Book Library (hereafter Fisher), Ontario Election Pamphlets, HC-D, Ballad Collection, *Build Up Ontario: Campaign Songs of the Ross Minstrels, Provincial Elections, 1902*. Also available at University of Toronto, Fisher Library Digital Collections, Canadian Pamphlets and Broadsides Collection, available at http://link.library.utoronto.ca/broadsides/digobject.cfm?Idno=CAP00677 (accessed 14 September 2016).

31   Greater Manchester County Record Office (hereafter MCRO), Ballad Collection, 1868/5/s.

32   Huntington, Civil War Songbooks Collection, *The Little Mac Campaign Songster* (New York: T. R. Dawley, Publisher for the Million, 1864).

33   Bishopsgate Institute, George Howell Collection, Howell Collection Pamphlet Box 39, 324.24106, *Liberal Election Song* (Bacup: Isaac Leach, n.d. [1880]).

34   *Ibid.*, no. 2.

35   *Ibid.*, no. 20.

36   *Ibid.*, no. 3.

37   MCRO, Manchester Broadside Collection, 1856/3/b, 'The Manchester Elector's Song'.

38   Gerald Massey, 'Labourer's Election Song', *My Lyrical Life* (London: Kegan Paul, 1889), pp. 422–3. See also Bishopsgate Institute, Howell Collection 39 (33), Gerald Massey, *Election Lyrics* (London J. Burns, n.d.).

39   MCRO, Manchester Broadside Collection, 1868/5R, 'How We Must Vote'.

40   *Hummer* (26 March 1892).

41   *Glasgow Herald* (February 1874). See Paul Pickering, 'Mercenary Scribblers and

Polluted Quills: The Chartist Press in Australia and New Zealand', in Joan Allen and Owen R. Ashton (eds), *Papers for the People: A Study of the Chartist Press* (London: Merlin Press, 2005), pp. 190–215. Songbooks could be attuned to the exigencies of a particular campaign. The *Non-Electors Hymn* (sung to *Auld Lang Syne*) in the *Liberal Song Book* in 1888, for example, provided space for local activists to insert the names of places and opposing candidates. See *Liberal Election Songs*, no. 5.

42   A. Nimmo, *Songs and Ballads of Clydesdale* (Edinburgh: John Menzies and Co., 1882), p. 154.

43   Howard Evans, *Radical Fights of Forty Years* (Manchester: Daily News & Leader, 1913), p. 42. See Kate Bowan and Paul Pickering, 'Singing for Socialism', in Laurajane Smith, Paul Shackel and Gary Campbell (eds), *Heritage, Labour and the Working Classes* (New York: Routledge, 2011), pp. 192–215.

44   Frank Trentmann, *Free Trade Nation* (Oxford: Oxford University Press, 2009), p. 101.

45   For Thatcher see Hugh Anderson, 'Thatcher, Charles Robert (1831–1878)', *Australian Dictionary of Biography*, National Centre of Biography, Australian National University, available at http://adb.anu.edu.au/biography/thatcher-charles-robert-4705/text7799 (accessed 12 September 2016). As one editor noted in 1865, writing about Thatcher had 'occupied so many able pens'. See State Library of Victoria, MS 5004, Ms. Charles Robert Thatcher Papers, *c.*1850 – *c.*1870 (hereafter Thatcher Papers), Newspaper cuttings.

46   Madden, vol. 23, fols. 403–553.

47   State Library of New South Wales, *Thatcher's Invercargill Minstrel, Containing Several Popular Local Songs As Written and Sung by Him at the Theatre Royal* (Invercargill: Invercargill Times, n.d.), pp. 12–14.

48   Thatcher Papers, MS Box 141/1(a), 'Private Dispatch of Captain Bumble'. We also know that while in New Zealand Thatcher performed a free benefit concert for Lancashire operatives caught up in the Cotton Famine. See Thatcher Papers, Box 141/1(d), Newspaper cuttings.

49   *Daily Southern Cross* (27 November 1862).

50   *Daily Southern Cross* (6 November 1862).

51   Ashton, *Modern Street Ballads*, p.v.

52   [Charles Dickens], *Household Words: A Weekly Journal*, vol. 8 (1854), p. 348. See also Robert Darnton, *Poetry and the Police* (Cambridge, MA: Harvard University Press, 2010), p. 79.

53   *Morning Chronicle* (14 September 1802).

54   See, inter alia, *Globe* (17 January 1874); *Globe* (17 September 1878).

55   *Globe* (20 September 1878).

56   *Globe* (18 February 1887).

57   *Poverty Bay Herald* (30 November 1896).

58   *Sydney Morning Herald* (27 June 1843); *Australian* (26 June 1843).

59   *Sydney Morning Herald* (19 February 1857).

60   *Scotsman* (22 December 1832).

61   *Lyttleton Times* (1 April 1863); *South Australian Advertiser* (24 April 1865); *Leeds Mercury* (27 November 1900).

62   *Sydney Morning Herald* (7 December 1885).

63   [Thomas Morell], *Judas Macchabaeus, an Oratorio. Set to Music by Mr. Handel* (Durham: P. Barwick, 1770), p. 58.

64   [Morell], *Judas Macchabaeus*, pp. 15, 21. See Bowan and Pickering, 'Singing for Socialism'.

65   *Hansard* [House of Lords], col. 1587 (27 December 1819).

66   *Daily Mail* (25 July 1891).

67   *Argus* (26 September 1891).

68   *Moore's Poetical Works* (London: Longman, Brown, Green and Longmans, 1853), pp. xxx, 178.

69   *Sydney Morning Herald* (19 September 1891). See also *Pall Mall Gazette* (27 July 1891).

70   See California State University Folklore Traditional Ballad Index, available at www.
      fresnostate.edu/folklore/ballads/PGa084.html (accessed 12 September 2016); 'The
      Wearing of the Green', *Era* (12 May 1900); Andrew Carpenter, *Verse in English from
      Eighteenth-Century Ireland* (Cork: Cork University Press, 1998).

71   Bodleian Ballads, 2806 c.16 (209), 'Wearing of the Green' (Manchester: T. Pearson,
      n.d.), available at http://ballads.bodleian.ox.ac.uk/view/sheet/28049 (accessed 12
      September 2016). The Bodleian collection contains several other editions; the earli-
      est is *c.*1850. In some American versions a third pro-US verse was added. Some ver-
      sions use the correct name, Napper Tandy, an Irish revolutionary; earlier versions
      use Napoleon in this role.

72   *Scotsman* (28 July 1891); *Argus* (26 September 1891).

73   Brand (3979 votes), Duncan (3719 votes). At the previous election in 1884 the
      Conservative candidate had secured a majority of 1087.

74   If, as one commentator put it, the song 'stirs the heart like the sound of a trumpet',
      we need to ask who was being so moved? *Era* (26 March 1886).

75   Bodleian Ballads, fol. 1259, 'Songs for the Electors: The Creed of the Labourers'
      (London: J.C. Durant, London, n.d.), available at http://ballads.bodleian.ox.ac.uk/
      view/edition/19263 (accessed 13 September 2016).

76   *Worker* (4 April 1891).

77   Michael Davitt, *Life and Progress in Australasia* (London: Methuen, 1898), p. 206.
      For O'Connor see Paul A Pickering, *Feargus O'Connor: A Political Life* (London:
      Merlin, 2008).

78   *Observer* (26 June 1897); *Mercury* (17 June 1897); *Sydney Morning Herald* (17 June
      1897); *North Eastern Daily Gazette* (9 June 1897); *Colonist* (17 June 1897); *Evening
      Post* (16 June 1897).

79   *Observer* (26 June 1897).

80   Dion Boucicault, *Arragh na Pogue, or the Wicklow Wedding*, scene 4 (Dublin: n.p.
      1864).

81   Ironically, if Seddon had waited until 1900 he could have sung a 'patriotic' version
      of the song that was released to coincide with the Queen's visit to Ireland in April.
      See *Birmingham Daily Post* (19 March 1900); *Glasgow Herald* (3 April 1900). This
      version did not outlive the Queen.

82   *Globe* (14 June 1882); *Globe* (15 June 1882); *Globe* (18 June 1882).

83   Fisher, Ballad Collection, Campaign Song, no. 2, 'Ontario, Ontario'.

84   *Globe* (14 June 1882); Hector Charlesworth, *Candid Chronicles: Leaves from the
      Note Book of a Canadian Journalist* (Toronto: Macmillan, 1925), pp. 196–7.

85   *Globe* (15 June 1882). Notably, the song was explicitly based on a line – 'Rouse thee,
      England, great and free' – a song critical of the British Government's treatment of
      Ireland, which had been published in the reformist *People's Journal*, vol. 5 (1848),
      p. 36. We are grateful to Liz Fitch for tracking this down for us.

86   *Globe* (15 June 1882). See also Fisher, Ballad Collection, Campaign Songs nos. 3 and
      4.

87   *Ibid.*, Campaign Song no. 4.

88   *The Times* (20 March 1894); *The Times* (2 April 1894); *The Times* (4 April 1894); *The
      Times* (5 April 1894). Brand was returned with a greatly reduced margin.

CHAPTER FOUR

'Sing a Song of Sixpence'

Sing a song of sixpence,
A pocket full of rye.
Four- and Twenty blackbirds,
Baked in a pie.
When the pie was opened,
The birds began to sing;
Wasn't that a dainty dish,
To set before the King.

Traditional[1]

[H]is experience had taught him that the employment of bands of music at elections was a frightful source of bitterness and dissention.

Edward Ball MP (1854)[2]

Colin Fox, one of Mr Sheridan's five party colleagues in parliament, sang Robert Burns' egalitarian 'A Man's a Man for A' That' as his protest before being moved to the end of the queue by Presiding Officer Sir David Steel. He sang for nearly a minute while Sir David told him: 'I'm sorry, there's no singing in parliament. Order.'

BBC News (2007)[3]

'They are about to abolish our old-fashioned Nomination Days – and not before due time,' lamented Thomas Cooper in his memoirs published in 1873. 'But I must confess I enjoyed the old days.' Cooper went on to admit that he had particularly fond memories of a contest in Nottingham in 1841, which was characterised by violence.[4] The occasion was an election involving a prominent middle-class 'moral radical', Joseph Sturge, and a less well-known Tory, John Walter. Sturge's participation was sufficient to attract national interest as well the attention of the pre-eminent leader of the Chartists, Feargus O'Connor.[5] The irascible Cooper was, at this time, one of O'Connor's most loyal and effective lieutenants and he commanded a highly disciplined group of working men based in Leicester who referred to themselves as the

Shakespearean Chartists. Cooper's Shakespeareans were renowned for their autodidactic endeavours, including their singing, and for their ferocity. Unsurprisingly, nomination day in Nottingham was memorable for a brutal clash between the notorious 'Tory Lambs' ('butchers in blue linen coats') and the Chartists, led by Cooper and O'Connor. 'It was no trifle to receive a blow from O'Connor's fists', Cooper remembered, and he 'floored' the Lambs 'like nine-pins', contributing to a bloody victory. But the interregnum between breaking bones at the nomination and casting votes the following day was a time for vigilance animated by music. 'It was agreed', Cooper recalled, 'that it would be well to watch during the night whether any of the Tory agents were slily [sic] creeping about to try to bribe voters':

> O'Connor said he would not sleep. 'We will parade the town, Cooper,' said he; 'and you shall lead the singing...'. And parade the town we did we did, singing 'The lion of Freedom [O'Connor] is come from his den' ... and

> 'We won't go home till morning – till Walter runs away!
> We won't go home till morning – till Sturge has won the day!'[6]

A contemporary report in the *Northern Star* provided more detail, further emphasising music's central role in the performance of politics. At eight, the reporter noted, a 'procession of about ten deep was formed', which 'traversed the whole town'; 'Cooper with his stunning tenor led the musicians'. Satisfied with their peregrinations over two and half hours the Chartist leaders retired to what they called the 'Guard House'. Soon, however, the 'music of the Blue band struck their ears'. 'Instantly', the report continued, 'it was proposed to muster the Chartist band', but unfortunately the musicians had dispersed. Faced with this dilemma O'Connor called for 'fifers and drummers' or French horns, and he contributed to the resolution of the problem himself by recruiting an Irish piper accompanied by a 'fine mountaineer' with a shillelagh, who danced the 'crack-skull exercise, to the tune of the fox-hunter's jig'. 'Turn out the guard!' was the command and, once assembled, they fell in behind the piper and set off in pursuit of the Blue band: 'By twelve o'clock the procession was immense, the Blue band silenced, and even the pipes smothered in the chorus of Spread, spread the Charter! spread the Charter through the land.' Upon arriving at the Conservative Assembly Rooms, the 'full melody of a Chartist song burst from every throat, which appeared as if by magic to extinguish the shining light of faction inside'. At 2.30 a.m. Sturge had been woken up and, the *Star*'s correspondent noted, the 'procession again formed, and, as if by mutual consent, struck up – We won't go home till morning, Till Walter runs away'. The musical contribution to the episode was concluded when Chartist singers arrived from the nearby village of Sutton and 'regaled' the local Chartists with 'some excellent glees'.[7] Clearly, music was a potent – even magical – weapon and winning the musical contest, together with and as part of the physical combat, was an analogue for the struggle itself. Indeed, given the inequities of the electoral system against which they campaigned, a musical victory could supplant an inevitable political defeat in prospect.

A constant din

Cooper's lament was for an era when music-making was a ubiquitous part of the political process and often used as a weapon. On some occasions the nature of the violence was aural and the only damage was to the senses and, no doubt, the odd eardrum. In Cathcart on the Victorian goldfields, for example, rival bands supporting five candidates circled the town before converging on the hustings, which, according to one witness, created an extraordinary cacophony (the only recognisable tune being the *Marseillaise*).[8] Nevertheless, volume was a powerful weapon. Imagine how difficult it was for the Conservative candidate in Northampton in 1891 to get his message across when confronted by Charles Bradlaugh's supporters in full voice. 'Mr Germaine essayed to deal with the general political questions', noted the local newspaper reporter, 'but was many times forced to stop, the repeated appeals of the chairman … for order passing unheeded'. The report continued: 'At length – as the constant din was kept up at the back of the hall, the interrupters shouting an old electioneering song with the refrain "Hurrah for Bradlaugh" – Mr Germaine finished by expressing the confident belief that, though he had not been given justice in this speech, he would obtain it at the polls.'[9] He didn't. Similarly, during Sydney's election in 1854, Henry Parkes, the former Chartist (and later Premier of New South Wales), stood by while his supporters behaved as legions of Chartists in his native Birmingham had done throughout the previous decade by drowning out his opponent's speech with 'ribald songs'.[10] Parkes's enthusiasts were still singing twenty years later but this time the victims included another former Chartist, David Buchanan.[11] Writing in 1903, W. E. Adams, a Cheltenham Chartist, summarised the practice usefully. Elections are 'pleasanter to remember than they were to witness'. Speeches were 'performed, often in dumb show' amidst 'shouting, fighting, band-playing and processioning'.[12]

The shoe was regularly on the other foot. In his campaign for the prime ministership in Canada in 1887, to take one example, Edward Blake was speaking to a packed house in Bowmanville in southern Ontario when a Tory procession arrived from nearby Newcastle and 'entered upon deliberate attempt to break up the meeting'. 'The band played and the mob shrieked and howled,' lamented the reporter.[13] Similarly, during the Colchester by-election in 1870, meetings in support of the hapless Henry Stokes, a Gladstonian Liberal, were repeatedly broken up by the incessant chanting of the nursery rhyme *Remember, Remember the Fifth of November* and raucous choruses of 'We'll hang old Stokes from a sour apple tree' (adapted from the iconic *John Brown's Body*) and *Poor Old Stokes*, undoubtedly a contrafactum of some sort set to an undisclosed air.[14] Raucous choruses of *Oh, You Beautiful Doll!* rendered inaudible successive speakers at a large suffragist rally in Guilford in 1913.[15]

As well as providing the soundtrack to political action, music-making was frequently the catalyst for violence. This can be seen by a glance at what was arguably the most notorious place in England for electoral hubbub: Wakefield in West Yorkshire. For half a century elections in Wakefield were synonymous with electoral violence, sometimes incited by marauding bands in both senses of the word. The town was the epicentre of the contest not just for a hotly contested borough seat but also for the all-important West Riding county seats and thus at every election after 1832 it was a focus of national attention. For our purposes two campaigns stand out. During the 1837 poll a day of brutal rioting was sparked off when a Liberal band of music (accompanied by a small band of Liberal 'Yellows' armed with 'walking sticks') marched headlong into a massive crowd assembled before the hustings. Ironically, Lord Morpeth, the Liberal candidate for the county seat and a national figure in Whig–Liberal politics, was speaking at the time of the sonic-cum-physical assault. A detailed diagram of the streetscape published in the *Leeds Mercury* illustrates that the crowd had been carefully separated into designated areas (much like football crowds today) and how wilfully, therefore, the Liberals careened into enemy territory, playing as they went. The ensuing scuffle developed into a pitched battle, drawing into the fray a significant group of supporters of the local Orange Order and a large contingent of radicals headed by Feargus O'Connor and Richard Oastler, a well-known Tory-radical. It is unclear on which side the radicals fought. Possibly both. By the time the army arrived from Leeds one of the combatants had been killed.[16] Presumably the band had played on throughout.

In 1852 the 'perambulations of the Tory and Liberal Bands' through the streets of Wakefield again precipitated a serious melee, in the first instance over a set of drumsticks. When the opposing bands marched past each other on the campaign trail the Tory drummer snatched the sticks from his counterpart and 'broke them to pieces'. The ensuing violence continued over several days during which 'bludgeon-men' attacked the rival bands in a vicious cycle of retaliation. Several participants were seriously injured, forcing the local mayor to ban bands for the duration of the campaign.[17] According to Daniel O'Connell the flashpoint for confrontation was often when bands passed each other as they marched.[18] Certainly, the 'bludgeon-men' accompanying bands were invariably well armed with various lengths of timber but musical instruments also made for excellent weapons. In Manchester in 1873, for example, members of rival temperance bands were brought before the court charged with 'being drunk and fighting and battering each other's heads with their instruments, which were shown in court bruised and indented to a considerable extent'.[19] These scenes would have been familiar throughout the length and breadth of the colonies. The election in Montreal in 1832, to take another example, was compared to the Massacre of Peterloo and, during Sydney's first poll in 1843, campaign organisers employed 'music wherever they could find it' for the hustings, which helped to provoke a riot. '*Only* one person died [emphasis added]', reported the *Sydney Morning Herald*, describing the victim as 'democracy's first martyr'.[20]

The use of music as a weapon in all its manifestations was undoubtedly frustrating, terrifying and even life-threatening but we should not lose sight of the fact that the presence of music was also integral to the fun – the carnivalesque – that suffused popular politics. In Tiverton in 1841 the 'excellent bands of music' amused the electors as they attended the poll at the Guildhall; the *Liberal Election Songs*, published in 1880, were lauded for the way that they 'entertained' the crowd before the candidates commenced their orations.[21] Even in Wakefield before the 'Yellow' band helped the event to spiral out of control in 1837, the *Mercury*'s reporter had noted that music had added 'an extremely lively effect to the scene', complemented by Morpeth's appearance as a 'Knight of the Shire', wearing court dress and sporting a sword and spurs.[22] Notably, a journalist in Melbourne in 1855 even used these apposite words: 'bands of music, flags and cockades', he wrote, 'made the event a kind of carnival'.[23] Hawkers and vendors, food-sellers and performers often milled around the crowds at the hustings and, as we have seen, playing, singing and dancing were often part of a broader agenda of sports, smoking and free-wheeling consumption of food and drink. In this way an election was political in both a specific and a broader sense. Having drawn attention to the merriment – and music's part in it – we should not lose sight of the subversive potential of popular culture expressed in this way. By incorporating quasi-political counter-theatre, a carnival can be a site of resistance to authority (to borrow Mikhail Bahktin's conception), the place where cultural, and potentially political, change could take place, or at least be conceived.[24]

Like the demands for the control of street noise discussed earlier, calls to use legislation to address the sound of political violence inevitably resonated inside the walls of Parliament. For much of the nineteenth century successive governments had struggled to regulate processions in Ireland, including attempting to control the use of inflammatory music and singing in the context of an annual calendar of commemorations familiar down to our own day.[25] The parliamentary debates almost invariably teetered on the brink of absurdity. Speaking in 1860 in relation to the Party Emblems Bill, Edwin James QC, the radical MP for Marylebone who had gained national notoriety for successfully defending one of the conspirators charged with plotting the assassination of Napoleon III, excoriated the government for failing not only to provide a schedule of banned songs but also for inanely attempting to police songs *and* the manner of their singing. 'So', he told the House in a tone dripping with sarcasm,

> a person might be singing the most loyal song – 'God Save the Queen' or 'Rule Britannia' for instance – and yet a constable might come up and object to the manner of the vocalist, and say, 'You have been singing through your nose', or 'You gave a curl of your lip, and I shall therefore seize you and your music too'.[26]

An Irish Tory, John Pope Hennessy, offered a broader context. 'The most despotic monarch in Europe', he fulminated, 'would be deemed insane if he proposed a penal law to prevent the singing of party songs.'[27] The measures directed at Ireland, however, were part of a broader attempt by the State to come to grips with street politics, which began in England and Scotland with the infamous Six Acts promulgated by a panic-stricken Tory regime in the aftermath of Peterloo. Music was not exempt; on the contrary, it was seen as part of a syndrome of activities, which, in the words of Lord Grenville, 'were calculated to produce intimidation'. Accordingly, the Seditious Meetings Prevention Bill prohibited attendance at public gatherings 'in military array, or with arms or weapons of every description or with drums or any kind of music, or with flags, banners, emblems, or other insignia'.[28] At least one reformer would later pointedly note the hypocrisy of these measures. In 1836 Thomas Potter, the doyen of Manchester liberalism and formative advocate of free trade, reminded the House of the time when 'street ballad singing was encouraged by the government – he alluded to the period of the French revolution, when persons were encouraged to sing loyal songs in the streets'.[29]

The principal focus of parliamentary efforts to control the use of music in political culture on the English side of St George's Channel, however, was in connection with electoral politics. As we have noted, at one level this was part of a broader campaign against unwanted public music (increasingly defined as 'noise'). At the same time, a number of parliamentarians – across the political spectrum – were particularly determined to legislate to suppress music at elections. Some were simply attempting to tidy up 'corrupt practices', which the Reform Bill had failed to address. For them, hiring bands to produce an air of festivity was nothing more than good old-fashioned treating and thus a thinly veiled form of bribery. For many others, however, the most compelling reason to silence electioneering was precisely because it was one of the major catalysts for conflict. Like the desire to expunge the last vestiges of the corrupt practices characteristic of pre-Reform politics, the intention was a modernising one. The 'scenes of violence which occurred between the two rival parties ... with their display of party emblems, and their bands of music', Henry Berkeley told the House of Commons in 1853, 'were perfectly disgraceful to a civilized community'.[30] One MP pointed out that special legislation was actually unnecessary as it was already possible to prosecute those guilty of disorderly proceedings under the common law and others even defended it albeit with tongue in cheek. 'When it was proposed to prohibit the use of bands, flags and ribbons,' recalled Henry Vizetelly, a sketch artist renowned for his contributions to the *Illustrated London News*, one parliamentarian had pleaded with mock exasperation, 'if this were done, the electors would not know whose heads they were breaking', and added that it was 'downright folly to attempt to make an English election as demure and orderly as a Methodist love-feast.'[31] Another MP complained that it would turn elections into funerals. Other members, however, clearly felt the need for a high profile gesture.[32]

The attempt to proscribe music as either a dangerous provocation or a corrupt practice, or both, proved difficult. The introduction of a succession of bills and amendments had decidedly mixed results. As we have seen, music was the cornerstone of Edith Brand's triumphs in Wisbech in the 1880s, but as well as votes she attracted volleys of stones from disgruntled Tories. Moreover, alongside the legislative architecture in Britain was a range of regulatory powers available to local authorities to prevent singing in public but these too proved difficult and fractious to police. By 1865 in Britain it was clear that music-makers were being prosecuted only if there was an outbreak of violence linked to their performance.[33] Indeed, in 1873 a disgruntled Tory MP complained that not only were radical bandsmen escaping prosecution, they were effectively being chaperoned by the State. Referring to a demonstration in Hyde Park, he complained:

[171]

One of the Park Rules said that there must be no unauthorized playing of any music in the Park. If an organ-grinder had attempted to play the 'Old Hundredth' he would soon have been taken to prison. There were bands however – one playing the 'Marseillaise' and another the 'Wearing of the Green' – under the protection of the guardians of public order.[34]

Ostensibly, the efficacy of attempts to control 'outmoded' electioneering was thought to be greater in the colonies. On the one hand, some commentators believed the fundamental constitutional change taking place would regulate cultural practices without further intervention of parliament. As one optimistic correspondent wrote to the *Sydney Morning Herald* not long after the ink on the colony's constitution had dried, the 'old days' were over. 'The elector, in the exercise of his most grave and sacred duty which he owes to his country and his fellow man', he wrote with solemn certitude, 'is protected from the exciting influence of noisy bands of music, the pestering of importunate canvassers, the childish parade of flags and ribbons, and the intimidation of the mean tribe of "exclusive dealers".'[35] In 1871 the editor of the *Queenslander* put the positive view more emphatically: 'Those who can remember what a contested borough election was in the old country and in "the good old times" will for the most part admit that these things are managed better by us now.' Gone, he continued, were 'party processions, bands of music, flags, banners, rosettes, open public-houses, an unlimited flow of beer, and consequent black eyes and broken heads'.[36]

These prognostications proved to be overly optimistic and the colonial parliaments were forced to intervene. Although the editor of Melbourne's *Argus* reminded readers of Daniel O'Connell's well-known boast that he could 'drive a coach-and-six through an Act of Parliament', he was nevertheless sanguine when assessing the prospects of the 1856 Election Regulation Act in attaining what it described as the hitherto 'Utopian dream viz. a thoroughly pure election'. The Victorian Act outlawed a range of practices intended to place voters under duress and proscribed a range of payments, including for 'cockades, ribbons, chairing, bands of music, flags or banners'.[37] It is difficult to be precise, but an extensive examination of press reports suggests that polling days in Victoria were quieter with bands less frequently engaged in the formal proceedings. Notably, however, the same is not true of the broader campaigns, which continued to feature music. Indeed, music-making remained a common feature of campaigns throughout the Anglophone world.

From the 1850s, for example, the New Zealand parliament had successively enacted a raft of laws designed to regulate the conduct of elections. Much as in Britain some critics complained that they were turning elections into 'something between a Quaker's meeting and a Venetian Council' and when the 1881 Corrupt Practices Prevention Act was tabled one commentator suggested that it was now 'almost impossible' for a candidate not to fall foul of what he considered a 'Draconian Act'.[38] However, nothing much appears to have changed; certainly, the repeated attempts of the legislators over several decades suggest that they had failed to achieve their objective. Events in Wellington during the general election of 1899 are a case in point. Although the editor of the *Evening Post* argued that a visitor from the 'Old Country' would find the colony's elections dull by comparison, this was certainly not so in Wellington. Here, in the seat of Newtown, the final election rally for the independent candidate, Richard Knight, unravelled according to a familiar refrain. Music was the currency of the evening. Knight's initial attempt to address the crowd was frustrated for about an hour by a large contingent of 'larrikins' who were incessantly shouting, hooting and singing. In an effort to change the course of the proceedings Knight finally called upon his wife, Mrs Gertrude Knight, who had been seated at a piano on stage the entire time, to 'give the boys a song'. Order was restored but it lasted only as long as Gertrude's playing, after which the interrupters began singing 'snatches of popular melodies'. The hapless candidate again 'asked the fair pianist to oblige'. Finally, in exasperation, Knight sought, to no avail, to strike a bargain – ten minutes of playing and singing for a ten-minute respite during which he might give his address. The 'chape of yells, cheers, and singing', ran the press report, 'caused a fearful din'. Knight didn't get his ten minutes and, no doubt more dispiriting, at the poll the following day he only received nine votes.[39]

The 'August Chamber'

For many MPs the reforming impulse was, at least in part, buttressed by the strains of the confrontational music they could hear from their seats. Marching on Westminster-style parliaments with bands and banners was a ubiquitous element in the dramaturgy of popular politics throughout the length and breadth of the British world, which, since the mass campaigns in favour of the Reform Bill, were underpinned by a threat of mass violence.[40] The symbolic challenge was particularly pointed when the protesters included members of self-styled 'alternative' parliaments, such as the Anti-Corn Law League's national conference in 1838, the Chartists' national convention a decade later and the national convention of the Women's Social and Political Union sixty years on in 1907. In each of these instances the processors claimed a greater legitimacy to speak on behalf of the people than those within the cosseted walls of the parliament that they approached.[41] Described by the Tory press as 'Determined Raids by Suffragettes', the 1907 march is an example of how episodes of this kind could easily spiral out of control with music-making a feature worthy of comment. The 'Wild Scenes at the House of Commons' involved police on horseback charging into the crowd of several hundred protesters and the arrest of thirty-four women singing *Glory, Glory Hallelujah*.[42] A similar pattern can be found throughout the Anglophone world. The detention of the leaders of the bitter miners' strike in Broken Hill, New South Wales in 1892, for example, produced a wave of protest throughout the Australian colonies. In Sydney it provoked a massive 'indignation' meeting, which culminated in a march on parliament. The protesters were estimated to have numbered over 30,000 and as they marched they cried 'Advance Australia' and sang *Marching through Georgia* with 'immense enthusiasm'. Whether or not the marchers deliberately sought to invoke an image of Sherman's army leaving a trail of carnage through the heart of the Confederacy by selecting this song is unclear but the inference must have occurred to at least some members of the colony's legislative class (particularly as leaflets urging protesters to give up on the ballot box and take up rifles were being widely distributed). Despite being halted short of its intended destination by police and mounted troops, according to one report the sound of the protest 'penetrated' the walls of the 'sacred enclosure' in Macquarie Street.[43] In Melbourne in 1858, at a time when progressive delegates were holding a traditional radical-like convention, explicitly styled as an analogue to the Colonial Legislature, supporters marched by torchlight with a band up Bourke Street to the reserve adjacent to the House. 'The sounds of the music and the mob', ran one report, 'were distinctly heard within the Assembly Chamber'.[44]

A variation of this ritual formula saw some MPs grasp the opportunity to emphasise their right to speak on behalf of their constituency by marching with their supporters to the House to announce their presence. When, to take a famous example, the newly elected Keir Hardie trudged to Westminster in 1892 to take up his seat inside the privileged walls he was accompanied by a large contingent of his fellow radicals, trade unionists and socialists and a band playing the *Marseillaise*. Among friend and foe alike, few that heard the music would have misinterpreted the message it was intended to deliver: according to a report in the *Westralian Worker*, Hardie was 'ever after regarded with the gravest suspicion'.[45] But in an important sense the music did not penetrate the 'sacred chamber' irrespective of the volume at which it was being made outside the walls. Indeed, in musical terms MPs were mute. Of course, Members could – and often did – use music as a metaphor within speech. For instance, when Dadabhai Naoroji, a Parsi who was the first Asian Member of the House of Commons, demanded equality for the Queen's Indian subjects, he asserted their right to sing 'Britons will not be slaves'.[46] The Standing Orders were, somewhat ironically, silent on the question of singing in the mother of parliaments. However, a prohibition of vocalising was a time-honoured convention. In fact, singing was not permitted in a Westminster-style parliament, be it in London, Toronto, Wellington or, to this day, Edinburgh or Canberra.[47]

Admittedly, there were some exceptions during the long nineteenth century. During the debate over a Reform Bill sponsored by the Liberal Ministry of Graham Berry (renowned as veteran militant radical earlier in his political career) in the Victorian Legislative Assembly in 1879, one Member 'parodied an old English election song' at the expense of the leader of the opposition, John O'Shanassy.[48] This light-hearted moment may have been little more than the upshot of a bacchanalian dinner break: there were notable exceptions, however, when musical behaviour was employed with more serious intent. Examining these rare attempts to break the musical silence of the parliamentary space is instructive. One the one hand, music was clearly introduced to denote unity and shared values. The inauguration of the Federal Parliament in Melbourne in 1901, for example, included performances of the oft-used hymn the *Old Hundredth*, Handel's 'Hallelujah Chorus', *Rule, Britannia* and *God Save the Queen* (referred to as the 'National Anthem') performed by an orchestra and singers, including the recently sworn-in Members and Senators.[49] Similarly, there were at least two notable instances in St Stephen's when music was used to indicate common purpose. On the final day of the session in September 1914 a letter from the King outlining the circumstances leading to the declaration of war a month previously was read in both Houses. At the conclusion of the address in the Commons an over-exuberant Labour MP, Will Crooks (a well-known trade unionist and Fabian socialist), encouraged by the leader of the Irish Nationalists, John Redmond, wondered 'if it would be in order to sing "God Save the King"?' All the members present, reported *Hansard*, 'joined in singing the National Anthem, the occupants of the Press and other galleries standing'. Crooks then proclaimed 'God Save Ireland' and Redmond, 'And God Save England, too'.[50] Redmond's gesture reflected the mood across the Irish Sea. As the volunteers in Dublin marched off to war in August the band played *God Save the King*. Without intending the pun one commentator described this as an 'unheard of thing',[51] but in fact he was incorrect: it had been heard before. Speaking in the House of Commons during the second reading of the Home Rule Bill in 1886,

Thomas Sexton pointed to successive performances of God Save the Queen and God Save Ireland – a song discussed below – in Ireland as a metaphor for the dawn of 'unity and loyalty'. Apparently the Dublin band played the former badly, but, Sexton quipped with understandable exaggeration, it 'hadn't been played since 1795'.[52] In fact, Crooks and his colleagues had been slow off the mark. Early in August the members of the South Australian House of Assembly produced what was described as a 'scene of unprecedented enthusiasm' when they stood in their seats to sing God Save the King.[53]

On other occasions, however, when music was introduced into parliamentary institutions it was, implicitly or explicitly, confrontational: from a means of resistance to a flashpoint for violence. In New Zealand, music played a complex role in inter-cultural politics, highlighting both a capacity for affirmation and at the same time a means of asserting agency and serving as a tool for resistance. In the aftermath of the bloody Māori Wars of the early 1860s there were successive attempts to provide for formal Māori representation within the colony's political structures. They also saw the establishment of parallel institutions: the well-known Māori parliaments, otherwise called Runanga or Paremata Maori. The details of the legislative ad hocery need not detain us; the institutions are worth lingering over. The parliaments sat intermittently and in several configurations from the 1860s. The 'first' District Runanga took place in 1862 in Wiamate. In this case it was 'duly constituted' by the government and comprised appointed members; thus it is not surprising that the proceedings closely mirrored those of a Westminster-style parliament, including an opening prayer, codified standing orders and a 'document much like a constitution or a Magna Charta'. 'A more orderly assembly was never convened', commented one observer, 'and many of the English spectators marveled to see how very quickly the members learned how to carry on the business according to European regulations.'[54] Later iterations were not government-sponsored but, in many respects, also embraced the forms and procedures of the mother of parliaments. The Paremata convened in Auckland in 1879, for example, opened with the 35th Psalm, following which the presiding officer, 'Chief Paul', asked members to conduct their business in the 'same manner as the European Parliament'.[55]

In April 1892 numerous tribal leaders formed Te Runanga o Te Kotahitanga mo Te Tiriti o Waitangi, which presaged the opening of a Māori parliament later in the year (it met annually for several years thereafter). Sessions of these Runanga were almost invariably inaugurated with the pomp and circumstance redolent of that in London. In June 1892, to take one instance, a Māori band played the National

Anthem.[56] But here there is also evidence of local agency. The parliament in Hastings in 1893, for example, opened with a food ceremony, the performance of a *haka*, funeral *tangis* and a rendition of a march by Ricardo Linter played by the Heretaunga Band. According to the correspondent from the *Daily Telegraph* the musicians performed with a 'skill and precision that many European bands might envy'. The bandsmen sported kilts but, the report continued, 'the pattern and color seemed to be according to the fancy of each'.[57] The parliament which opened in Gisborne in 1894 closely resembled New Zealand's Pākehā political institutions (which had themselves been transplanted from Britain) in many respects: from the configuration of the chamber to the employment of Hansard-style reporters to record the proceedings in the Māori language.[58] In a highly significant departure, however, the Paki Paki Brass Band, comprising thirty members, performed 'at intervals between the speeches'.[59] From the official record of the proceedings it is clear that the band were present in the assembly to mark the adjournment of business and, on at least one occasion, called upon to mark the farewell of a prominent Member. Furthermore, one evening the House was 'given over' for 'entertainment', leading to an early adjournment the following day because the Members' heads were 'in a bad state'.[60] On another occasion, in 1895, it was noted that a Member responded to the reading of the King's speech with 'hip hip hooray, hip hip hooray, hip hip hooray', followed by a performance of a rhythmic chant (*ngeri*) 'with action'.[61] In 1906, the proceedings opened with a prayer and a Māori song sung by the presiding officer in a 'delightful tenor'.[62] At least one Māori MP ('Maori Joe') in the Bay of Plenty area used song to expound upon his political exploits. A translation of one of his songs, in pursuit of an unpopular land agent, was published in 1913:

> Time I go to, long time I make to stay.
> I talk all my talk away, Kapai Hori Grey;
> No me like Mr _____, by-by down he go;
> Tenei te korero tangata pai Ingola Maroi Joe [This is the talk of a very good man, his name is Maori Joe].

'The stuff loses its effect in print', noted the translator, but it 'never failed to bring the house down'.[63]

Of course, press reports of the proceedings of the *Paremata Maori* were often composed with tongue firmly in cheek, literally mocking 'mock' parliaments, but it is important for the historian to not simply join in the fun. On the contrary, for the student of counter-theatre and cultural resistance it is important to ask who was doing the appropriating. On the one hand, the *Paremata Maori* in general can be seen as an institutional and cultural polyphony, a synthesis of the introduced institutions of the coloniser with structures of indigenous governance and culture. At the same time, the introduction of a vibrant musical and performative culture within the walls of the chamber provides a clear indication of the incorporation and appropriation of the essential features of a Westminster-style parliament into the rituals of Māori governance and not the other way around. In this way music-making both denoted and abetted a reversal of the relationship between coloniser and colonised.

At about the same time as the eclectically kilted Māori bandsmen were entertaining their parliamentary representatives in Waitangi, an example of the way in which the disruptive effects of singing on the campaign trail could be brought into a parliamentary chamber occurred in July 1902 in the Australian Senate, then barely a year old. The action unfolded during a heated debate over the relative virtues of free trade and protectionism. The Speaker at the time was John Cash Neild, an insurance agent, colonel in a volunteer regiment and ardent free-trader known for sporting a Garibaldi beard and for his extraordinary capacity to 'stonewall' (he had once spoken for nine hours continuously, earning him the sobriquet 'Jawbone').[64] After an hour of stentorian endeavour by Neild, Senator Gregor McGregor, no doubt fearing another extended oration, ceased interjecting and began singing. McGregor was a veteran agricultural labourer and Clydeside shipbuilder who was the first Labour man elected to the Senate from South Australia. Urged on by a group of other Labour senators (notably James Stewart, a socialist and trade unionist who described himself as a Jacobite), McGregor chose not a political song but *He Was A Gallant Man* from the comic-opera *Ma Mie Rosette* (composed in 1892).[65] McGregor's colleagues prompted him to sing *The Boyne Water* instead (or to use comb and paper to play *The Wild Colonial Boy*); inflammatory music in both cases no doubt. But perhaps from McGregor's perspective the irony of the title of his selection suited the occasion. Notwithstanding the mirth enjoyed by the 'Labour Corner', Neild was understandably not impressed: 'I never heard of singing being permitted before,' he pleaded. According to one report the 'senatorial machine ... creaked terribly' under the pressure of what was clearly an uncommon experience for keen observers of Parliament.[66] The Senate President asked McGregor to 'desist at once', noting that, 'It certainly is very improper'. McGregor defied the chair but before the episode escalated the disruption proved effective. Speaker and singer refrained and a vote was taken.[67]

Music was in the air in manifold ways in the Quebec Legislature during a constitutional crisis in March 1879. Lieutenant Governor

Luc Letellier de Saint-Just had dismissed the ministry on the grounds of incompetence in respect of railway concessions (there was also a whiff of corruption).[68] In a bi-partisan response, Members proceeded to filibuster on a motion condemning the Governor, combined with what we would nowadays call a 'sit in' lasting over twenty-four hours. Describing the scene as 'Ludicrous in the extreme', one newspaper report told of MLAs engaged in 'blowing tin trumpets, whistles, singing, cat-calls, Jews' harps, and all kinds of unmelodious sounds'. At dawn, the report continued, 'the drowsy occupants … struck up the "Marseillaise" and a variety of other chorus songs'. Coffee and 'other stimulants' heralded the return of music: 'as the day wore on, songs loud and lengthy were indulged in, drowning for the time the voice of whoever then had the floor'. When the Governor's wife arrived to witness the extraordinary scene with her own eyes the parliamentarians began singing the *National Anthem*. After a 'moment's hesitation' the 'whole House, including the Speaker' joined. One commentator suggested that this 'ebullition of loyalty' prevented the 'probably unheard-of-before occurrence' from 'drifting into demoralisation and disorder'.[69] The *National Anthem* was undoubtedly an expression of loyalty, but to what? The Governor's wife would undoubtedly have approved but perhaps was not entirely justified in so being. As we shall see below, radicals and reformers often claimed a higher loyalty to their 'British' rights and in this way their singing could easily have been an expression of a kind of counter-aurality: a taunt rather than a tribute.

A further example of singing – or at least of attempting to sing – in a parliamentary chamber, however, highlighted deep fissures in the body politic that neither William Crooks and John Redmond's duet nor McGregor's annoying disruption had. Shortly after midnight on the morning of 5 March 1901, A. J. Balfour, a leading member of Salisbury's Tory government, moved that 'the question be put' to bring to an end a protracted discussion of an Education Amendment Bill. This provoked outrage by a clutch of members of the Irish Parliamentary Party on the grounds that they had not been given the opportunity to speak on a Bill directly affecting their constituencies. The fact that Balfour was Chief Secretary for Ireland (known as 'Bloody Balfour' for his administration of the Crimes Act) and a determined opponent of Home Rule undoubtedly helped to inflame the situation. The Speaker duly put the question but sixteen Members refused to either vote or leave the chamber and were thus suspended. Soon the situation spiralled out of control. Faced with the continuing refusal of the MPs to leave the House, the Speaker ordered the Sergeant-at-Arms to eject them. When this proved beyond his capacity a contingent of police was summoned and one by one the so-called miscreants were dragged kicking and screaming from the House.[70]

Reports of the incident – referred to variously as a 'Free Fight on the Floor of the Chamber', a 'disgraceful exhibition', 'extraordinary scenes' and 'Imperialistic Tyranny' – quickly echoed around the Anglophone world.[71] Although *Hansard* remained silent it is clear that as the Members were removed, other radical MPs (English, Scottish and Welsh) shouted 'Shame, Shame' and the Irish MPs stood in their seats singing *The Wearing of the Green* and *God Save Ireland*.[72] The import of the former we have discussed at length; the genealogy of the latter makes clear that its use in this context is suffused with equal significance. The title was drawn from Edmund Condon's defiant words in court in 1867. He had been sentenced to death for his part in the sensational rescue of two Fenian prisoners in Manchester, during which a police constable was killed. The 'Manchester Martyrs', as they became known, were hanged on 23 November; the song was published in Manchester on 7 December.[73] The words had been penned by T. D. Sullivan, a well-known Irish journalist, and struck a chord of furious defiance:

> God save Ireland said the heroes,
> God save Ireland said they all,
> Whether on the gallows high, or the battlefield we die,
> No matter when for Erin dear we fall.[74]

The song to which it was set – *Tramp! Tramp! Tramp! (The Prisoner's Hope)* – was entirely apposite. The music and lyrics had been composed across the Atlantic in 1864 as a protest against conditions in the Confederate prison camp at Andersonville:

> Tramp, tramp, tramp, the boys are marching,
> Cheer up comrades they will come,
> And beneath the starry flag
> We shall breathe the air again,
> Of the free land in our own beloved home.[75]

God Save Ireland retained its potency into the twentieth century. As with *The Wearing of the Green*, *God Save Ireland* was regarded as inflammatory in Britain as well as in the colonies. The celebrated Irish tenor John McCormack, for example, recorded *God Save Ireland* in 1906 (and *The Wearing of the Green* in 1904 and 1912), which, according to his biographer, caused tension and, together with his failure to sing *God Save the King*, precipitated a noisy crowd interruption during a performance in Adelaide, ultimately leading to cancellation of the tour.[76]

Armed to the teeth with bitter hatred

Policemen have been mounted on guard, armed conspicuously with wooden bludgeons and, secretively, with revolvers. Union pickets have been posted with orders to do their duty with 'civility,' but armed to the teeth with that bitter hatred – which is a just hatred – towards all who blackleg upon the union principles.

Barrier Truth (1909).[77]

An examination of the persistent conflict associated with electoral politics has provided a starting point to consider the intersection between music and music-making and the institutional structures of politics, the law and authority more generally. The long nineteenth century, particularly the final quarter of Queen Victoria's reign and the years leading up to the Great War, was marked by major strikes and lockouts, which almost invariably involved violent confrontation exponentially more serious than most election scuffles and ejecting bilious MPs from the House. No part of the radical Anglophone world escaped: from Vancouver Island to Wellington; from London to Broken Hill. Typically, the dispute was protracted and violent and although the issues were different they unfolded according to a remarkably similar template. Music and music-making had a consistent place in the repertoire of direct action undertaken by strikers and their supporters; in this way it provides an important vantage point from which to consider lived experience.

Notwithstanding the protracted and bitter maritime and shearers' strikes in 1890–91, the 1889, 1892 and 1909 miners' strikes single out Broken Hill, 1,100 kilometres from Sydney in far west New South Wales, as Australia's *ne plus ultra* of industrial confrontation before the Great War. These events will be our point of entry. White settlers founded the town of Broken Hill in 1883 on what was the land of the Wiljakali people, following the discovery of silver and zinc ore. By 1889 the population had grown to 3,000, most of who were employed by the Broken Hill Proprietary Mining Company (BHP, now BHP-Billiton, which would become the world's largest mining company as a result of what was one of the world's most extensive mineral deposits). The mining population was heavily unionised, being the home of an extensive branch of the militant Amalgamated Miners' Association of Australasia (AMA). The 1889 dispute resulted from an attempt by the miners to enforce a 'closed shop' to ensure that only union members would be employed. The strike lasted a week and ended with agreement in the union's favour, but in other ways it was a portent of the future. For the student of transnational history and political culture the 1892 and 1909 strikes demand closer attention.

In 1892, faced by declining ore prices, BHP (followed by the smaller mining companies) sought to reduce costs by employing contract labour, which effectively repudiated the agreement concluded in 1889. Although resistance to 'blacklegging' and wage cuts was the catalyst for the strike, the miners' grievances included growing concern with the conditions under which they worked. In particular, lead poisoning was being raised as an issue, as was the demand for a reduction in working hours.[78] The strike excited considerable international attention within and beyond the labour movement, as did the 1909 dispute. The notoriety of the latter was undoubtedly enhanced by the presence of Tom Mann. Mann arrived in Broken Hill in September 1908 to take up the position of AMA organiser. As we have seen, Mann had been one of the heroes of the London Dock Strike of 1889 and by the time he migrated to Victoria in 1901 he had spent most of the previous twenty years as an itinerant agitator, advocating a potent mix of socialism, democracy and trade union activism. He was ready-made for the looming crisis. According to Ben Tillett, his friend and fellow veteran of the iconic London strike, Mann 'combined the qualities of whirlwind and volcano. His was the genius of sheer energy'.[79] In Australia comrades and commentators alike struggled to find sufficient superlatives: Mann was 'beloved'; a 'modern John the Baptist', the 'greatest organiser in the world' and even the 'ideal entertainer', a reflection of his power as a platform orator. As one witness recalled: from 'the first word uttered he gripped his audience and kept them spell-bound until the end.'[80] To opponents Mann loomed large as a combination of 'Machiavelli, Mephistopheles and Frankenstein's Monster'. He did little to endear himself to them, boasting that he was a 'Dangerous Agitator, and a Dangerous Man'.[81]

Within weeks of arriving in Broken Hill Mann had increased membership of the AMA by 1,600 to approximately 6,000, which meant that the union was at its peak when the flashpoint came in January 1909. The catalyst was a precipitate 12.5 per cent wage reduction instigated by BHP with the smaller mining companies following in its wake. The miners went on strike; the mining companies sacked them to a man, creating a lockout. As in 1892, in 1909 the fulcrum had become the proposed use of non-union labour and it is in the context of this stand-off that we have an opportunity to explore the role of music and musical behaviour in conflict. Unlike 1889 both the 1892 and 1909 strikes dragged on interminably: the former for just over eighteen weeks, the latter for close to five months.[82] During both strikes action was centred on two key demotic hubs – the public meeting and the picket line. Music was often present at meetings and almost invariably a part of the ritualised behaviour of picketing.

[182]

Examining the music-making that underpinned the industrial action allows us firstly to see and better understand the strength of the community which undertook it. Much has been made, rightly, of the role of women in the prosecution of the strikes in Broken Hill.[83] In both 1892 and 1909 women-only rallies and parades were organised (even though on one occasion the company allegedly included a male spy in women's clothing) and women also became embroiled in violent action. At a rally in 1892, William Ferguson, secretary of the Trades and Labor Council, entreated the women not to mingle with the men on pickets, but his request was ignored. In August, for example, the 'Amazon Brigade' (as the *Sydney Morning Herald* dubbed them), 'armed with sticks and other weapons', headed an assault by a 'howling, yelling mob' on 'blacklegs' attempting to cross the picket line.[84] Indeed, reflecting upon these events a year later during the debates over women's suffrage in the South Australian parliament, one Member argued that at Broken Hill the 'women got much more excited and acted with more violence than the men did'.[85] In 1909 there is photographic evidence that women were also among the pickets.[86] And they sang. This is not an isolated occurrence. On the picket during the 1912 gold miners' strike in Waihi on New Zealand's North Island, for example, about fifty 'women-folk' brandished banners proclaiming 'Workers of the World Unite', abused 'scabs' and 'blacklegs' and sang *The Red Flag*.[87]

A venerable word coined originally in a military context – both for an advance guard and a defensive stockade – 'picket' had first been used in connection with industrial action in the late 1780s and when referring to strikes came into popular usage in the third quarter of the nineteenth century. Picketing was the only effective response to a lockout and, as one of the Broken Hill leaders put it, the cordon sanitaire had to be secure enough so that not even 'a young rabbit could get through'.[88] This required tremendous discipline and commitment in the form of round-the-clock vigilance. Notwithstanding the elements – 'bitter winds' in mid-1892 and the blistering sun in 1909 – teams of between 100 and 300 men changing every four hours stood guard. According to Mann, at its peak the Broken Hill picket extended over an area of three miles.[89] Music-makers played a conspicuous part on the front line of industrial action. Milling around one of the factory gates during the massive Preston lockout in the cotton industry in 1853, Charles Dickens told readers of *Household Words*, was a 'knot of young girls ... singing and offering for sale some of the Ten Per Cent Songs, taking their name from the origin of the strike. ... The songs are not remarkable for much elegance and polish', he continued, 'but they possess some earnestness and fire, and are undoubtedly composed by the operatives themselves.' At the same time, reported a local liberal newspaper, a protest meeting in the nearby Temperance Hall, which had been 'literally besieged' by the press of those seeking entry, concluded 'after a song on the subject of the present agitation had been sung'.[90]

Striking workers, and pickets in particular, received tremendous succour from kith and kin, neighbours and fellow workers across the labour movement, including those who made music. As soon as the London Dock Strike commenced in 1889, Tillett recalled, the pickets were being recruited, funds collected for the struggle ahead and 'a band was rapidly improvised to provide marching music'. 'Presently', he continued, 'more bands, more collectors, and more banners'.[91] At its peak 180,000 dockworkers were on strike, with 15,000 of them on the pickets. The organisers convened weekly meetings in Hyde Park, drawing huge crowds and up to fifteen bands. Similarly, in New Zealand throughout the course of the 1913 dispute on the docks the Wellington Waterside Workers' Band was a constant feature of the public meetings in nearby Newton Park; during a transport workers' strike in Winnipeg it was the St Boniface brass band that performed this role.[92] Secondly, at every changing of the guard throughout the lengthy struggles in Broken Hill the incoming pickets marched in formation to the line headed by a band. Indeed, the single occasion when the band was absent required a public explanation lest it be misinterpreted as a loss of resolve: they had inadvertently (and somewhat ironically) locked themselves out of their band room.[93] More broadly, bands were a ubiquitous feature of rallies in support of the strike. And, in Broken Hill in 1890, Bartley's Barrier Band (discussed below) religiously attended the daily strike meeting, assuming its post in front of the offices of the *Barrier Miner* and playing 'excellent selections' while the 'throng' awaited the arrival of the Labour Defence Committee.[94]

The presence of a band was a tangible and measurable index of community support, which provided affirmation and promoted solidarity. As one perspicacious commentator in Broken Hill noted: the 'usefulness' of the 'daily turning out of the Combined Band cannot be overestimated'. The music itself, he continued, 'expresses the feeling of the people, viz. that though oppression is rife ... the people are not despondent, but are filled with that innate conviction that to keep a still upper lip is necessary, for the justice of their cause must ultimately prevail.'[95] Another observer celebrated the band's 'valiant and yeoman service, which, throughout, has been rendered by them so freely and loyally'.[96] As such, the music and musical behaviour provided an auditory cover over the strike; to celebrate it and to anticipate ultimate victory. At one and the same time it not only helped to articulate and promote the cause to anyone within earshot but it also created a safe space within which the introspective culture of radical politics could sustain common purpose. Of course, 'blacklegs' and 'scabs' (as noted, an epithet dripping with hatred and loathing without equal in the international labour movement) were themselves workers. Often strike-breakers were brought in from outside the local area. To take one of countless examples, in 1844 the 'regular men' at the Chapelton Ironworks near Rotherham in South Yorkshire were 'supplant[ed]' by 'blacks from Derbyshire'. Sometimes the distances were great: in St John, Nova Scotia, in 1905 the waterside dispute was broken by workers from England while workers from Italy were used to break a mineworkers' strike in Montreal.[97] But in other cases their presence could reflect an internecine conflict between rival unions within a community. The industrial dispute in Waihi in 1912 is a case in point. Here was a bitter feud between members of the union refusing to take industrial action and 'Red Raggers' committed to prosecuting it. It is worth noting that there was singing as well as stone-throwing on both sides.[98]

Quite apart from the logistical effort that must have been involved in chaperoning pickets three and four times a day or performing at daily strike rallies, the fulfilment of these tasks is a testament to the tenacity and fidelity of the bandsmen themselves. It could be arduous work. According to one observer, members of the Waterside Workers' Band in Auckland during the Waihi strike were beginning to show signs of 'feeling the effects of their strenuous efforts' but upon reaching their destination they 'again blared forth, and enlivened the proceedings with strains of the Red Federation's battle song'.[99] As we have seen, in 1909 the AMA's eponymous band – open only to members of the union – performed these roles. The band had been formed in 1896 and was typical of the union bands discussed in a previous chapter in that they undertook extensive work in the community beyond their union duties.[100] According to one enthusiastic local antiquarian writing in 1908, the AMA Band 'has collected hundreds of pounds from time to time for charitable purposes'.[101] Strike reports from 1909, however, usually referred to a Combined Band, which was drawn from no less than four local bands: the AMA Band, the City Band, the Alma Band and the Broken Hill Band.[102] In 1892 strike duty was performed by Bartley's Barrier Band. It had been founded in 1888 by William Bartley, himself a miner, and had no 'official' status whatsoever within the AMA. And yet the campaign could not have sought a more committed group of men, as they were a ubiquitous presence throughout the long struggle. Moreover, their commitment to fellow workers extended well beyond even Australia: they are listed as contributing to a disaster relief fund for the families of workers killed in a mining accident in New Zealand in 1896. Within the Barrier district Bartley's is reputed to have raised £3,000 for charity over its life.[103] When, after more than a decade, Bartley himself removed to Western Australia to mine for gold, the band continued in his name, only later becoming the City Band; it was in this guise it participated in the Combined Band of 1909.[104]

Industrial campaigns also drew upon a range of concerts and other activities for support – spiritual and financial – and music obviously contributed significantly to the necessary reservoir of cultural capital. The extant accounting ledgers of the Broken Hill Defence Committee for the period January to June 1909 list contributions that attest to the Australia-wide and transnational support for the strikers. Here, we can see the extent of the radical and reformist Anglophone world: donations were received from places as far removed as Perth and Bundaberg, Otago and Glasgow.[105] In January the *Worker* reported that £5,000 had been donated overseas.[106] As the case of New Zealand illustrates, a number of these donations were generated by dances and concerts.[107] Among the fine-grained detail of the accounts, however, we can also break the contributors down to micro-level. Inter alia the accounts record donations by Casey's Court Band (6s.), the Demo Concert Party (£13. 6s. 3d.), the Tin Can Band (2s. 6d.) and the proceeds of a children's concert (£11. 6s. 3d.).[108] This gives us a better sense of the real people in Broken Hill playing and singing, as well as those donating scarce shillings and pennies. As Winnipeg's *Voice* put it, most individual donations in support of Lawrence textile workers in 1912 were between 5 and 25 cents.[109] In this way, relief funds followed another time-honoured pattern, as a glance at the columns of practically any edition of a radical newspaper would attest: from the *Charter*, which reported in 1839 that the London Operative Stonemasons had donated £50 to the Defence of the Glasgow Cotton Spinners and £16. 13s. for the Dorchester Labourers (transported in 1834), to the *Westralian Worker*, which noted seventy years on in 1909, that the Eastern Goldfields Women's League in Kalgoorlie had 'hurriedly arranged a euchre party and dance' that raised £5. 5s. for the Broken Hill strikers. There are shards in the mainstream press too, such as the account in the *Toronto Daily Mail* in July 1893 of striking telegraph workers who would receive free tickets to a benefit concert at the zoo, and the *Auckland Star*'s notice of the £30 collected by the Ohinemuri branch of the miners' association from a concert held at Paeroa.[110]

The concerts and socials themselves follow a script well known to any student of transnational popular politics over the long nineteenth century. This involved a mixture of singing, instrumental performance – including keyboard, string ensemble, mixed orchestral, brass, bagpipes and tin whistles – poetry recitations, dancing, vignettes from popular plays, magic lantern slide shows, magic tricks and even calisthenics, all sustained by abundant eating, drinking and toasting. As we have seen, the festivities sometimes included political speeches at various intervals; at other times politics was left at the door. Sometimes, the repertoire was not obviously political – on the contrary, it appears determinedly so. On other occasions there was a sprinkling of inspiriting-cum-ideological content. These could be contrafacta, parodies and original compositions.

The performers in these events included professional and semi-professional artistes (almost invariably donating their services) as well as card-carrying activists. Leaders, from Feargus O'Connor to Mann, sang too. In Broken Hill itself, a series of benefit concerts held at the Theatre Royal in Argent Street by the Empire Vaudeville Company in January 1909 in aid of the AMA and Combined Unions lockout fund were typical of the former. The impresario was Los C. Hayward, recognised for his long-standing and 'sterling support of the workers' cause' and 'service to the working classes'; the master of ceremonies was Mayor Harry Ivey, himself a trade unionist of twenty years standing. Following a 'catchy overture by the orchestra' the evenings featured Tom Mann (in a speaking rather than singing role) and a series of performances by the Company who had all donated their services.[111] By contrast, the advertisement for a 'Series of Weekly Entertainments' held by the branch of the Socialist League in Farringdon, which commenced in March 1888 in aid of their strike fund, makes clear that they were in-house affairs. Earlier in the month the *Commonweal* issued a call for 'friends' to 'assist with songs, recitations, instrumental music, etc.'. The 'talented Artistes' who responded included William Morris, John Burns, Mary Gostling and H. Halliday Sparling (Morris's son-in-law and publisher, as well as editor of a collection of Irish songs, lyrics and ballads). This was to be supplemented with dancing lessons and the Socialist League Choir singing 'Glees and Madrigals'.[112]

Like the girls singing at the Preston factory gates, Mary Gostling was young. She was a member of the Socialist League's Junior Educational Society in London and the fact that she sang (as well as lectured) is not exceptional. In fact, children's choirs were a notable feature on many playbills at the time. This is also not surprising. With the words of Byron's *The Giaour* ringing in their ears – 'For Freedom's battle once begun,/ Bequeathed by bleeding Sire to Son,/ Though baffled oft is ever won' – radicals invested considerable effort into educating the next generation to continue the struggle or protect hard-won gains.[113] In Britain, these efforts reached an apotheosis with the late nineteenth-century Socialist Sunday School movement. This was an important – if

understudied – feature of popular politics. The movement was formed
in the early 1890s in London and Glasgow and by the 1910s there were
approximately 120 schools operating under the auspices of the National
Council of British Socialist Sunday Schools.[114] The schools generated
cultural production on an impressive scale – from educative plays to
a socialistic version of the Ten Commandments. In terms of pedagogy
music-making was central, which was evident in a plethora of song
sheets and hymnbooks. The following lyrics with accompanying score,
published in the programme for the Huddersfield Sunday School's fourteenth anniversary celebrations in 1910, are typical of the genre:

> Oh, we are little soldiers in the world's great fight,
> We can't do much to overthrow the foes of right;
> But we remember those who've laboured hard and long,
> And we mean to fight for justice as we march along.[115]

As we shall see below, using music to communicate political ideas
to young people – including in nursery rhymes familiar down to our
own day – was a practice venerable by antiquity. It is thus not surprising that during the widespread children's strikes that occurred in the
industrial districts of Britain in 1911, the scene of students parading
the streets 'singing to the accompaniment of tin whistles and mouth
organs with snatches of "Tramp, Tramp, the boys are marching" and
"Fall in and follow me" (the favourite strike song all over the country)'
was not uncommon:

> Fall in and follow me, fall in and follow me!
> Come along and never mind the weather,
> Altogether, stand on me boys,
> I know the way to go,
> I'll take you for a spree.
> You do as I do and you'll do right,
> Fall in and follow me![116]

Inevitably, Socialist Sunday Schools were also established in Australia
and New Zealand, including in Broken Hill. Indeed, having previously
enthused about the Socialist Sunday Schools in Melbourne, 'Comrade
Mary' reported in the Brisbane *Worker* in 1907, 'in many parts of
the world now young Socialists are banding together'. Isn't it nice to
think', she continued, 'that young Labour boys and girls are not going
to be behind the door when socialism comes around?'[117]

Fundraising events and internal meetings more generally were
rarely a place for dissent. Within secure walls, music served not only
to foster solidarity but also to buttress common purpose and replen-
ish resolve. Although political songs were important in this context,
comedic parodies and apolitical contributions – simply popular songs –

also had a role in promoting an atmosphere of inclusivity. Admittedly, the tendency to fissiparousness and factionalism, which plagued the radical, labour and socialist movements during the long nineteenth century (and beyond), meant that music could occasionally provoke an argument. Take, for example, the denouement of a lecture by Mann held in the Trades' Hall in Carlton, an inner suburb in Melbourne in 1903. According to the reporter from the *Worker*, a large audience was not disappointed by Mann's performance: the 'hearty and con-tinued applause that was extended to him exceeded anything that I have ever heard'. To open the proceedings the audience sang what were described as 'Labour songs set to familiar tunes, with a zest that is encouraging'.[118] Following Mann's speech, however, William Ferguson MP (dubbed a 'renegade Labour MP' by the *Worker*) got to his feet to voice a serious objection. Despite the condemnatory epithet, Ferguson could boast a proud record as a Labour stalwart. As we have seen, he was among the leaders of the 1892 miners' strike, serving a ten-month prison sentence for conspiracy. In 1894, shortly after his release, Ferguson was elected to the New South Wales parliament, but in 1899 he supported the protectionist government against the deci-sion of the Labour caucus, becoming an 'Independent Labour member'. It was a display of defiance and intransigence worthy of Tom himself. Importantly, in Melbourne Ferguson did not criticise Mann's words, at least not directly; his complaint was against the songs.[119]

The two 'democratic hymns' sung under Mann's 'conductorship' were part of the radical-cum-socialist canon, both appearing in Edward Carpenter's iconic *Chants of Labour* published in 1888.[120] The first was Edith Nesbit's *Hope of the Ages*, sung to the tune of *Red, White and Blue*. Nesbit was a well-known Victorian author of children's literature – including *The Railway Children* and *The Enchanted Castle* – who combined this with a deep commitment to socialism. Written in the 1880s, Nesbit's lyrics were a potent admixture of defiance and optimism:

> We laugh in the face of the forces
> That strengthen the flood they oppose!
> For the harder oppression the fiercer
> The current will be when it flows.
>
> Our watchword is 'Freedom' – new soldiers
> Flock each day when her flag is unfurled,
> Our cry is the cry of the Ages,
> Our hope is the hope of the World.

The authorship of the tune was the subject of a transatlantic contro-versy, being claimed by two composers in the 1840s. And, there are at least two other sets of lyrics that also date from this time: *Columbia, Land of the Brave* and *Britannia, Gem of the Ocean.*[121]

The other song that was sung by the crowd on that night was *What Ho! My Lads*. Described by one commentator from Sydney as a 'wild democratic hymn' the words had been written by J. L. Joynes in the 1880s. Joynes was a Master at Eton and an expert on German Literature who had jeopardised his career by embracing socialism and composing radical poetry.[122] The words could be sung to either *Auld Lang Syne* or *Partant pour la Syrie* (composed half a century earlier by Napoleon's sister-in-law to celebrate the Emperor's campaign on the Nile, it had replaced the *Marseillaise* as the French national anthem under Louis-Napoleon).[123]

Joynes's sentiments are much like Nesbit's – note the juxtaposition of the image of slavery and tyranny with an infectious air of confidence:

> What ho! My lads, the time is ripe,
> Away with foolish fear!
> The slave may dread his master's stripe –
> We'll have no tyrants here!
> We'll have no tyrants here, my boys,
> Nor, lords to rule the roost;
> Their threats are naught but empty noise,
> And naught but breath their boast.

It is important that the lyrics of both these poems struck a similar chord – in fact, they are typical of the sentiments of many reform-cum-radical songs – which provided an affective platform for Mann's oratory. These words were intended to be sung precisely because in unison they promoted solidarity and a shared sense of mission with the promise of victory. For a hostile commentator in the *Argus* the song warranted withering parody. Speculating that Mann had penned the words himself, 'Oriel' of 'DOGGEREL & Co. UNLIMITED' lamented the promulgation of this 'cheap foreign-made trashy article', offering instead a local version in Mann's voice:

> When from the economic fight
> (I once more say, 'What-ho')
> The capitalist talks of flight
> I answer, 'Let him go'
>
> And if you should bemoan your loss,
> To this grand motto cling –
> 'No wife, no kids, no purse, no boss,
> No blooming anything!'[124]

Musical parody was, as we have seen, part of the use of counter-theatre and appropriation, which underpinned demotic politics in the

Anglophone world and, as already discussed, was often introduced into crises in a way which suggests that it served as an analogue when the stakes were high. Here, however, the parody provoked no response (Mann probably found it funny). Indeed, it is unlikely that either it or the note of discord from a 'renegade' that was introduced in the Melbourne proceedings would have done anything to dispel the prevailing air of affirmation, resolve and optimism produced by the combination of Mann's mellifluous oratory and inspiriting music. On the contrary, reports of activities taking place among the faithful, either explicitly or implicitly, suggest that a good time was had by all. The use of music and music-making to bookend a meeting allows us to better appreciate the expression of movement culture diachronically – as it happened – but also bounded by place and time.[125]

Outside a safe space where, almost invariably, music promoted solidarity, the public sphere was a place where music could be used in an aggressive way to challenge and intimidate and thus it is not unusual for there to be a direct connection between music-making and violence. We have seen this in the context of elections and even on the floor of the House of Commons, but there was undoubtedly more blood spilled and resources of the State far more extensively engaged in that grey area where industrial action, processions and rallies shaded into riot and rebellion. Just as Lord Grenville had used the word 'terror' when describing a form of cultural intimidation (which included music close to the top of the list) of polite society in 1819, so too the word 'terror' came to lips of a correspondent during the General Strike which convulsed Britain in mid-1842. As a contingent of Chartist strikers passed through Castle Donnington en route to Birmingham, the reporter noted that they commenced singing a Chartist hymn 'much to the terror of the old ladies and nervous gentlemen, who secured their doors and fled into the cellars for safety, imagining that the "Revolution" was coming'. At the same time John Bright wrote hastily to Richard Cobden, fellow industrialist and leader of the Anti-Corn Law League, to relate the vaguely threatening sight (and sound) of 'several hundred women' at the gates of his house singing 'Chartist hymns'.[126]

As the battle lines were being drawn in Broken Hill in January 1909, the *Sydney Morning Herald* noted that even the so-called 'moral suasion' of a picket is generally intimidation of a pretty effective type and, as the *Sydney Mail* observed, a band playing helped a lot to turn out workers in support of the strike.[127] The miners also emulated the Chartist practice – soon proscribed – of undertaking 'monster' processions by torchlight accompanied by 'massed bands'.[128] On another occasion Premier Charles Wade, who had come out in support of the mine owners, was burned in effigy in the main street to the strains of *John Brown's Body* adapted to the task at hand: 'We'll burn old Wade on a sour apple tree', sang the crowd. Effigies of a blackleg and a police-man were also consumed.[129]

In fact, an outstanding example of the intimidatory power of music again emerges from an analysis of the Broken Hill lockout. As events unfolded in 1909 reports referred increasingly to the *Barrier Anthem*. But this song was no inspirational *Marseillaise*-like call-to-arms; on the contrary, it was a highly popular ragtime ditty, *Bill Bailey, Won't you Please Come Home*, penned in 1902 by Hughie Cannon.[130] The song was pressed into service simply because the unfortunate under-ground foreman at the Proprietary Mine was named Jim Bailey. Bailey attracted the ire of the miners because he agreed to give evidence before hearings of the Federal Arbitration Commission, which were held in Port Pirie, a seaport 200 kilometres north of Adelaide where the mining giant owned and operated a large smelting works. Bailey was often besieged at the mine gates and required constant police protec-tion. One miner wrote to the *Barrier Truth* suggesting words to be sung with the band while Bailey took refuge:

> Won't you come out, Jim Bailey?
> Won't you come out?
> Won't you come out come out to me?
> There's thousands of people waiting
> Down the street,
> Jimmy, your face to see.
> You know, Jim Bailey, you're doing wrong!
> You're not the man you ought to be![131]

In fact, there were several 'parodies upon Bill Bailey', which were played at strike concerts to the great amusement of the crowd. Indeed, it is important to ponder the effect of playing and performing an up-beat music-hall patter song on the affective dimension of a meeting: rather than a solemnity reflecting a bitter struggle, the meeting must have had, at least in part, a light and breezy atmosphere that brought a smile to the faces of those present. At the same time the use of *Bill Bailey* had a sinister edge. Under the heading 'The Charm of Music' one story (widely-syndicated throughout New South Wales) told of alarmed children disturbing a snake drinking water in their garden. While the children ran for help, the snake went into hiding:

A neighbour, however, with a knowledge of the influence of music on serpents, produced a concertina, and played the Barrier National Anthem ('Wont You Come Home, Bill Bailey') – The Snake reappeared and was killed.[132]

Although Bailey had travelled to Port Pirie surreptitiously, the miners were waiting for him; they induced the hotelier to vacate his room and at one point he was forced to take refuge in the prison.[133] The striking miners had not taken the AMA band with them. Fortunately, technology came to their aid in the form of the gramophone. The strikers had already been forced to confront this problem following Tom Mann's arrest and bail early in 1909. A condition of his bail was that he not give public speeches in New South Wales. Initially, the unions had circumvented this by what they called a 'unique enterprise' of organising rallies forty miles away where Mann could literally stand inches over the border in South Australia and address a crowd that remained in New South Wales.[134] His audience had travelled by train – known as the Tom Mann Express – but soon organisers realised that it would be easier to bring Mann to them.

In this case, however, their solution was not strictly an innovation. In the run-up to the November presidential election of 1908 William Taft and William Bryan had, for the first time in US politics, recorded their speeches to increase exponentially their ability to campaign wherever a gramophone was at hand.[135] A few short months later the Broken Hill strikers also enlisted the gramophone; in this case to evade the law. Early in February gramophone recordings were completed and subsequently played to crowds to great effect.[136] The mainstream press speculated that Mann was 'sailing close to the wind' in respect of his bail conditions and by 1914 another journal was lamenting that notwithstanding the fact that troublemakers such as Mann had been physically removed their voices lingered.[137] The AMA's decision to emulate the US presidential candidates was, moreover, undertaken simultaneously with another auditory innovation when they recorded the AMA Band, allowing it to be in two places at the one time.[138] In particular, a gramophone recording of the *Barrier Anthem* allowed the miners to serenade 'Bill' Bailey in Port Pirie. Bailey was understandably distraught at his rough treatment, telling the court that 'a gruesome fate awaited him if he dared leave his property'. After he left for South Australia one correspondent suggested that perhaps Bailey should not come home.[139]

Whether Bailey returned to Broken Hill is unclear, but he was not physically molested despite the vitriol directed against him. In this respect, he fared better than many bandsmen: being in the vanguard often put musicians at risk. As Mann recalled, on one celebrated occasion a large contingent of police attacked the picket relief column, broke the poles holding their banners and attacked the miners, including the bands.[140] Writing in 1880, Frank Peel recalled a serious melee in Halifax in 1842 when, as a ten-year-old, he had witnessed a very large crowd of women turn-outs standing 'in front of the magistrates and the military' daring 'them to kill them if they liked'. 'They then struck up THE UNION HYMN', he continued. 'Singing this stirring hymn they defiantly stood in their ranks as the special constables marched up, but their music did not save them, for the constables did not hesitate to strike them with their staves.'[141] The danger level increased exponentially as the conception of the conflict on the part of the State, and in some cases, the perpetrators slipped from strike and riot into sedition, subversion, rebellion and revolution. For some, music was portentous. For example, a young W. E. Gladstone, quoting Sir John Colbourne, told the House of Commons in 1838 that 'the game which M. Papineau is playing cannot be mistaken; and we must be prepared to expect, that if 400 or 500 persons are allowed to parade the streets of Montreal at night, singing revolutionary songs, the excited parties will come into collision.'[142] Within six months the colonial authorities responded, decreeing that 'any person found loitering in the streets, or on the footpaths, or pulling down papers posted up, or whistling or singing, or causing a disturbance in the streets by screaming or crying out, should be sent to prison for a period not exceeding two months'.[143] Of course, this did nothing to prevent the bloody outbreak later that year. In this sense music was predictive. In other cases it was symbiotically connected to the crack of rifles and the unsheathing of sabres.

The details of the Massacre of Peterloo in 1819 do not require rehearsal but it is important to note that the tragedy was bookended by music. According to the harrowing account by the well-known weaver-poet Samuel Bamford, the contingent from his native Middleton set off on their fateful four-mile march to Manchester to the strains of an 'excellent band' and animated by dancing and singing by the 'handsomest girls and sweethearts to the lads who were with us'. They later took their place in the massive crowd (estimated at 70,000–80,000) assembled on St Peter's Fields in Manchester. As is well known the denouement of the meeting was the vicious and unprovoked assault by the Yeomanry Cavalry – armed gentlemen on horseback, to borrow E. P. Thompson's famous characterisation – which included not only attacking the crowd indiscriminately but also a systematic attempt to destroy the radicals' banners and, as Bamford recalled, their instruments. 'On the first advance of the Yeomanry', he recalled, 'one of the horses plunging at the crowd, set its fore-feet into the head of our big drum' and it was 'kicked to pieces in the melee'.[144] The conservative *Morning Post* reported the scene for its metropolitan audience: 'The Caps of Liberty, and the standards of sedition, were instantly torn down, and the confusion created was almost beyond description; hats, clubs, shoes, handkerchiefs, and instruments of music lay scattered and broken in every direction.'[145] Ever defiant, however, Bamford noted that the contingent of 1,000 surviving radicals from Middleton marched home to the 'sound of fife and drum', their only remaining banner waving.[146]

The tumult in Glasgow during 1848 displays the range of musically inflected action at a moment of crisis. The *Glasgow Examiner* reported that among the bands of armed rioters looting shops and small business in the streets of Scotland's largest city, some sang 'the Marselles [sic]' and proclaimed '"Vive are the Publics" (elegant French)'. Weeks later the massive crowd assembling for a Chartist protest meeting on Glasgow Green, the epicentre of demotic politics in the city, were entertained by numerous bands marching around the periphery. When the Chartist platform party sought to commence the meeting with a rendition of the *Scotch Marseillaise*, however, apparently very few among the estimated 50,000 present joined in.[147] 'This attempt at imitating the French', noted the reporter, 'turned out a melancholy affair'. The Tory press was quick to scoff at both episodes: the malcontents were insufficiently familiar with the contrafactum to sing along or even how to correctly pronounce the song's original title. They clearly missed the point. The participants knew (however imperfectly) by a process of audiation that the *Marseillaise* represented sonically a set of values, aspirations and intent. The relationship was thus highly complex and warrants far more than a sneer. Three case studies provide an opportunity to explore more systematically the symbiosis between music and musical behaviour and rebellion and revolution.

'Sing a Song of Sixpence'

Sing a song of sixpence a bag full of lies,
Four and twenty witnesses all prov'd to be Spies,
Before the bag was open the Ministers began to sing,
There we have a dainty dish to set before the King.
But when the bag was opened the Lords began to stare,
To see their precious evidence vanish into air.[148]

Published in 1820, *A BOTTLE OF SMOAK or a Song of Sixpence* was a none-too-subtle adaption of the traditional nursery rhyme *Sing a Song of Sixpence*. It was designed to highlight the government's discomfiture as their attempts to discredit the popular Queen Caroline and thereby secure a divorce for the corpulent and profligate George IV fell apart. In 1889 the striking London dockworkers dipped into the same cultural reservoir:

Sing a song of sixpence,
Dockers on the strike.

Guinea pigs are hungry,
As the greedy pike.
Till the docks are opened,
Burns will speak for you.
Courage lads, and you'll win,
Well within the week.[149]

The crude play on the words 'guinea pig' and the reference to the large predatory fish known for choking itself to death by excessive gorging – thus a traditional euphemism for rapacity – are relatively straightforward. Moreover, given that the dockworkers' principal demand was for an increase in the minimum hourly rate from 5d. to 6d., their choice of song to use as a contrafactum seems particularly apposite.

What is far less obvious, however, is that the original words of the rhymes themselves could be deeply political. As the *Literary Gazette* commented in 1847, 'Nursery Rhymes are not the modern nonsense some folks may pronounce them to be. They illustrate the history and manners of the people for centuries.' 'Here, for instance,' the essayist continued, 'is a relic in the form of a nursery rhyme, but in reality part of a political song, referring to the rebellious times of Richard the Second':

'My father he died, I cannot tell how,
But he left me six horses to drive out my plough!
With a wimmy lo! wommy lo! Jack Straw, blazey-boys!
Wimmy lo! wommy lo! wob, wob, wob!'

The author's point was that by the 1840s it was not well understood that Jack Straw had been a contemporary pseudonym for Wat Tyler, leader of the Peasants' Revolt in 1381, an episode that fascinated nineteenth-century radicals from a youthful Robert Southey to William Morris. For the latter, the tale warranted ballads sung to a 'sweet wild melody'.[150]

Sing a Song of Sixpence is a case where the political message was entirely encoded and thus available only to the initiated. According to Charles Mackay, the 'lines are political and written in the time of the Commonwealth to a popular melody'. The Cavaliers had introduced the song 'even in the cradle' to cement the 'loyalty of the children'. The assumption, of course, is that the children would simultaneously imbibe the code. 'The pocket full of rye is a correct allusion to the fugitive monarch, who made his escape at Horsham, very near Rye, after the battle of Worcester,' Mackay revealed. 'The blackbirds, who were so ignominiously cooked up' were the 'Roundhead regicides forming, indeed, a very "dainty dish" when cut up "to set before a king".'[151] Thus, in *Redgauntlet*, published in 1824, Sir Walter Scott depicts a number of prominent Jacobites sitting in a public house singing coded rebel songs, notwithstanding the fact that the clientele included a number of Redcoats who were entirely oblivious to the sedition in the room.[152]

'The patriotic in music': Britons never, never shall be slaves[153]

If melody and song could be used to create an auditory veil that obscured sedition, there were other equally effective instrumental roles that music and music-making played in rebellion and revolution. An examination of the agitation on the goldfields in central Victoria, which culminated in the rebellion at Eureka in December 1854, offers an example of how music could summarise one of the core issues and direct our attention to its ideological underpinnings. What began as a peaceful protest movement led by Chartist émigrés and conducted according to their political repertoire – petitions, 'monster meetings' and furious oratory – culminated with a bloody attack by British troops on armed miners in a makeshift stockade. The wider protest movement demanded democratic reform and an end to the oppressive regime of taxing miners as enumerated in a hybrid version of the People's Charter. The familiar phrase 'No Taxation Without Representation' was a capsule statement of their demands. Much as with the Chartists in 1839, a faction prepared to resort to 'physical force' emerged. These men – a collection of Irish, British, Americans and Europeans – armed themselves, built a fortalice, swore allegiance to a rebel flag (the Southern Cross) and awaited the inevitable assault. Australia's 'little revolution', as it has been called, has produced numerous songs (mainly since the 1890s).[154] At the time, however, two musical incidents resonate. These can be heard thanks to the account of the rebellion penned by one of its participants, Raffaello Carboni, published in 1855. Carboni had been an active member of the Young Italy Movement and was seriously wounded in the Rome campaigns of 1849 before migrating to Melbourne in 1852 to mine for gold. He brought with him a talent for languages, a literary disposition and a harp. Awaiting trial for high treason, Carboni penned 'Victoria's Southern Cross', the name given to the flag of independence that flew over the palisades of the stockade, weaving it into an homage to Peter Lalor, the leader of the rebellion:

> For brave Lalor –
> Was found 'all there'
> With dauntless dare:
> His men inspiring:
> To wolf or bear,

Defiance bidding,
He made them swear –
Be faithful to the Standard, for victory or death.[155]

Lalor's Irishness (he was a brother of James Fintan Lalor, a veteran of
the 1848 rebellion) did not influence Carboni's choice of music, opting,
as he did, for *The Warrior Bard, or the Standard Bearer*, composed by
the German, Peter Josef von Landpainter, and translated in 1847 by
an American, W. F. Brough. The lyrics suited the events in Victoria's
golden triangle and clearly appealed to Carboni's self-image as a
musical chronicler-cum-freedom fighter:

The night is past, the conflict's come with dawn,
The minstrel knight has seen its fortifying;
'Midst the death and carnage onward still are borne,
His song is heard 'midst thousands around him dying.

Stern death now sated quits the gory-lain,
The lifeblood from the warrior-bard is streaming;
While on his flag he rests his head with pain,
And faintly sings his eyes with fervor beaming.[156]

The fact that Carboni was not actually in the stockade when the troop-
ers attacked was obviously not allowed to get in the way of a good
story.

Carboni's first mention of music in his account, however, comes by
way of complaint, specifically about the number of diggers incessantly
singing *Rule, Britannia*: 'DO NOT LET the word "British" become
a bye-word', he pleaded, 'AND ABOVE ALL LEAVE OFF SINGING
"Britons never, never shall be slaves" until you leave fondling the
chains which prove the song a lie, a mockery, a delusion, a snare'.[157]
What do we make of this? *Rule, Britannia* was written in 1740 for
an aristocratic musical essaying Alfred the Great, but it soon gained
a broader audience, including politicians of all stripes. Almost from
the first time it was performed in London in 1745 it attracted contrafacta, beginning with the Jacobites.[158] By the nineteenth century the
tune had been pressed into service many times. From his prison cell,
Bamford, 'the Burns of Lancashire', used it for the basis of a paean to
the people's favourite, Queen Caroline:

To Caroline we'll tune the sring [shepherd's flute],
In music we will sound her praise,
With heart-felt loyalty we'll sing
God bless our Gracious Queen always!
Rejoice, ye Britons, ye Britons, all rejoice
And bless our Queen with heart and voice.[159]

[198]

A version in the *Commonweal* in 1891 employed the tune for class struggle:

> When Labour first in strength awoke,
> And smote to break the galling chain,
> No self-linked fetters stayed the stroke,
> But rebel workers sung this strain –
> Rule, O masters, henceforward in your graves!
> We will never, never, never more be slaves.[160]

But alternate lyrics were not always necessary, even for radicals. Indeed, few radicals would have disagreed with the core libertarian sentiment: Britons never, never shall be slaves. For some, this meant the song could be appropriated in its original form into an oppositional repertoire. As *Reynolds' News* noted in its report of the massive celebration of the victory in the London Dock Strike in 1889: 'The music was eloquent of a victory won':

> The 'Marseillaise', 'God save Ireland,' and 'Rule Britannia' were the *pièces de résistance*, the latter played with a big drum *fortissimo* at 'Britons never, never shall be slaves'.[161]

Similarly, at a massive torchlight parade culminating in a public meeting in front of the Victorian Legislative Assembly in June 1858 those gathered to demand political reform and access to land were serenaded by bands playing the *Marseillaise, Mourir pour la Patrie, Partant pour la Syrie, Yankee Doodle, St Patrick's Day* and *Rule, Britannia*. The report underscored the fact that *Rule, Britannia* was being appropriated by noting what was not played: '"The "National Anthem" was frequently called for by foolishly loyal people at the outskirts of the crowd', the journalist records, 'but was not performed.'[162] Following the execution in 1885 of Louis Riel, the leader of the Métis rebellion in Red River, a crowd of Québécois burned an effigy of the Prime Minister of the Canadian Federation, John MacDonald, to the strains of the *Marseillaise* at the base of Queen Victoria's statue in Montreal.[163]

On other occasions, however, the use of *Rule, Britannia* in a radical context – original lyrics and melody – points not to appropriation but to an insistence on a higher loyalty expressed within a monarchical framework. The transcript of the trial of Henry Hunt published in the aftermath of Peterloo, for example, includes testimony from several witnesses that the assembling radicals were singing *Rule, Britannia* and *God Save the King*, heads bared out of respect. It would be a mistake to underestimate what has been called popular constitutionalism-cum-monarchism among radicals. With reference to the original context, Alfred the Great was to become a favourite for generations of radicals and reformers. For example, Carboni's fellow scribe Ebenezer

Syme, who was co-editor of the miners' colonial Chartist newspaper, the *Diggers' Advocate*, lauded Alfred in public lectures as a man of 'character complete on every side': his many achievements included establishing 'tribunals of justice' and he 'completed a new code of laws'. Picking up the theme of the anthem, Syme also noted that the Great King 'made a first effort at a defense of England by sea'.[164]

Beyond this there is ample evidence that many Chartists, radicals, reformers and even socialists subscribed to a form of popular constitutionalism in which a 'good' monarch could be celebrated or mourned. Upon the death of Edward VII in 1910, to take one example, a crowded meeting of suffragists, in the teeth of a bitter struggle against Asquith's Liberal government, gathered in Prince's Hall in London to hear the redoubtable New Zealander Anna Stout speak. 'Let not the public imagine we do not feel the loss of our beloved King less than other people,' wrote one correspondent: 'On the contrary. Everyone was in black – even the most militant young Pankites were without their purple and green. Before the speaking commenced, we stood as one while the "Dead March in Saul" was played as a mark of respect to the memory of the dead Monarch.'[165] In these circumstances singing *Rule, Britannia* (or *God Save the King*) could be part of a claim to a higher loyalty; a claim to the time-honoured 'Rights of the Free Born Briton' on behalf of Britons and against their governors.[166] Unsurprisingly, in 1851 reformers in Hobart (opposed to the transportation of convicts to the Australian colonies) sang *God Save the Queen* as they burned effigies of Her Majesty's Secretary of State for Colonial Affairs, Earl Grey, and the Queen's representative in Tasmania, Governor William Denison; in the aftermath of the rising in Upper Canada in 1837–38 William Lyon McKenzie, the 'firebrand' leader of the rebellion, published *God Save the Queen* in his eponymous gazette; when eight suffragettes were released on bail following what was described as an 'attack on the House of Commons' in 1908 their supporters sang *Rule, Britannia*.[167] And, Louis Riel took an oath of loyalty to Queen Victoria following his election to the Canadian House of Commons in 1874.[168] For all his fulmination and earache, even Carboni could not ultimately resist the trope, incorporating into the final stanza of his anthem:

> The Southern Cross will float again the same,
> UNITED BRITONS, Ye are OMNIPOTENT.[169]

At Eureka music points us directly to the keystone of an overarching constitutionalist framework. By listening to the singing at the barricades we can hear not only what the *Glasgow Examiner* sneeringly referred to as radical efforts to offer 'the patriotic in music' – dismissing it as cynical appropriation – but also a chorus underpinned by a purer loyalty. When they sang 'Britons never, never shall be slaves', they meant it.[170]

A night with the Kellys

Three decades after the smell of cordite from the miners' rebellion in Ballarat dissipated, we find another example from the colony of Victoria which ties the previous two case studies together by highlighting the way that 'patriotic' music could at one and the same time be employed as a cloak, a proclamation and as what we would nowadays call a public relations strategy. In a previous chapter we have seen the power of *The Wearing of the Green* (including the original lyrics) when used in a political contest remote in time and place. In the Australian colonies the melody most famously attracted new words to tell the story of the anti-authoritarian exploits of a fictional bushranger named Jack Doolan or Duggan – *The Wild Colonial Boy*:

O come along, me hearties, and we'll roam the mountains high –
Together we will plunder, together we will die.
We'll wander over valleys and we'll gallop over plains,
And we'll scorn to live in slavery, bound down by iron chains.[171]

Doolan, however, was less of a rebel than a cocky larrikin. But the song's political potential was easily exploited. For example, its title (together with the original tune) was pressed into service by striking shearers in Queensland during the 1891 depression:

'So it's come along, me hearties,
Let's all do as we like,
Since shearin's worse than slavery
Let Union shearers strike
We'll rob the lordly squatter
And his flocks we will destroy,
For we're heroes with the nurse-girls,'
Said the wild colonial boy.

'Bring forth the loud stage thunder,
High let the red flag fly,
Though we saw – we'll ne'er sawrender;
Though we run we'll ne'er die.
Then shout me lusty 'ringers;'
Your deliverance is nigh
For I'm bustin' up the empire,'
Said the wild colonial boy.[172]

The association of the song with union politics reverberated as far as Canada where, presumably, the name Jack Doolan meant nothing. A

[201]

socialist songster, first published in 1902 in Buchans, Newfoundland, told the story of a 'bold young Union boy named Don Head' set to the tune.[173]

Arguably the first recorded performance of the song in Australia was when it featured in popular accounts of the feats of the notorious Kelly Gang. Opinion was divided on Edward 'Ned' Kelly and his coadjutors. For many, the son of an Irish convict was an 'execrable miscreant', a 'manslayer and thief' who, among other crimes, murdered three policemen. For others, the activities of the Kelly Gang had the patina of 'rebellion'. Here was a colonial rebel who stood up to the tyranny of a venal government enforced by an unscrupulous and corrupt police force. Kelly's manifesto – a rambling screed known as the 'Jerilderie Letter' – invoked *The Wearing of the Green* and, indeed, the song was closely associated with his legend. According to the account written by one of hostages who survived the gang's infamous siege in a hotel at Glenrowan in central Victoria in 1880, which ended with Kelly's arrest (and the death of the remainder of his gang), there was singing and dancing involving captives and captors: 'the redoubtable concertina was brought into requisition, and with the player perched upon a chair in the corner of the room from where he dispensed crude music'. During the siege, one of the hostages remembered, Ned's brother Dan 'gave us a sample of his vocal abilities in the shape of a song about the Kelly gang'. The song was written by a member of the gang, Joe Byrne. The hostage continued: 'I only remember one verse of it which is as follows; tune Wearing of the Green':

> Oh, Paddy, and did you hear the news that's going round?
> On the head of bold Ned Kelly they have placed ten thousand pound;
> On Hart, and Joe Byrne a similar they'll give;
> But though the sum was doubled, sure the Kelly boys would live.[174]

Other accounts suggested that Ned and Dan also sang *The Wearing of the Green* itself.[175]

The Kelly legend was undoubtedly promulgated by music and music-making. This was true of *The Wild Colonial Boy* more broadly. As one commentator noted, rendering Doolan's exploits in verse – 'set to a melancholy air' – created a song which became a 'favourite with every stockman and boundary-rider between the Darling Downs and the Wombat Ranges'.[176] At least half a dozen Kelly songs were penned before 1900 and, according to oral tradition, the police often attempted to prevent them being sung as they were 'treason songs'.[177] Linking the Kelly Gang's activities to *The Wearing of the Green* certainly would have helped to valorise and for some legitimise them.

'Our comrades within the walls'[178]

The dock provided activists with an almost uniquely uncensored (if understudied) platform to express their views, and 'speeches from the dock' became a popular genre found in books, newspaper columns and performed on stage. *The Trial of Robert Emmett* was undoubtedly the best-known example of the latter for most of the nineteenth century. A measure of potency of the practice was the restrictions put on it in some cases. Kelly, for example, did not speak; Riel, on the other hand, did.[179] Far rarer are examples of singing in court. Perhaps the outstanding example when the dramaturgy of a speech from the dock was combined with music-making was the trial of Emmeline Pankhurst in April 1913. Before she was sentenced to three years' imprisonment for malicious damage (blowing up Lloyd George's house), Pankhurst gave a defiant address during which she was frequently interrupted by the judge insisting upon restraint. Pankhurst was planning a hunger strike – not for the first time – and thus there was no false gravitas when she suggested that a custodial sentence might be tantamount to sending her to her death.

What is less well known is that as the recalcitrant activist was taken down her followers turned the august institution into an oppositional music hall by taunting the judge with a chorus of *For He's a Jolly Good Fellow*. And, as they marched out, Pankhurst's cadre sang what was known as their *War-Chant*, *War-Song*, *March On!*, or to give it its correct title, the *Women's Marseillaise*.[180] The chorus was apposite for the occasion:

> To Freedom's cause till death
> We swear our fealty.
> March on! March on! Face to the dawn
> The dawn of liberty.
> March on! March on! Face to the dawn
> The dawn of liberty.[181]

Pankhurst recalled that it was 'absolute pandemonium': 'The Judge flung after their retreating forms the dire threat of prison for any women who dared repeat such a scene.' 'The women's song only swelled the louder', she remembered, 'and the corridors of the Old Bailey reverberated with their shouts.' She had a sense of history in the making: 'Certainly that venerable building had never in its checkered history witnessed such a scene.'[182]

The spectacle was repeated in Glasgow in October when Dorothea Smith and Margaret Morrison were sentenced to eight months' imprisonment for attempting to set fire to a house. As the verdict was pronounced, their supporters in the packed courtroom pelted the judge

[203]

with 'apples and other missiles' and 'bundles of suffragist literature were hurled at counsel's table'. The police sought to quell the disorder, noted one horrified reporter, resulting in numerous 'exciting scuffles' and 'the chorus of a suffragist song was sung to the "Marseillaise" with great gusto'. Accounts of this episode flashed around the Anglophone world – from Manawatu to Kalgoorlie – although by this stage the song was simply reported as the *Marseillaise* without any reference to lyrics dedicated to the cause. As with the Glasgow Chartists half a century previously, undoubtedly it didn't matter.[183]

Pankhurst's brutal experience of incarceration – shared by more than 1,000 suffragists – was one common across time and distance and one in which music-making offered a shard of comfort and an avenue for ongoing resistance. Commentary about the incarceration of radicals and reformers – among contemporaries and historians alike – is underpinned by two well-worn tropes: that they often found prison an opening for study otherwise denied to them and that solitude provided a platform for creative endeavour.[184] Even the harshest conditions could not thwart the exercise of the life of the mind. Of dubious authenticity as it might be, Ernest Jones's claim among the Chartists that he wrote poetry in his own blood (including, as we have seen, the enduring radical canticle, *Song of the 'Lower Classes'*) is matched by Thomas Cooper's determination to commit his original versifying to memory: 'I thought I could defeat their purpose by composing a poem and retaining it in my mind,' he recalled.[185]

For radicals the cell was also an opportunity to compose and perform music. Carboni contrived his anthem awaiting trial for treason: 'Thus I spanned the strings of my harp', he wrote, 'but the strain broke them asunder in the gaol.'[186] At the height of the Wellington miners' strike, the well-known Australian socialist H. E. Holland composed *The Burden of our Song*, set to the southern gospel song, *Beulah Land*, from his cell. Here was a rousing panegyric of defiance for those continuing the struggle:

> O, workers of all Maoriland,
> As one big union firmly stand,
> Through bolted door and prison's bar
> Shines Freedom's light that gleamed star!
> O, comrades, be ye brave and strong
> And stand united 'gainst the wrong.[187]

Well over a century earlier, in 1794, Thomas Spence incorporated the act of composition into the musical narrative of his incarceration in London's infamous Newgate Prison. To be set to a traditional merry jig, *Maid of the Mill*, Spence wrote:

As for me though in Prison I oft have been cast
Because I would dare to be free
And though in black Newgate I did pen this song
My theme I've not alter'd you see.
In jail or abroad whatever betide
My Struggles for Freedom shall be
Whatever Fate bring I will think, speak and sing,
The Rights of Man Boys for me.[188]

Alongside composition was custodial performance. Bamford's first brush with the law in 1817, for example, was accompanied by music-making at every stage. During the journey to London in leg irons to face a possible charge of high treason, he and his fellow prisoners sang through the night. The sound of pieces of 'solemnity and pathos', he recalled, 'brought the singing parties of our own homes to our recollection.' And, later, when confined to a cell in Coldbath Fields, they 'spent the evening in conversing about our families and friends' and at the 'hour of rest' they concluded by singing his *The Union Hymn*:

Oh! worthy is the glorious cause,
Ye partiers of the union;
Our fathers' rights, our fathers' laws,
Await a faithful union.
A crouching dastard sure is he
Who would not strive for liberty,
And die to make Old England free
From all her load of tyranny;
Up! Brave men of the union.[189]

A generation later R. G. Gammage recalled the first hours following his arrest: 'I laid myself down that night on a hard mattress, but not to sleep, for I could not get a wink, so I rose up and sang the song of my friend, John Leatherland: – Base oppressors, leave your slumbers.'[190] Many years later again, Pankhurst, weak from a hunger strike, wiled away the hours in her cell at night feebly singing Ethel Smyth's *March of the Women* and *Laggard's Dawn*.[191] Music-making may well have been good for the soul, a means of fortifying individual resolve and an act of temerity; it also provided succour for those within earshot and aided communication between prisoners. In her memoirs Pankhurst provides an example of this in operation: 'The remand prisoners demanded that I be allowed to exercise with them, and when this was not answered they broke the windows of their cells. The other suffrage prisoners, hearing the sound of shattering glass, and the singing of the Marseillaise, immediately broke their windows.'[192] Perhaps the most vivid example of the collective place of music within the prison walls comes again from the annals of the suffragists. As 400 of her fellow prisoners stomped around the exercise yard singing her most famous suffragist composition – *The March of the Women* – Ethel Smyth was reputed to have conducted them with a toothbrush from a window above.[193]

The sound of music was equally important outside the prison walls. In much the same way as it provided succour and affirmation to pickets and strikers more generally, sound provided an aural canopy for those in the hands of the State. Indeed, the *Barrier Times* noted in February 1909 that after marching to the gaol the combined bands had 'proceeded to encircle this modern Jericho' (quipping that the walls had not fallen, probably because they had not circled it seven times). The 'music of the combined bands must have penetrated the capitalist stockade', the editor confidently predicted. The recently sentenced prisoners, ran another report, would know 'by the presence of the band in that vicinity, and the chorus from a thousand throats, that they were not likely to be forgotten'. A correspondent for the *Sydney Morning Herald* made much the same point to the journal's unsympathetic readership by conceding that the sound of the music must comfort the prisoners. A souvenir postcard produced by the AMA captures a Sunday procession to the gaol on 14 February 1909 (see figure 4.1). As can be seen, the march is headed by the band of approximately twenty-five musicians who do not wear uniforms; they are followed by an extensive phalanx of supporters disappearing into the distance and are flanked by children, some carrying parasols against the fierce kiss of the sun. The inscription on the rear of the card tells us somewhat prosaically that the band is marching with the intention of cheering up the unionists in captivity (and, notably, it indicates that the postcard had been purchased from the union photographer just over a week after the event had unfolded) (see figure 4.2). Taken together the two sides of the card tell us much: it is a snapshot of an episode – visual and sonic – in which there is a shared understanding of the primary purpose as well as an opportunity to raise funds; that it involved not only performers, marchers and prisoners but also the broader community.

At least one of the strike organisers felt that '[s]erenading our comrades in gaol', as it was called, had 'never before been witnessed in Australia'.[194] This may well have been true in Australia but it was not with respect to Britain. In fact, using singing to communicate from either side of the foreboding walls of stone was almost venerable by antiquity. In the 1770s, for example, Sir John Hawkins had recounted the story of Richard I's faithful minstrel Blondel serenading the King, captured on his return from the Holy Lands, and of Richard's response in kind, leading to a mutual composition notwithstanding the bars between them. This tale was republished in the 1820s and 1830s.[195]

4.1 A postcard showing the AMA band marching to the gaol in Broken Hill in February 1909 to support the imprisoned miners' union leaders during the protracted lockout of 1909. Image: 'Procession to the Gaol [Broken Hill], Sunday, Feb. 14[?] 1909'.

Nevertheless, it must be said that in Broken Hill, taken together with the escort provided at every changing of the pickets, the contribution of radical and trade union bands was extraordinarily tenacious and deserving of a special place in the annals of struggle during the long nineteenth century. There is no evidence that the suffragists benefitted from their example but they too used music to create a sonic connection with their myrmidons within. At the gates of London's Holloway Prison, for example, they kept up a vigil (described by the press as 'picket duty'), which was bolstered by marchers with bands playing the *Marseillaise* and the *Women's March*, 'their object being to encourage the Suffragette prisoners still confined'.[196] The crucial point is that although the bands and choirs were not in sight of 'victims' of the State they *were* within earshot. Sound could do what sight could not. The facility to establish an aural interdependence between those inside and outside places of confinement highlights again one of the key themes of this book: music's capacity to mediate the relationship between the individual and the collective.

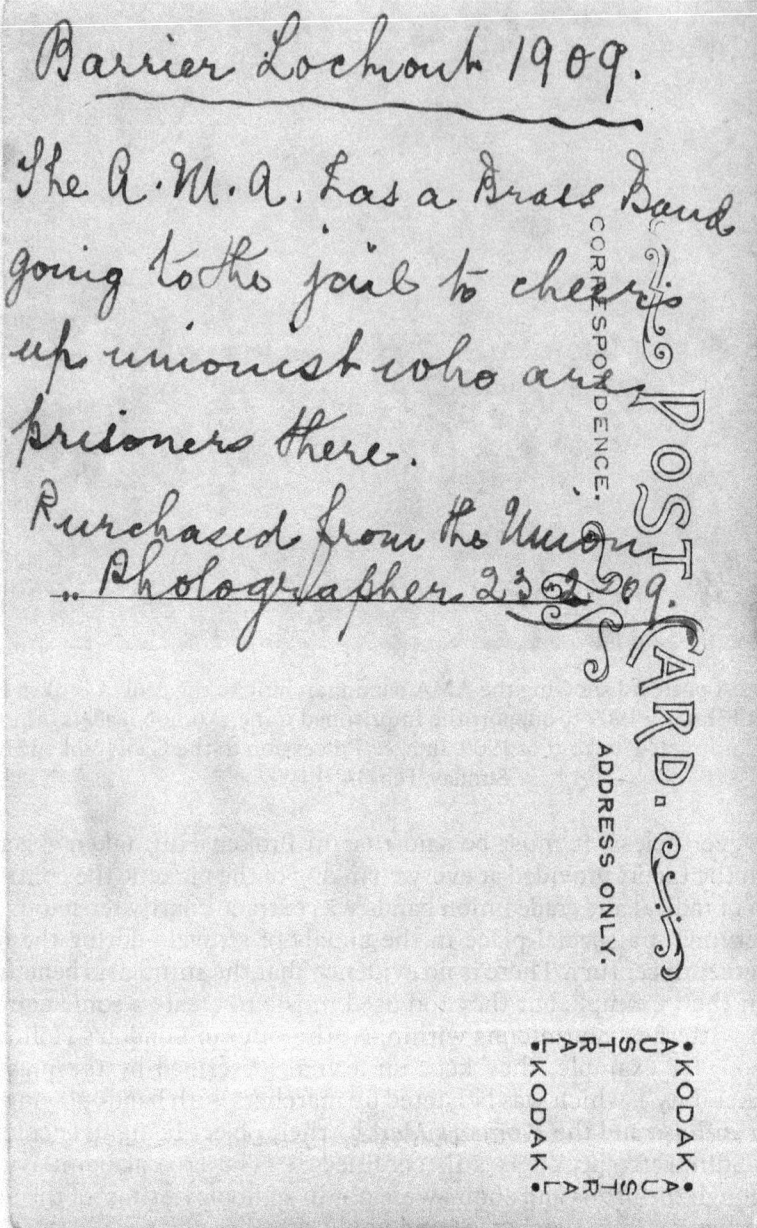

4.2 The inscription on the reverse of the postcard reads: 'The A.M.A. has a Brass Band going to the jail to cheer up unionist [sic] who are prisoners there. Purchased from the Union Photographer 23 2 09'. Image: 'Procession to the Gaol [Broken Hill], Sunday, Feb. 14[?] 1909'.

For many radical prisoners incarceration ended with a collective celebration tinctured with defiance and enlivened by a statement in musical shorthand. Henry Hunt's 'triumphal entry' into London in 1822, for example, involved banners, an ornate coach and two bands playing the *National Anthem*; when in January 1913 Arthur Doyle was released from Mount Eden Prison in Auckland where he had been held for his part in the Waihi miners' strike he was treated to a smoke, a haircut and a jollification replete with 'toasts drunk with enthusiasm and musical honours'. Doyle himself contributed to the programme of songs, which concluded collectively with *The Red Flag*.[197] Similarly, when John Frost arrived at the 'immense demonstration' in Todmorden to be welcomed home after sixteen years transportation by the radicals of Yorkshire and Lancashire he was serenaded by an apposite Chartist hymn, *Great God, is this the Patriot's Doom?* and the universally serviceable *See, the Conquering Hero Comes*. In London, Frost was welcomed by a brass band playing *Partant pour la Syrie*. In this case, however, it was Frost's detractors that opted for a musical precis: the editor of *Lloyd's London Daily* quipped that, given Frost's politics, *Ça Ira* would have been more appropriate.[198]

Some radical prisoners (as we shall see) died silently in custody; for a few political prisoners, however, their period of imprisonment terminated abruptly at the end of a rope. In common parlance hanging was sometimes referred to as the 'jig without music', but even at this moment, which represented the most extreme intersection of oppositional politics and the authority of the State, music could be present. According to several accounts, before Kelly was hanged in November 1880 he wiled away the precious time in his cell singing. His repertoire was apparently 'ribald songs'. Without needing to explore the complex relationship between rebellion and banditry – essayed eloquently by Eric Hobsbawm, among others[199] – the fact that Kelly did not sing of rebellion does not necessarily suggest that his career had less to do with politics than plunder. By singing while facing death Victoria's rebel-cum-murderous thug was not alone. When seven leaders of the machine-breakers or 'Luddites', the so-called followers of 'Ned Ludd', were led to the gallows at York in January 1813 they sang a 'well-known hymn' based on Psalm 63:

> Behold the Saviour of mankind
> Nail'd to the shameful tree!
> How vas the love that Him inclined
> To bleed and die for me.[200]

Writing in the 1880s, Frank Peel, one of West Yorkshire's pioneering antiquaries and oral historians, noted that despite relentless and savage official persecution (and thus a time when the need for anonymity was at a premium), the Luddites often publically proclaimed their cause by singing. He recounts an impromptu performance of the *Cropper's Song* by John Walker, 'a true specimen of the old rollicking race of croppers', in a public house in the hamlet of Hightown:

> And night by night when all is still
> And the moon is hid behind the hill,
> We march forward and do our will
> With hatchet, pike and gun!
> Oh, the cropper lads for me,
> The gallant lads for me,
> Who with lusty stroke
> The shear frames broke
> The cropper lads for me!

'Long before Walker had come to the end of his song', Peel wrote, 'the rollicking chorus was eagerly caught up by his delighted audience, and when the end was reached the refrain was twice repeated with extraordinary vigour, many of the men beating time on the long table with their sticks and pewter mugs.'[201]

The fact that the song was an easily identifiable contrafactum of a popular contemporaneous ballad, *The Gallant Poacher*, highlights again the nexus between radical protest and criminality. The point here, however, is that it was the Luddites themselves who were making the connection by effectively adding poaching – albeit at one remove – to their list of offences. It is not surprising that they should do so. Poaching in blackface was, as E. P. Thompson has famously shown, an act of defiance at the core of the early eighteenth-century popular resistance to what was seen an encroachment on the people's right to hunt deer and poach hares in the King's forests. The Waltham Black Act (1723) was one of an increasing number of legislative attempts to protect 'private property' irrespective of popular rights enshrined in custom attached to it.[202]

As noted, some of the Luddites sang hymns as they awaited the noose. Unlike Kelly and the Luddites, however, singing on the gallows could be a decidedly political final act. The most famous example of this within the annals of the labour movement was undoubtedly the execution of the 'anarchists' – George Engel, Adolf Fischer, August Spies and Albert Parsons – speciously found guilty of involvement in the explosion of an incendiary device at an eight-hour day rally in Chicago in 1886. Their execution in November 1887 resonated around the Anglophone world and remained a source of bitterness for decades. As H. E. Holland ranted in the Australasian *International Socialist* in 1910, these men had died on the 'gallows-trees of Capitalism'. Prior to the execution, Holland recounted, 'while the carpenters hammered away at their work of scaffold building', Parsons spent his final hours singing the Scottish folk song *Annie Laurie*.[203] Reputed to be Keir Hardie's favourite song, *Annie Laurie* is a lament for lost love, originally written in the 1740s. The song was entirely befitting of the coming event and had only the faintest echo of Jacobitism attached to it. On the scaffold, however, Parsons and his fellow hooded prisoners had overtly stood by their politics, defiantly singing the *Marseillaise*.

The use of unambiguously political music on the scaffold had also been explicit in the case of the so-called Cato Street Conspirators. As is well known, in February 1820 a plot to assassinate the British cabinet was uncovered, leading to thirteen arrests. The affair was controversial due to the significant role of agents provocateurs, but this did not save five of the conspirators who were hung, drawn and quartered in April. As several contemporary accounts made clear, one of the unfortunate radicals, Joseph Ings, used his final moments to sing 'in a hoarse voice' the familiar song *O Give Me Death or Liberty*.[204] The original lyrics had been published as early as 1780 in a collection of *English Songs, Duets & Cantatas*. The editor indicated that it had been part of a musical interlude titled 'The Election' by Miles Andrews (music composed by François-Hippolyte Barthélémon, a one time collaborator of David Garrick) in 1774.[205] Andrews was a client MP who vacillated between the Whigs and Tories but his lyrics would have appealed to anyone wedded to the trope of the rights of the free-born Briton:

> WHILE happy in my native Land,
> I boast my Country's Charter;
> I'll never basely lend my Hand,
> Her Liberties to barter ...
>
> Each free-born Briton's Song should be,
> 'Or give me Death or Liberty.'

This version appeared in 1783 in collection compiled by Joseph Ritson, but the version that the hapless Ings is likely to have known is that which appeared in *A Tribute to Liberty: Or a Collection of Selection Songs*, published in 1795. This contrafactum left nothing to the imagination, promising the guillotine for peers and that knights would be hung in garters:

> These despots long have trod us down,
> And judges are their engines,
> Such wretched minions of the crown
> Demand the people's vengeance.

Each patriot Briton's song will be
O give me death or liberty.[206]

Some executed rebels, such as Ned Kelly, were buried in unconsecrated ground without a funeral (when Kelly's was finally held 130 years later the cortege was headed by a lone piper).[207] Similarly, Samuel Lount and Peter Matthews were executed and dissected in Toronto for their role in the Upper Canada Rising in 1838 and buried beyond the sight of their families and coadjutors. Louis Riel's body, on the other hand, was released to his mother, albeit on the condition that there was no public event. This proscription was ignored. On the contrary, a major procession was held in St Vital, Winnipeg. Admittedly, the local press referred to it as a 'novel sight' but at the same time 'one that revived memories of days long gone by'. On the morning of the obsequies a crowd assembled at Riel's home, where his body had 'laid in state'. The Métis pallbearers carried Riel's casket six miles to St Boniface's churchyard. The local newspapers were particular interested in their attire, which comprised 'buffalo coats' and 'beaver caps and moccasins'. 'Red colored sashes encircled their waists' with a 'white sash across their shoulders and breast', the reporter continued. Riel's brothers – 'both stalwart specimens of their race' – headed the cortege, 'one wore a heavy buffalo coat the other an ordinary frieze coat'. Anticipating trouble, a guard of thirty 'half-breeds' marched alongside the bier. The service comprised a 'standard' requiem mass with the music provided by a conventional church choir as well as chants – presumably of Métis origin – described by the press as 'Gregorian'.[208]

For many more radicals death within prison was not at an appointed time, but as a result of the capriciousness of fate. These events gave rise to radicalised funereal rites in which music played a central role by providing a synoptic view of popular outrage and lamentation. Again, the composition and course of the rituals of martyrdom was strikingly similar across the Anglophone world. Joseph Mairs, for example, was one of fifty miners sent to prison in August 1913 for their involvement in the bitter miners' strike in Ladysmith on Vancouver Island, British Columbia, which had commenced the previous September. Mairs, a few days shy of his twenty-second birthday, died in captivity in January 1914. The ensuing public funeral, comprising a cavalcade of more than a mile in length, was headed by a brass band.[209]

Arguably the most famous funeral following the death of a radical in prison during the nineteenth century – in Britain at least – was that of Samuel Holberry, a Sheffield Chartist. Holberry had a brief efflorescence in the public eye in January 1840 when, in the wake of the Chartist rising in Newport, he was arrested for his part in a conspiracy to capture Sheffield Town Hall and burn the local military barracks. Sentenced to four years in prison, where he was subjected to the fashionable 'separate and silent' system, including extended periods on the treadmill, Holberry's health quickly began to fail and in June 1842 at age twenty-seven he died. Holberry's treatment had been a matter of public controversy – including in Parliament – and his death caused a sensation.[210] Memorial services for the 'Martyr to Liberty' were held in Chartist communities across Britain, but the principal 'Funeral of the Victim' took place in his native Sheffield. The organisers urged mourners to recall the motto 'Peace, Law and Order', refrain from intoxicating drink and 'observe that strict decorum which the solemnity of the occasion demands'.[211] A band playing the 'solemn air' of Ignaz Pleyel's *German Hymn* headed the procession. Some sources had – incorrectly – credited Pleyel with composing the *Marseillaise*; nevertheless, he certainly had composed numerous pieces for the French Republic in the 1790s, including a variation of *Ça Ira*. According to *Grove Music Online*, however, by the time of Holberry's internment the *German Hymn* was 'ubiquitous' and thus the selection was more likely a coincidence than a deliberate political statement.[212] The most notable musical element of Holberry's funeral occurred at the graveside. Here, a 'hymn composed for the occasion' by James Henry Bramwich, a Leicester Chartist, was distributed (critics alleged it was sold for a halfpenny) and sung by the mourners. Bramwich's lyric, set to a well-known sixteenth century hymn, the *Old Hundredth Psalm*, was caught somewhere between sentimentality, defiance and the prosaic:

> Great God! is this the Patriot's doom?
> Shall they who dare defend the slave,
> Be hurl'd with a prison's gloom,
> To fit them for an early grave?
>
> Is this the price of Liberty?
> Must Martyrs fall to gain the prize?
> Then be it so! we will be free.[213]

Encounters with the State involved an ever-present risk of dying for the cause. The Massacre of Peterloo, as we have seen, led to loss of life; indeed, death during clashes in the streets was not uncommon. These events often led to the performance of funerary rites, wherein music-making helped to encapsulate and sustain the tone, a template that, again, concatenated across space and time. The reports of the funeral procession (reputed to be one of the largest in the history of Auckland) for Frederick Evans, a worker caught up in a brutal clash during the Waihi strike in November 1912, could easily have appeared in the columns of a newspaper in Glasgow published fifty years previously or in Adelaide a few short weeks later.[214] When James Kavanagh died as a result of wounds sustained in the 'battle for freedom' on the streets of Toronto in December 1837, his comrades published a song entitled *The Widow's Woes* in his memory.[215]

Perhaps the most compelling fusion of scribal genius and a simple dirge was created in the aftermath of what became known as 'Bloody Sunday'. The rioting, which occurred in London's Trafalgar Square in November 1887, plucked Alfred Linnell from obscurity. Linnell was one of a crowd of 30,000–40,000 protesters gathered to demand an end to government coercion in Ireland and the release of the Irish MP William O'Brien. As the rally degenerated into a serious affray, Linnell was trampled by police horse and later died. His demise prompted comparisons with Peterloo and demands for a public funeral.[216] The subsequent event was much more than this. From newspaper accounts we witness a cultural extravaganza of sound and vision: from the sight of a vast assemblage of up to 200,000 mourners shoulder to shoulder against a backdrop of driving rain to an iconic engraving by Walter Crane on the facia of the printed memorial-slip ballad clutched by many present; from the reverberation of a socialist brass band playing the 'Dead March' in *Saul* to the mass singing of Linnell's *Death Song* with William Morris's text and music composed by Malcolm Lawson (best known for his arrangement of the Jacobite anthem *The Skye Boat Song*). Morris's inspirational lyrics went hand in glove with Lawson's music, modulating from an evocation of the tragedy of the present in E minor to the optimism for the future expressed by a shift to the tonic major for the refrain:

> They will not learn; they have no ears to harken;
> They turn their faces from the eyes of fate;
> Their gay-lit halls shut out the skies that darken.
> But lo! this dead man knocking at the gate.
>
> Not one, not one, nor thousands must they slay,
> But one and all if they would dusk the day.[217]

The editor of the hostile *Aberdeen Weekly Journal* complained about endless 'weeping black ink' over Linnell's decease. He had a point: accounts of the funeral were spread far and wide – from Perth, Western Australia, to Boston, Massachusetts; from Wrexham, North Wales, to Tuapeka, New Zealand.[218] Unsurprisingly, the sound of Morris and Lawson's *Death Song* resonated too. Even in the sparsely populated Riverina district of south-western New South Wales the local paper treated its readers to the text in full.[219]

Morris and Lawson's melding of sorrow and hope is a reminder that radical funereal rites were part of a broader category of rituals of martyrdom, commemoration and revelry. The report in the *Northern Star* referred to Samuel Holberry's funeral as a 'celebration' – a word with a complex etymology denoting both pathos and joy. On the one hand, these rites served to renew collective anger by connecting the injustice of an unnecessary death and the purity of sacrifice (and even a signal defeat) with the abiding justness of the cause. At the same time they were festive – an affirmation of a positive link to the past and relevance to the present and the future. But if death (by misadventure or otherwise) was tinctured with ambiguity, birth was unequivocally a cause for celebration. Tom Paine's birthday, as we have seen, was a favourite for radicals and also for socialists. The *London Intelligencer*, edited by Robert Cooper, an Owenite socialist and notorious atheist, proclaimed a Paine birthday dinner in 1855 the 'greatest meeting ever held in Bradford'. The festivities included toasts and speeches by secularist luminaries, such as G. J. Holyoake and Cooper himself, and fifteen unnamed songs and recitations.[220] The Bradford commemoration, and the place of music-making in it, is typical of hundreds held in Britain during the long nineteenth century (and down to our own day), but this is true not just in Paine's native land but also throughout the Anglophone world. In Melbourne in 1874, for example, Paine's admirers gathered at Stutt's Hotel to enjoy speeches interspersed by songs; in Christchurch in 1896 a 'Grand Musical Programme by Full Orchestra' enlivened an anniversary lecture.[221]

During the first half of Queen Victoria's reign arguably the most common commemorations among radicals, particularly among working men in the north of England, were those devoted to Henry Hunt, the white-hatted hero-cum-victim of Peterloo. Joining the revellers at a November 1849 dinner in Ashton-under-Lyne, seventy-six years after Hunt's birth, allows us to make three points. The walls of Mr Dewsnap's pub in Victoria Street were decorated with oil paintings of the 'principal Chartist and republican characters', Hunt's family home and Peterloo. After the 'cloth was withdrawn' there was ample eating and drinking.[222] The evening's entertainment opened with a reading from Hunt's memoirs; the first toast to the immortal memory of Hunt was proposed by Samuel Walker, a right he claimed on the basis of the fact that this was the twenty-ninth anniversary he had attended in a row – a significant revelation for the historian to note about the continuity of cultural form. Fortunately, at least part of the musical repertoire was recorded: *In Wiltshire a Fair Child was Born; Ye Wealth Producers; Peterloo*, an original composition, by John Stafford, the Charlestown poet, 'being one of his own compositions after having been at the Peterloo massacre'; *Henry's Ghost*; *The Life and Death of Henry Hunt*; and *My Emmett's No More*.[223] The report concluded: 'Other songs, toasts and recitations were given in the course of the evening.'[224] Getting inside the episode further – in the Thompsonian sense – is difficult. We know that one of Stafford's songs, *The Life and Death of Henry Hunt*, was of long-standing notoriety, having featured in a Hunt birthday celebration a decade earlier.[225] And, of course, *My Emmett's No More* was a well-known Irish lament penned following his execution in 1803:

> O, Erin, my country, your glory's departed;
> For tyrants and traitors have stabbed thy heart's core;
> Thy daughters have laved in the streams of affliction,
> Thy patriots have fled, or lie stretched in their gore,
> Ruthless ruffians now prowl thro' thy hamlets forsaken,
> From pale hungry orphans their last morsel have taken;
> The screams of thy females no pity awaken;
> Alas! my poor country, your Emmett's no more.[226]

Most of the evening's repertoire, however – even those selections with names – is a form of intangible cultural heritage that is obscured by the dense mists of time. As Frank Peel lamented in the 1880s, many of the Luddites' 'rude home-spun songs' are 'now remembered only in disjointed fragments by the few old people who have a personal knowledge of those unhappy times'.[227]

The second point – one of the key observations made several times in our book thus far – is that we can join the celebration knowing that many of those present would understand our attempts to historicise the repertoire. Many would know the history of the songs they sang. For example, undoubtedly the song most often associated with Hunt was the rollicking ballad, composed in the immediate aftermath of the Peterloo massacre, *With Henry Hunt, We'll Go, We'll Go*:

> With Henry Hunt we'll go, we'll go,
> With Henry Hunt we'll go;
> We'll raise the cap of liberty,
> In spite of Nadin Joe.[228]

Those singing lustily would have done so with a combination of defiance and bemusement at what was essentially an act of appropriation and counter-aurality. They would have known that the song was a parody of a popular song devoted to Wellington:

> With Wellington we'll go, we'll go,
> With Wellington we'll go;
> For Wellington commanded
> On the Plains of Waterloo.

Some present might have also been aware that an earlier iteration of the song was a satire 'in ridicule of the American army' abroad in 1775 entitled *The Brags of Washington*. They may have also been familiar with the county-folk version, *A-Nutting We Will Go*.[229] Historicity was important. It can be seen in the endless convivial toasts, the choice of banner inscriptions – both of which often laid claim to a direct connection to the past – as well as the ubiquitous use of historical intertextual references in platform oratory. This was also true of music. As Sylvia Pankhurst recalled, suffragette events often included '[o]ld London cries, arranged after tremendous research by willing enthusiasts', which were 'delightfully sung'.[230]

Thirdly, it is abundantly clear that music-making not only helped to contextualise the purpose of the Hunt dinner but also served as a precis of both the ideas and the intention. Far from being surplus to requirements when measured against the extended oratorical contributions, music-making was supremely efficient in providing a form of musical shorthand to help the process of ideation. This was particularly the case when the challenge to state power was direct and was thus met with 'sovereign' acts of domination or coercion, ranging from legislation to the edge of a blade. One of the defining characteristics of the Hunt celebration in Ashton-under-Lyne was the memory of a violent clash with the State. For many of those eating, drinking, toasting, reciting, dancing and making music on the night, the memory of that encounter would have been visceral: of terror, persecution, prosecution, imprisonment or all of the above. For others present the affective knowledge of Peterloo was second- or third-hand but keen nonetheless. The acute experience of politics was present in many of the episodes examined in this chapter – from strikes to riots, from uprisings to revolutions – and music-making helped to define the challenge, shape the action as it unfolded in real time and condition the response. Having said that, overwhelmingly political contests and a broader reformist impulse in Britain, and the colonies of settlement more generally, were conducted within a shared constitutionalist paradigm in which petitions were more prevalent (and perhaps even more potent) than pikes. Any dividing line between what was called 'physical' and 'moral' force is, by definition, arbitrarily drawn and, irrespective of the methods, the challenge was, typically, no less confronting and the agenda every bit as capacious. Moreover, the prosecution of politics with less tumult and disorder did not make it quieter.

Notes

1 Charles Mackay, *Forty Years' Recollections of Life, Literature and Public Affairs from 1830 to 1870* (London: Chapman and Hall, 1875), pp. 198–9. According to the *Literary Gazette* (6 February 1847), the song was quoted by Beaumont and Fletcher during the reign of James 1 (1603–25).

2 *Hansard* [House of Commons] (21 July 1854), col. 503.

3 'Oath Protest as MSPs Start Work', BBC News (7 May 2007), available at http://news.bbc.co.uk/2/hi/uk_news/scotland/3006175.stm (accessed 15 September 2016).

4 Thomas Cooper, *The Life of Thomas Cooper* (Leicester: Leicester University Press, [1872] 1971), p. 154. As his account makes clear, by this time there had been a metonymic shift in the meaning of 'hustings' from the place where the act of open voting took place to a word that encompassed the collective activities performed during a campaign. For the history of the hustings see Frank O'Gorman, 'Campaign Rituals and Ceremonies: The Social Meaning of Elections in England 1780–1860', *Past and Present*, 135 (1992), pp. 79–115.

5 The term 'moral radical' is drawn from the work of Alex Tyrrell. See Alex Tyrrell, *Joseph Sturge and the Moral Radical Party in Early Victorian Britain* (London: Croom Helm, 1987).

6 Cooper, *Thomas Cooper*, pp. 154–60.

7 *Northern Star* (13 August 1842).

8 See Lorna L. Banfield, *Green Pastures and Gold: A History of Ararat* (Canterbury, Vic.: Mullaya Publications, 1974), p. 114.

9 *Sheffield and Rotherham Independent* (9 February 1891).

10 *Maitland Mercury* (3 May 1854).

11 *Sydney Morning Herald* (13 February 1872). For Buchanan see Paul Pickering 'A Wider Field in a New Country: Chartism in Colonial Australia', in M. Sawer (ed.), *Elections, Full, Free & Fair* (Sydney: Federation Press, 2001), pp. 28–44.

12 W. E. Adams, *Memoirs of a Social Atom* (London: Hutchinson, 1903), pp. 150–4.

13 *Globe* (22 February 1887). Similar recollections were recorded throughout the Anglophone world. See, for example, *Argus* (22 June 1880).

14 *Essex Standard* (28 October 1870); *Essex Standard* (4 November 1870). For Josephine Butler's harrowing account of the election see Josephine Butler, *An Autobiographical Memoir* (Bristol: J. W. Arrowsmith, 1909), pp. 98–109.

15 Hocken Library, University of Otago, NZ, Noeline Baker Papers, MS-0619-9, album containing mounted letters, pamphlets, newspaper clippings (hereafter Noeline Baker Papers), *Surrey Weekly Press* (25 July 1913).

16 *Leeds Mercury* (5 August 1837); *Morning Chronicle* (11 August 1837); *Morning Chronicle* (12 August 1837).

17 *York Herald* (3 July 1852); *York Herald* (10 July 1852). For later violence at Wakefield elections see *Scotsman* (18 November 1868); *Newcastle Courant* (20 November 1868).

18 *Hansard* [House of Commons] (25 June 1832), col. 1041.

19 *Co-operative News* (10 May 1873).

20 *Vindicator* [Montreal] (22 May 1832); *Sydney Morning Herald* (5 June 1843).

21 *Morning Post* (29 June 1841); Bishopsgate Institute, George Howell Collection, Howell Collection Pamphlet Box 39, 324.24106, *Liberal Election Songs* (Bacup: Isaac Leach, n.d. [1880]).

22 *Leeds Mercury* (5 August 1837).

23 *Sydney Morning Herald* (16 November 1855).

24 Mikhail Bakhtin, *Rabelais and His World* (Cambridge, MA: M.I.T. Press, 1968).

25 See Neil Jarman, 'For God and Ulster: Blood and Thunder Bands and Loyalist Political Culture', in T. Fraser (ed.), *The Irish Parading Tradition: Following the Drum* (Basingstoke: Macmillan, 2000), pp. 158–72; Katy Radford, 'Drum Rolls and Gender Roles in Protestant Marching Bands in Belfast', *British Journal of*

Ethnomusicology, 10:2 (2001), pp. 37–59; Dani Garavelli, 'Orange Flare-up', *Scotsman* (10 June 2012).

26 *Hansard* [House of Commons] (10 August 1860), col. 1155.
27 *Ibid.*, col. 1153.
28 *Hansard* [House of Lords] (30 November 1819), col. 486–7; *Hansard* [House of Commons] (7 December 1819), col. 843.
29 *The Times* (12 July 1836).
30 *Hansard* [House of Commons] (6 July 1853).
31 Henry Vizetelly, *Glances Back Through Seventy Years: Autobiographical and Other Reminiscences*, vol. 1 (London: Kegan Paul & Co., 1893), p. 7.
32 *Hansard* [House of Commons] (28 July 1862).
33 *Hansard* [House of Commons] (17 February 1865).
34 *Hansard* [House of Commons] (27 March 1873).
35 *Sydney Morning Herald* (20 October 1856).
36 *Queenslander* (29 April 1871).
37 *Argus* (15 April 1856).
38 *New Zealander* (14 July 1858); *Evening Post* (9 December 1881). See also Appendix A of the Report of the Royal Commission on the Electoral System 1986, which provides a detailed outline, available at www.elections.org.nz/sites/default/files/bulk-upload/documents/appendix%20a.pdf (accessed 16 September 2016).
39 *Evening Post* (6 December 1899); *Evening Star* (7 December 1899). For Richard Knight see *The Cyclopedia of New Zealand* (Wellington [Wellington Provincial District]: Cyclopedia Co. Ltd, 1897).
40 See Paul Pickering, 'Peaceably if we can, forcibly if we must: Political Violence and Insurrection in Early-Victorian Britain', in Brett Bowden and Michael T. Davis (eds), *Terror: From Tyrannicide to Terrorism in Europe, 1605–2005* (St Lucia, Brisbane: University of Queensland Press, 2008), pp. 114–33.
41 See Paul Pickering and Alex Tyrrell, *The People's Bread: A History of the Anti-Corn Law League* (Leicester: Leicester University Press, 2000), chap. 7; Paul Pickering, '"And Your Petitioners &c": Chartist Petitioning in Popular Politics 1838–48', *English Historical Review*, 116:466 (2001), pp. 368–88; *The Times* (14 February 1907).
42 *Courier and Argus* [Dundee] (14 February 1907).
43 *Barrier Miner* (19 September); *Barrier Miner* (20 September 1892). The crowd also sang *The Flag That Sets You Free*.
44 *Adelaide Advertiser* (12 June 1858).
45 *Westralian Worker*, 19 October 1900.
46 *Hansard* [House of Commons] (12 February 1895).
47 We are grateful to the former Speaker of the Australian House of Representatives, Harry Jenkins MP, for his interpretation of the standing orders on this point. In 2016, however, the election of Linda Burney, the first indigenous women to the Australian House of Representatives, saw a relaxation of the rules by Speaker Tony Smith, to allow her to be 'sung into parliament' from the public gallery by a Wiradjuri woman, Lynette Riley. See 'Indigenous MP Linda Burney Slams Calls for Changes to Race Hate Laws', ABC News, available at www.abc.net.au/news/2016-08-31/first-female-indigenous-linda-burneys-passionate-maiden-speech/7802942 (accessed 15 September 2016). Notably, however, the episode was not recorded in *Hansard*.
48 *Queenslander* (13 September 1879). For Berry see: Geoffrey Bartlett, 'Berry, Sir Graham (1822–1904)', *Australian Dictionary of Biography*, Australian National University, available at http://adb.anu.edu.au/biography/berry-sir-graham-2984/text4355 (accessed 15 September 2016).
49 *Hansard* [Senate of Australia] (9 May 1901).
50 *Hansard* [House of Commons] (18 September 1914), col. 1019–20.
51 Michael MacDonagh, *The Home Rule Movement* (Dublin: Talbot, 1920), p. 264
52 *Hansard* [House of Commons] (1 June 1886).
53 *South Australian Register* (5 August 1914).

54 *Empire* (22 May 1862).
55 *Queanbeyan Age* (12 March 1879).
56 Alexander Turnbull Library, Wellington, NZ, Maori Manuscripts MS – 6373–26, Te Kotahitanga Papers, *Nga Korero o te hui o te Whakakotahitanga i tu kit e Tiritio o Waitangi*, [typescript draft translation of the proceedings of the Maori Parliament of New Zealand (hereafter Te Kotahitanga Proceedings), first sitting, 1893, p. 2.
57 *Daily Telegraph* (12 April 1893).
58 *Evening Post* (17 April 1894).
59 *Ibid.*
60 Te Kotahitanga Proceedings, 21 April 1893, p. 8; Te Kotahitanga Proceedings, 18 May, 20 May 1893, p. 122.
61 Te Kotahitanga Proceedings, 7 March 1895.
62 *Fielding Star* (30 October 1906).
63 Reprinted in Rona Bailey and Herbert Roth (eds), *Shanties by the Way* ([Christchurch]: Whitcombe and Tombs, 1967), p. 103.
64 By this time Garibaldi affectations had become largely meaningless symbols in Australian politics. See Paul Pickering 'Garibaldi's Shirt: The Influence of Garibaldi and Mazzini on Popular Politics after 1850' (unpublished paper, Sydney University, XI World Italian Language Week, August 2011).
65 *Argus* (19 July 1902); *Ma Mie Rosette: a Romantic Opera in 2 acts*, English version by George Dance, which debuted in Melbourne in 1894, available at www.aus stage.edu.au/pages/event/101914 (accessed 16 September 2016).
66 *Argus* (19 July 1902); *Euroa Advertiser* (25 July 1902).
67 *Argus* (19 July 1902).
68 *Colonist* (13 March 1879). See Robert Rumilly, 'Letellier de Saint-Just, Luc', in *Dictionary of Canadian Biography*, vol. 11, (Toronto: University of Toronto/ Quebec: Université Laval, 2003), available at www.biographi.ca/en/bio/letellier_ de_saint_just_luc_11E.html (accessed 15 September 2016).
69 *Colonist* (13 March 1879).
70 *The Times* (6 March 1901); *Hansard* [House of Commons] (5 March 1901), cols. 686–696.
71 *Scotsman* (6 March 1901); *New York Times* (8 March 1901); *Argus* (7 March 1801); *Manchester Guardian* (6 March 1901); *Worker* [Brisbane] (20 April 1901).
72 Possibly the only parallel occurred in South Carolina in 1876 when eight 'negro' Republican members occupied the house in protest. *The Times*'s correspondent reported that they wiled away the time 'singing political songs to religious airs' and 'by other grotesque buffoonery of a kind never, I suspect, witnessed in a hall of Legislature before'. *The Times* (20 December 1876).
73 Oxford University, Bodleian Library, Broadside Ballads Online (hereafter Bodleian Ballads), 2806 c.16(184) and Harding B 11(3577), *God Save Ireland* (Manchester: T. Pearson, n.d.), available at http://ballads.bodleian.ox.ac.uk/search/?query=Hardin g+B+11%283577%29 (accessed 15 September 2016). Condon was not among them; his sentence had been overturned.
74 Bodleian Ballads, Harding B 11(3577), *God Save Ireland*.
75 Library of Congress, Civil War Ballad Collection, George F. Root, *Tramp! Tramp! Tramp! (The Prisoner's Hope)* (Cleveland: S. Brainard's Sons, 1885), available at www.loc.gov/item200001912 (accessed 15 September 2016).
76 See Gordon Ledbetter, *The Great Irish Tenor* (London: Duckworth, 1977), pp. 103–6.
77 *Barrier Truth* (2 January 1909).
78 See *Barrier Miner* (24 September 1892); *Sydney Morning Herald* (22 September 1892).
79 Ben Tillett, *Memories and Reflections* (London: John Long, 1931), p. 125.
80 *Flame* (10 December 1906); *Barrier Miner* (1 February 1909); *Barrier Miner* (8 February 1909); *Barrier Miner* (25 August 1909); Chas Glyde's serialised 'Thirty Years' Reminiscences in the Socialist Movement' cited by Mann himself. See Tom Mann, *Tom Mann's Memoirs* (London: Labour Publishing, 1923), p. 68.

81   *Socialist* (15 January 1909); *Socialist* (12 February 1909).
82   The 1918–19 Broken Hill strike lasted for eighteen months.
83   See, inter alia, Joy Damousi, *Women Come Rally: Socialism, Communism, and Gender in Australia, 1890–1955* (Oxford: Oxford University Press, 1994).
84   *Adelaide Advertiser* (26 August 1892); *Sydney Morning Herald* (27 August 1892).
85   State Library of South Australia, 324.623, 'Women's Suffrage in South Australia [scrapbook]: Parliamentary Debates 1893–1894'.
86   *Barrier Miner* (25 August 1892); *Barrier Truth* (5 January 1909); *Sydney Morning Herald* (27 August 1892); *Sydney Morning Herald* (13 September 1892). Cf. the photograph in Paul Adams and Erik Eklund, 'Representing Militancy: Photographs of the Broken Hill Industrial Disputes 1908–1920', *Labour History*, 1001 (2011), p. 11.
87   *Ashburton Guardian* (3 October 1912).
88   *Barrier Miner* (4 July 1892).
89   *Barrier Miner* (14 January 1909).
90   [Charles Dickens], 'Locked Out', *Household Words: A Weekly Journal*, vol. 8 (1854), p. 347; *Preston Guardian* (10 October 1853).
91   Tillett, *Memories and Reflections*, p. 123.
92   See *Reynolds' News* (15 September 1889); *Maoriland Worker* (5 November 1913); *Voice* [Winnipeg] (8 August 1902).
93   *Barrier Truth* (26 March 1909).
94   *Barrier Miner* (11 September 1890).
95   *Barrier Truth* (27 January 1909).
96   *Barrier Truth* (12 January 1909).
97   *Northern Star* (11 May 1844); *St John Daily Sun* (29 November 1905).
98   *Poverty Bay Herald* (11 October 1912); *Grey River Argus* (13 November 1912).
99   *Poverty Bay Herald* (11 October 1912).
100 See Leonard Curtis, *The History of Broken Hill: Its Rise and Progress* (Adelaide: Fearson's Printing, 1908), p. 152.
101 *Ibid.*
102 Again, as in Wellington, there is some evidence of disquiet because the union was covering the AMA Band's expenses whereas those of the other players were not. However, this did not affect their role in the strike. See *Barrier Truth* (11 September 1908); *Barrier Truth* (25 September 1908).
103 *Barrier Truth* (13 May 1899); *Barrier Miner* (18 June 1890); *Barrier Miner* (21 August 1890); *Barrier Miner* (16 September 1890); *Grey River Argus* (2 July 1896).
104 Curtis, *Broken Hill*, pp. 152–3; *Barrier Miner* (15 September 1890).
105 Mitchell Library, Sydney, M3331-B, Broken Hill Strike 1909, volume of cuttings (hereafter Broken Hill Cuttings), 'Combined Unions Lockout: Balance Sheet from 1st January to 26th June 1909'; *Industrial World* (24 April 1909); *Otago Daily Times*, 24 April 1909.
106 *Worker* (21 January 1909). See also *Barrier Daily Truth* (9 January 1909).
107 *Otago Daily Times* (24 April 1909).
108 Broken Hill Cuttings, 'Combined Unions Lockout'.
109 *Voice* (10 May 1912).
110 *Charter* (1 December 1839); *Westralian Worker* (14 May 1909); *Toronto Daily Star* (26 July 1893); *Auckland Star* (18 September 1890). For the receipts one fundraising concert played by the Waterside Workers Band, see Alexander Turnbull Library, Wellington, NZ, Herbert Otto Roth Papers MS-Group-0314 (hereafter Roth Papers), Notes and Clippings – Waihi Strike, 94–106–41/05.
111 *Barrier Daily Truth*, four reports Jan–Feb 1909; *Barrier Miner* (14 January 1909). For Hayward see also *Barrier Miner* (22 December 1911); *Barrier Miner* (24 February 1913).
112 International Institute of Social History, Amsterdam, Socialist League (UK) Archives, Items SL 3456/4, Handbill; *Commonweal* (10 March 1888); *Commonweal* (31 March 1888); *Commonweal* (6 October 1888); *Commonweal* (26 October 1888).

113   Byron, *The Giaour: A Fragment of a Turkish Tale* (1813), line 016. Nineteenth-century radicals often invoked the words as quotation, inter-text and on banners. See Paul Pickering, *Chartism and the Chartists in Manchester and Salford* (Basingstoke: Macmillan, 1995), Appendix A.

114   Labour History and Archives Centre, Manchester, Socialist Sunday School Collection (Ivy Tribe Collection), GB 394 SSS (hereafter Tribe Collection), 1892–1970.

115   Tribe Collection, *Huddersfield Socialist Sunday School Fourteenth Anniversary Service, on April 20th, 1910 in the Town Hall* (Huddersfield: Worker's Press, 1910).

116   Dave Mason, 'Children's Strikes in 1911', *History Workshop Pamphlet*, 9 (n.d.), p. 34; Billy Corville and Dave Mason, 'Fall in Follow Me: A Play about the Children's Strike of 1911', *History Workshop Pamphlets*, 13 (c.1973). The lyrics were penned in 1910 by Whit Cunliffe, a music hall comic singer known for his Tory songs. See Dave Russell, *Popular Music in England, 1840–1914*, 2nd edn (Manchester; New York: Manchester University Press, 1997). For a student strike in Dunedin, see also Roth Papers, 94–106–29/4, newspaper cutting (1889).

117   See *Flame* (July 1907); *Worker* (2 May 1907); *Worker* (12 October 1907); *Worker* (6 January 1908); *Worker* (11 January 1908); *Evening Post* [Wellington] (13 February 1909); *International Socialist* (7 May 1910).

118   *Worker* (2 May 1903).

119   See *Ibid.*; *Argus* (21 April 1903); *Argus* (22 April 1903). For Ferguson see Parliament of New South Wales, available at www.parliament.nsw.gov.au/members/Pages/member-details.aspx?pk=1053 (accessed 14 September 2016).

120   Edward Carpenter (ed.), *Chants of Labour: A Song Book of the People with Music* (London: Swan Sonnenschein, 1888), nos. 7 and 16.

121   See *American Notes and Queries* (1 February 1857), pp. 57–8; Vera Brodsky Lawrence, *Music for Patriots, Politicians and Presidents* (London: Macmillan, 1975), chap. 9. For Nesbit see Julia Briggs, 'Nesbit, Edith (1858–1924)', *Oxford Dictionary of National Biography* (Oxford: Oxford University Press, 2004), available at www.oxforddnb.com.virtual.anu.edu.au/view/article/31919 (accessed 15 September 2016).

122   *Truth* [Sydney] (17 May 1903). For Joynes see Henry Salt, 'J. L. Joynes – A Tribute', *Social Democrat* (August 1897), available at www.henrysalt.co.uk (accessed 28 May 2015).

123   The lyrics of *Partant Pour la Syrie* by Alexandre de la Borde are not at all political and certainly not radical. The words tell the story of a crusader, Dunois, who, just before leaving for the crusades in Syria, prays to the Virgin Mary that he will be the bravest and that his love will be the most beautiful. His prayers are answered: he is the boldest in battle and on his return he is granted the hand of his lord's very beautiful daughter, Isabelle.

124   *Argus* (25 April 1903).

125   In part this is what Manuel DeLanda calls a social assemblage. See *A New Philosophy of Society: Assemblage Theory and Social Complexity* (New York: Continuum, 2006). We are grateful to David Worrall for drawing our attention to DeLanda's work.

126   *Hansard* [House of Lords] (30 November 1819); *Northern Star* (27 August 1842); John Bright to Richard Cobden, 11 August 1842, quoted in G. M. Trevelyan, *The Life of John Bright* (London: Constable and Company, 1913), p. 80.

127   *Sydney Morning Herald* [5 January 1908?], Broken Hill Cuttings; *Sydney Mail* (25 November 1882).

128   *Barrier Miner*, 8 March 1909.

129   *Barrier Truth* (6 September 1908); Broken Hill Cuttings. For Wade see John M. Ward, 'Wade, Sir Charles Gregory (1863–1922)', *Australian Dictionary of Biography*, National Centre of Biography, Australian National University, available at http://adb.anu.edu.au/biography/wade-sir-charles-gregory-8938/text15707 (accessed 15 September 2016).

130   It appears that the song was first published in Australia in the *Crackerjack*

Songster in 1904 but had undoubtedly been available in imported songbooks prior to this. See *Brisbane Courier* (11 June 1904). The earliest edition in the National Library of Australia dates from 1905.

131   *Barrier Daily Truth* (14 January 1909).

132   *Barrier Daily Truth* (15 January 1909); *Northern Star* [Lismore] (26 February 1909).

133   *Adelaide Advertiser* (3 March 1909).

134   *Socialist* (12 February 1909).

135   *Harp Week* (29 August 1908), available at www.harpweek.com (accessed 15 September 2016).

136   See *Barrier Miner* (8 February 1909).

137   *Sydney Evening News* (16 February 1909); *Table Talk* (12 March 1914).

138   *Barrier Daily Truth* (27 January 1909).

139   *Barrier Truth* (23 January 1909); *Barrier Miner* (19 February 1909).

140   Mann, *Memoirs*, p. 236.

141   Frank Peel, *The Risings of the Luddites, Chartists and Plug-drawers* (New York: Routledge, [1880] 1968), pp. 333–4. *The Union Hymn* referred to by Peel was written by Samuel Bamford on the wall of his prison cell in 1817. It is not the song of the same name (also known as *The Gathering of the Unions* or *God is Our Guide*) discussed in later chapters. See Samuel Bamford, *An Account of the Arrest and Imprisonment of Samuel Bamford, Middleton, on Suspicion of High Treason* (Manchester: George Cave, 1817), pp. 5–6.

142   W. E. Gladstone quoting Sir John Colborne, *Hansard* [House of Commons] (23 January 1838), col. 436; *The Times* (12 January 1838).

143   John Leader, quoting from the Public Ordinance for Quebec and Montreal, *Hansard* [House of Commons] (14 August 1838), col. 1246.

144   Samuel Bamford, *Passages in the Life of a Radical, and Early Days*, vol. 1 (London: T. Fisher Unwin, 1893), p. 158.

145   *Morning Chronicle* (21 August 1819).

146   Bamford, *Life of a Radical*, p. 160.

147   *Glasgow Examiner* (18 March 1848); *Glasgow Examiner* (22 April 1848). See also *Scotsman* (8 March 1848); *Scotsman* (11 March 1848); *Scotsman* (19 April 1848).

148   Bodleian Ballads, Johnson Ballads fol. 307, 'A BOTTLE OF SMOAK or a Song of Sixpence' (London: Marshall, 1820), available at http://ballads.bodleian.ox.ac.uk/search/?query=Johnson+Ballads+fol.+307 (accessed 15 September 2016).

149   See Mann, *Memoirs*, pp. 86–93. The Burns in the song was John Burns, one of the leaders of the strike, not Robbie.

150   See Robert Southey, *Wat Tyler: A Dramatic Poem* (London: William Hone, 1817); William Morris, *A Dream of John Ball* (London: Reeves and Turner, 1888), p. 19. Notably, it was included in the pageant described in our introduction.

151   Mackay, *Forty Years' Recollections*, pp. 198–9. As noted, the song had actually been circulation since at the reign of James I, suggesting the possibility of an even earlier encoded message.

152   Sir Walter Scott, *Redgauntlet. A Tale of the Eighteenth Century* (Edinburgh: Constable and Company, 1824). We are grateful to the late Susan Manning for this reference.

153   *Glasgow Examiner* (22 April 1848).

154   As we have seen, the *Battle of Eureka* was often played. We are grateful to Jeff Brownrigg for his view on this matter.

155   Raffaello Carboni, *The Eureka Stockade* (Melbourne: G&G, [1855] 1984), pp. 114–15.

156   Peter Josef von Landpainter, 'The Warrior Bard, or The Standard Bearer', trans. W. B. Brough (Boston: G. P. Reed, 1847).

157   Carboni, *Eureka Stockade*, p. 44.

158   See Murray Pittock, *Poetry and Jacobite Politics in Eighteenth-Century Britain and Ireland* (Cambridge: Cambridge University Press, 1994), p. 83.

159   Bodleian Ballads, Harding B 25(339), 'Excellent New and Popular Songs on Queen

Caroline of England' (Newcastle: J. Marshall, n.d.), available at http://ballads.bodleian.ox.ac.uk/view/sheet/4246 (accessed 15 September 2016).

160   *Commonweal* (26 September 1891).

161   *Reynolds' News* (22 September 1889).

162   *Adelaide Observer* (12 June 1858).

163   *Daily News* (17 November 1885).

164   State Library of Victoria, Melbourne, Ebenezer Syme Papers, MS 17354, Box 132/1. See Paul Pickering, 'Confronting the Good Monarch: Searching for a Democratic Case for the Republic', in Benjamin T. Jones and Mark McKenna (eds), *Project Republic* (Melbourne: Black Inc., 2013), pp. 128–9; *Northern Star* (5 June 1841).

165   Noeline Baker Papers.

166   Paul Pickering, 'The Hearts of the Millions: Chartism and Popular Monarchism in the 1840s', *History*, 88:290 (2003), pp. 227–48; Neville Kirk, 'The Conditions of Royal Rule: Australian and British Socialist Attitudes to the Monarchy', *Social History*, 30:1, 2005, pp. 64–88.

167   Paul Pickering, 'Loyalty and Rebellion in Colonial Politics: The Campaign Against Convict Transportation', in Philip Alfred Buckner and R. Douglas Francis (eds), *Rediscovering the British World* (Calgary, Alberta: University of Calgary Press, 2005), p. 87–9; *Mackenzie's Gazette* (3 November 1838) in John Moir, *Rhymes of Rebellion* (Toronto: Ryerson Press, 1965), p. 79; *Manchester Courier* (14 February 1908).

168   See Michel Bédard and James Robertson, 'Oaths of Allegiance and the Canadian House of Commons', Parliamentary Information and Research Services, Background Paper, BP-214 E, Ottawa, 2008, p. 7. Apparently the Clerk of the Parliament did not recognise Riel who quickly left the building to avoid arrest.

169   Carboni, *Eureka Stockade*, p. 145.

170   *Glasgow Examiner* (22 April 1848).

171   Cited in Robert Hughes, *The Fatal Shore: A History of the Transportation of Convicts to Australia, 1787–1868* (New York: Vintage, 1986), p. 243.

172   *Australasian* (19 September 1891).

173   University of British Columbia, Rare Books & Special Collections, *Come Hell or High Water* (New York: Workers Library Publications, 1932), p. 13.

174   *Richmond Gazette* (5 January 1889); *Argus* (1 December 1881); *Ned Kelly: Man and Myth* [a symposium] (North Melbourne: Cassell, 1966), pp. 93–5. The entire song was read to the symposium and is reproduced in the proceedings. As one of the participants notes, it has obviously been rewritten many times since.

175   In the 1970 film of the Kelly story directed by Tony Richardson the song was sung by Mick Jagger.

176   *Clarence and Richmond Examiner* (26 December 1899). It even made it as far as British Columbia where a trade union songster included 'The Bold Young Union Boy' set to the tune. See *Come Hell or High Water*.

177   John Meredith (ed.), *Songs from the Kelly Country* (Woolloomooloo, NSW: A Bush Music Club Publication, [1955]).

178   *Barrier Daily Truth* (3 February 1909).

179   See Hans Hansen, *Riel's Defence: Perspectives on His Speeches* (Montreal and Kingston: McGill-Queen's University Press, 2014), pp. 25–44; Paul Pickering, 'No Witnesses. No Leads. No Problems: The Re-Enactment of Crime and Rebellion', in Iain McCalman and Paul Pickering (eds), *Historical Re-enactment: From Realism to the Affective Turn* (Basingstoke: Palgrave, 2010), pp. 109–33.

180   *Manchester Courier* (4 April 1914).

181   Florence E. Macaulay, *The Women's Marseillaise* (London: Furnival Press, [1909]).

182   Emmeline Pankhurst, *My Own Story* (London: Eveleigh Nash, 1914), p. 302.

183   *Aberdeen Daily* (16 October 1913); *Manawatu Standard* (17 October 1913); *Evening Post* [Auckland] (21 October 1913); *Kalgoorlie Miner* (17 October 1913); *South Australian Register* (17 October 1913).

184   Timothy Randall, 'Chartist Poetry and Song', in Owen Ashton and Stephen Roberts (eds), *The Chartist Legacy* (London: Merlin, 1999), pp. 171–95; Christopher

Godfrey, 'The Chartist Prisoners 1839–41', *International Review of Social History*, 24 (1999), pp. 189–236; Pickering, *Chartism and the Chartists*, chap. 8.

185 See Miles Taylor, *Ernest Jones, Chartism and the Romance of Politics* (Oxford: Oxford University Press, 2003); Cooper, *Thomas Cooper*, p. 184.

186 Carboni, *Eureka Stockade*, p. 145.

187 *Maoriland Worker* (19 November 1913).

188 Reprinted in Alistair Bonnett and Keith Armstrong (eds), *Thomas Spence: The Poor Man's Revolutionary* (London: Breviary Stuff Publications, 2014), pp. 163–4. See also Michael T. Davies, 'Meet and Sing and Your Chains Will Drop Off Like Burnt Thread: The Political Songs of Thomas Spence', in the same volume.

189 Bamford, *Arrest and Imprisonment*, pp. 5–6; *Life of a Radical*, pp. 90–1, 98–9.

190 Robert Gammage, *Reminiscences of a Chartist* (1883), ed. W. H. Maehl (Manchester: Free Press, 1983), p. 23; Timothy Randall reports Chartist prisoners singing 'extempore'. See 'Chartist Poetry and Song', pp. 172–3.

191 June Purvis, *Emmeline Pankhurst: A Biography* (New York: Routledge, 2002), p. 217.

192 Pankhurst, *My Own Story*, p. 220.

193 E. Sylvia Pankhurst, *The Suffragette Movement: An Intimate Account of Persons and Ideals* (London: Virago, [1931] 1977), p. 377. See also Ernest Newman (ed.), *Impressions that Remained: Memoirs by Ethel Smyth* (London: Longmans and Green, 1919), p. ix. The song was composed in 1911 with the words later written by Cicely Hamilton, herself a notorious suffragist, and, at Pankhurst's instigation, replaced the *Women's Marseillaise* as the anthem of the cause.

194 *Barrier Truth* (12 January 1909); *Barrier Truth* (4 February 1909); *Sydney Morning Herald* (9 February 1909); *Barrier Miner* (15 February 1909).

195 Sir John Hawkins, *Science and Practice of Music*, vol. 2 (London: Payne, 1776) p. 57; *The British Poets*, vol. 67 (Chiswick: C. Whittingham, 1822); *Gentleman's Magazine*, 101:2 (1831), p. 131.

196 *Courier & Argus* (14 April 1913).

197 *Morning Post* (12 November 1822); *Maoriland Worker* (31 January 1913).

198 *People's Paper* (30 August 1856); *Daily News* (26 August 1856); *Lloyd's London Weekly* (21 September 1856).

199 Eric Hobsbawm includes a brief reference to Kelly, giving him, at least vaguely, the status of a rebel. See Eric Hobsbawm, *Bandits* (London: Weidenfeld & Nicolson, 1969), p. 131.

200 Peel, *Risings of the Luddites*, p. 263.

201 Peel, *Risings of the Luddites*, pp. 47–8.

202 For *The Gallant Poacher* see, inter alia, Bodleian Ballads, available at http://ballads. bodleian.ox.ac.uk/search/?query=Gallant%20Poacher&f_Themes=Poaching&f_ Collections=Bodleian%20Harding (accessed 15 September 2016); E. P. Thompson, *Whigs and Hunters: The Origin of the Black Act* (New York: Pantheon Books, 1975). We are grateful to Keith Laybourn for information in relation to the *Cropper's Song* and *The Gallant Poacher*.

203 *International Socialist* (12 November 1910). See also *Barrier Socialist Songster* (Broken Hill: Truth Print, n.d.), p. 15. The story was later embellished to suggest that Parsons's wife, prevented from visiting him prior to his execution, had faintly heard the song and joined in. See *International Socialist* (18 December 1915).

204 *The Trials of Arthur Thistlewood, J. Ings, J. T. Brunt, W. Davidson, and R. Tidd, On a Charge of High Treason ... To Which is Appended a Copious Account of the Execution*, 2nd edn (London: John Fairburn, 1820), p. 136; *Morning Chronicle* (2 May 1820).

205 *The Minstrel, Being a New and Select Collection of the Most Admired English Songs, Duets and Cantatas* (London: Richardson, c.1780), p. 129. Note that the wording was 'Or give me death or liberty' not 'O give' etc. It was also published in *Roundelay, Or the New Siren, a Collection of Choice Songs* (London: W. Lane, c.1780), p. 92. For Andrews see History of Parliament, available at

www.historyofparliamentonline.org/volume/1790–1820/member/andrews-miles-peter-1742–1814 (accessed 16 September 2016).

206   Joseph Ritson, *A Select Collection of English Songs with their Original Airs*, 2nd edn (London: J. Rivington, 1813), p. 214; [R. Thompson], *A Tribute to Liberty: or a Collection of Select Songs* (London: n.p., 1795), pp. 80–1.

207   *Border Mail* (12 December 1915).

208   *Winnipeg Free Press* (12, 13, 14 December 1885); *Daily British Whig* (12 December 1885).

209   *Daily Colonist* (21 January 1914). See also Mark Leier, 'Mairs, Joseph', *Dictionary of Canadian Biography*, vol. 14 (Toronto: University of Toronto/Quebec: Université Laval, 2003), available at www.biographi.ca/en/bio/mairs_joseph_14E. html (accessed 16 September 2016).

210   See the biographical sketch of Holberry (probably written by George Julian Harney) in *English Chartist Circular*, pts 14–15 [1843].

211   *Northern Star* (2 July 1842); *Northern Star* (9 July 1842).

212   Rita Benton, 'Pleyel (i)', *Grove Music Online, Oxford Music Online* (Oxford: Oxford University Press), available at www.oxfordmusiconline.com/subscriber/article/grove/music/21940 (accessed 16 September 2016).

213   *Northern Star* (2 July 1842); *Sheffield and Rotherham Independent* (2 July 1842). It was sold as a slip ballad subsequently. See *Northern Star* (23 July 1842).

214   *Maoriland Worker* (22 November 1912).

215   Toronto Public Library, Research Collection, 'To the memory of James Kavenaugh' (Rochester: Daily Union Office, 1837).

216   One commentator argued that a significant display would convince the government of the people's anger and resolve, adding that 'what the eye sees is fastened on the memory in a much greater degree than all the ear can hear'. *Pall Mall Gazette* (8 December 1887).

217   University of Warwick, Modern Records Centre, Papers of William Wess, MSS. 240W/4/2/6 (hereafter Wess Papers), William Morris, *A Death Song*; Wess Papers, *Alfred Linnell Killed in Trafalgar Square, November 20, 1888* (London: Richard Lambert, 1888), p. 8. For Lawson see Discogs, available at www.discogs.com/artist/2198664-Malcolm-Lawson (accessed 16 September 2016).

218   *Aberdeen Weekly Journal* (14 December 1887); *West Australian* (13 January 1888); *Boston Daily Globe* (17 December 1887); *Wrexham Advertiser* (19 December 1887); *Tuapeka Times* (31 March 1888).

219   *Riverine Grazier* (10 February 1888). The death of a comrade from natural causes was sometimes marked by a public funeral. After James Bennett died suddenly while working at his forge in Broken Hill in 1909, for example, he was given what was described as a 'socialist funeral'. His comrades marched to the graveside where an oration was given and the mourners sang *The Red Flag*. See *Socialist* (26 June 1909).

220   *London Intelligencer* (March 1855).

221   *Age* (25 January 1874); *Press* [Christchurch] (25 January 1896).

222   *Northern Star* (17 November 1849).

223   *Ibid.*

224   *Ibid.*

225   *Northern Liberator* (14 November 1840).

226   *Hyland's Mammoth Hibernian Songster* (Chicago: Hyland & Co., 1901), p. 41.

227   Peel, *Risings of the Luddites*, p. 123. This is true elsewhere in the radical Anglophone world. For example, a Chartist jubilee in Melbourne in 1898 was punctuated by selections from the Bootmakers' Band and the Labour Church. See *Worker* (23 June 1898).

228   'A Blackbird', *Musical Times* (May 1895), pp. 301–2. Joe Nadin was the deputy-constable who arrested Hunt at Peterloo having called in the military to assist him.

229   *Ibid.* What they would have obviously not known is that the musical and lyrical shape of the song continued in popular politics long after as the basis for election

ballads as well as a comedic street ballad: 'She reckoned up and showed him | And the answer gave complete | How five-and-twenty shillings | Were expended in a week'.

230 Pankhurst, *Suffragette Movement*, p. 355.

CHAPTER FIVE

Music, morals and the middle class

In 1860 Hugh Reginald Haweis arrived in Naples as part of the British volunteer legion ready to join Garibaldi in his fight for independence. At barely five feet tall and with a club foot, Haweis presented as an unlikely freedom fighter and, as it eventuated, the British had arrived too late for active battle. Not too late, however, as Haweis remembered in his published account, to be almost killed by Neapolitan sharpshooters on the hills outside Capua or to witness the peace celebrations with Victor Emmanuel.[1] But it is not through this ill-timed adventure with the Garibaldians that Haweis achieved his enduring fame, but rather through the publication in 1871 of his enormously popular book, *Music and Morals*, which by 1903 had reached its twentieth edition.[2]

Haweis, the son of a clergyman, grew up in Brighton. His early interest in music led to his study of the violin at the Royal Academy of Music with Antonio Oury, an erstwhile student of Paganini. He read German poetry and philosophy at Cambridge, graduating in 1859. After his return from Italy he followed in his father's footsteps and became a curate, ultimately securing a position at St James's, Marylebone. In addition to religious duties, Haweis was active as both a popular lecturer and writer on many subjects, but above all on music. He was music critic for *Pall Mall Gazette* and *Truth* and produced other major works including *My Musical Life* (1891) and a travel account, *Travel and Talk* (1896).[3] Haweis's account of his globetrotting as a popular lecturer to such far-flung corners of the Empire as Australia and New Zealand is of particular relevance to this study.

Despite his diminutive size and physical disability, Haweis was a charismatic figure with olive skin, green eyes and black hair, always preaching in a black cloak. He quickly rescued St James's from a moribund state, and for the next thirty-five years filled it to capacity. A Broad Churchman, he was known for his unconventional attitudes expressed throughout his life: from his youthful surrender to 'the hot breath of revolution' or, as he also called it, 'Garibaldi fever' (one enduring result of which was his collection of Garibaldi and Mazzini ephemera exhibited in the St James's vestry during his tenure), to his extended expositions on the relationship of music and morality, and from his support of Sabbatarianism with his 'Sunday evenings for the people', comprising edifying orchestral and oratorio concerts and exhibitions of sacred art, to his interest in spiritualism, participations in seances, and membership of the Society for Psychical Research. His wife, Mary Haweis, a renowned artist and illustrator, shared some of his inclinations and participated in various social movements, particularly women's suffrage. Together they embody many of the themes of this chapter.

Haweis is but one of many examples of individuals who combined progressive political and social tendencies with a strong interest in music and a belief in its power to shape human behaviour. It is well known that the nineteenth century saw profound shifts in religious belief brought about by what has been generally understood as the Victorian crisis of faith. Scholars such as Mark Bevir have explored so-called 'spiritual immanentism', defined as a 'belief in a God present throughout the world'.[4] This was a crucial concept for those seeking new modes of understanding, from radical forms of religious theology, to a new conception of secular humanism and on to, as Bevir argues, ethical socialism. This chapter will examine the role of music in the reform culture of middle-class liberals such as Haweis and John Pyke Hullah.[5] Common to the two organisations examined here in detail, London's South Place Chapel and Melbourne's Australian Church, was both an eschewal of orthodoxy, dogma and creed replaced by openness and inclusiveness in outlook, and a vibrant musical culture. Thus we look at the ways that musical performance was used by these organisations to create their own internal cultures and shape and express their own particular identities. The intention is not to argue a position of primary importance for music, but rather to evaluate its place in the everyday life of these societies, its role in the various agendas for moral improvement and to use it as a window onto differing and changing cultural values. The hymn will be one unit of analysis. A consideration of the unconventional, even radical hymnbooks produced by these societies in this and subsequent chapters will reveal how the genre was appropriated by a multitude of progressive causes, both political and social. This is immediately apparent by the broad range of authors represented within these collections, which included advanced thinkers, reformers, political radicals and even anarchists. These hymnbooks reflect the ongoing changes in religious practices and beliefs, and most suggestively demonstrate the carrying over of religious ceremony and ritual into the secular sphere. They also raise interesting questions as to what constituted a hymn.

Music and Morals, as noted by Dave Russell, became 'the classic Victorian text on music and social reform' even though Haweis himself stated in a discussion of sacred music within the book that 'the social effects of music', although interesting, 'lie a little outside the purpose of our present article'.[6] Significantly, while traversing a range of subjects from musical psychology to the relationship of sound and colour, the work has at its heart a particular understanding of the relationship of music and emotion. The result: a confusing and contradictory treatment of a problematic subject, but one that was of enormous interest to many Victorians. Beginning with the 'popular assertion that music is the language of the emotions', Haweis proposed that there were 'many points of contact' between art and morals.[7] For Haweis, music had a 'mysterious command ... over the realm of abstract emotion', also described as 'the temperatures or atmospheres of the Soul'. Given that these 'atmospheric states' could be 'wholesome or the reverse', music therefore possessed 'vast capacities for good or evil' and 'must be held responsible for the manner in which it deals with that realm, and the kind of succession, proportion, and degrees of the various emotional atmospheres it has the power of generating'.[8] The potential role of music in moral uplift is made explicit in the following words: 'People think and feel on different planes of thought and feeling. There are different Planes of Emotion. If your character is base, the plane of your emotion will be low. If your character is noble, the plane of your emotion will be high.'[9] Controlling emotion determined moral health, and music had a central role to play. For those who upheld art for art's sake (Haweis was himself a champion of 'great' German music, in particular the music of Wagner), he adjusted his argument: 'The morality lies in the administration, and comes from a quality which belongs ... to the agent who administers it.'[10] Furthermore, this morality 'must depend upon the way in which the conception, as presented, is calculated to affect the moral health of society.' Not simply in terms of either good or evil, 'but to the proportions in which the two are mixed, and above all to the kind of sympathy with which they are intended to be viewed.'[11]

It is no coincidence that the sacralisation of the arts occurred during the age of secularisation. The sacralisation of music came about in part through its power to elicit sympathy. This power to speak directly to the emotions, which for many relegated it to the realms of the transcendental, ironically also made it a powerful tool of social utility. Underlying the strengthening belief in the importance of 'serious' music and the cultivation of taste to promote societal health felt throughout Haweis's writing, we can also detect the thinking of Thomas Carlyle, John Ruskin and Matthew Arnold.

One place in which many of these radical liberal tendencies coalesced and cohabited was South Place Chapel. The move from radical religion to progressive secularism is expressed clearly through its long history. South Place Chapel was established in London during the French Revolution by a dissident congregation of Universalists led by the American minister Elhanan Winchester.[12] The society came into its own a few decades later in the early nineteenth century under the leadership of the charismatic Unitarian minister W. J. Fox, renowned for his tireless work in political and social reform and for being one of the great orators of the Anti-Corn Law League. From 1824, when it moved from Parliament Court to the purpose-built South Place Chapel in Finsbury, the Chapel teemed with progressive ideas concerning religion, politics and social reform. By the end of the century, South Place Chapel had, under the leadership of two more Americans, Moncure Daniel Conway and Stanton Coit, transformed into the South Place Ethical Society, which moved to Red Lion Square in the heart of Bloomsbury. It is still active today as Conway Hall Ethical Society. From its beginnings it developed a vibrant culture with a range of facilities, such as the Lending Library and the Orchestral Society, and an array of offerings including the South Place Reading Class, the Children's Sunday Afternoon Society and the soirees (also known as *conversazione*). Over the course of the century, with its South Place Sunday Popular Concerts (still running today) and its choir, it also gained international recognition as a place of music.

The 1924 Centenary of South Place provided an opportunity for the society to celebrate its history, one it proudly upheld as a 'microcosm of the general movement of liberal thought between 1824 and 1924'.[13] The extended historical accounts found in the *Souvenir of the Centenary Celebration* were infused with the rhetoric of toleration and political and social freedom. For C. J. Pollard, then editor of the South Place Ethical Society's *Monthly Record*, the history recounted in the *Souvenir* 'has interest not only as a record of the life of one individual Society, it has also a much wider interest owing to the fact that South Place Chapel, throughout the hundred years of its existence, has played a not unimportant part in the liberation of religion, politics and art from all forms of tyranny.'[14] Another contributor, well-known reformer and social commentator John A. Hobson, echoed these sentiments, outlining many of 'the great causes of Liberty' South Place had fought for, including: 'Catholic Emancipation, the Anti-Corn Law Movement, the Anti-Slavery Movement, the Movement of Toleration for Dissenters, for Deists, for Atheists, and the ever expanding

[231]

movement in the wider field of Politics'.[15] For socialist and Labour MP Harry Snell, South Place stood for the ideals of 'truth without fear or limitation; dignity of doubt and for the courage of dissent'. He made much of its 'reforming zeal', noting that in its continued efforts 'to widen the opportunities for man and to remove political and social barriers to his development', it was the 'first to protest against the oppression of women' and to agitate for education for both sexes and for the extension of the franchise.[16]

Fox and Conway, in particular, are celebrated as the heroes of South Place. A weaver's son and autodidact, whose own education had been gleaned from a variety of piecemeal sources, Fox was acutely aware of the importance of education for the lower classes. He made it a chief objective to bring together the classes and was many things to many people. In the words of his biographer, Richard Garnett, in 1909, he was a '[f]ree-thinker in the widest sense of the word, a religious teacher of morals, an educationalist, a Radical propagandist, a literary journalist, a Corn-law reformer, and a man of the people at heart'.[17] As such, he synthesised the ideological underpinnings of many of the emancipatory reform movements of the period. However, Fox's position at South Place was to bring about unexpected and fundamental change, not because of his world view but because of events in his personal life. In 1834 the Chapel went through considerable upheaval caused by a highly charged scandal involving the breakdown of Fox's marriage and questions about the nature of his relationship with South Place's composer Eliza Flower. Fox's relationship with Flower split the congregation and led to his expulsion in 1835 by the Body of Presbyterian Ministers. A minority of the congregation left, leaving South Place more radicalised as a result.[18]

Fox was one of a succession of fascinating personalities who were to lead the institution; another was Moncure Daniel Conway. Conway was, like South Place's founder, an American. Despite the fact that he grew up in a slave-owning Virginian family, he became an abolitionist early on. Raised as a Methodist, Conway came under the influence of Emersonian transcendentalism. He turned to Unitarianism in 1855 while still in America, but by 1864 when he assumed his appointment at South Place he had turned away from progressive Unitarianism to embrace an increasingly humanist vein of freethought. On this ideological journey he was to embrace the republican heresiarch Thomas Paine, whose biography he was to write later in life.[19] He remembered 1869 as the year where he decided he 'was unwilling to offer prayers to an all-wise Being', so bringing the practice permanently to an end at the society.[20] Thus the generous Catholicism of Fox was continued by Conway, and South Place consequently became a 'clearing house' in which a wide array of scientific and religious beliefs intermingled. It provided a meeting place for intellectual, artistic and politically radical circles. Conway gave a vivid sense of the milieu in his own history of South Place, published in 1894.[21] He lists, for example, the 'South Place friends' who had sat at his predecessor's feet in the Chapel. This included many leading intellectual figures of the period: 'Hazlitt, Thomas Campbell, J. S. Mill, Douglas Jerrold, Leigh Hunt, Talfourd, Pemberton, Horne, John Forster, Crabb Robinson, Browning, Macready, the Novellos, Hennells, Brabants, Brays, Howitts, Cowden Clarke … Helen Faucit, Sarah Flower Adams, and her sister Eliza Flower'.[22] Conway went on to evoke a 'far larger movement' that he saw the Chapel being linked to when he imagined the 'cloud of witnesses' that surrounded him during important memorial services. Again he provided a lengthy list that included, apart from Fox himself, leading figures from politics and culture, such as 'Lincoln, Cobden, Dickens, Maurice, Mazzini, Mill, Strauss, Darwin, Longfellow, Carlyle, Emerson, Louis Blanc, Harriet Martineau, Mary Carpenter, Colenso, Renan, Tennyson, Huxley'.[23] Many of the above, including Mill and Martineau, became regular contributors to the *Monthly Repository* after Fox became its editor in 1831.

Conway also clearly identified the predominantly middle-class makeup of South Place's congregation, recalling that it 'contained no workingmen so-called, and the few artisans in it were persons of fair education'. He characterised the members as 'mostly middle-class people of literary tastes, and trained in families whose vital religion was the new Reformation.'[24] There were, however, notable exceptions such as the former moral force Chartists, William Linton and William Lovett. Conway remembered Lovett with affection as 'the old [C]hartist, who wrote several useful books on sociological and educational subjects, [and] was a charming old radical to talk with.' Another member, Mrs Fletcher, recollected Lovett as 'the first person who really affected me … He taught me to change my views about Chartists. He was charming, a gentleman … He was an Educationalist, and had classes at St Martin's Hall.'[25] Other veteran radicals included James Watson, whose memory extended back to the prosecutions of Thomas Paine and his friends, and who had himself been in prison for selling Paine's works.[26]

The 1924 centenary celebrations concluded with a concert of music composed a hundred years earlier, the main feature of which were the 'hymns and anthems associated with the names of W. J. Fox, Dr Conway, and the sisters Flower'.[27] What follows is an account of music in the life of this small society throughout the nineteenth century, looking at how music functioned in this semi-public, semi-private space in terms of both repertoire and musical practice, taking account of the ways in which it helped to structure and organise an internal culture and its role in building a 'way of life' for this group of like-minded individuals.

Central to South Place's early musical culture was the composer, Eliza Flower. Flower was born in 1803 at Harlow in Essex, followed by her sister Sarah two years later. After the death of their mother in 1820, they were raised by their father and had by all accounts an 'original and erratic' upbringing.[28] Their father, Benjamin Flower, was a radical journalist and printer who edited first the *Cambridge Intelligencer* and later *The Political Register*. He was also to serve a term in Newgate Prison on charges of libelling Bishop Richard Watson. Unitarianism brought Fox into contact with the Flower family during the 1820s and he became such a close family friend that, on the death of their father, he was appointed the two sisters' guardian. Eliza was acclaimed as 'the most distinguished hitherto among English female composers' and Sarah 'not the least among English poetesses'.[29] Sarah produced many literary works but earned lasting renown for her hymn *Nearer my God to Me*. In 1834 Sarah married William Bridges Adams, another radical writer, and took the name Sarah Flower Adams. Eliza, however, never married and lived with Fox until her death in 1846. Garnett employed full-blown Romantic language in his characterisation of Eliza. She was, he declared, 'a child of nature': 'ardent, unworldly and passionate ... careless to a fault of discomfort and disadvantage' who 'existed by preference in a world of beautiful sound'.[30] Eliza was an accomplished performer, and had early on shown an aptitude for musical composition, although apparently she never received adequate training in composition. Despite this lack of education, none other than Felix Mendelssohn while on a trip to London had, according to Conway, 'recognised Eliza's genius'.[31]

The two sisters were remembered by Linton as 'two of the most beautiful women of their day'. His encomium was unrestrained: 'With their love and feeling for music and pictorial art, they were such women in their purity, intelligence, and high-souled enthusiasm, as Shelley might have sung'.[32] Eliza, in particular, caught the imagination of many leading literary and intellectual figures, including the young Robert Browning, Harriet Martineau and John Stuart Mill.[33] Himself a pianist and singer of airs, Mill adhered to the popular Victorian notion of music. The Utilitarian was not unmoved by its powers, echoing the popular Victorian conception of music as 'that art, so peculiarly the expression of passion'.[34] It was music alone of the 'imaginative arts' that had given the philosophical radical pleasure as a child because of its properties of 'exciting enthusiasm ... winding up to a high pitch those feelings of an elevated kind which are already in the character, but to which this excitement gives a glow and fervour, which, though transitory in its utmost height, is precious for sustaining them at other times.'[35] Mill considered Eliza's genius on a par with his beloved wife, the philosopher Harriet Taylor, and glowingly reviewed many of her compositions in the *Examiner*.[36] According to Conway, Eliza was Browning's first love. And he had, as he told her in a letter written shortly before her death of tuberculosis, nothing but 'entire admiration' for her music. He saw it as quite set apart from existing English music and declared complete belief in it 'as the music we all waited for'.[37]

Flower's output consists primarily of vocal music. In addition to her major contribution to South Place's *Hymns and Anthems*, which shall be considered separately, she wrote a substantial body of work that takes the form and style of early nineteenth-century art song. Much of it appeared in Fox's *Monthly Repository* as part of the series 'Songs of the Month'. Flower drew upon the work of poets such as Walter Scott and of Letitia Elizabeth Landon, a poet and novelist known by her initials L. E. L. This was evidenced in her first publication of 1831, which was a set of fourteen songs entitled the *Musical Illustrations of the Waverley Novels*, and her setting of L. E. L.'s 'Sleep, Heart of Mine'; both were published by Novello, another member of the South Place congregation.[38] They were well received in the press. Other musical settings included 'Vectis Benedicta' by Fox and 'When Thou Were Here' by her sister.

Flower also wrote politically inspired music, much of which represented the inclinations of many in South Place. She was particularly influenced by the radical views of Fox, as seen by her hymn *Lo! We Answer: The Gathering of the Unions, March and Song*, written in 1832 for the 'monster meeting' of political unions at Newhall Hill in Birmingham in support of the Reform Bill.[39] *The Gathering of the Unions* (subsequently known variously as the *Union Hymn* and *God is Our Guide*) became an anthem for generations of radicals; in fact, for many it supplanted the *National Anthem*.[40] Unsurprisingly, Flower's hymn found a place in song collections such as the working-class *Labour Church Hymn Book* (to be discussed in a later chapter). In 1893 the humanitarian socialist H. S. Salt included the hymn – unattributed – in his collection of *Songs of Freedom*, declaring it to be 'familiar to every child in the land'. The fact that it was written by a young middle-class woman from Finsbury had long been forgotten. There are two further contributions to this genre worth considering in more detail: another part-song setting of Harriet Martineau's poem *Hymn of the Polish Exiles by the Siberian Sea*, published by both Novello and the secularist Charles Fox in 1833, and her collection of *Free Trade Songs* with words by her sister.[41] In both these instances the genteel drawing-room genre of art song was harnessed to a political cause.

Martineau, a former Norwich Unitarian, radical liberal, writer and journalist, had become closely associated with South Place and became part of Fox's inner circle.[42] She had met the Flower sisters earlier in 1820 through the Unitarians at Dalston, before furthering the friendship at South Place. The two were close friends until the scandal that later consumed Fox and Flower.[43] The *Hymn of the Polish Exiles* can be understood as a sign of solidarity and support from within the radical liberal intellectual and artistic world for the Polish political refugees living in London. It appeared in 1833, three years after the November Uprising (itself coming on the heels of the July Revolution in France) led by Polish radicals against imperial Russia. The revolt was quickly put down in the Russo-Polish war of 1831. In the post-1832 Reform period, Polish exiles in London had established a London Bureau and Thomas Campbell, one of those who had sat at Fox's feet in 1832, founded a Literary Association of the Friends of Poland. The fate of Poland then was very much in the front of the minds of progressive types.

The scene is set by Martineau's florid preface:

A little band of Poles is assembled at midnight by the Charmed Sea (Siberia), where the imprisoned winds are moaning under the ice. They are allowed liberty in this vast solitude, and may therefore chaunt their hymns, without danger from being overheard.

This bleak, frozen environment is reflected in the sombre and proud character of the simple but effective music, which is created by key, tempo, a pervasive funereal rhythmic motive and a certain declamatory style. The refrain sees the chorus join the soloist with the impassioned plea to 'Give us our heritage again!' (see figure 5.1).

The *Free Trade Songs* also promoted a political cause. They were written for the League Bazaar of 1845, undoubtedly influenced by the fact that Fox had begun lecturing for the Anti-Corn Law League in 1843. They take their place among a large corpus of Anti-Corn Law songs. The political force is often hidden behind the tender qualities of the genteel music. Far from the serious and stark intention of the Martineau setting, the *Free Trade Songs* stand as simple, mimetic musical portrayals of the four seasons: 'Spring, the Descent of the Lark'; 'Summer, The Song of the Brook'; 'Autumn, Harvest Home'; 'Winter, Promise'. Stylistic conventions typical of the genre, such as the running figures to represent the babbling brook in 'The Song of the Brook' (not unlike those found in, for example, Franz Schubert's

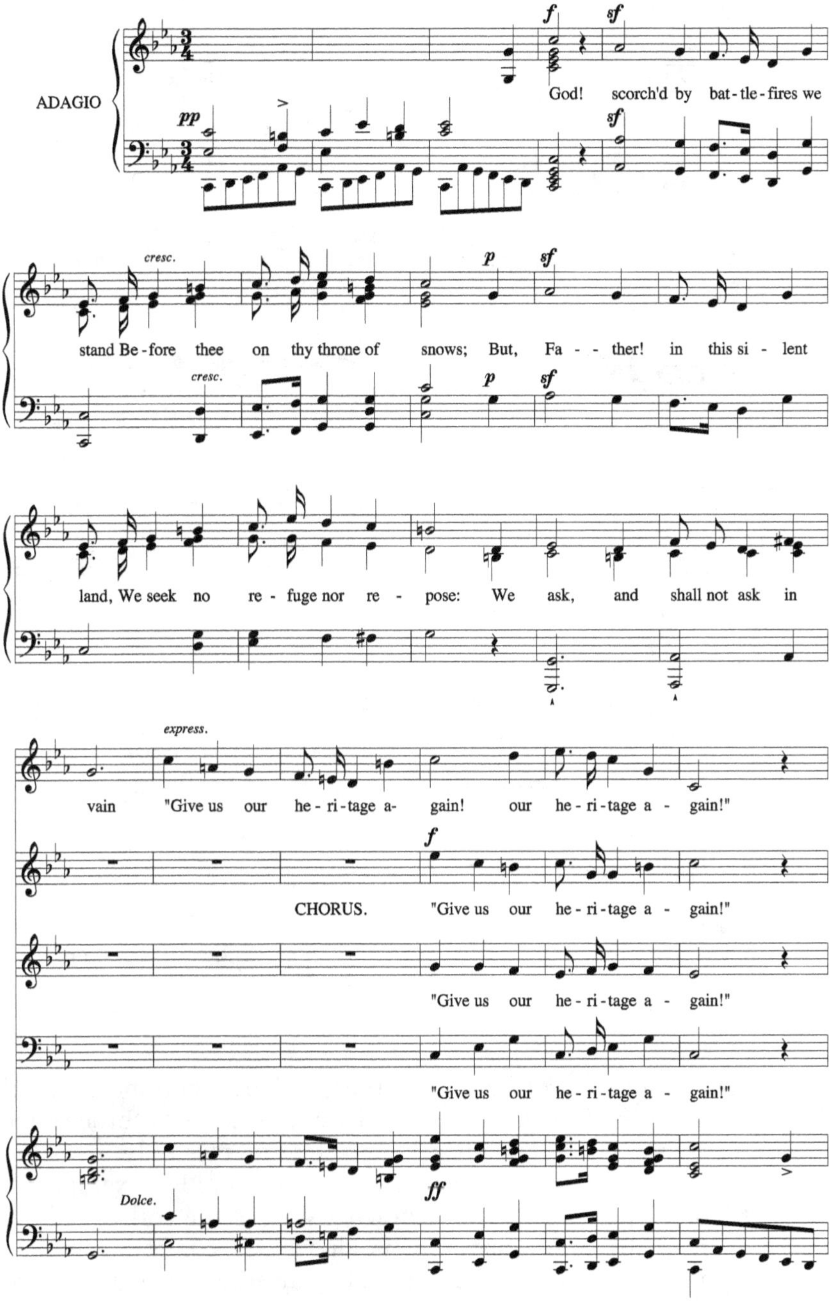

5.1 Eliza Flower, *Hymn of the Polish Exiles* (1833), bars 1–22.

5.2 Eliza Flower, 'Summer, Song of the Brook', *Free Trade Songs*, no. 2 (1845), bars 12–15.

song cycle *Die schöne Mullerin*) and other easily recognisable musical devices designed to denote particular affective states, run through the music (see figure 5.2). The political character emerges only occasionally and more by implication than direct instruction. For example, in 'Harvest Home', perhaps the most moving song of the collection, the theme of inequality and starvation is eloquently communicated in the final bars. With a dead child offered as an unwilling sacrifice to the landlord's greed, it stands as a direct allusion to Schubert's song *Erlkönig*, which also finished tragically with a dead child in the arms of a devastated father (see figure 5.3).

5.3 Eliza Flower, 'Autumn, Harvest Home', *Free Trade Songs*, no. 3 (1845), bars 33–44.

Flower was a central force in the creation of South Place's internal musical culture. She produced the first iteration of *Hymns and Anthems*, a collection that was to provide the music for South Place services for decades to come. 'Lizzie is in the thick of the torment with publisher, music engraver, and such like,' wrote Sarah Flower Adams. 'Notwithstanding all this', Adams continued, 'she is arranging a new hymn book to supersede the old collection which has long annoyed her at the chapel; and this ... and the establishment of a new choir, are all upon her head, and within her very soul.'[44] Flower's *Hymns and Anthems*, which appeared in 1841, quickly became, as Linton put it succinctly, 'the music of South Place Chapel'.[45] He was one of many

[239]

who had great admiration for the chapel's 'musical services' and was particularly approving of the hymnbook's contents, making special mention of 'the selections of Scripture' and 'old divines and poets', all of which, he remarked, were 'set by Flower to worthy music of notable originality and excellence'.[46] Its performance, however, demanded a high level of musicianship and, as such, required professional choristers and a musically able congregation. These requisites were to shape the content and delivery of the musical service for many decades after Flower's death.

Flower managed the musical side of the collection, arranging existing music and composing her own, while Fox and Adams were the literary editors and often took the opportunity to include their own work. Garnett pointed to the collection's distinctive character owing much to the fact that 'the text was seldom derived from the founts ... of professional hymn writers, but from the wide ocean of poetry, wherever sufficiently inspired with spiritual feeling'. [47] By 1874 the *New York Graphic* was describing it as a 'collection of moral verse' rather than an overtly religious collection.[48] In the review, much was made of the inclusion of canonical poets such as Milton, Byron, Shelley, Shakespeare, Browning and Tennyson, but less notice was made of the appearance of the female authors Mary Howitt, Mme Barbauld and Harriet Martineau and the working-class poets Robert Nicoll and Ebenezer Elliott, the 'Corn-Law Rhymer'. Fox admired what he characterised as the 'manlier and more direct utterance' of these so-called 'singers of the people' and had endeavoured to feature their poetry in the *Monthly Repository*. As early as 1832 he had celebrated Elliott's poetic achievements in an article entitled 'The Poor, and their Poetry'.[49] This was part of Fox's wider engagement with working-class culture as he sought to build a bridge between the classes. Indeed, he dedicated an issue of *Monthly Repository* to 'the working people of Great Britain and Ireland; who, whether they produce the means of physical support and enjoyment, or aid the progress of moral, political, and social reform and improvement, are fellow-labourers for the well-being of the entire community.'[50]

Flower produced three handsome leather-bound books of manuscript music.[51] Cramer, Addison and Beale published two volumes: the first in 1842 and second in 1846, which provided musical scores to accompany the text-only versions that Charles Fox had been producing since 1841.[52] It is significant that the first volume was a gift from Flower to the South Place stalwart Vincent Novello, with the inscription dated 4 November 1843. Approximately half of the hymn settings are attributed to Flower. The progressive political tendencies exhibited in her *Free Trade Songs* and *Hymn of the Polish Exiles* are felt here also. Conspicuous among her settings are poems produced by her intimate circle (among the group dubbed by Conway as the 'South Place friends'), she provided almost all of the music for Fox, her sister, Browning and Martineau. Noteworthy too are her decisions to set many of the working-class poets, Elliott and Nicoll, the philosophical radical and Unitarian John Bowring, as well as female poets in addition to Howitt, Barbauld, Martineau and Adams, such as Elizabeth Gaskell and Felicia Hemans.

Flower's musical taste in *Hymns and Anthems* does not betray an equivalent embrace of democratic culture or interest in social and political reform. Popular songs are notably absent. In addition to her original contributions and established hymn tunes, she selected various works by composers including Bach, Purcell, Handel, Beethoven, Mozart, Haydn, Hummel, Mendelssohn, Spohr and Gluck, as well as English composers including Richard Farrant, Charles Avison, Thomas Moore, Battishal Boyce and Thomas Tallis.[53] These musical decisions reveal a distinct political and aesthetic typology that took its place as part of an emerging middle-class taste.

The poetic and musical repertoire of this collection, despite constant adjustments and additions over the years, reveals a sustained commitment to appropriately reflecting the beliefs of the society. For example, the revised edition of *Hymns and Anthems* in 1889 for what was by then the South Place Ethical Society sought better to reflect the group's more secular philosophy. The preface is imbued with references to an immanent spirituality as the editors made clear their determination to produce a volume in which a wide range of beliefs could find common ground based on ethical humanism. They also make clear that the inclusion of the more overtly religious content was intended for performance by the choir only and served to provide a link with 'the religious life of the past, and because of their musical and literary merit'.[54] In 1874, long after Flower's death, Honorary Music Director H. Keatley Moore wrote a detailed report of the year's work, most of which had been dedicated to reorganising the musical collections of South Place. While bemoaning the state of much of it, he was more impressed when appraising the Flower collection, finding it to be 'at least the work of a person of great musical taste'. He was less complimentary of her compositional abilities (certainly than Browning or Mill), but did remark on her gift for melody. Keatley Moore was generally pleased with the selection of composers present in the Flower collection, although he did take her to task for supplying too much of her own music and 'using the great masters so sparingly'.[55] To the sixty composers already represented in the 110 hymns, Keatley Moore went on to add Schubert, Weber, Schumann, Arne, Webbe and Crotch as well as several 'modern'

English composers who had come to prominence after Flower's death, including Sullivan, Barnett, Dykes and Barnby.

The discerning Keatley Moore's term at South Place was, however, short-lived. After a dispute with the committee he left the post.[56] Despite the clash, he has remained one of several individuals who played an important role in creating the musical culture of South Place. Other notable South Place musicians included Collet Dobson Collet, the musical director, radical freethinker and opponent of taxes on newspaper, with whom Flower worked directly, as well as his sister Sophia, who also contributed some hymns and tunes for the service.[57] A later director, J. Trousselle, also composed a number of hymns and anthems, as did E. J. [Emily Josephine] Troup, another prominent musician and composer. At South Place Troup's role was chiefly to run the Children's Sunday School service. She composed much music for this purpose as well as adding to the general musical service.[58] In the *Souvenir of the Centenary Celebration* she was remembered as a 'most accomplished musician who took an immense interest in our music and movement ... showing a sense of continuity and tradition'; particular note was made that Troup 'became in Conway's time, what the Flower sisters had been in the days of Fox'.[59] Troup's songs travelled beyond the borders of South Place and found themselves in later socialist song literature, from the countless iterations of Socialist Sunday Books to songbooks printed for the New Zealand Socialist Party at the opposite end of the Anglophone world. We can likewise track South Place's journey from Unitarian chapel to Ethical Society through the Conway Hall Library's quite remarkable collection of freethought literature that includes not only *Hymns and Anthems* but also the subsequent compilations, the *Ethical Hymn Book* and *Hymns of Modern Thought*.[60]

In 1888 Stanton Coit, like Winchester and Conway before him, crossed the Atlantic and became South Place's minister. It was under his direction that the name was changed to South Place Ethical Society. An acolyte of Felix Adler, the founder of the Ethical Movement in the United States, Coit worked with his mentor to produce the *Ethical Hymn Book* intended for the Union of Ethical Societies. The hymn-book saw many editions and its contents overlapped significantly with South Place's *Hymns and Anthems*. Coit and Adler explained their choice of the term 'hymn' over the more open-ended genre of 'song': 'Hymns', they asserted, 'are songs in praise of what is held to be supremely sacred; and the poems in this collection are in praise of Duty, Truth, Beauty, Nature, and Life.'[61] Although the preface to the fourth edition announced a forthcoming version with words and music, this edition supplied only the hymn metres for each poem and

[242]

thus emulated the common practice for conventional hymn-singing. To a large extent, this decision was certainly made from convenience – the hymn tune books were easily available and widely known, and providing the metres alone allowed for a flexibility of musical choice. This approach, which as we will see is repeated in many similar publications, nonetheless created a curious and paradoxical tension between secular words and sacred music. Whether determined by questions of convenience, contest or continuity, or a combination of all three, the practice had the effect of sacralising the secular.

The semi-private, semi-public nature of the society was expressed through the mixture of music of the 'greats' and music by South Place composers. During the last decades of the nineteenth century a music sub-committee was established. The surviving minutes between 1877 and 1888 reveal the on-going presence of these South Place composers' music in the repertoire of the chapel.[62] They all continued to feature on the programmes until at least 1888; Flower more so than any of the others. In 1887 her works still appeared regularly throughout the monthly repertoire list. As Conway recounted, the weekly lecture had been 'a feature of South Place in Fox's time so that public teachers could be heard there who could be heard nowhere else'.[63] And as the society shifted from religious worship to a kind of freethinking ethical humanism, the lecture came to supplant the weekly sermon. We can see a process occurring here in which the ritual patterns of the religious service in relation to musical performance and speech are maintained but the content moves from the sacred to secular. During the late 1870s and 1880s, Flower's anthems were frequently called into action to provide appropriate musical commentary for the week's address. 'The Limits of Liberty' of 9 January 1881 was supported by Flower's Anthem no. 119, *Life May Change, But it May Fly Not*; 'The Growth in History of the Moral Ideal' of 24 May 1885 was accompanied by Anthem no. 59, Flower's setting of Martineau's *Beneath this Starry Arch*; 'The Ethics of Socialism' presented the following week was partnered with no. 139, *More Sweet Than Odours Caught by Him Who Sails*, just to give some examples.[64] Her music, along with that of Trousselle, Keatley-Moore, Sophia Dobson Collet and Troup had become part of a discrete internal musical canon.

In keeping with the South Place tradition, the committee were vigilant in their determination to ensure that the music accurately mirrored the society's principles. They resolved to meet once a month 'to settle the music for the following month', and also asked 'that the Organist be requested to attend same, bringing a list of High class pieces from which to make a Selection'. The organist/musical director's choices were not accepted outright. They were scrutinised carefully and some

[243]

rejected (on one occasion, for example, excerpts from Handel's oratorios *Judas Maccabeus* and *Israel in Egypt* were deemed unsuitable).
The monthly schedule was then given to Conway for approval.[65] The
committee minutes also underscore the importance of both the quality
of performance and the patterns of the musical service itself. They
reveal that both the music and musical culture of South Place were
closely controlled. Choices in repertoire were very carefully considered, as was the engagement of professionals for the choir. Positions
were advertised in the *Musical Times*; leading conservatoires such as
the Royal Academy of Music were directly approached for candidates
and singers underwent audition often to be rejected outright or hired
on probation with a strong likelihood of dismissal.[66]

With quality foremost in mind, the committee were determined to
improve the balance of participatory and passive musical experience
within the service itself. There was considerable discussion about
the balance between congregational singing and that sung only by the
choir. It was decided that 'the second hymn be rather more ornate, and
more of the character of an anthem'; it was also suggested these hymns
should 'be sung by the Choir only' and 'the opening and closing hymns
be so far as possible of a congregational character'.[67] The anthem, the
central non-participatory work, assumed a special place of importance
within the service. Middle-class taste was in a state of rapid development and in order to find a continued supply of suitable 'high-class'
anthems, the committee agreed to look beyond the existing collections. The final run of minutes are primarily lists of repertoire by
Schubert, Schumann, Hummel, Spohr, Rossini, Weber, Beethoven,
Tchaikovsky, Boyce, Sterndale-Bennett, Berlioz, Mozart, Haydn and
Gounod, although music by Trousselle, Sophia Dobson Collet, Troup
and Flower is still present.

In keeping with its long-standing objectives of moral improvement
and education for the working classes, South Place Chapel offered
itself as a venue to the newly formed People's Concert Society (PCS)
in 1878. The PCS was established to run cheap concert series of 'good'
music all over London as an improving recreational past-time. It was
by no means the first of its kind (Haweis, for example, had started his
Sunday Concerts for the People several years earlier). Nine years later,
in 1887, the South Place Concert Committee took over the concert
series, leaving the PCS free to find another venue. The South Place
Sunday Popular Concerts ran approximately twenty-six concerts a
season. Admission was free, although a collection was taken to defray
costs. It was (and remains) an extraordinarily successful undertaking,
quickly becoming one of the leading series of elite chamber music
in London with a reputation spreading as far afield as Australia and

India. The programming ranged from conventional holdings of the canon to concerts showcasing a single nationality or single composer. Towards the end of the nineteenth century, concerts were dedicated to premiering the works of contemporary British composers, including Charles Villiers Stanford, Joseph Holbrooke, Samuel Coleridge-Taylor, Frank Bridge and Richard Walthew.[68] Prominent performers such as Henry Wood appeared alongside members of his orchestra; the young Australian Percy Grainger made an appearance; and South Place went so far as to promote the budding historical music performance movement by featuring 'Concerts of Ancient Music' by the Chaplin Trio complete with harpsichord.[69]

From the outset the aim was to elevate, and chamber music itself was understood to stand at the more highbrow end of classical music-making. As W. S. Meadmore maintained in his history of the concert series, the title itself was a 'misnomer'; the music had in fact always been, he insisted, 'of the most consistently *unpopular* character'. In his opinion, South Place had done 'a vast amount of spade work' in the shifting of public taste from the 'lighter forms' to 'an appreciation of chamber music'.[70] Richard Walthew, a frequent participant as composer, performer and lecturer, wrote in 1894 of the 'great good' done by these concerts in 'making known the masterpieces of music to a public fed mostly on comic songs and shop ballads'.[71] The notes for the twenty-fifth season (1910–11) betray a certain ambivalence towards the series' 'frankly educational' origins, which were 'not altogether unconnected with the "uplifting of the masses!"'; but still managed to claim that the concerts, while no longer 'didactic', had not lost any of their 'democratic character'.[72] The history of this series shows the development of the modern concert. Extensive programme notes were supplied to educate the listener about the works they were about to experience. We also see changing patterns of listening. Whereas earlier in the series (and more generally) the audience was not expected to listen to an entire string quartet (or any multi-movement work) 'without some light respite', by 1887 the programmes included an instruction for audience members to remain silent throughout and only leave between works.[73]

Much was made of this audience: it was held up as exemplary. An extended description of it found in the *Daily Graphic* of 1898 gives both a sense of its makeup, but also the importance placed on conveying the success of improving ventures such as these in turning people away from the popular to the 'serious'. The account begins with the audience queuing outside the doors of South Place 'with an anxiety which is more often associated with the pit door of a popular theatre than with a place of worship'. The 'interesting' and 'distinctive' audience consisted of a minority of trades people and young couples looking for an opportunity to sit together, and a majority of 'the rather pale-faced people who attend evening lectures, and very seldom miss going to chapel on Sunday mornings', presumed to be 'suburban'; an amusing characterisation of the lower middle classes in the pursuit of respectability. The journalist then elected to speak on their behalf: they did not listen to the music (in this instance Beethoven's 'Kreutzer' Sonata) 'so intelligently and patiently' out of any 'polite affectation', but because they genuinely liked it and understood it to be 'very good'. This 'real appreciation' of 'classical' music stemmed from an education borne of regular attendance over a period of twenty years.[74] Through examples such as the South Place Sunday Popular Concerts we can see the audience becoming increasingly passive consumers of music as well as the ever-widening gulf between 'popular' and 'classical' music, with the latter gaining purchase as a marker of respectability, upward mobility and good taste.

As well as pursuing such social experiments, South Place contin-ued to welcome and support a wide range of views, both religious and political. During the same period that it was presenting concerts of fine chamber music, it was also freely providing a platform for many late Victorian socialists. The Fabians, the Social Democratic Federation (SDF) and the Socialist League all took advantage of this generosity and it became a popular venue for their annual Commune celebrations. South Place's openness to difference can be heard through the music that sounded under its roof. For example, between May and June of 1885, earnest listeners appreciated the chamber music of Mendelssohn, Schubert and Beethoven; South Place's own congrega-tion listened to their choir singing Flower's and Martineau's anthem *Beneath This Starry Arch*; and the socialists had risen as one to join the International Working Men's Choir 'in the intonation of the HYMN OF REVOLUTION', the *Marseillaise*.[75] And of course it was the same venue that over fifty years later hosted the Festival of Music for the People which was to programme Jones's *Song of the 'Lower Classes'*.

Although South Place stands as an exceptional example of a confluence between progressive and reformist thought and a rich and carefully constructed musical culture, it is by no means alone, and neither was the phenomenon confined to the British Isles. The Australian Church established by Charles Strong in Melbourne on 11 November 1885 stands as another example. Although there is no trace of Strong's church in the records of South Place, the similarities are both numerous and striking: they both had at their core a concept of religion that was free from dogma and creed and so accommodated a broad spectrum of religious and doctrinal beliefs; they had gained this unorthodox character through a profound schism with formal religion; they were defined in large part by the philosophy of a charismatic and controversial leader; through their congregations they had many connections to radical political and social reform movements; they sought to create an ethical way of life through a strong and distinctive internal culture; and music played a role in all of their many diverse activities.

Originally from Ayrshire and educated at Glasgow University, Strong travelled to Melbourne in 1875 with his wife Margaret to take up the post at the Scots Church on Collins Street. Within three years Strong had come under fire from the Presbytery for heretical behaviour. 'The Strong Case', as it came to be known, dragged on for the next five years. His relationship with Liberal politician and Chief Justice George Higinbotham from 1883 was one of the main catalysts for the Presbytery's censure, in particular Strong's support of Higinbotham's Sunday Liberation Society and the politician's lecture on religion and science delivered in the Scots Church.[76] The controversy was followed closely in the *Argus* and *The Age*; both newspapers came out in support of Strong.[77] Strong refused to denounce Higinbotham's lecture and was expelled at the end of 1883. The following year, after a short visit to Scotland, he could be found preaching to considerable audiences in Melbourne's Temperance Hall. He established the Australian Church soon after, and it moved into its new building two years later. The aims and objectives found in the annual reports and elsewhere are strongly reminiscent of South Place. The Australian Church advocated 'tolerance of diversity of theological belief'; it believed that 'genuine religion [was] confined to no one form of belief', that sectarianism was 'not only a ridiculous folly, but a sin'. The concept of liberty underpinned its 'Basis of Union', which sought a 'free, progressive, and unsectarian Religious Brotherhood ... untrammelled by a final dogmatic theological creed'; this 'Brotherhood and Catholicity [was] essentially ethical and spiritual'.[78] It had much in common with the progressive Unitarianism that shaped South Place's earlier outlook before its shift to an Ethical Society. Although never a Unitarian, Strong was well versed in the writings of Emerson and William Channing. He was also an admirer of James Martineau, a leading Unitarian, philosopher and brother of Harriet Martineau.[79]

The name 'Australian Church' itself suggests a possibility of renewal. Like many political radicals, Strong saw an opportunity to start afresh in a new country. The *First Annual Report* imparted this excitement; the Australian Church could become a 'national church' capable of 'embracing all shades of religious thought', and as such had 'the potential to escape old ways of thinking'.[80] Strong made this even more explicit: 'The name ... was adopted to avoid old theological or

sectarian associations and to express the free spirit of a young democratic people desirous of leaving behind them old world divisions and
quarrels.'[81] It thus became part of the emergent radical nationalism of
late nineteenth-century Australia. Others shared his optimism. The
Argus embraced it as 'an experiment' – 'a church of the future' that
could 'show the way' in a 'new and hopeful land'.[82] Strong's powerful
sense of optimistic nationalism is found in an alternative to *God Save
the Queen* printed at the bottom of a children's concert programme of
1890 that celebrates at once a sense of idealistic universalism and love
of country:

> God bless Mankind! we pray.
> O may Heaven's morning ray
> Dispel earth's night!
> Bless our Australian Land;
> Firm may her children stand,
> A free and noble band,
> For Love and Right.[83]

Many from the large and enthusiastic congregation that had accumulated around Strong at the Scots Church followed him after his
expulsion. They included leading figures in business and politics, representatives from intellectual and artistic circles and working people.[84]
Strong had close friendships with many in his congregation, including
high-profile politicians; the musicians George Marshall-Hall, Alberto
Zelman (the elder) and the internationally renowned singer Ada
Crossley (who was principal contralto in the Church's choir); the poet
Bernard O'Dowd; and the Goldsteins – a family of social reformers,
perhaps most famous for producing Vida Goldstein, one of Australia's
leading feminists and suffragists. Jacob Goldstein was on the committee of the Australian Church for many years, and his wife, Isabella
Goldstein, a temperance advocate and suffragist, was deeply involved
with the Australian Church's welfare work. She encouraged her daughters Vida and Elsie in the same direction. Vida was later to found the
Woman's Political Association; and in 1898, Strong married Elsie to
British socialist H. H. Champion, former Secretary of the SDF and a
key organiser of the London Dock Strike, who had come to Australia
some years earlier.

A key figure on the general committee was Samuel Mauger. Mauger,
who performed other major roles in the workings of the church,
was another important Victorian reformer and radical Liberal politician. Alfred Deakin, a lawyer, journalist and already by that time a
prominent parliamentarian (he later became Australia's second prime
minister), left the Theosophical Society to join Strong's congregation.
He became Strong's close friend and actively assisted in the church's

reform endeavours. George Marshall-Hall, a composer and Ormond Professor of Music at Melbourne University, was married in the Australian Church. Marshall-Hall was a controversial public figure known as an outspoken socialist and atheist, as well as an author of bawdy verse. Poet, socialist and radical nationalist Bernard O'Dowd was, from an early stage, deeply involved with the church. A committed socialist, O'Dowd had, like Deakin, been a member of the Theosophical Society; he was also a friend of Marshall-Hall's. O'Dowd was involved in many clubs and societies and epitomised in many ways the sociability that characterised the vibrant radical and reform culture of late nineteenth-century Melbourne.

The Australian Church then was, in many respects, a nexus, bringing together people who were active across a whole range of reformist causes. It also built its own structures of sociability that included a Dramatic Society, a Literary Society, an Orchestral Society, a Religious Science Club,[85] a Children's Sunday School, a Young People's Guild and a Social Improvement Society. The Young People's Guild, whose object was to 'organise the young life of the Church for its own improvement' and to assist the Minister in 'carrying out the programme of a free, active and living Church of to-day', ran their own debating society, nature excursion club and choral union which in turn became a glee club.[86] As we shall see, the Social Improvement Society ran several initiatives out in the working-class suburbs of Collingwood and Richmond.[87]

The hundreds of extant programmes attest to the centrality of music in creating and sustaining this culture of sociability.[88] Music was a constant presence. In addition to the music that formed an intrinsic part of the morning and evening services, there were sacred concerts, organ concerts, glee club concerts, orchestral concerts, choir festivals, 'at homes', *conversazione*, young people's festivals and children's parties. Music featured prominently at the laying of the Church's foundation stone in 1885, and it shaped the annual general meetings. The opening lines of the first annual report mentioned the string band that enlivened the proceedings under Herr Weinberg and thanked the artists who supplied the vocal music. The programme of the 1899 annual meeting further illustrates the importance of music in these settings. It opened with a performance Mendelssohn's Sixth Organ Sonata. The annual report, financial statement and reports of the various societies were heard. The choir and tenor soloist then performed 'In Splendor Bright' and 'The Heavens are Telling' from Haydn's *Creation* before an address by Deakin and Reverend Wollenden. The choir followed with Spohr's chorus *God Thou art Great* and a hymn brought the meeting to its end.[89]

The programmes were eclectic, revealing a broader taste than South Place; one that incorporated the popular ballads of the day, Rossini's *Stabat Mater* and the organ works of Wilhelm Friedrich Bach. The repertoire covered a broad range of composers and musical styles and genres: from canonical classical composers such as those heard in South Place – Schubert, Schumann, Bach and Stanford – to lighter fare, including music by Henryk Wienawski, Karl Popper and Louis Gottschalk. Arrangements of operas by figures such as Wagner and Donizetti were also featured on occasion. These well-known figures were found among a wider field of now lesser-known counterparts, including Raff, Fischer, Papini, Lacantoni, Ciro Pinsuti, Édouard Batiste and Gaetano Braga, to name but a few. As the musical directors were without exception organists, organ specialists such as Alexandre Guilmant and Charles-Marie Widor featured throughout the programmes, as did works by those with a reputation for sacred music such as Joseph Barnby, John Stainer, Henry Leslie and Bertholt Tours. More significant events demanded a more 'highbrow' repertoire, whereas the social evenings and glee club concerts featured more of an eclectic mix: songs by Pinsuti, Sullivan, Balfe and many drawing-room ballads by popular music composers such as Stephen Adams and Wilford Morgan were heard alongside piano works by Schubert and Chopin or part-songs by Mendelssohn. With the more 'serious' concert series such as the Sunday Afternoon Concerts, the Australian Church, like South Place, sought to control the audience's behaviour, issuing instructions in the programme to refrain from applause and not to leave during the numbers. For example, in the programme for a concert in collaboration with Melbourne's Lyric Orchestra of Rossini's sacred work *Stabat Mater*, the audience was 'respectfully requested to refrain from applause during the singing of the "Stabat Mater"' as 'such music' was 'best listened to in silence'.[90] In mid-1897 the programmes began to include more extended programme notes to introduce the works by Meyerbeer, Mendelssohn and Beethoven.[91] In such episodes we see the making of middle-class musical culture in action.

The public lecture was central to this culture, as it was to South Place, and it was inevitably surrounded by music. Over the years the Australian Church presented countless lectures on a range of subjects – religious, philosophical, literary, political, artistic, musical – by an equally broad range of speakers. It was the central feature of the Sunday Afternoon Concerts, which tended towards more 'highbrow' music, and it was here that chamber music was heard in addition to choral and vocal music often of a sacred nature. The exalted, even sacralised, position of music in the Australian Church is seen by the frequent inclusions of uplifting quotations by leading British intellectuals scattered throughout the programmes. For Reverend John Watson, 'Music, with its subtle suggestions and perfect harmony' was 'part of that unseen world where every ideal is real'.[92] Carlyle acknowledged its power when he declared that, 'Not only was Thebes built by the music of an Orpheus; but without the music of some inspired Orpheus was no city ever built, no work that man glories in ever done.'[93] Ruskin was more direct in his prose: 'The great purpose of Music is to say a thing that you mean deeply, in the strongest and clearest possible way.'[94]

Music featured constantly in the events of the many societies run by the Australian Church, particularly their social meetings and *conversazione*. In 1892, those present at the Literary Society's evening event could hear both an essay on women and democracy and a lecture-recital on the 'Songs of Shakespeare' with musical examples given by the church choir.[95] Singing was often used in the discussion of poetry and instrumental music would support recitations. The Young People's Guild was equally musically active. Not only did they run their own choral union-cum-glee club and give concerts at charitable institutions, but they also organised Guild festivals. A lecture on Schubert and 'Music as Emotional Speech' were included in their lecture series.[96]

The Orchestral Society was established in 1888 with the object of developing the 'Musical and Social element' among the members and to help the church in 'every good work so far as convenience will allow'.[97] It appears on many of the programmes, such as the aforementioned Dramatic Society concert, but struggled with numbers and was relatively short-lived. In addition to the Orchestral Society, the Australian Church engaged with the wider musical community and presented concerts in conjunction with Melbourne's Lyric Orchestra.

The operational meetings of the Church also featured musical performance. The annual general meeting of 1889, for example, featured Mrs and Miss Strong playing a piano arrangement of the march from Wagner's *Rienzi*, music by Handel, various comic songs and Sullivan's enormously successful ballad, *The Lost Chord*.[98] In 1893 during a Tennyson Evening organised to raise money for the Church Service Book Fund and Strong's own newspaper, the *Australian Herald*, songs were featured by the English and Irish composers Balfe, Barnby and Villiers Stanford, alongside recitations and tableaux.[99] The annual budgets show that a considerable amount of money went on supporting the choir, paying for the organ and the procurement of musical instruments and scores, particularly the hymnbook.

The Australian Church choir was central to this culture, performing not only at church services but also at the wide range of events that occurred throughout the week. The general committee had a strong interest in the standard of music and went to some trouble every year to thank the choir for their services in its report: 'The Musical Services of the Church are of a superior order, and the Committee desires to assure the Ministers, Organist, and Choir that their efforts for the improvement of the Church Service are highly appreciated.'[100] Several years later, Strong echoed these sentiments in a 'Pastoral Letter' expressing his desire 'that the musical part of the service should be devout and impressive, and the Choir and people should feel themselves to be one.' He then went on to say that while congregational singing could sometimes be 'hearty and good' there was still much 'to be desired'.[101] His anxiety possibly explains why at the top of some programmes for the evening service, the congregation was 'earnestly invited to join heartily and audibly in the Hymns and Responses'.[102] As with South Place, the employment of professionals was important. During a time of financial difficulty the church dispensed with the professional choral quartet. They quickly reversed the decision, however, and on announcing their reinstatement expressed their hope that this would 'strengthen and encourage the Choir, and enable them to produce at our sacred concerts music of a more interesting character, and, at the same time, more satisfactory to themselves, than could otherwise be sung.'[103]

The Strongs were themselves trained musicians and were committed to providing high quality music in the services. Charles provided the text of an original cantata, *The Day of Rest*, for organ, solo voice and chorus, composed for the inauguration of the new organ by the church's organist. He also supplied extensive programme notes and translations of foreign texts, as seen in the programme for Rossini's *Stabat Mater*, another co-production with the Lyric Orchestra.[104] Margaret Strong, 'an excellent musician' according to Strong's biographer C. R. Badger, ran the musical programme for the children's Sunday classes and Miss Strong was a constant as a pianist at a wide range of events.[105] Charles also lectured on music and religion on more than one occasion. As part of a choir festival that featured Gounod's *Gallia* and Schubert's 23rd *Psalm*, he gave an address on 'The Place of Music in Church', and, in 1900 as part of a concert of sacred of music featuring Gounod's psalm setting, *Out of Darkness*, he again presented, as an interlude, 'Ten Minutes on Church Music'.

Although the Australian Church did not build its own body of original music as South Place had, Strong, like Fox, nonetheless did edit his own hymnal. In 1892, partly in response to the costliness of producing service sheets, but more because of his determination not to see the 'prayers and hymns of a Church ... become stereotyped', Strong published *Church Worship: Hymns, Psalms and Prayers*. This was followed up in 1903 with a *Church Worship Supplement and Young People's Hymnal*.[106] In a memoir of the church, Annie Worsley remembered that Strong's hymn choices were guided by the belief that they must be selected 'in the light of modern knowledge and experience', for, as he insisted, 'we must not sing what we do not believe'.[107] Strong sought in his selections to embody the 'Spirit of Christian Religion' so as to appeal to a wide spectrum of religious thought. 'Variety, and adaptation to the special wants and feelings of changing times and circumstances, are necessary to make them living.'[108] Many of his choices echo those found in South Place's *Hymns and Anthems*: W. J. Fox, Sarah Fox Adams, Adelaide Procter, T. W. Chignell, Horatius Bonar, Whittier, Lowell, Samuel Longfellow and Gerald Massey among many others. There are many similarities again in the musical repertoire in the anthem section; along with Mendelssohn, Haydn, Beethoven, Gounod, Rossini, Spohr and Mozart we find the English composers, Sullivan, Sterndale Bennet, Barnby, Frederick Cowen, Charles Horsley and C. Francis Lloyd. The church, as with many similar movements, placed great importance on educating the next generation. Hymns played a pivotal role in the Young People's Sunday Morning Class. The Strongs worked as a duo in this setting, with Charles 'drilling' the children in 'carefully selected, or specially composed, hymns' that ultimately appeared in the *Young People's Hymnal*, while Margaret presided at the organ. She also copied out a collection of 'suitable tunes' for the hymn-singing.[109]

Strong saw the Australian Church as 'comprehensive': it was both 'spiritual and practical'. In his annual 'Pastoral Letter', Strong would repeatedly remind his congregation of the importance of the 'practical', urging them to participate in the church's reform activities. 'We have striven to put social improvement at the foreground of our church life.'[110] The conditions of the working class preoccupied Strong and he became deeply involved in Melbourne's wide network of social reform. In so doing, the Australian Church moved to the centre of radical political and social activity. From the early 1880s he was a member of the Australian Health Society and the Society for the Promotion of Morality. In 1892 he and the Anglican clergyman Horace Finn developed the Tucker Village Settlement Scheme, a utopian settlement plan to resettle the unemployed in rural Victoria (it resulted in financial ruin for both men). Strong joined Mauger and Champion in the Anti-Sweating League, becoming its vice president in 1895.[111] In 1900 he, along with others including H. B. Higgins (the Liberal politician and judge famous for the 1907 'Harvester Judgement', which paved the way for the granting of the basic wage), founded the Peace Society. Strong remained a committed pacifist throughout the First World War.[112]

Prison reform was also important to him and he became president of the Criminology Society.

The Australian Church was involved with various bodies within the early women's movement through various individuals. Through her own work with working-class women, Margaret Strong had become closely involved in the women's movement and was appointed vice president of the National Council of Women (NWA) in 1903. Charles Strong lectured to the NWA and offered the Australian Church as a platform for lectures by leading suffragists including Vida Goldstein, Catherine Spence and Alice Henry. In the early years of the twentieth century Strong fostered close connections with the Socialist Party, who invited him to lecture on 'Idealism and Crime'. None other than Tom Mann attended his church lecture on unemployment that was duly reported in the *Socialist*.[113] These activities and possibly his connections to the Victorian Socialist Party rendered Strong for many an increasingly 'dangerous radical'.[114]

In addition to participating in this wide raft of reform movements, the Australian Church established its own Social Improvement Society (SIS) through which it conducted its own dedicated programme of social reform. It was initiated in 1885, and by the following year was producing its own publication, *Our Good Words*. In its tireless efforts to improve the lives of those in the working-class suburbs of Collingwood and Richmond, the Australian Church put into action its commitment to the 'practical' application of religion. This welfare operation was initially almost entirely a female undertaking with very few male committee members (although, of course, Strong was president and Mauger and O'Dowd contributed). Margaret Strong was the honorary treasurer, Isabella Goldstein served at times as vice president and the Goldstein daughters were prominent members. In the early years it was very much a society run by women for women, and working women's agency was a consideration as the members of the Auxiliary Society consisted of sixty of the 'most hardworking women from Collingwood'.[115] The object of the society, as outlined in the report for 1892, was 'to promote good fellowship between all classes, and enlighten social opinion and to improve by every means in it power social conditions'.[116]

The SIS ran a raft of welfare programmes to alleviate the hardship of working women and their children. Using funds raised in part through entertainments, it started Melbourne's first crèche in Collingwood as well as a home for children in need. A grand concert was held under the auspices of the SIS on 23 December 1885 as a benefit for the Collingwood crèche. The Young People's Guild also provided their services to the SIS as seen in their entertainment of popular songs, dramatic tableaux and recitations produced in aid of the children's home in 1892.[117] In addition the SIS ran a Dorcas Society, sewing classes, a Ladies Reading Club, and opened a district library in Collingwood, intended to 'to create an intelligent interest in social questions'.[118] Church members ran elocution and singing classes for the Collingwood children and produced 'musical and elocutionary' entertainments, during which the children could display their new improved oratory and singing skills.[119] A singing class for young women was raised as a possible venture, but instead they were encouraged to join the singing class already well attended at the Working Man's Club that Strong, along with Deakin and Higinbotham, had been instrumental in establishing in 1891.

The Ladies Reading Club, presided over by Strong, provided the women with a challenging diet of improving literature by a wide range of authors including Charles Kingsley, Dickens, Eliot, Browning, Whittier, Tennyson, Emerson, Lowell, Thoreau, Whitman, Kropotkin, Mazzini, Shelley's earlier radical poems, as well as Blatchford's *Merrie England*, Edward Carpenter's *England's Ideal*, Henry George's *Social Problems*, Ruskin's *A Joy For Ever* and Thomas More's *Utopia*. The club organised a monthly 'at home', hosting visiting lecturers such as Catherine Spence, who spoke on the reform treatment of criminals, as well as others who spoke on women's education, Dickens as social reformer, Rousseau, pianoforte literature, landmarks of toleration, music in relation to national character and Chopin. They were made 'doubly agreeable by the instrumental and vocal music given'.[120] In addition to these, there were monthly social meetings, the object of which was 'not only to bring together different classes in a friendly way, and to unite the Members of the Auxiliary Society in Collingwood, but also to create an interest in questions affecting the health and progress of the people.'[121] Part of the purpose was to bring to the participants' attention some of the most 'burning social questions' of the day.[122] Again, each meeting featured an address. Goldstein and Champion spoke on women's unions and co-operation. Annie Besant's daughter, Mabel Besant-Scott lectured on women's suffrage and Strong lectured on socialism. Other subjects were temperance and children's education. Members took care to distribute a range of literature at these meetings, including issues of Strong's *Australian Herald* and a specially prepared 'Collingwood Series Tracts'. As with the club's 'at homes', there were lectures on musical subjects, including one on Mendelssohn illustrated by the organist and the church choir.[123] The educational lecture was supported by '[e]xcellent entertainments, consisting of songs, instrumental music, recitations, and comediettas' provided by members of the congregation and other 'friends'.[124]

This strategy of combining 'instruction and amusement', though in no way original, was expressly intended to increase the society's popular appeal.

Music was thus crucial to many of the SIS programmes as it was to the other activities of the Australian Church, but importantly the musical repertoire and practices that the Australian Church utilised in this working-class context were *fundamentally different* to the way music operated within the church's own internal culture and in its wider engagement with Melbourne's middle- and upper-class public. Although a selection of what can be termed 'light' classical music formed part of the many entertainments, the Australian Church drew upon the use of parody and appropriation of popular song, in particular the setting of new improved texts to familiar tunes, in their engagement with the population of Collingwood and Richmond. It almost seems as they were trying in a sense to speak, or rather sing, their language – a tactic of translation to cultivate the cross-class sympathy they sought. The programmes suggest that they were not trying, as seen so power-fully in the South Place Sunday Afternoon Concerts, to elevate the working class through modifying musical taste, but instead were hoping to effect social change by co-opting working-class musical behaviour.

There was a strong emphasis on participatory singing. Uplifting moral verse concerned with overcoming hardship was set to *Yankee Doodle*, the *Last Rose of Summer*, *Auld Lang Syne*, *Home, Sweet Home* and *John Brown*, as well as the popular Moody and Sankey hymn tunes, *Sweet By-and-Bye* and *Hold the Fort*. The meetings would open and close with group singing and the central part of the programme would feature short 'lecturettes' and recitations as well as music (including, on one occasion, solos on the zither)[125] by Australian Church volunteers. For example, the social meeting of 16 June 1890 was summarised as follows: 'Hymn 1 – (Sung by All). Short Address by the President ... Songs and Instrumental Music, Readings and Recitations; Exhibition of Sciopticon Views,[126] Hymn 2 – (Sung by All)'.[127] Again in this context the idea of a hymn became flexible. On this evening, *Marching On* set to *John Brown* was the opening hymn, while the hymn *Good Night* set to *Home, Sweet Home* closed the meeting. Yet another contrafactum of the *National Anthem* was desig-nated as a final hymn for the social meeting of 12 June 1892:

> God bless and keep our land;
> Firm may she ever stand,
> For truth and right.[128]

The substitution of 'the land' as 'she' instead of the reigning monarch is a none-too-subtle reminder of the nationalist-separatist impulse underpinning Strong's enterprise. The hymns *Marching On* to *John Brown* and *Do Your Best* set to *Yankee Doodle* were utilised on more than one occasion. Both convey a sense of movement from dark to light, suggesting a shift from hardship to a better time. *Marching On* begins with the grim lines:

> From the busy city sad moans of pain arise,
> Poverty and want wring salt tears from weary eyes;
> Progress seems but shewn in some Moloch sacrifice;
> So we go marching on.[129]

The final line makes clear the link to *John Brown*. But as 'the gleams of a better day' rise 'o'er the eastern mountains' in the next verse the singers are imbued with a sense of optimism. Both in the title and final line of each verse ending with 'marching on' there is an important allusion to another iconic political song: William Morris's renowned song *The March of the Workers* from his *Chants for Socialists* of 1885. Likewise, *Do Your Best* opens with a bleak admission rather at odds with jaunty character of *Yankee Doodle*:

> Tis true the world is very bad,
> No mortal soul can blink it!

But again 'dark shadows' are replaced by light and in the final verse the singers are encouraged to 'cease this everlasting growl':

> And since the world is bad, let's join
> And do our best to mend her.[130]

On another occasion an adaptation of Lowell's well-known poem 'The Present Crisis' was again set to *John Brown*:

> Though the cause of evil prosper, yet
> The truth alone is strong,

Each stanza ended with the triumphal proclamation, 'The Truth goes marching on!'[131]

According to the annual report of 1893–94, Strong had produced a small book of *Social Songs* for use at the SIS monthly social meetings. Badger mentions another collection of Strong's called *Songs of Hope and Progress*, which followed the same practice as found in the programmes of being set to 'good rousing tunes'.[132] Of the three examples given by Badger, two are instantly recognisable. The first is *Sons of Labour* by the Chartist poet John Macleay Peacock, which appeared frequently in ethical, secularist and socialist song collections most often set to the tune *Austria*, Haydn's famous *Emperor Hymn*, which is now best known as the melody for the German national anthem. The second is Charles Mackay's hit song, *There's a Good*

Time Coming, Boys, also found in countless songbooks. Despite the good intentions that drove these reform initiatives, there is no sense of how successful these attempts to create intra-class sympathy were, and there is no strong presence of working-class participants in the Australian Church records, apart from the occasional remark in the annual reports that attendance at SIS events was not always as it might have been.

Music, both in terms of repertoire and practice, was instrumental in the making of the distinctive internal cultures of these two progressive middle-class institutions on either side of the globe. Both the Australian Church and South Place Chapel were consequences of the nineteenth-century crisis of faith and both were driven by the same core set of beliefs produced in part by a reaction against conventional theology and a subsequent turn to 'spiritual immanentism'. The place of the hymn and music in the service was recognised by the members as defining their identity; they worked as a kind of social glue, providing cohesion and solidarity. From the late eighteenth century onward to late Victorian socialism, institutions such as the Australian Church and South Place Chapel not only produced hymnbooks but also provided the venue for numerous musical performances by radical dissenters and progressive thinkers alike. Both sought in quite different ways agendas of social reform in which music played an important part. As we will see in a subsequent chapter, there was a significant working-class equivalent to these two case studies: the Labour Church, which also used music and musical practice as way of constructing a clear identity and cohesive internal culture. But before moving on to a consideration of the Labour Church, we will continue to explore the ways in which the hymn and hymnbook operated in other political and reformist contexts.

Notes

1 Haweis published his experiences with the Garibaldians as three instalments in the journal *Argosy*. See Hugh Reginald Haweis, 'Garibaldi', *Argosy*, 2:9 (1866), pp. 207–16; 2:10 (1866), pp. 260–777; 2:11 (1866), pp. 349–59. Haweis's adventures in Italy are less well known than his musical work and, for example, do not rate a mention in Rosemary Williamson's article in the *Grove Dictionary of Music and Musicians*. See Rosemary Williamson, 'Haweis, Hugh Reginald', *Grove Music Online, Oxford Music Online*, Oxford University Press, available at www.oxford musiconline.com/subscriber/article/grove/music/46470 (accessed 8 July 2016).

2 Hugh Reginald Haweis, *Music and Morals* (London: Strahan, 1871).

3 Hugh Reginald Haweis, *My Musical Life* (London: W. H. Allen, 1891); Hugh Reginald Haweis, *Travel and Talk* (London: Chatto, 1896).

4 Mark Bevir, 'British Socialism and American Romanticism', *English Historical Review* 110:438 (1995), p. 879.

5 See, for example, Ian Bradley, 'The Theology of the Victorian Hymn Tune',

in Martin Clarke (ed.), *Music and Theology in Nineteenth-Century Britain* (Farnham, UK: Ashgate, 2012), p. 8.

6 Dave Russell, *Popular Music in England 1840–1914: A Social History*, 2nd edn (Manchester; New York: Manchester University Press, 1997), p. 23; Haweis, *Music and Morals*, p. 115.

7 Haweis, *Music and Morals*, p. 9, p. 41.

8 *Ibid.*, pp. 49–51.

9 *Ibid.*, p. 97.

10 *Ibid.*, p. 40.

11 *Ibid.*, p. 44.

12 The Universalists, or, as they were also known, the Philadelphians, were a dissenting religious group who rejected the concept of eternal damnation.

13 Conway Hall Library, London, South Place Chapel and South Place Ethical Society historical records (hereafter SPES Collection), *Souvenir of the Centenary Celebration of the Opening of South Place Chapel, February 1st, 1824* ([London]: n.p., 1924), p. 2.

14 *Ibid.*

15 *Ibid.*, p. 5.

16 *Ibid.*, p. 8.

17 Richard Garnett, *The Life of W. J. Fox, Public Teacher and Social Reformer* (New York: John Land Company, 1909), p. 253.

18 There is a considerable body of contemporary material on this highly fraught and divisive issue in the SPES Collection. See, for example, the folder 'Fox and Flower', which includes: W. J. Fox's letter of resignation, 15 August 1834; 'Resolution of the Finsbury Congregation asking Fox to withdraw Resignation', 1 September 1834; 'Declaration of members of Finsbury Congregation replying to minority protest', 14 September 1834; 'Resolution of Finsbury Chapel regarding Expulsion of Fox from Body of Presbyterian Ministers', 26 May 1835 among other related items. See also Kathryn Gleadle, 'Flower, Eliza (1803–1846)', *Oxford Dictionary of National Biography* (Oxford: Oxford University Press, 2004), available at www.oxforddnb.com.virtual.anu.edu.au/view/article/9762 (accessed 10 July 2016); R. K. Webb, 'Fox, William Johnson (1786–1864)', *Oxford Dictionary of National Biography* (Oxford: Oxford University Press, 2004; online edn, May 2009), available at www.oxforddnb.com.virtual.anu.edu.au/view/article/10047 (accessed 10 July 2016).

19 See Moncure D. Conway, *The Life of Thomas Paine*, 2 vols (New York: G. P. Putnam's and Sons, 1908).

20 Moncure D. Conway, 'Story of Old London Society', *Open Court*, 7:317 (7 September 1893), p. 3795.

21 The serialised account Conway gives in the *Open Court* is similar to that found in his own separately published history of South Place. See Moncure D. Conway, *Centenary of the South Place Society: Based on Four Discourses Given in the Chapel in May and June, 1893* (London: Williams and Norgate, 1894).

22 Conway, 'Old London Society', p. 3795.

23 *Ibid.*

24 Moncure D. Conway, *Autobiography, Memories and Experiences of Moncure Daniel Conway*, 2 vols (Boston; New York, Houghton, Mifflin and Co., 1904), pp. 39–40.

25 SPES Collection, *Souvenir of the Centenary Celebration*, p. 10. Fox and Lovett had met when the latter engaged Fox to run a series of lectures for the working classes at his National Hall between 1844 and 1846.

26 Conway, *Autobiography*, pp. 39–40.

27 SPES Collection, *Souvenir of the Centenary Celebration*, pp. 19–20.

28 Garnett, *W. J. Fox*, p. 64.

29 *Ibid.*, p. 63.

30 *Ibid.*, pp. 156–7, 64.

31 Conway, *Centenary of the South Place Society*, p. 90.

32 W. J. Linton, *Threescore and Ten Years, 1820 to 1890* (New York: Scribner, 1894), pp. 25–6.

33 Eliza is believed to have inspired two of Browning's poetical characters, Pauline and Pippa. It is ironic that Flower should have been the inspiration for *Pauline*, his first publication and his greatest critical and commercial failure. This is made more so when one compares Mill's brutal treatment of *Pauline* with his fulsome praise for Flower's music. See Charles Perquin, 'Robert Browning's Dramatic Monologues: Masks, Voices and the Art of Confession', *Cercles*, 2 (2001), pp. 3–11.

34 John Stuart Mill, *Autobiography and Literary Essays*, ed. John M. Robson and Jack Stillinger (Toronto: University of Toronto Press, 1981), p. 350.

35 Ibid., p. 146.

36 See, for example, *Examiner* (3 July 1831); *Examiner* (20 April 1834).

37 Conway, *Autobiography*, p. 26.

38 Eliza Flower, *Musical Illustrations of the Waverley Novels* (London: Novello, [1834]); 'L.E.L's Song, Sleep Heart of Mine' (London: Novello, [1839].

39 This is the song referred to by G. J. Holyoake discussed in chapter 2. Another example of her political interests is her part-song *Now Pray We for Our Country*, written soon before her death in 1846. This song was first printed in the *Musical Times* in 1846, then as separate sheet music by Novello in 1886 and 1897. It achieved a renewed popularity as a patriotic song during the First World War. Curwen published it in 1915 with tonic sol-fa notation so as to make it more widely accessible, and again in 1916.

40 H. S. Salt (ed.), *Songs of Freedom* (London: Walter Scott Publishing, n.d. [1893]), p. 80. As noted in the previous chapter, Flower's song is not to be confused with Samuel Bamford's *Union Hymn* composed in 1817.

41 Eliza Flower, 'Hymn of the Polish Exiles by the Siberian Sea' (London: Novello; Charles Fox, 1833); Eliza Flower, *Free Trade Songs* ([London]: For the League Bazaar, 1845). According to Conway, Flower had collaborated with Martineau on another occasion to produce one of the first original South Place hymns for the 1833 memorial service held at South Place for the Rajah Rammohun Roy, a leading Indian social reformer and founder of the reformist Brahmo Sabha movement. See Conway, *Centenary of the South Place Society*, p. 60.

42 For Martineau see R. K. Webb, 'Martineau, Harriet (1802–1876)', *Oxford Dictionary of National Biography* (Oxford, Oxford University Press, 2004; online edn, Oct 2006), available at www.oxforddnb.com/view/article/18228 (accessed 23 September 2016).

43 Fox and Flower's controversial relationship placed a great strain on their friendship with Martineau. They no longer saw each other and some time passed before Martineau once more began writing to Fox. She never spoke to Flower again.

44 Garnett, *W. J. Fox*, p. 219.

45 Linton, *Threescore and Ten Years*, p. 25.

46 *Ibid*.

47 Garnett, *W. J. Fox*, p. 222.

48 SPES Collection, H. Keatley-Moore, 'Annual Report on the Music of the Chapel from the Honorary Musical Director, South Place Chapel' (31 December 1874), p. 4.

49 See Garnett, *W. J. Fox*, p. 127.

50 See *Monthly*, 7 (1833). Repository.

51 These are held in the SPES Collection and the published editions are in the British Library with the second half of volume two still in manuscript.

52 *Hymns and Anthems* (London: Charles Fox, 1841; 1845).

53 This is, however, only the first volume. The music for the second volume was not ready by the time of the 1841 publication.

54 *Hymns and Anthems* (London: South Place Chapel, 1889), p. ii.

55 SPES Collection, Keatley-Moore, 'Annual Report on the Music of the Chapel from the Honorary Musical Director, South Place Chapel', p. 7.

56 Keatley-Moore was not the first musical director to clash with the South Place committee. Conway reminds us that an earlier dispute had arisen between Mr Smith, the music director/organist, and the committee over the kinds of music that were appropriate for performance during the service. Notably, the situation reached crisis point on the occasion of Fox's inauguration as South Place minister. Smith and some of the more 'progressive' choir members rebelled against the strictures imposed by the committee, resulting in a fifteen-month stand-off, during which time South Place had no organist. Ultimately the committee won out, and an arbitration forced Smith's resignation. Conway singles the 'rebellious' Smith out as 'a pioneer of the artistic music for which our Society afterwards became famous, and those who opposed him and his progressive minority were survivals from the Puritan *regime*'. See Conway, *Centenary of South Place Society*, pp. 35–7.

57 Sophia Dobson Collet was remembered as a cultured woman. She had known Emerson and the Novellos, and had been a close friend of the Flower sisters. In 1848, Collet Dobson Collet had been among the Linton's delegation to Paris following the revolution discussed in the first chapter. For Collet Dobson Collet, see Miles Taylor, 'Collet, Collet Dobson (1812–1898)', *Oxford Dictionary of National Biography* (Oxford: Oxford University Press, 2004), available at www.oxforddnb.com/view/article/42336 (accessed 23 September 2016).

58 For example, Troup's *Everyday Songs for Boys and Girls* (London: Novello, 1897), a set of sixteen two-part songs, was used by the SPES Sunday Society.

59 SPES Collection, *Souvenir of the Centenary Celebration*, p. 11.

60 The Conway Hall Library holds the fourth edition of the *Ethical Hymn Book* edited by Felix Adler and Stanton Coit (London: Swan Sonnenschein, 1905); *Hymns of Modern Thought* (London: South Place Ethical Society, 1900).

61 Coit and Adler, 'Preface' to the third edition of the *Ethical Hymn Book*, p. i.

62 See SPES Collection, Music Sub-Committee Minutes 1877–1888, MS Min 4/1.

63 Conway, 'Old London Society', p. 3795.

64 SPES Collection, Music Sub-Committee Minutes of 12 September 1886.

65 SPES Collection, Music Sub-Committee Minutes of 21 November 1879.

66 SPES Collection, Music Sub-Committee Minutes of 19 April and 5 July 1879.

67 SPES Collection, Music Sub-Committee Minutes of 19 July 1879.

68 Notably, early on in the series, Troup's 'Romance for String Quartet' was programmed.

69 For a comprehensive list of works and artists see SPES Collection, W. S. Meadmore, *South Place Sunday Popular Concerts (Chamber Music): The Story of a Thousand Concerts (1887–1927)*. See also SPES Collection, *Concert Annual Reports 1887–1997*.

70 Meadmore, *South Place*, p. 5.

71 *Ibid.*, p. 10.

72 *Ibid.*, p. 20.

73 *Ibid.*, p. 5.

74 Extract from *Daily Graphic* (12 December 1898) quoted in Meadmore, *South Place*, p. 12.

75 International Institute of Social History, Amsterdam, Socialist League (UK) Archives, Items SL 3453, 3455–3458. Programme for Socialist League Meeting held at South Place Institute [*sic*], 11 June 1885.

76 Strong's attitudes to Sabbatarianism were not clear cut, but he did support Sunday openings of public libraries and art galleries.

77 This support is noted by Strong's biographer, C.R. Badger. See C. R. Badger, *The Reverend Charles Strong and the Australian Church* (Melbourne: Abacada Press, 1971). See also *Argus* (16 November 1883); *Argus* (29 November 1884) and *Age* (27 April 1881); *Age* (25 September 1883).

78 National Library of Australia, Papers of Charles Strong, 1875–1961, MS 2882 (hereafter Strong Papers), Annual Reports, 1887–1955, Series 2, MS2882/2, Folder 4, *The Australian Church: First Annual Meeting*.

79   Earlier in Britain the two men had had a brief correspondence involving offers from Martineau for Strong to take up a position within the Unitarian church. See Badger, *Reverend Charles Strong*, pp. 159–60. We thank Frank Bongiorno for the reference.

80   Strong Papers, Folder 4, Series 2, MS2882/2, *First Annual Report 1886*, p. 6.

81   Badger, *Reverend Charles Strong*, p. 107.

82   *Argus* (9 November 1888), quoted in Badger, *Reverend Charles Strong*, p. 104.

83   Strong Papers, MS 2882/3, Minutes, Programmes and Reports of Social Improvement Society, 'Two Hours with the Boys and Girls', 30 May 1890.

84   Badger notes that Strong particularly sought to establish close links with the working class. See Badger, *Reverend Charles Strong*, p. 107.

85   The Religious Science Club hosted a remarkable series of lectures that clearly showed the open-mindedness of the church. Strong was himself interested in comparative religion and there were lectures on theosophy, the Qur'an (by Deakin), and in 1910 a visiting Buddhist monk gave three lectures on Buddhism. See Strong Papers, MS2882/2, Series 2, Folder 4, Annual Report 1910/11, p. 8. Strong, a good linguist, also translated Henri Bergson's address to the London Psychical Research Society. See Strong Papers, MS2882/2, Series 2, Folder 4, Annual Report 1895/96, p. 11.

86   Strong Papers, MS 2882/2/6, Series 2, Folder 6, Programmes of the Church, 'Young People's Guild Sunday Evening Service, 12 July, 1903'.

87   See Strong Papers, MS 2882/3, Series 3, Folder 2, Social Improvement Society Minutes.

88   See Strong Papers, MS 2882/2/6, Series 2, Folder 6, Programmes of the Church.

89   See Strong Papers, MS2882/2, Series 2, Folder 4, See Annual Reports, 1885–1899.

90   Strong Papers, MS 2882/2/6, Series 2, Folder 6, Programmes of the Church, 'A Sacred Concert of Vocal and Orchestral Music including Rossini's *Stabat Mater*, 30 September 1897'.

91   Strong Papers, MS 2882/2/6, Series 2, Folder 6, Programmes of the Church, 'An Orchestral and Vocal Concert', 12 May 1908.

92   Strong Papers, MS 2882/2/6, Series 2, Folder 6, Programmes of the Church, 'Sunday Afternoon', 29 August 1897.

93   Strong Papers, MS 2882/2/6, Series 2, Folder 6, Programmes of the Church, 'Sunday Afternoon', 12 September 1897.

94   Strong Papers, MS 2882/2/6, Series 2, Folder 6, Programmes of the Church, 'Sunday Afternoon', 1 May 1898.

95   See Strong Papers, MS2882/2, Series 2, Folder 4, *Annual Report 1892/93*.

96   Strong Papers, MS2882/2, Series 2, Folder 4, *Annual Report of the Young People's Guild 1906/7*, p. 8.

97   Strong Papers, MS2882/2, Series 2, Folder 4, *Annual Report 1888/89*, p. 28.

98   Strong Papers, MS2882/2, Series 2, Folder 4, Australian Church Literary Society, 'Annual General Meeting, 27 November 1889'.

99   Strong Papers, MS2882/2, Series 2, Folder 4, *Annual Report 1892/93*, p. 15.

100   Strong Papers, MS2882/2, Series 2, Folder 4, *Annual Report 1886/87*, p. 9.

101   Strong Papers, MS2882/2, Series 2, Folder 4, 'Pastoral Letter', *Annual Report 1903/4*, p. 13.

102   Strong Papers, MS2882/2, Series 2, Folder 4, 'The Australian Church [Evening Service]', 19 April 1891.

103   Strong Papers, MS2882/2, Series 2, Folder 4, *Annual Report, 1905/6*, p. 6.

104   Strong Papers, MS 2882/2/6, Series 2, Folder 6, Programmes of the Church, 'A Sacred Concert of Vocal and Orchestral Music including Rossini's *Stabat Mater*, 30 September 1897'.

105   Badger, *Reverend Charles Strong*, p. 27.

106   Charles Strong, *Church Worship: Hymns, Psalms and Prayers* (Melbourne: Melville, Mullen & Slade, 1892); Charles Strong, *Church Worship Supplement and Young People's Hymnal* (Melbourne: Fraser and Jenkinson, 1903).

107   Strong Papers, MS2882/1/1, Series 1, Folder 1, Annie Worsley, 'The Australian Church 1885–1955 and Rev. Charles Strong, D. D. 1844–1942' (1958).

108 Strong Papers, MS2882/2, Series 2, Folder 4, *Annual Report 1886/87*, p. 13.
109 See Strong Papers, MS2882/2, Series 2, Folder 4, 'Young People's Sunday Morning Class', *Annual Report 1899/1900*, p. 17; 'Young Peoples Class Report', *Annual Report 1900/01*, p. 15.
110 Strong Papers, MS2882/2, Series 2, Folder 4, *First Annual Report 1886*, p. 6.
111 The Anti-Sweating League was founded to fight for the rights of the underpaid workers toiling in the appalling conditions of what were known as sweatshops.
112 Strong spoke out publicly against the singing of the *National Anthem* in his church in 1916 on the grounds that it would create an offensively jingoistic atmosphere. It was a defiant act for which he was lucky only to be publicly criticised.
113 'The Rev. Dr. Strong and the Unemployed', *Socialist* (30 June 1906).
114 Badger, *Reverend Charles Strong*, p. 127.
115 Strong Papers, MS 2882/3, Series 3, Folder 2, Social Improvement Society Minutes, *SIS Annual Report 1903/4*, p. 17.
116 Strong Papers, MS 2882/3, Series 3, Folder 2, Social Improvement Society Minutes, 'Social Improvement, Friendly Help & Children's Aid Society, Social Meeting', 13 October 1892.
117 Strong Papers, MS 2882/2/6, Series 2, Folder 6, Programmes of the Church, 'Young Peoples' Entertainment. In aid of "THE HOME", Collingwood', 11 July 1892.
118 Strong Papers, MS 2882/3, Series 3, Folder 2, Social Improvement Society Minutes, *SIS Annual Report 1897/98*, p. 11.
119 See Strong Papers, MS 2882/2/6, Series 2, Folder 6, Programmes of the Church, 'A Musical and Elocutionary Entertainment,' 5 December, [no year].
120 Strong Papers, MS 2882/3, Series 3, Folder 2, Social Improvement Society Minutes, *SIS Annual Report 1899/1900*, p. 14; *SIS Annual Report 1900/1*, p. 10; *SIS Annual Report 1902/3*, p. 19.
121 Strong Papers, MS 2882/3, Series 3, Folder 2, Social Improvement Society Minutes, *SIS Annual Report 1892/93*, p. 8.
122 Strong Papers, MS 2882/3, Series 3, Folder 2, Social Improvement Society Minutes, *SIS Annual Report 1899/1900*, p. 19.
123 Strong Papers, MS 2882/3, Series 3, Folder 2, Social Improvement Society Minutes, *SIS Annual Report, 1897/98*, p. 18.
124 Strong Papers, MS 2882/3, Series 3, Folder 2, Social Improvement Society Minutes, *SIS Annual Report 1892/93*, p. 9.
125 Strong Papers, MS 2882/3, Series 3, Folder 2, Social Improvement Society Minutes, 'Social Evening under the Auspices of the Social Improvement Society of the Australian Church', 12 June 1889.
126 The sciopticon was a type of magic lantern projector. Magic lantern slides were a popular form of entertainment at this time.
127 Strong Papers, MS 2882/3, Series 3, Folder 2, Social Improvement Society Minutes, 'The Social Improvement, Friendly Help & Children's Aid Society, Social Meeting, Wellington Hall, Collingwood', 16 June 1890.
128 Strong Papers, MS 2882/3, Series 3, Folder 2, Social Improvement Society Minutes, 'Social Evening', 12 June 1889.
129 Strong Papers, MS 2882/3, Series 3, Folder 2, Social Improvement Society Minutes, *Collingwood Series: Tract IX* [n.d.].
130 Strong Papers, MS 2882/3, Series 3, Folder 2, Social Improvement Society Minutes, 'The Social Improvement Friendly Help and Children's Aid Society Social Meeting', 13 October 1892.
131 Strong Papers, MS 2882/3, Series 3, Folder 2, Social Improvement Society Minutes, 'The Social Improvement Friendly Help and Children's Aid Society' [n.d.].
132 See Badger, *Reverend Charles Strong*, pp. 111–13.

CHAPTER SIX

The challenges of uplift

The presence of women has been evident throughout the previous pages. In the last chapter this was manifested not only in their political and reform activities, but also in their work as musicians and the ways in which their musical activities contributed to the formation of the distinct internal cultures of South Place Chapel and the Australian Church. Women from a range of social backgrounds were important participants in the Australian Church's social reform programmes, and the church was, as we have seen, a strong and long-standing supporter of women's rights. Vida Goldstein acknowledged a debt of gratitude to Charles Strong in her address on women's suffrage, celebrating the fiftieth year of the Women's Christian Temperance Union (WCTU) in Victoria.[1] And it was, of course, in the Antipodes where women first successfully fought for and won suffrage. The WCTU, a branch of the broader Temperance movement, which intersected in important ways with the suffragette campaign, is one example of the many social and moral reform movements that were not touched by any 'crisis of faith' and remained firmly within established modes of religious practice. Like the Temperance movement more widely, it used popular song, familiar classical music and the hymn as important parts of its repertoire of action in pursuit of its moral and evangelical crusades. After examining the uses of music in the WCTU, thereby taking account of the close interactions that occurred between its New Zealand branches and Māori women, we will look at some Christian missions in detail to consider the place of music and music-making in colonial engagements with the indigenous peoples of New Zealand, Canada and Australia. The hymn plays a central part in this uncomfortable and complex area of colonial history.

A large-scale non-denominational religious movement, the WCTU was formed to promote temperance with a particular agenda of improving the lives of women and children. Just as the Temperance movement spread quickly across the Anglophone world in the first half of the nineteenth century, so the WCTU did in the second. Founded in Ohio in 1873, the WCTU opened its first branch in Ontario the following year, and arrived in Australia and New Zealand in 1882 and 1884, respectively. The World WCTU was formally established in 1883.[2] Anna A. Gordon made this global dimension clear in the title of her substantial collection, *The White Ribbon Hymnal or the Echoes of the Crusade compiled for The National and World's Woman's Christian Temperance Unions*. Gordon was the fourth national president of the American WCTU and companion to the renowned Frances Willard, founding member of the WCTU and a leading suffragist. Gordon, known for her musicality, had been asked to prepare a temperance hymnal that was to 'embody the "psalms, hymns and spiritual songs" that had inspired the movement'. This collection and earlier ones such as *Songs of the Young Woman's Christian Temperance Union* use a combination of well-known hymns and original songs set to 'well-known airs' written from within the ranks. In addition to popular tunes, there was music composed specially for the collection and the occasional arrangement of works by Mendelssohn, Mozart and Schumann. They were intended to be disseminated across the world. Given that the copies used here were found in the State Library of Queensland suggests that her objective was realised. Gordon demonstrated the centrality of singing in the movement culture by providing a list of possible events at which the hymnal could be used: 'the quiet prayer meeting, the earnest gospel temperance gathering, the great mass meetings and temperance entertainments, the memorial service, pledge-signing meetings and rousing prohibition and home protection rallies'.[3] The importance of appropriate choice of song comes through unambiguously. 'How many times in Miss Willard's pilgrimage', Gordon asked, 'has the power of her meeting been enhanced by music that harmonized with the spirit of the hour'; 'it is no exaggeration', she claimed, 'that the effectiveness of a meeting for religious or reformatory purposes is imperilled by the failure to provide intelligently for the service of song.'[4]

The *Ontario Women's Christian Temperance Union Prohibition Songs* suggest close cultural ties between Canada and the US at this point. Not only was the collection edited in Chicago, it also draws heavily upon Civil War songs.[5] *Cheer up, Prohibition Men, Vote for Me, Just a Little Ballot* and *Loyalty to Christ* are all set to *Marching Through Georgia*; *Vote for Prohibition* and *On to Victory* are set to *Tramp! Tramp! Tramp!*; *White Ribbon Rally* was sung to the *Battle Hymn of the Republic*; *King Alcohol Must Go* to *John Brown*; *What's the News* to *Maryland, My Maryland*; and *Our Trust is in the God of Battles* to *Just Before the Battle, Mother*.[6]

Memoirs such as the one by Mrs E. H. Ward, a member of the WCTU from 1884 who was instrumental in establishing a Young Women's Christian Association branch in the working-class Sydney suburb of Surry Hills, reveals both the ways that music functioned in this particular culture of moral reform and also the extent to which the temperance platform was used to advocate for women's suffrage.[7] Meetings were punctuated with music and singing, there was a choir of Ladies' Committee members, singing classes were run, funds were raised to buy a piano and when a fifth Monday in the month occurred 'social past times and music' were organised.[8] Singing was also heard at a public meeting in Temperance Hall in 1893, when the members of the WCTU intoned the hymn *Praise God from Whom All Blessings Flow* to congratulate the women of New Zealand on winning the vote.

Commanded by such energetic and effective agitators as leading suffragette Kate Sheppard, New Zealand's WCTU assumed an ascendant position in the women's movement. It rapidly established branches across both islands and was a highly organised and cohesive national body. Similar patterns of musical behaviour can be gleaned from the pages of the New Zealand WCTU's national journal, *The White Ribbon* (1898–1913), which reveal a middle-class and predominantly female musical culture of occasional music – vocal, instrumental and choral – that accompanied meetings, picnics, socials, afternoon teas, *conversazione* and 'at homes'. Fundraising concerts were a staple for a range of causes, as was performing at old people's homes, hospitals and Sailors' Rests. Particular attention was given to retired sailors, who were perhaps seen as more vulnerable than most to the demon drink. The women of Greymouth, a town on the west coast of South Island, decided to make concerts a regular feature after two sailors were so taken with the musical entertainment that they went on to sign the pledge.[9]

Songs and poems appeared in the pages of *The White Ribbon* and in a dedicated WCTU page in its predecessor, *The Prohibitionist*. We can again see a familiar repertoire. For example, the satirical poem 'An Appeal from Celie, Melie and Velie' by Eliza Sproat Turner, which appeared in *The Prohibitionist* in 1892, could be sung to Engels's favourite ballad, *The Vicar of Bray*, while another wryly humorous dig at the male sex, *The Woman's Sphere*, could be sung to *Auld Lang Syne*. Other more earnest texts such as *Vote As You Pray* and *The Glorious Nineteenth* were set to traditional hymn tunes, namely *Caritas* and *We Plough the Fields and Scatter*. Hymns were a constant presence. On Sunday evenings in Lyttleton women would spend an hour singing Sankey's hymns at the Sailors' Rest and the factory girls of Wellington were given a clear directive with the hymn that closed their meeting: *I Surrender All*. Certainly, after 1893 it appears as though music assumed a diversionary role in the WCTU's activities; nonetheless, some songs were so ubiquitous that it was often highly effective to invoke them in spoken addresses. Margaret Sievwright, when president of the National Council of Women in 1904, took such an opportunity when she invoked Burns to make her point:

> For a' that and a' that
> Her Edenship and a' that,
> In a' that makes a living soul
> She matches man for a' that.[10]

In New Zealand, temperance, one of the main objectives of the rational recreation movement, cut not just across class but also gender and race. From 1898 the WCTU devoted much time, energy and ink to the promotion of temperance among Māori women. Their efforts paid off and several Māori branches opened. Māori women had a high level of agency in this world and politics more generally. Like their European counterparts, they had won the vote in 1893, and several years before this they had been granted voting rights in the Māori parliaments. Many of the organisers of the Māori unions were themselves Māori. It was recounted with great excitement, for example, that Mrs R. Davis had agreed to act as president of the Putiki Union. Known not only as a 'strong Temperance advocate', she was also 'the greatest chieftainess of the Wanganui River' and as such exerted 'great influence among her people'.[11] Perhaps because of the high level of literacy that had existed for decades among the Māori, *The White Ribbon* began to print the Māori branch reports in their own language. Miss Stirling, another worker in the Putiki Union, was also seen to be of 'great value' due in part to the renown she achieved 'throughout the colony' as a Māori singer with the Salvation Army.[12] The printing of music appeared as an item of expenditure in the budget for the WCTU Maori Fund, suggesting a notable level of musical literacy among the Māori temperance women. Music, in the form of congregational hymn-singing in both languages and the performance of Māori songs, was an important element of what was a cross-cultural dialogue. An entertainment held in 1911, organised by Mr and Mrs Munro, transformed the stage of the Ashburton Oddfellows Hall into a Māori whare (hut) 'replete with objects' and Mrs Munro 'fully justified her distinction of being one of New Zealand's leading vocalists, with her "beautiful" performances accompanied by local musicians. Shortly after she impressed an audience in Wellington with her rendition of a Māori *poi* song and as an encore sang the hymn, "The Better Land".'[13]

Anna Stout, married to Robert Stout, well-known freethinker and twice premier of New Zealand, was a central figure in New Zealand's WCTU. As we have seen already with Elsie Harker, Edith Brand and Margaret Strong, Stout was herself a formidable political actor. Like so many suffragists of this period, she was an international player, and was later to join Vida Goldstein on the board of the British Dominions Woman Suffrage Union that ran between 1914 and 1922.[14] Stout worked closely with Māori women on issues such as education, employment and, of course, temperance. In 1908 she spoke on several occasions, including an address to the 1908 Maori Convention, outlining her scheme for domestic training colleges for Māori girls. The attitudes found in these lectures typify the kind of contradictory, essentialist paternalism of Pākehā thinking at this time. She rejoiced in the 'new pride of race' that the Young Maori Party (which included luminaries such as Ngata and Carroll) was 'fostering', and exhorted her audience 'as the descendants of the noblest race the British have ever met' to 'battle the demon drink'. She determined that the Māori 'should not burden themselves with the trammels of our civilisation' but asked them to exchange weapons for 'pen, voice and vote', and ended her speech with a Māori battle cry. At a later event in Wellington, again attended by leading Māori and Pākehā figures, she contended that the old laws, *tapu*, no longer worked and that the Māori needed to take up 'the new methods of their Pākehā friends'.[15] She wholeheartedly supported education for Māori women, but added that they should not take up sedentary work as this would make them 'mentally and morally degenerated'; instead they should focus on cooking, sewing, laundry work, infant and old-age care and nursing. While she thought Māori and Pākehā were mentally and physically equal, she nonetheless deemed inter-racial marriage inappropriate.[16] The subsequent musical offerings that closed the meeting – a Māori choir singing the hymn *It is Finished* in Māori and a male vocal quartet performing *Work for Prohibition, Men* and *Vote as you Pray* – only added to the air of cross-cultural confusion overlain with double standards.

The concerted effort by the WCTU to enlist Māori women to the temperance cause takes its place as part of a much broader and long-standing project of religious conversion, moral and social improvement and control initiated from the early years of colonisation. The imposition of moral reform upon the working classes from above was already a troubled undertaking. Although many within the working classes assumed active roles in the sphere of self-improvement, for example within the mechanics' institutes, and divested the middle classes of much of their paternalistic control, moral reform became an even more complex project when it reached the inter-cultural contact zone in which the European determination to dispossess indigenous peoples of their land was paramount. The shadow of reform culture is found in the deeply fraught world of the Christian mission in the colonies of settlement. Saving souls assumed a particularly brutal and frightening dimension when taken to the indigenous people of New Zealand, Canada and Australia (although it must be remembered that despite the often devastating cultural cost these missions functioned for many as refuges from settler violence).

European music often assumed an uneasy, even insidious, role in the contact zones in the colonies of settlement. Here, the hymn took on more sinister functions. For Christian missionaries it had the potential to become an almost devious weapon of colonial oppression and deculturation, while simultaneously providing an enormously valuable index to prove their civilising successes to potential benefactors. The teaching and singing of hymns was a central element of this process. The musicality of indigenous peoples was often cited by missionaries as evidence of their capacity to be 'civilised'. The singing of hymns particularly was a sign of civilisation – an index of the progress that had been made. It was therefore central to the cultural work of many missionaries.

From 1820 missionaries made rapid strides in translating the Bible into Māori and early on were holding services in the indigenous language. Māori hymns were a part of this enterprise from the beginning, as seen in early translations from the 1830s onwards. In 1830 William Yates, an Anglican missionary, sent a small pamphlet containing biblical extracts, including the Ten Commandments and nineteen hymns, to Sydney to be printed. At this time New Zealand was still without a printing press. It was William Colenso, who was to become a renowned naturalist, politician and authority on Māori culture, who brought out the first printing press four years later as an employee of the Church Missionary Society. By 1837 Colenso's translation of the New Testament was printed in New Zealand,[17] and in 1847 he produced a stand-alone Māori hymnbook of twenty-seven hymns.[18] The strategy of translation was successful and the demand for religious texts and hymns in Māori was high. The 1883 edition of *Himene e mot e karakia ke te Aurua* (hymns in the Māori language) had grown to over 180 hymns. Although the language was different, the *rangi* or melodies stayed the same, as seen by the inclusion of familiar hymn tunes or names of composers such as Mendelssohn or Tallis. An earlier report of 1853 by Thomas Samuel Grace in his memoir, *A Pioneer Missionary Among the Māoris*, recounted how 'Hullah's system of singing' was introduced at the industrial boarding schools in the Turanga district, providing strong evidence to suggest that the same musical tools and strategies central to the rational recreation project of social control and improvement based around the choir and the brass band were also used to 'civilise the savages' in the colonies as well as at home. According to Grace, the musical progress was 'satisfactory', unlike that made in English lessons, and after six months the Māori students were able to sing a numbers of songs in parts, including *God Save the Queen*.[19]

It was none other than Reginald Hugh Haweis who provided a vivid picture of this bilingual religious world in his *Travels and Talk*, which details his Australasian tour of 1895. After indulging in a moment of self-congratulation on discovering that his *Music and Morals* was to be found 'in almost every town' in Australia and New Zealand, he provided a description of congregational singing during a Māori church service in Wanganui led by Rev. Mr Williams, who, Haweis noted, spoke 'their language like a native':

> One or two pretty Maori girls and some more elderly native students led the singing, and all joined in. The tunes were plaintive, the voices full, rich and pathetic in timbre ... Mr Williams assured me that the chants were adapted from native tunes, but they sounded to me very much like most other Negro revival or even Salvationist melodies.[20]

By the end of the century the musical repertoire had broadened to include other types of music, including perhaps their own. Haweis' experience was by no means unusual. As we have already seen Māori choirs performed at an array of events, and hymns took their place among a range of musical genres and styles. Musical performance provided a way of enacting cross-cultural conviviality that often happened in dedicated reformist and communal spaces such as Temperance and Oddfellows Halls, for example the Maori–Pakehi Concert that was hosted by the Oddfellows Hall in Waikato in 1906. This 'novel entertainment' featured music from both cultures. 'Striking' *poi* dances were performed after the Kauaeranga orchestra had opened the concert. Of particular note among the ensuing performances by the brass band and songs and choruses by Europeans and Māoris was a 'Maori hymn, "Onward Christian Soldiers,"' which was purportedly 'splendidly sung by a Maori choir'.[21] This pattern of cross-cultural engagement continued. Two thousand Pākehā turned out in 1911 to support the equivalent number of Māori for the unveiling of the memorial to Māori leader Tamahau Mahupuku. After the 'welcome *haka*' was danced, a Māori choir sang hymns in both Māori and English.[22]

The Māori had been the target of the Temperance movement well before the WCTU's campaign. Two editions of a temperance songbook in Māori compiled by Charles Oliver Bond Davis appeared in 1873 and 1884. Davis was a complicated and contradictory character. After moving from Sydney to the Wesleyan mission in Hokianga as a child, he became fluent in Māori and spent many years working closely with the Māori people on land issues, often angering settlers and other Māori in the process. In 1840 he assisted at the meeting in Hokianga which saw the signing of the Treaty of Waitangi, before taking up a long career in the Native Department under his close friend Donald McClean. Davis wrote at least two biographies of prominent Māori figures and helped produce Māori-language newspapers, including the official newspaper *Te Karere Maori* (The Māori Messenger). During the 1870s he became closely involved in the temperance movement and in 1873 produced *He Waiata Pehi Waipiro etc. I Te Reo Maori* or *Temperance Songs, etc., in the Maori Language*. An expanded edition, *Te Honae*, appeared over a decade later.[23]

Davis takes his place among a group of Pākehā who were aware of and remorseful about the great wrongs inflicted upon the Māori by Europeans. Nonetheless, this group was insistent that the way forward was not through political agitation but rather through personal improvement, and temperance was key to this agenda. An unidentified newspaper report pasted into one extant copy of the songbook, however, expressed some reservations as to the effectiveness of the strategy of singing in achieving this end:

> There are few Europeans who can appreciate what has been done, and it is to be feared that the natives, although they will sing the songs, will drift along, running after will-o'-the wisps about appeals to the Home Secretary and deputations to London, but leaving unreformed their social and personal habits, although reform in that direction is the only means that will save the race.[24]

The reporter still hoped that these songs 'would have greater influence in moulding a people than the laws'.

The songbook was published 'by request of friends who take a lively interest in the good cause of Total Abstinence among the Maoris'.[25] Davis was explicit that the aim of the songs was to 'ameliorate the moral and social condition of the Maori Nation'. There is evidence of Māori participation: Hori Ropiha and Mihaka Makoare are among those thanked as subscribers and one hymn was purportedly 'by a native, occasioned by the death of a relative'.[26] The music given for the temperance songs is an eclectic mix of traditional English and evangelist hymn tunes,[27] and popular European, American and Māori songs. In the first edition Davis often gave both the hymn metre and a possible tune. In some instances, such as the song *Te Pai o Te Kore Kei Waipiro*, two tunes are given. Somewhat incongruously, in this case the hymn tune *Palestine* and the popular Scottish melody *There's*

Nae Luck About the House are suggested.[28] The second edition contains more American music, particularly revolutionary and Civil War melodies. The collection was acclaimed as 'absolutely unique' and 'a wonder of Maori scholarship' in the same report, which went on to describe and translate some of the songs. The opening song, set to *Johnny Comes Marching Home*, relates 'in approving terms' the Māori leader Tawhiao's signing of the temperance pledge with Sir George Grey, his adherence to the pledge during his travels in England and his continued advocacy of temperance among his people. The second, sung to no. 72 from *Sacred Songs and Solos*, expressed gratitude to the people of Waikato and Wanganui, and Ngāti Maniapoto and Māori leaders who came out in support of the Prohibitory Liquor Law. The third, set to the *Star Spangled Banner*, was written 'in honour of the Governor and his Ministry, regarding their action on the temperance question'. Politicians thanked by name included Premier Robert Stout and Finance Minister Julius Vogel:

> The Governor, truly, established good will
> And banished intoxicants all from the border;
> And Stout too, and Tole displayed their great skill,
> Courageously silencing taunts and disorder.
> And Vogel and Buckley upheld the same rights,
> While Reynolds and Richardson worked with their might.
> Speed on, O Prosperity, through the whole land,
> O'er hills, plains, and rivers, and ocean-bound strand.

These translations reveal the songs to be similar to the journalistic style of ballads composed and performed, as we have seen, by the likes of Charles Thatcher. By delivering detailed point-in-time commentary on local events they in effect both chronicled and editorialised to music.

Missionaries were necessarily among the most peripatetic citizens of the Anglophone world and so gained first-hand experience of many indigenous cultures. On 15 June 1904 the *Wanganui Chronicle* reported the address, 'People of Other Lands', given by Bishop Ridley about mission work in British Columbia, which demonstrated the many parallels in the colonial and missionary history of Canada and New Zealand. The Putiki Maori Choir's opening rendition of *When I Survey the Wondrous Cross* in Māori prompted the Bishop to ruminate on the many (around twenty-three, he supposed) different languages he had heard the same hymn sung in, before going on to comment on how the Māori reminded him of the 'Indians' in British Columbia who were also 'wonderful linguists and excellent musicians'.[29]

British Columbia was a hive of missionary activity for much of the nineteenth century. As in New Zealand, the translation of scripture and hymns into the local languages was undertaken in Canada. One missionary who immersed himself in the study of Tsimshian languages was William Duncan, an Anglican lay minister. In 1862 he founded Metlakahtla [sic], a utopian Christian community comprising several hundred Tsimshians from the fourteen Tsimshian tribes on Metlakatla Pass, near Prince Rupert. Duncan's unconventional religious beliefs led to his expulsion from the Christian Missionary Society, and in response he founded his own Independent Native Church. Duncan pursued the strategy of hymn translation as seen in his report of Christmas in 1873, when he recounted 'the first attempt of the Indians at part-singing in their own tongue'. He had spent Christmas Eve with twenty young men practising a 'new Christmas hymn in Tsimshean [sic]', and at 1.30 a.m. on Christmas morning the men paraded around the 'illuminated' village singing hymns in 'hearty and solemn' voices, accompanied by himself and his colleague, William Henry Collison, on harmonium and concertina.[30] The harmonium, a small pneumatic keyboard instrument, was commonly found in the colonies as it was portable and durable. The concertina had been adopted for similar reasons by many Victorians as 'an instrument of rational recreation', and 'concertina bands were to become part of organised working class music making'.[31] Some Canadians took it up with obvious enjoyment (and perhaps for reasons of status and respectability). Admiral Prevost recalled in his report of a visit to Metlakatla, an invitation from a Tsimshian elder 'to hear him perform on a parlour organ [harmonium], which he had bought at Victoria for 80 dollars'. 'It was a wondrous sight,' Prevost pronounced, 'the Indian and his wife at his side playing and singing many of the well-known Sankey's hymns [sic]!'[32]

Indigenous attitudes to Britain and Empire were various and not always, or at least not always obviously, oppositional, as seen in the vivid account of Governor General Lord Dufferin's visit to Metlakatla in September 1876. The native people helped their 'energetic white chief' prepare for the event:

> Several Union Jacks were hoisted throughout the village, and a red cloth, with 'God save the Queen' worked on it, was stretched across between two houses near the landing. ... The next thing was the singing of the National Anthem to an accompaniment supplied by some of the members of a brass band which exists among the young men of the community.

The latter, he continued:

> were gorgeous in cast-off uniforms of United States soldiers, purchased at a sale of condemned military clothing recently held in Alaska. ... Subsequently all the people were assembled in the open air, and the

younger portion of them sang, under the direction of Mr. Duncan and Mr. Collison, a number of songs and hymns, both in their native tongue and in English.[33]

Music was used as a way to negotiate, enforce and articulate power relations and structures of authority between cultures. It was also used, as seen in the Māori–Pākehā concerts and the Cooper–Selby concert to be discussed later in this chapter, as a way of generating cross-cultural engagement and mediating cultural differences. As we have seen (and this was the case with much history of indigenous peoples), the one-sidedness of the overwhelming majority of available evidence makes it difficult to hear the indigenous voice and to assess indigenous agency and motive.

Not far away in Kitamaat Village, located 120 kilometres southeast of Prince Rupert (now the centre of the Haisla First Nation), the indigenous Canadians were, as we have noted, also becoming proficient bandsmen. In this case there is further evidence in the missionary George Raley's journal, *Na-Na-Kwa*, to suggest the First Nation Canadians were active agents in this. While preparing a submission for special subscriptions for the acquisition of new band instruments, Raley wrote:

> The band instruments, for which the people had subscribed a year ago, arrived on the 15th of August. They are of the 'Ideal' series from Whaley, Royce and Co. of Toronto. The natives are natural musicians, and better judges of a good instrument than one would expect. They are delighted with the new band. Every Christian village has its band.[34]

When A. Jackson, a new missionary, arrived in October 1900 he received a hearty welcome: the 'band turned out in full force and played several selections in good style'.[35] Children's entertainments were held at the Children's Home, featuring songs, choruses, quartets and motion songs. They were 'drilled' in choral singing by Miss Long, who ran the Children's Home. In 1900 it was reported that they had learnt several anthems, including Gounod's *Praise ye the Father*. They were praised for their musical ability, as were the young men who also participated in concerted singing.[36]

During this period many First Nations people were living in missions and working in the canneries and fisheries that dotted the coastline. Music was as important to the workers from Kitamaat Village as it was to the Tsimshians at Metlakatla, and in 1899 they pulled together and raised enough money to buy an organ. The subsequent concert of an 'excellent programme of vocal and instrumental music' was 'rendered very creditably'.[37] From the final decades of the nineteenth century, many First Nations people continued to take great pride in their brass bands and the bands exerted a considerable degree of agency in their dealings with the Department of Indian Affairs.[38] Not only did they request funding for instruments, uniforms and music, but some band leaders produced their own music. Job Nelson, a First Nations conductor who worked in Metlakatla during the 1890s, composed the *Imperial Native March* that was performed during the 1905 Dominion Exhibition and an arrangement for piano was published in 1907.

It is important to keep in mind when considering these kinds of musical events that they occurred in a context of extreme hardship for indigenous people, who were suffering not only cultural loss, in part through the assimilationist endeavours of missionaries and governments, but also dispossession of their land and massive loss of life through settler violence and associated problems of disease and food shortage. Consequently, the history and historiography of settler colonialism is profoundly fraught and deeply troubled, presenting conceptual and evidential challenges of considerable complexity to do with agency, appropriation, subversion, assimilation, defiance and adaptation within grossly unbalanced power structures.

Since the establishment of the journal *Aboriginal History* in 1977 the Aboriginal history of Australia has grown exponentially as a subfield of inquiry. Scholarship on the history of missions takes its place within this disciplinary field.[39] Much has been written, for instance, about Coranderrk, one of the first Victorian missions situated just outside Melbourne, and its notable and influential Aboriginal leader, William Barak.[40] As is well known, Barak was an active advocate for his people during a time of enormous hardship. His paintings of corroborees (indigenous ceremonies, which included singing and dancing) are now understood as important cultural-historical documents as well as art objects. He was also known for his fine baritone voice, but unfortunately the musical element of the many deputations he and his associates made to government officials has not survived in the historical record.

This is not true, however, of a mission on the New South Wales side of the Murray River, not far from the small town of Echuca where Wesleyan lay preacher Daniel Matthews established Maloga Mission in 1874. Matthews stands among a group of missionaries, including John Green at Coranderrk and John Gribble at Warrangesda, who have been characterised by one leading scholar of Aboriginal history, Bain Attwood, as 'humanitarian'. Attwood argues that these men were driven by a genuine sympathy for indigenous Australians, and were passionately committed to their moral and social improvement.[41] There were close ties between the Coranderrk, Maloga and Warrangesda missions, reflected in the continual movement of people between the missions and the shared outlook of the Europeans who worked there. The missionary commitment to what has been called 'Aboriginal uplift' did not go unacknowledged by some indigenous people who spent time on these missions. For example, an Aboriginal activist, Shadrach L. James, unequivocally acknowledged the contribution of many missionaries at Cummeragunga and Maloga: 'Whatever efforts have been made to help us have been by the missionaries. They are the only people who have attempted to lift us to citizenship.'[42]

Matthews emigrated to Australia with his parents and brother from Cornwall in 1851. Soon after his arrival he went to try his luck on the goldfields. His humanitarian sympathies were aroused by the treatment of Aborigines he witnessed there. From then on he felt 'an irresistible call to give time and strength to the interest of these Aborigines'.[43] By 1864 he had abandoned his quest for gold and opened a store in Echuca. Ten years later, in response partly to the colonial government's decision to move Aborigines onto reserves managed by missionaries,[44] Matthews and his wife, Janet, decided to dedicate their lives to what he described as an 'unsectarian movement for the moral and spiritual elevation of the native Blacks of Australia'.[45] The store was closed and land bought twenty kilometres from Echuca. The site chosen for the Maloga Mission on the banks of the Murray was Yorta Yorta ceremonial ground. Maloga Mission was privately run, subsisting on private donations and small grants from the New South Wales government. In 1880 Matthews was instrumental in establishing the New South Wales Aborigines Protection Association (APA), which in turn provided financial support for the mission. By this time Maloga had transformed into a small settlement with a church, schoolhouse and cottages with land for livestock and agriculture.

The mission's annual reports that were published from the late 1870s survive as rich historical records.[46] They are not, however, without their interpretative challenges. These reports were a central part of Matthews's fundraising activities and were shaped accordingly. They focussed equally on tales of tragedy (the many deaths that occurred with awful regularity throughout the decades) and the tales of success (the conversions, the marriages, the births). The former were intended to arouse sympathy and the latter to show progress. What comes through clearly in the reports is the importance of music in achieving what he saw as civilising objectives. He and his wife saw their duties as including 'the protection, education, and evangelization of the aboriginal natives of Australia, especially of the children'.[47] For them Maloga was a site where the Victorian notions of morality, hard work, honesty, sobriety (Matthews had long been committed to temperance) and education coalesced to bring about Aboriginal 'uplift'. His attitudes towards Aborigines are summarised by one of the American revivalist hymns he chose to teach them, being in his opinion 'so singularly applicable to the case of the Aborigines of Australia':

> Rescue the perishing, care for the dying;
> Snatch them in pity from sin and the grave.[48]

Maloga offers a rich case study of music on missions as well as its use in reform and political activity. Here, the recollections of William Cooper provide an essential point of entry. As the founder of the Australian Aborigines' League in 1934 Cooper was perhaps the most important indigenous activist of the early twentieth century. Born around 1861 he lived for a number of years with his extended family on Maloga Mission (and later at Cummeragunga station).[49] The years he spent at Maloga were formative both politically and musically, an influence he was later to acknowledge.

As seen in a letter to Matthews's daughter, written shortly before his death in 1941, Cooper remembered the missionary and his wife, Jane, with affection and respect:

> It was very unfortunate for the Aborigines to lose your dearly beloved father and mother. Had they lived and worked till now, we would have had Aboriginal doctors, lawyers, mechanical engineers and other professional people, and would also have had educated natives capable of representing our people in Parliament.[50]

Song was central to life at Maloga and it shaped Cooper's memories of the place. 'We never had singing like we had at Maloga,' he recalled. The 'beautiful singing' stayed with him and was to inform his own activism.[51] The Matthews both had a deep love for music. Janet was proficient on the keyboard, whether it was piano, harmonium or organ. (Later in life she and her daughter were to teach music in the district to support themselves.) Despite a palpable sense of unhappiness and resentment felt by many Aborigines as a result of Matthews's often-severe approach, the singing of hymns remained popular throughout the life of the mission and beyond. The Aborigines often sat with the Matthews in the school house 'and sang without much intermission for two hours'. 'They all love music', Matthews reported, 'and display a measure of taste and talent'.[52] Committing hymns to memory formed a significant part of the children's general education. In his reports Matthews noted the ever-increasing number they could sing by heart.[53] Singing classes, including sacred concerts and instruction in part-singing, were held on Monday and Tuesday evenings. His annual reports repeatedly mention singing in the most favourable terms, making much of the Aborigines' natural aptitude for music. This abundance of music-making resulted in the formation of a choir, which quickly became celebrated across the region as the Maloga Choir and was an important asset for Matthews with regard to raising money.

Maloga thus provides us with an important example of the way that singing provided a sounding index of 'improvement'. For many at that time the ability to harmonise was a marker of difference between so-called civilised and native peoples, and musical complexity was equated with racial superiority. Polyphony was seen as the music of civilisation and therefore more sophisticated and superior, and monophony the province of the 'natural' or 'uncivilised'. We can see clearly this woefully ill-conceived construction of racial hierarchy through musical 'complexity' in Matthews's determination to teach the Maloga Aborigines part-singing. As noted, it was constantly referred to in his reports.[54] Matthews believed that part-singing lifted Aborigines to a higher cultural level; once again providing sounding proof of their potential to be 'civilised'. His reports supplied further examples of what he believed to be the moral benefits of hymn-singing. For example, the young Aboriginal men returning from sheep-shearing did not 'as formerly go away to the nearest shanty and spend their money recklessly among the people of their tribe'; rather, they came back to the mission and sang hymns.[55] Matthews also attributed the power of the hymn in recruiting to the mission two young Aboriginal women he had met while on a tour at Conargo, north of Deniliquen. He and two Aboriginal men had entertained the women with 'some of the Maloga hymns' that apparently 'gave them much delight'.[56]

As we have seen from examples in New Zealand and Canada, the use of music at Maloga was by no means an isolated example. Many missions in Australia also had a strong musical life. For example, the Benedictine mission in New Norcia run by Dom Salvado, a monk and composer, is remembered for its music.[57] According to one newspaper report, 'The Blacks at New Norcia' held string and brass performances every evening.[58] Lutheran missions in south and central Australia, such as Hermannsburg, demonstrated a marked interest in Aboriginal languages and had from the outset translated hymns. The Hermannsburg or Ntaria Ladies Choir is still singing to this day, with Arrentje translations of Lutheran hymns a staple of their repertoire.[59] Late nineteenth-century reports of mission life in Poonindie, South Australia, made special note of the competent playing of flutes, concertinas and violins by the Aborigines and acknowledged a level of musical literacy.[60] After a visit to Warrangesda a reporter for the *Southern Cross* commented that Aboriginal children were 'as fully apt and teachable as average European and colonial youngsters whilst in the matter of musical sensibility and mimetic melody they left their ordinary white rivals far behind'. The article went on to make an equivalent point about the adults:

> when you follow them to church and hear them singing the wild sweet melodies of the American revivalists with such native gusto and force, you can hardly resist the conviction that this latest attempt to civilise and Christianise the outcast race is fully as worthy of New South Wales as her Garden Palace or her extension of the political electorate.[61]

A brass band was formed at Yarrabah Mission in Northern Queensland, established by John Gribble and taken over by his son, Edward, in 1884. The band's public performances from the early years of the twentieth century were well received by correspondents to the local press, who again used musical aptitude as a measure of improvement:

> To those who have been accustomed to regard the Australian aboriginal as a wretched specimen of humanity so far as intellect and fixity of purpose is concerned, no greater surprise could have been experienced than to have encountered the Yarrabah Brass Band as it marched through Abbot–street on New Year's Day playing in perfect time and tune.

Much was made of their 'clean smart new uniforms of white faced with red' and given that they had had their 'cast off' instruments for at most eight months, the performance was reckoned, therefore, as 'nothing short of marvellous'.[62]

It was again music's ability to create affect, to elicit an emotional response, which in these contexts (certainly with hindsight) gains a somewhat sinister character. From countless references it is clear that many of the indigenous people enjoyed singing and playing European music. For Aboriginal people, the singing of hymns provided reprieve and momentary pleasure in lives otherwise filled with disease, persecution and violence; the act of singing itself provided some coherence in a rapidly changing world. Although Matthews was, in Attwood's sense, a humanitarian, he was authoritarian and often resorted to physical punishment. This doctrinaire approach extended to the issue of language. Unlike other missionaries, he did not translate hymns into indigenous language so as to increase their power as a tool of conversion. Rather, he frowned upon the use of language and banned traditional ceremonies, seeking to replace them with European customs. His reports are scattered with what he regarded as small successes. He was particularly pleased to report a funeral during which no one 'cut their flesh or burned themselves'; instead relatives 'covered up the grave decently' and hymns were sung.[63] On another occasion involving the burial of a woman who had refused conversion he was less successful. She was buried in traditional fashion covered in blankets without a coffin; nonetheless, a hymn was sung. Episodes such as this reveal music as an essential part of the assimilationist agenda and demonstrate its instrumentality in the hegemonic processes of colonialism and destruction of culture.

Music's role in cross-cultural encounter and exchange is thus not straightforward. As something all cultures do, singing could reach across considerable barriers and play a key role in the communication between strangers as wonderfully described by scholars such as Inga Clendinnen and Vanessa Agnew.[64] What happened at the missions, however, was not a transient exchange but was rather part of a consistent and determined programme of cultural dispossession and disempowerment. Missions such as Maloga provided some indigenous people a refuge from settler brutality but at considerable cultural cost. Many missionaries sought to eradicate certain cultural practices and supplant them with European culture.[65] However, the fact that the people at Maloga enjoyed singing hymns did not mean that they did not practise their own rituals and ceremonies without Matthews knowing. In a sense the European music augmented their musical practice rather than replace it.

If Maloga was a place of music, it was also a place of political action. This came from two directions: the first from Matthews himself and the second from the many Aborigines who had come to Maloga as refugees from Coranderrk and Warrangesda. Attwood has identified Coranderrk as a place where Aborigines 'learned humanitarian and liberal political precepts, which gave them the means to protest their plight'. [66] These refugees, already politicised through their past experiences of protest, brought this knowledge to Maloga and Warrangesda and later to Cummeragunga.[67] Through Coranderrk leaders such as Barak and Simon Wonga (who were, as Attwood has observed, 'adept students of the colonial political system and adroit exponents of its techniques of lobbying'), the next generation of Aborigines, including Cooper, learned strategies to deal with colonial authority.[68]

Matthews also encouraged the Aborigines to take political action. He was a rare individual who stood apart from the majority of his contemporaries in his attitudes to Aborigines in significant ways. For example, he questioned the 'popular idea' of the vanishing race. In a report intended for a London audience, he included an extract of a particularly extreme articulation of the 'dying race' theory by Charles Kingsley, a British author and Christian Socialist, in which Kingsley claimed that Aborigines, like Africans, were too 'stupid' to understand the Gospel and must 'perish off the face of the earth as brute beasts'.[69] Matthews's response was to inform his readers that not only were many Aborigines now 'intelligent Christians, some of who evangelised among their own people', but also that around thirty men 'had their names on the register of voters for the election of Parliamentary representatives'.[70] This statement makes clear the importance Matthews placed on Aboriginal men (this was, of course, before universal suffrage) claiming their rights as British subjects in terms of political representation and citizenship. He regarded them as 'equally entitled to the privileges of British subjects' as 'the colonists themselves'.[71] In 1877 he proudly noted that four men, who had been 'drinking men', rode into Moama 'to record their votes for the Parliamentary election'.[72] European settlers constituted a problem for Matthews as they considered Aborigines 'as animals to be exterminated', rather than 'human beings to be saved, and fellow subjects of the Queen to be protected'.[73]

Maloga was a place where music and politics converged. Matthews was tireless in his efforts to gain public support for Aborigines and his mission. He lobbied leading Sydney politicians, spoke at meetings and wrote to the press. Singing was an integral part of this crusade. During the 1880s he took delegations to several meetings with former radicals John Robertson and Henry Parkes. The Maloga Missionary Band, a group of five aboriginal men, accompanied him on these ventures. During one visit in March 1887 Matthews and the Maloga Missionary Band combined appearances at the annual meeting of the APA, numerous 'Evangelistic and Missionary meetings' and a meeting with Parkes, then Colonial Secretary. Singing was heard throughout. At the annual meeting '[a] considerable amount of sympathy was aroused on behalf of the Australian Aboriginal race, surprise was evinced at the intelligence of these men, the clearness and fluency of their addresses, and the true Christian ring that characterized their singing.'[74] This sympathy was also shown by Parkes on hearing the aborigines speak 'of the wants of their race'. The 'missionary hymn' they sang seemed also, according to Matthews, 'to give the aged statesman some pleasure'. As it did to his colleague, Robertson, who received the men in an adjoining waiting room where he and his two granddaughters 'spoke kindly to the Blacks, and heard them sing'.[75]

The following April Matthews joined forces with the secretary of the APA and a group of Aboriginal girls from Warrangesda in a deputation to Government House. They sang 'several melodies' which gave Governor and Lady Carrington 'evident satisfaction' and produced a promise to help.[76] Carrington was called to make good this promise only a few months later on 19 July when a deputation from Maloga met him at the small town of Moama. Jack Cooper, a relative of William's and also educated at Maloga, read out an address and presented to the Governor the now renowned Maloga petition of 1887 requesting 100 acres of land for Aboriginal men.[77] Carrington promised government support 'in every legitimate direction' and was given three cheers and a verse of the *National Anthem* sung by the children 'with such sweetness as to elicit general applause'.[78]

The inclusion of Aborigines in Matthews's various deputations was part of his fundraising strategy. What is less clear is what the Aborigines sought in these meetings. The petitions of the 1880s clearly show that they had their own parallel agendas centring on landownership, but their voices are not heard in Matthews's accounts. Song was, and remains, central to the indigenous cultures of settler colonies: it holds and preserves vast bodies of ancient knowledge, documents and facilitates everyday life and articulates the societal, legal and political structures. Given the importance of song in these indigenous cultures, its use in such a formal context may have made excellent sense to them precisely because it mapped onto their own cultural practices.

The legacy of these interactions resonated in direct ways well into the twentieth century. We can see this in a telling example in the life of William Cooper, which also reveals an unexpected and highly significant transnational story beginning in the late nineteenth century and extending until today. Although beyond our chronology, the best way to start this story is to join the audience gathered at Melbourne's Australian Church on Russell Street on the evening of 31 May 1937 to listen to a concert by an Aboriginal choir. The concert was part of the celebration of Melbourne's 102nd anniversary and was to feature English and Aboriginal songs as well a harp and gum leaf orchestra. It was the result of a collaboration between William Cooper and Isaac Selby, founder of the Old Pioneers' Memorial Fund. Cooper had insisted on Aboriginal representation at such displays of public remembrance and the programming was his. The fact that this groundbreaking example of indigenous musical intervention was held at Charles Strong's Australian Church is a wonderful convergence of reformist cultures.

This was the first of a series of concerts Cooper and Selby organised for important commemorative events and is understood by historians to have been instrumental in Cooper's idea for the Day of Mourning, which was held on Australia Day the following year. It also informed Cooper's institution of Aboriginal Sunday, held the first Sunday after Australia Day, which featured singing by Aboriginal choirs. Cooper's programming for what was essentially the Coomeragunga Choir (a direct successor of the Maloga Choir) included both indigenous and European songs.[79] A parallel to the Māori–Pākehā musical concerts decades earlier is evident in his bilingual programming with its inclusion of indigenous and European repertoire. Cooper repeatedly cited the arguments made by Māori and indigenous Canadians for citizenship and legal rights when arguing for similar rights for Australian

Aborigines.[80] Echoing Matthews's rhetoric of British subjecthood and justice, he promoted a discourse of Aboriginal uplift, seeing political representation and self-determination as its logical outcome.[81]

In addition to Aboriginal and English songs and a harp and gum leaf orchestra, the programme was notable for its inclusion of African American spirituals. The concert ended with a rendition of *Burra Phara*, a translation into Yorta Yorta of the African American spiritual *Turn back Pharaoh's Army*.[82] Tracing the appearance of this spiritual, which is still sung today in Yorta Yorta, takes us back to Maloga Mission in 1887 to a quite extraordinary and little-known encounter with the world-famous Fisk Jubilee Singers. The choir was established at Fisk University, one of the first southern black universities founded in 1865 in Nashville, Tennessee, by the American Missionary Society. The aim was to provide higher education for emancipated slaves. In Tennessee, as in other parts of world, the ability to sing was held up as 'evidence that the negro was susceptible of education'.[83] The student choir was quickly identified as a lucrative source of fundraising and it began to tour from 1871. The Fisk Jubilee Singers, as they became known, are seen as largely responsible for introducing northern US audiences to African American spirituals described by them in one instance as 'the prayer-meeting hymns which they had learned in bondage'.[84] They aligned themselves closely with reform movements such as temperance, and worked alongside former British abolitionists and the American revivalists Moody and Sankey. By the time of their three-and-a-half-year tour of Australasia between 1886 and 1889 they had already attained international fame through their highly successful tours of Britain and Europe (which had included performances for the Prince of Wales, Prime Minister Gladstone and Queen Victoria). Their concerts of spirituals were received with enormous enthusiasm in the major Australian and New Zealand cities. Despite their busy schedule they found time in late August 1887 to accept an invitation 'from a missionary at Meloga [sic], a Mission Station, to come out and sing to them'.[85]

One can only guess at the motives behind Matthews's invitation, but it seems clear that the African American singers were to serve as an example of cultural uplift, and more specifically, moral and social improvement through musical achievement. They made their way through a strange and isolated landscape to the mission at what must have seemed to be the end of the world. When they arrived there was no immediate identification between the African Americans and the Aborigines. It is manifestly clear from the opening lines of manager Frederick J. Loudin's account that he viewed them with a mixture of disdain and curiosity not dissimilar to many white commentators of the time:

[283]

The aborigines of Australia are said to be the lowest type of the human family; they are very black, with long, wavy hair and very coarse features.[86]

Initially, they found 'these black people far from cordial'. It was only when they began to sing the hymn *Steal Away to Jesus* that the situation changed. The 'tones of the old slave song' brought tears of joy and expressions of gratitude.[87] They left to a sustained farewell accompanied by the singing of apposite hymns. The Aborigines sang *Blest Be the Tie that Binds* and Americans responded with *Good-Bye Brothers, Good-Bye Sisters*.[88]

Despite the positive close to this visit, Loudin went on to draw an unfavourable comparison between them and the Māori, who '[u]nlike the Aborigines of Australia' were 'a strong, vigorous, intelligent people'.[89] The struggles that the Fisk Jubilee Singers had themselves endured left them with a firm adherence to the ideology of racial uplift. White middle-class aspirations, such as the acquisition of education and professional occupations, were their models. They quite possibly would have resisted identification with the people they met at Maloga, who they so clearly saw as less civilised. This encounter did not then result in mutual recognition of similarly oppressed people as Matthews might have hoped for, but none of the initial awkwardness of the meeting comes through in his report. By his account it was a 'memorable day'; moreover, the Americans had been 'astonished' by their visit to the school, especially as during their Australasian tour 'they had heard such depreciating stories of the Australian coloured people'.[90] The initial unfriendliness of the Aborigines was also overlooked; instead, their rapturous response to the singing was recorded.

The visit to Maloga had culminated in an exchange of gifts. Loudin was presented with a pair of carved emu eggs and in return offered two photographs of the singing troupe and, in a decision that was to have long-term consequences, a dozen Jubilee songbooks containing 'copies of their sweet melodies in music'. The influence of this repertoire was immediate. The Jubilee songs were taken up in the Tuesday night part-singing classes. Matthews reported soon after that 'two or three of the Jubilee songs' had been mastered 'with tolerable effect'.[91] A report the following year noted further improvement: 'The Jubilee Singers paid Maloga a visit last year; they were so nice and kind and sang some of their hymns for the Black people here, who have since learnt to sing some of them so well.'[92]

Turn back Pharaoh's Army, which in turn became *Burra Pharra*, the finale of Cooper's 1937 concert, is the eighth song in the collection left at Maloga Mission by the Fisk Jubilee Singers fifty years earlier (see figure 6.1).[93] It was appropriated and translated (presumably after Matthews had left Maloga), and found an enduring place in the culture. Over the decades *Burra Pharra* became part of indigenous culture and its inclusion in Cooper's 1937 concert is one long-term consequence of a fleeting but significant encounter. Its position in Yorta Yorta song culture was made manifest by Cooper's decision to use it as the finale for his symbolic public event; in so doing he moved it from the realm of self-improvement to the arena of political agitation. The act of translation stands as an example of indigenous agency, and the choral performance as an act of self-determination. Cooper's choice could also have been influenced by the subject matter. The Maloga Aborigines strongly identified (encouraged by Matthews) with the Jews' escape from Egypt, as described in the Book of Exodus, which has long been interpreted as marking a new beginning for a persecuted people. The text chosen for the translation that became *Burra Pharra* were the verses specifically concerned with Moses and the Pharaoh. Cooper was convinced by the parallel between the plight of the Jewish people and his own, and later was to speak out publicly against the Nazi persecution of the Jews. Drawing on Matthews's rhetoric of British rights and justice and continuing the patterns of predecessors such as Barak in the adoption of European political techniques, Cooper promoted a discourse of Aboriginal uplift centring on political representation and self-determination. The lessons learned at Maloga are evident in the 1937 concert in which music was used strategically to advance a political agenda.[94]

A continuous thread extends from the improbable 1887 meeting between the Yorta Yorta people and the Fisk Jubilee Singers through to the choral concert at the Australian Church in 1937. This continuity was encapsulated by the Aboriginal choir who performed that evening. It is music-making that provides us with a window. The Maloga Choir survived Matthews's departure, becoming the Coomeragunga Choir that toured and broadcast well into the twentieth century. This was the 'Aboriginal choir' that performed at the church in 1937, and undoubtedly many of its members also participated in the historic 'Coomeragunga walk off' two years later.

The Fisk Jubilee Singers's visit had occurred at the height of difficulties for Maloga and the Matthews family personally. Not only was this a period when many Aborigines were beginning to express their profound discontent with Matthews's autocratic demands, the Matthews were also being subjected to a vicious smear campaign in the newspapers, which ultimately saw the withdrawal of major funding. On 22 May 1887 the APA reduced Matthews's role to that of religious teacher and appointed a secular manager to run the mission. The evangelising

No. 8. Turn back Pharaoh's Army.

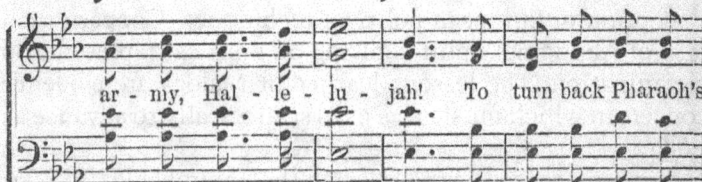

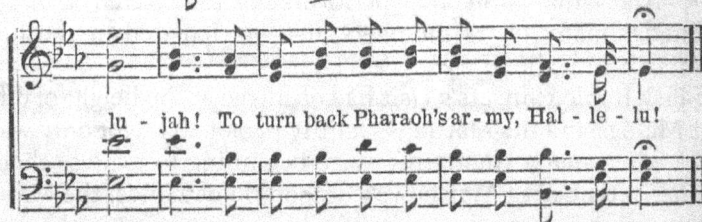

6.1 'Turn Back Pharaoh's Army', *Jubilee Songs*, no. 8 in J. B. T. Marsh, *The Story of the Jubilee Singers; With Their Songs* (London: Hodder and Stoughton, 1886), p. 132.

tours that had begun much earlier in the late 1870s increased in frequency when the financial situation at Maloga became dire. Singing was the 'chief attraction' of these tours.[95] Children were a special focus for missionaries in general; they were seen as *tabulae rasae* and more easily trained to European ways. Earlier, in 1878, the Colonial Secretary of Victoria gave free railway passes to twenty children from Maloga to attend the Juvenile Industrial Exhibition in Ballarat. At the Colonial Secretary's request, the children sang several hymns to an 'immense' audience'.[96] Matthews used the 'sweetness' of the children's voices to his advantage on many other similar occasions.[97] During the 1880s, the Matthews, the Missionary Band and the Maloga Choir undertook extensive tours, appearing in Mechanics' Institutes and Temperance Halls all over Victoria. Thousands of people turned up to hear them speak and sing. Newspaper accounts inevitably referred to the high quality of the singing. One claimed that the 'concerted and solos singing' of the Aborigines had 'entranced their large audience'. He went on to make the by now familiar observation:

> Had any one fifty years ago predicted that Australian aborigines would at this day, held spell-bound, assemblies of educated Europeans, both by their simple unadorned oratory, and exquisite vocalisation, such person would be so doing, have made himself an object of ridicule.[98]

After 1887 many accounts note the influence of the Fisk Jubilee Singers's repertoire.[99] Their impact was worldwide; they had had a similar effect in New Zealand and, before that, Britain.[100] Later, in 1900, in a moment of convergence exemplifying the close ties between global reform movements at this time, the Fisk Jubilee Singers performed at a WCTU convention in Edinburgh, during which, it was reported in *The White Ribbon*, Loudin made reference to his deep affection for New Zealand. Significantly, none other than the Putiki Maori Choir had taken up the Jubilee songs, making them a feature of their concerts, punctuating them with *poi* dances and *hakas*.[101] Haweis too had noted a similarity of vocal timbre between the choir he heard at the Wanganui church and the Fisk Jubilee Singers that had, he recalled, 'visited England some years ago'.[102]

In 1888 the APA once again stepped in with disastrous consequences for the Matthews. They dismantled the buildings at Maloga and moved them to Cummeragunga. Daniel and Janet Matthews lost their jobs and their mission. Daniel mourned through music. He told his readers that he and the few remaining Aborigines sang the first hymn he had taught at Maloga, *There is a Happy Land, Far, Far Away*, as the buildings were pulled down around them. He also included an extract from a letter by Jaspar, an old blind man who was missing Maloga: 'The sound of the old harmonium is still ringing in our ears, and we are praying for you all night and day.'[103] The Matthews's response was to organise a fundraising trip to London. They chose not to take the Missionary Band and instead took a married Aboriginal couple, Jenny and Paddy Swift, described as 'two converted Aboriginal natives ... who advocate their own claims, and sing'.[104] Much was made of the couple's singing in the accounts of their British reception.[105]

On his their return to Australia in 1899, Matthews began to travel further afield using the Maloga Mission Coach. He also established the Jubilee Quartette, who travelled with him. The vocal quartet consisted of his two daughters, his son and a young Aboriginal woman, Mable Pantonie, who he had trained especially to sing with the ensemble. After a tour to Adelaide, the Matthews family decided to leave Maloga permanently and founded the Manunka Mission in South Australia. After Daniel's death in 1902, Janet Matthews and her children continued their mission work. Music assumed a similar position in the culture of their new mission as it had at Maloga. The busy weekly music schedule was virtually identical. The same 'dear old piano' led the singing in the schoolhouse, and the Misses Matthews also accompanied on auto harp and violin. One notable difference was that, without the constraining presence of Daniel Matthews, the women began to translate to hymns and songs in the indigenous language.

It was a hegemonic trope to stress the 'natural' musicality of dispossessed and disempowered people, and much was made of the musicality of indigenous Australians, Canadians and the Māori, as it had been of the Scots, the Irish, the Gypsies and the Jews. The role of music in the mission built upon the importance of song in these indigenous cultures. As noted by one commentator on the Māori, their 'old songs composed all their literature'.[106] Many indigenous people then were actively engaged, and were pragmatic, quick to subvert and adapt these practices to advance their own situations (much as the British working class did with the musical forms of rational recreation). The records – the preponderance of which we have had to read against the grain, in Clendinnen's terms – suggest that they enjoyed it and were interested in it. We should not forget, however, that although there might be evidence of indigenous agency and genuinely productive interpersonal relationships between Europeans and indigenous people, they occurred within the confines of power structures that were fundamentally uneven. In the sounds of music-making we can hear limited choices, constrained agency, and unequal relationships between the coloniser and colonised.

Notes

1   National Library of Australia, Papers of Bessie Rischbieth, 1900–1967, MS 2004 (hereafter Rischbieth Papers), Vida Goldstein, 'The Struggle for Women's Suffrage in Victoria. For the 50th Anniversary of the WCTU', [typescript], 27 October 1937. Strong received general recognition for his role in a minor history of women's suffrage, in which he was described as 'always the first man to move to the front in any movement for social reform was one of the earliest advocates of Women's Suffrage'. See Rischbieth Papers, Folio 2004/97–134, Women's Suffrage Roll of Honour (n.d.).

2   For an account of the WCTU see Ian Tyrrell, Woman's World/Woman's Empire: The Woman's Christian Temperance Union in International Perspective, 1880–1930 (Chapel Hill: University of North Carolina Press, 1991).

3   Anna Gordon, The White Ribbon Hymnal or the Echoes of the Crusade compiled for The National and World's Woman's Christian Temperance Unions (Chicago: Women's Temperance Association, 1892), p. 5.

4   Ibid.

5   McMaster University, Hamilton, Archives & Research Collections, Pamphlet Collection, Rev. Elisha A. Hoffman, Ontario Women's Christian Temperance Union Prohibition Songs (s.l.: Ontario Woman's Christian Temperance Union, n.d.).

6   Notably, the borrowings from Britain and Ireland are far fewer. In addition to God Save the Queen, Make the Map All White was set to The Wearing of the Green and No Surrender was sung to Annie Laurie.

7   E. J. Ward, Out of Weakness made Strong: Being a Record of the Life and Labours of Mrs. E. J. Ward (Sydney: Christian World, 1903).

8   Ibid., see especially chap. 3.

9   See, for example, White Ribbon (March 1898), pp. 7–8; White Ribbon (April 1901), p. 11; White Ribbon (July 1901), pp. 4–5; White Ribbon (April 1902), p. 12, White Ribbon (October 1902).

10 'National Council of Women', White Ribbon (October 1904), pp. 8–9.

11 'A Maori Branch Formed at Putiki', White Ribbon (April 1905), p. 11.

12 Ibid.

13 'News of the Union', White Ribbon (January 1911), pp. 2, 8.

14 Rischbieth Papers, MS 2004/4/1–44, 'Letters from Australian Women's Suffrage Leaders 1900–1959', Letter from Emmeline Lawrence to Bessie Rischbieth, 25 August 1915.

15 Hocken Library, University of Otago, NZ, Papers of Anna Stout, ARC-0021 (hereafter Anna Stout Papers), 'Address to Māori Convention' 24 June 1908 [typescript].

16 'Maori Women', Evening Post [Wellington] (16 July 1908).

17 In the same year the Wesleyan Mission Press brought out a collection known as Harmony of the Gospels, which, in addition to extracts from the four Gospels and other prayers, included thirty-five hymns. See William Woon, Ko te Rongo Pai i tuhituhia e nga Kai Wakaako o Ihu Karaiti: me te Mahi o nga Apotoro: me nga inoinga, me nga himene hoki (Mangungu, NZ: Wesleyan Mission Press 1837).

18 William Colenso, Himene 100–126 (Waitangi: Heretaunga, 1847).

19 Thomas Grace, A Pioneer Missionary Among the Maoris, 1850–1879: Being Letters and Journals of Thomas Samuel Grace, ed. S. J. Brittan (Palmerston North: G. H. Bennett & Co., [1928]), p. 28.

20 Hugh Reginald Haweis, Travel and Talk, vol. 2 (London: Chatto, 1896), pp. 187–8.

21 'Maori-Pakeha Concert. A Novel Entertainment', Thames Star (24 March 1906).

22 'Memorial to a Native Chief', Hawera and Normanby Star (31 March 1911).

23 C. O. Davis, Temperance Songs, Etc., in the Maori Language [He Waiata Pehi Waipiro etc., I Te Reo maori] (Auckland, John Henry Field, 1873); C. O. Davis, Te Honae; Being a Small Collection of Temperance and Sacred Melodies, in Maori,

2nd edn enlarged [*He Tau Puru Ripene, Aha, Aha, Na Hare Reweti*] (Akarana: Brett, Evening Star Office, 1885).

24   *Ibid.*
25   Davis, *Te Honae*, pp. v–vi.
26   Davis, *Temperance Songs*, p. 25.
27   These include tunes from *Hymns Ancient and Modern*, Moody and Sankey's *Sacred Songs and Solos*, Wesley's *Tune Book* and the *Salvation Army Tune Book*.
28   Davis, *Temperance Songs*, p. 6.
29   *Wanganui Chronicle* (15 June 1904).
30   Eugene Stock, *Metlakahtla and the North Pacific Mission of the Church Missionary Society* (London: Church Missionary House, 1880), available at www.gutenberg. org/cache/epub/6976/pg6976-images.html (accessed 15 December 2015).
31   Stuart Eydmann, *The Life and Times of the Concertina*, p. 132, available at www. concertina.com/eydmann/life-and-times/eydmann-life-and-times-chap-08.pdf (accessed 14 August 2012).
32   Stock, *Metlakahtla.*
33   *Ibid.*
34   *Na-Na-Kwa* (8 October 1899).
35   'New Worker's Letter', *Na-Na-Kwa* (12 October 1900). For indigenous Canadian brass bands see Susan Neylan, 'Here Comes the Band! Cultural Collaboration, Connective Traditions, and Aboriginal Brass Bands on British Columbia's North Coast, 1875–1964', *BC Studies*, 152 (2007), pp. 35–66; David Mattison, 'On the March: Indian Brass Bands 1866–1916', *British Columbia Historical News*, 15:1 (1981), pp. 6–14.
36   *Na-Na-Kwa* (9 January 1900); *Na-Na-Kwa* (10 April 1900).
37   *Na-Na-Kwa* (8 October 1899).
38   For this correspondence, see Library and Archives Canada, Ottawa, Record Group 10 (RG 10), Records Relating to Indian Affairs. See for example: RG 10, vol. 2234, file 45549, the correspondence to the Indian Affairs Department from the Chippewas Brass Band; RG 10, vol. 2098, file 17103, the correspondence to the Indian Affairs Department from the Moravian Brass Band; RG 10, vol. 2978, file 210690, the correspondence to the Indian Affairs Department from the Royal Mohawk Brass Band; RG 10, vol. 2628, file 27530, the correspondence to the Indian Affairs Department from the Six Nations Brass Band; and RG 10, vol. 2092, file 15319, the correspondence to the Indian Affairs Department from the Cape Croker Brass Band.
39   See, for example, Deborah Bird and Tony Swain, *Aboriginal Australian and Christian Mission: Ethnographic and Historical Studies* (Bedford Park, South Australia: Australian Association for the Study of Religions, 1988); Leigh Boucher and Lynette Russell (eds), *Settler Colonial Governance in Nineteenth-Century Victoria* (Canberra: ANU Press, 2015); Richard Broome, *Aboriginal Victorians: A History Since 1800* (Crows Nest, NSW: Allen and Unwin, 2005); Christine Choo, *Mission Girls: Aboriginal Women on Catholic Missions in the Kimberley, Western Australia, 1900–1950* (Crawley, WA: University of Western Australia Press, 2001); Patricia Grimshaw and Andrew May, *Missionaries, Indigenous Peoples and Cultural Exchange* (Portland, OR: Sussex Academic Press, 2010); Jamie S. Scott and Gareth Griffiths (eds), *Mixed Messages: Materiality, Textuality, Mission* (New York: Palgrave Macmillan, 2005); Norman Etherington (ed.), *Missions and Empire* (Oxford: Oxford University Press, 2005).
40   See Bain Attwood, *The Making of the Aborigines* (Sydney: Allen and Unwin, 1989); Judith Ryan, Carol Cooper and Joy Murphy-Wandin, *Remembering Barak* (Melbourne: National Gallery of Victoria, 2003); Shirley W. Wiencke, *When the Wattles Bloom Again: The Life and Times of William Barak, Last Chief of the Yarra Yarra Tribe* (Woori Yallock: S. W. Wiencke, 1984).
41   See Bain Attwood and Andrew Markus, *The Struggle for Aboriginal Rights: A Documentary History* (Sydney: Allen and Unwin, 1999), pp. 8, 63; Bain Attwood, *Rights for Aborigines* (Sydney: Allen and Unwin, 2003), pp. 8, 11–13, 27–9;

Bain Attwood and Andrew Markus, *Thinking Black: William Cooper and the Australian Aborigines' League* (Canberra: Australian Institute of Aboriginal and Torres Strait Islander Studies, 2004), pp. 5–6, 11.

42 S. L. James, 'Address to the Australian National Missionary Council', *Sun* [Melbourne] (12 April 1929), quoted in Atwood and Markus, *Thinking Black*, p. 29. James was son of Thomas Shadrach James, a long-time teacher at Maloga, who later married Ada Cooper and lived with her family on both missions. Hereafter, variations in the spelling of 'Cummeragunga' reflect those used in the original sources.

43 Daniel Matthews, *From Darkness and Death. A Record of Sixteen Years of Gospel Work and its Result among the Aboriginal Blacks of Australia* (London: Woodford Fawcett, n.d.), p. 1.

44 Attwood, *Rights for Aborigines*, p. 8.

45 Daniel Matthews, *The Story of the Maloga Aboriginal Mission* (Melbourne: Rae and Munn, 1896), p. 10.

46 National Library of Australia, Papers of Daniel Matthews, 1866–1909, MS 2195 (hereafter Matthews Papers). These reports, all written by Daniel Matthews, are held as part of the Matthews Papers, Box 1, MS 2195/2/5.

47 *The Story of the Maloga Aboriginal Mission 1891–1893, Seventeenth Report* (Melbourne: Rae and Munn, 1893), p. 34.

48 *Fifth Report of the Maloga Aboriginal Mission School, Murray River, New South Wales, 1880* (Echuca: Riverine Herald Office, 1880), pp. 5–6.

49 See Diane Barwick, 'William Cooper (1861–1941)', *Australian Dictionary of Biography*, National Centre of Biography, Australian National University, available at http://adb.anu.edu.au/biography/cooper-william-5773/text9787 (accessed 23 September 2013).

50 Nancy Cato, *Mister Maloga* (St. Lucia: University of Queensland Press, 1993), p. 350.

51 Attwood and Markus, *Thinking Black*, p. 125.

52 *Third Annual Report of the Maloga Aboriginal Mission, 1878* (Echuca: Riverine Herald Office, 1878), p. 8.

53 *Ibid.*, p. 4. '[P]lenty of singing' was had by the children while Matthews read *Uncle Tom's Cabin* to the young men.

54 For a detailed account of race, colonisation and the question of polyphony see Vanessa Agnew, 'The Colonialist Beginnings of Comparative Musicology', in Eric Ames, Marcia Klotz and Lora Wildenthal (eds), *Germany's Colonial Pasts: An Anthology in Memory of Susanne Zantop* (Lincoln, NE: University of Nebraska Press, 2005), pp. 41–60.

55 *Fourth Annual Report of the Maloga Aboriginal Mission, 1879* (Echuca: Riverine Herald Office, 1879), p. 17; *Tenth Annual Report of the Maloga Aboriginal Mission, 1885,* (Echuca: Riverine Herald Office, 1885), p. 19.

56 *Sixth Annual Report of the Maloga Aboriginal Mission, 1881* (Echuca: Mackay and Drought, 1881), pp. 8–9.

57 Salvado wrote memoirs chronicling his experiences in Western Australia. See Dom Rosendo Salvado, *The Salvado Memoirs: Historical Memoirs of Australia and Particularly of the Benedictine Mission of New Norcia and of the Habits and Customs of the Australian Natives*, trans. and ed. by E. J. Stormon (Nedlands, WA: University of Western Australia Press, [1977]).

58 Australian Institute of Aboriginal and Torres Strait Islander Studies (AIATSIS), Canberra, Gribble, Ernest R. 1847–93, Collected Papers, 1892–1970, MS 1515 (hereafter Gribble Papers), Box 17, Item 179, Part 2: Collection of cuttings, mainly on the death of J.B. Gribble, 'The Blacks at New Norcia'.

59 State Library of South Australia, South Australiana Pamphlets Collection, *Souvenir Brochure 1967 Tour of Bethlehem Lutheran Church Choir, Hermannsburg Mission, N.T. Commemorating the 90th anniversary of the Mission's founding by the Finke River on June 8th, 1877* (Hermannsburg, NT: The Mission, 1967).

60 Mathew Hale, *The Aborigines in Australia: Being an Account of the Institution for their Education at Poonindie in South Australia* (London: Society for Promoting Christian Knowledge, [1889]), pp. 86–7, 97.

61 Matthews Papers, MS 2195, Box 1, Folder 5, Press Clippings, 'Work Among the Blacks' *Southern Cross* (1881).

62 Gribble Papers, Box 17.

63 *Third Annual Report of the Maloga Aboriginal Mission, 1878*, p. 4.

64 Inga Clendinenn, *Dancing with Strangers* (Cambridge: Cambridge University Press, 2005); Vanessa Agnew, *Enlightenment Orpheus: The Power of Music in Other Worlds* (Oxford: Oxford University Press, 2008).

65 We should point out here that the operation of a mission was determined in very real ways by the personality and outlook of those who ran it.

66 Attwood, *Rights for Aborigines*, p. 6.

67 Petitions have long been a political strategy used by indigenous people from the early years of Coranderrk, notably the address submitted to the governor of Victoria in 1863 by a deputation from Coranderrk including Barak and Simon Wonga. See, for example, 'Deputation of Aborigines', *Illustrated Melbourne Post* (25 June 1863), in Attwood, *Struggle for Aboriginal Rights*, p. 43–5.

68 Attwood, *Rights for Aborigines*, p. 19. Coranderrk during the term of John Green had been a more liberal and egalitarian place. Matthews would have been aware of the protest at Coranderrk. He had visited there in the 1870s during its success-ful period under the supervision of Green. He recalled one visit when he taught the children the gospel hymn *Shall We Gather at the River*. Particularly during the 1880s because of changed policies concerning mixed-race people, but also earlier, there was a steady influx of Coranderrk refugees arriving at Maloga and Warrangesda. See Matthews Papers, MS2195/3/4, Diaries, diary entry, 3 April 1870.

69 Matthews, *From Darkness and Death*, p. 2.

70 *Ibid.*

71 *Twenty-fifth Annual Report of the Maloga Aboriginal Mission, 1900* (Melbourne: Rae and Munn, 1900), p. 13.

72 *Third Annual Report of the Maloga Aboriginal Mission, 1878*, p. 25.

73 Matthews, *From Darkness and Death*, p. 4.

74 *Twelfth Annual Report of the Maloga Aboriginal Mission, 1888* (Melbourne: Rae and Foyster, 1888), p. 14. A fascinating but unexplained moment occurred when one of the delegation to Parkes in 1887 showed 'a spirit of resistance and left the room and only after much pleading grudgingly agreed to rejoin the group', suggest-ing that there were tensions, whether caused a lack of consensus or a moment of frustration with the process. This overt display of discontent occurred at a time when there was growing resentment against Matthews's stringent and restrictive paternalism and an increasing desire for autonomy and self-determination. It was around this time that many people left Maloga for nearby Cummeragunga.

75 *Thirteenth Annual Report of the Maloga Aboriginal Mission, 1888* (Melbourne: Rae and Foyster, 1888 [1889]), p. 4.

76 *Ibid.*

77 The petition is included in Attwood and Markus, *Thinking Black*, p. 27.

78 *Ibid.*, p. 11.

79 For a detailed description of the concert see also Bain Attwood and Helen Doyle, *Possession: Batman's Treaty and the Matter of History* (Melbourne: Miegunyah Press, 2009), pp. 246–7.

80 See 'William Cooper, Secretary, Australian Aborigines' League, to the Premier, New South Wales, Bertram Stevens, 15 November 1936, in Attwood and Markus, *Thinking Black*, p. 60. Touring missionaries speaking about Canada provided an avenue for Aboriginal people to learn about the situation for indigenous people in other colonies. In New Zealand there was the example of Bishop Ridley, whereas in 1887 Reverend Lucas of Canada gave a lecture in Echuca on 'The Native Tribes of North America'. Young Aborigines from Maloga were invited on to the plat-

form to sing. See *Tenth Annual Report of the Maloga Aboriginal Mission, 1885,* p. 22.

81 Cooper shared an assumption with many indigenous people in the British colonies that Queen Victoria had given them their reserves. Attwood explains this as a 'special relationship' based on indigenous traditions of reciprocity and exchange. See Attwood, *Rights for Aborigines,* p. 60. For Cooper on uplift see 'William Cooper, Secretary, Australian Aborigines' League, to the Minister for the Interior, Thomas Paterson, 31 October 1936', in Attwood and Markus, *Thinking Black,* p. 56.

82 *Burra Pharra* is now known as *Bura Fera.* See 'Aboriginal and Torres Strait Islander Languages and Culture, Language of the Month 08, October 1999 – Aretha Briggs and David Wirrpanda "Yorta Yorta [Victoria]"', available at www.fatsilc.org.au/languages/language-of-the-month/lotm-1996-to-2000/1998-oct---aretha-briggs-and-david-wirrpanda- (accessed 24 September 2013).

83 J. B. T. Marsh, *The Story of the Jubilee Singers Including their Songs, With Supplement containing an account of their six years' tour around by world, and many new songs by F. J. Loudin* (London: Hodder and Stoughton, 1903), p. 13.

84 *Ibid.,* p. 50.

85 *Ibid.,* p. 140.

86 *Ibid.*

87 *Ibid.,* p. 141.

88 *Twelfth Annual Report of the Maloga Aboriginal Mission Station, 1888,* p. 8.

89 Marsh, *Jubilee Singers,* p. 142.

90 *Twelfth Annual Report of the Maloga Aboriginal Mission Station, 1888,* p. 8.

91 *Ibid.,* p. 9.

92 *Ibid.,* p. 1.

93 Marsh, *Jubilee Singers,* p. 166.

94 The story of *Burra Pharra* does not end here. In 1967 Janet Matthews (possibly a descendent) recorded Yorta Yorta woman Geraldine Briggs singing the song. In 1998 as part of a language revival project, Briggs recorded it again, this time accompanied by the Yorta Yorta Singers who also played the didgeridoo and clapping sticks. More recently it featured in the successful play, and subsequent film, *The Sapphires,* which follows the lives of a group of singing sisters from Cummeragunga during the 1970s.

95 *Twenty-fifth Annual Report of the Maloga Aboriginal Mission, 1900,* p. 9.

96 *Fourth Annual Report of the Maloga Aboriginal Mission, 1879,* p. 8.

97 See *Eleventh Annual Report of the Maloga Aboriginal Mission, 1886* (Echuca: Mackay and Foyster, 1886), p. 1; *Thirteenth Annual Report of the Maloga Aboriginal Mission, 1888,* p. 1; *Twenty-first Annual Report of the Maloga Aboriginal Mission, 1896* (Melbourne: Rae and Munn, 1896).

98 *Twelfth Annual Report of the Maloga Aboriginal Mission, 1888,* p. 18. These tours also drew derogatory comments from detractors such as Reverend F. A. Hagenauer, one of the authors of the appallingly destructive Half Caste Act of 1886 that saw the removal of mixed-race children from their families. His contemptuous remarks singled out Matthews's use of singing on which to pour scorn: 'I understand he has got a black boy from Queensland and a few half-castes who ought to earn their living but who go about Melbourne singing and keeping what he calls Missionary Meetings'. See Cato, *Mister Maloga,* p. 296.

99 *Twelfth Annual Report of the Maloga Aboriginal Mission, 1888,* p. 18.

100 See *White Ribbon* (September 1900), p. 2.

101 'Putiki Maori Choir', *Wanganui Chronicle* (14 September 1895).

102 Haweis, *Travel and Talk,* pp. 187–8.

103 *Fourteenth Annual Report of the Maloga Aboriginal Mission* (London: Woodford, Fawcett and Co., n.d. [1890]), pp. 10, 16.

104 Cato, *Mister Maloga,* p. 254.

105 Matthews, *Maloga Aboriginal Mission Station,* pp. 20–5.

106 Unidentified newspaper cutting in Davis, *Te Honae.*

CHAPTER SEVEN

'Sing of the warriors of labour': radical religion, secularism and the hymn[1]

Hymns and Chartism

Hymns were powerful agents. Much in the previous two chapters has demonstrated the instrumentality of the hymn in a variety of contexts. As we have seen, religion was a central force within nineteenth-century social reform movements and music was a key part of their cultural practices. As faith in formal religion continued to weaken in the late nineteenth century there was a burgeoning interest in alternative belief systems; within secularist and ethical circles the desire for spiritual uplift remained strong. Ritual behaviour and the production of alternative hymnbooks provided a way of creating and affirming collective identity within these fringe movements and institutions.[2] As both cultural icons and agents,[3] hymns were central to what David Nash has described as the 'eclectic search for morality',[4] a search which was undertaken by a range of movements at different times and in different places. Hymn-singing and carefully selected hymn collections helped to construct internal identities. They could knit together communities, such as those found in London's South Place Chapel and Melbourne's Australian Church, and played a key role in their social reform initiatives. As we have seen in the previous chapter, for Daniel Matthews and other missionaries moving around Britain's colonies, hymns could, as effective tools of evangelicalism, do much towards 'civilising' the indigenous peoples of the Empire.

To extend this line of inquiry we examine expressions of radical religious ideas and moral reform within working-class political movements and explore the ways in which music was utilised in this context. The tension that permeates the questions of 'by' or 'for' is brought into play here. This was not a rational recreation initiative of the middle classes imposed from above; it was one driven by working-class agency and collective participation, forged in the radical working-class culture of self-improvement. Chartism continued to radicalise religion and in so doing produced a democratic hymnody, one that was infused with the rugged independence typical of the proud working-class tradition of self-help. Hymns then became part of radical political discourse and the fight for democratic reform. This chapter looks both at how Chartist hymnbooks operated as a kind of ideological manifesto and at how hymns worked in action. It will then examine how musical practices played out in the two main trajectories that emerged from the crucible of Chartist and Owenite moral and intellectual debate: the secularist movement that gained momentum in the 1860s and beyond (with figures such as G. J. Holyoake, Charles Bradlaugh and Joseph Symes), and the short-lived but significant religious articulation of late nineteenth-century socialism, the Labour Church movement. Not surprisingly, these two movements made their way out to the colonies of settlement accompanied by the music and musical practices that helped shape their identities.

As has become apparent throughout this study, musical genres elude fixed definition. The hymn is no exception. The hymn or song of praise was not necessarily or exclusively religious in terms of text or music. The patriotic song of praise was one popular variation, and explicit references to patriotic hymns are scattered throughout radical print culture, revealing in part the influence of French revolutionary hymns. In 1839, for example, the *Northern Star* made special mention of the patriotic hymn that opened the Female Chartist Association meeting.[5] John Peacock's *Conventional Hymn* set to *Rule, Britannia* is a kind of hybrid form, combining revolutionary hymn with patriotic song. The Lord is enlisted in the 'holy fight' against the 'impious tyrants' who dared to rule 'by their lawless might'. The chorus issued a clarion call to the multitudes:

> Hail ye people! All hail the firm decree!
> 'Tis said, we ever – ever shall be free.[6]

In setting their hymn texts to secular music, such as W. Mann's choice of *Snug Little Island*, Thomas Dibdin's popular stage tune of 1797, for his poem *The Charter Hymn*, many Chartists revealed the influence of Primitive Methodism.[7] There was also a strong tradition of serious and deeply religious hymn-writing and singing within Chartism that used well-known sacred tunes. Chartist poets, such as Thomas Cooper, John Bramwich and William Jones, were acclaimed for capturing the tenor of the movement in their hymns.

As is well known, Chartist thought was, in many ways, suffused with religious belief, which legitimised their struggle, transforming it into a crusade. In a statement that was to find echoes later in the

[295]

Labour Church movement, Rev. William Hill, editor of the *Northern Star*, believed 'the principles of Chartism to be Religious principles and every Chartist Society to be consequently a Religious Society'.[8] Of course, attitudes to religion within the movement varied considerably and included a rich infidel and secularist tradition to which Owenites often contributed. There was unanimity, however, in a rejection of the Anglican Church as a cruel and unjust adjunct to a corrupt State. A plethora of Nonconformist and schismatic sects (not including Wesleyan Methodism) drew upon support from communities of working people. Progressive ideas of equality and egalitarianism, combined with what many regarded as real religion, produced a form of 'democratic Christianity' (to borrow Eileen Yeo's words).[9] Just as they were 'true patriots', they were 'true Christians'. For them, Christ was the first Chartist and to paraphrase Rev. James Scholefield, otherwise known as the 'Chaplain of the Manchester Chartists', the Bible was the book most deserving of the title *Rights of Man*.[10] Many of these views, we have noted, echoed within the walls in South Place and in Melbourne.

It is not surprising then that many Chartists practised their own religious rituals and followed various home-grown theologians. Among the second lieutenants of Chartism were preachers of various stripes, well known to contemporaries and scholars alike. These ranged from the incumbents of the formal Christian Chartist Churches – attracting more detractors than supporters within and outside the movement – to a gaggle of 'charismatic' individuals who led schismatic congregations, including those sometimes called 'dotty sects'. Again, it is unsurprising that this led to the composition of dedicated hymns and the publication of Chartist hymnodies. In April 1841 a notice in the *Northern Star*, for example, announced the imminent publication in Leeds of *Hymns for Public Worship Suitable for Chartist Congregations*. According to the notice it was to meet a 'desideratum' that was 'seriously felt'.[11]

Several followed, including *Hymns for Worship*, produced in 1843 by Joshua Hobson, the publisher of the *Northern Star*. On this occasion, the desideratum was deemed to be '*severely* felt'. The claim that the book would be 'Without Sectarianism' makes clear the desire to avoid theological controversy. A careful line was observed: the hymns 'breathe the pure spirit of genuine, practical Christianity – pure Political Truth, without an atom of theological, sectarian dogmatism'.[12] These sentiments are repeated in a review of the collection. The hymns found in the 'little book' were pronounced to be 'genuine poetry and genuine Chartism'. There was 'no humbug, nor any theological sectarianism in them'. In the sample offered – 'God Will Avenge Oppression' – God is invoked as 'warrior and defender of liberty'.[13]

Of course, radical preachers had previously compiled hymnbooks for the use of their congregations. The seventh edition of a hymnody for Scholefield's flock, for example, was published in 1841.[14] What seems to have been missing, however, were hymnbooks compiled democratically and collectively, which would be a concrete expression of the fierce desire for independence that underpinned the Chartist *mentalité*. One notable attempt to meet this need commenced in 1844. A meeting of the regional leaders of Chartism in south-east Lancashire, one of the movement's heartlands, resolved to 'get out a selection of Hymns to form a Hymn-book'. A committee was empowered to oversee the production, making suitable selections from hymns solicited from the rank and file. Throughout the following year increasingly tetchy reports appeared updating the readers on progress. In December 1845 James Leach, the secretary of the National Charter Association (NCA), was called in to sort out the finances – the subscribers wanted the books or their money back. The plan to ensure that 'each locality receive their proportionate share of the hymnbooks' was an additional levy of twopence. The hymnody soon appeared, including compositions from many individuals. As with *Hymns of Worship*, the committee was instructed 'to omit all pieces touching on theology'.[15] Despite its rocky beginning the book was obviously very successful, going into its third edition in 1849.[16]

As early as September 1842 the *Northern Star* had announced that Thomas Cooper's hymnbook was ready to be ordered.[17] The following year the second edition of what was identified as 'The Shakspearian [sic] Chartist Hymn Book' was on sale for threepence; the first edition of 2,000 copies having sold out. This one was promoted as 'neater and with the addition of thirteen new hymns'.[18] Bootmaker, poet, journalist and inveterate squabbler Thomas Cooper was, as noted previously, one of the movement's central figures. His initial exposure to music had occurred during his years in Lincoln, where he had become closely involved with the newly formed Lincoln Mechanics' Institute. It was here, while learning (and later teaching) a selection of European languages including Latin, ancient Greek, French, Italian and German, as well as organising classes in geometry, algebra, botany, drawing and chemistry, that Cooper discovered music. Somewhere in his hectic schedule this extraordinary but irascible autodidact found time, with 'a few young men', to establish a Choral Society. On being appointed its secretary, he threw himself into it with his characteristic and all-consuming energy and passion. 'What mad enthusiasm I had felt for music!' he exclaimed in his wonderful memoir, published in 1897. 'The enjoyment – the rapture' he experienced through music was, he remembered, 'more than a reward' for his tireless work during which he wore out his own boots on the streets of Lincoln, acquiring new instruments, raising funds and selecting the best musicians for his society ('raw amateurs' were rejected).[19] Ever ready for a grandiloquent flourish, Cooper proclaimed that his 'heart and brain' were instantly aflame with 'the worship of Handel's grandeur'.[20] The singers quickly familiarised themselves with major musical works, including Handel's oratorios, Haydn's *Creation* and the choral works of Mozart and Beethoven. As with many of Cooper's interactions with people, confrontation was inevitable. He was, in his own words, accused of 'a most shameful tyranny'; his ranting staccato account gives a sense of his obsessive passion:

> I was opposed, – I was thwarted, – I was 'called to account', – I was advised to resign, – I was threatened with dethronement,– and so, eventually, I abdicated, and left the Lincoln Choral Society, which had been my idol and my passion, to conduct itself. [21]

Cooper's passion for music, which was 'something far above the mere indulgence of feeling', brought about his own Augustinian crisis. Whereas St Augustine anxiously admitted in his *Confessions* to sometimes being more moved by the music to which the text had been set than the words themselves, so too did Cooper later admit that he had been overwhelmed, even possessed by music: 'Oh, how easily I could again yield to it! But I dare not.' He concluded sadly, 'It was well that I broke my connection with music, for my passion would have been ruinous to me had I continued to let it sway me'. [22]

Cooper had become involved in compiling Chartist hymnbooks in the early 1840s after his return to the city of his birth to take up a position with the *Leicester Mercury*. Here, he became deeply involved with Chartism; by the sheer force of his powerful will he recruited many working people, particularly 'the poor stockingers', to the cause and the Leicester Chartists became recognised as a serious force on the national stage. As we have seen, he dubbed them the 'Shakespearean Chartists' and himself their General, and they sang and fought with equal enthusiasm. Like many working-class intellectuals, Cooper had a complex relationship with religion and during the 1830s he experienced a crisis of faith. As a young man he had been a popular lay preacher for the Wesleyans. At the time of his involvement in Chartist hymn compilation, however, not only had he rejected conventional Christianity for more radical religious ideas but he had also become what we might nowadays call an enforcer, if not a thug. During this period he eventually turned to freethought, on which he lectured until 1856 when he converted to the Baptist Church.

Cooper's ongoing commitment to the hymn is curious given that it persisted during his period as an apostate, illustrating once again that the genre could be used for a range of purposes and be adapted to range of beliefs, even non-belief. Although the hymn *O Thou Who Didst Create Us All* is a searing indictment of the clergy, it nonetheless implies an abiding belief in God.[23] His hymn *God of the Earth, and Sea, and Sky* calls directly upon an instrumentalist God:

> To us, – the wretched and the poor,
> Whom rich men drive from door to door,-
> To us, then, make Thy goodness known,
> And we Thy lofty name will own.

Nevertheless, Cooper was clearly struggling with his faith. The final stanza issues a challenge, culminating with a warning to God:

> Father, our frames are fading fast:
> Hast Thou our names behind Thee cast?
> Our sinless babes with hunger die:
> Our hearts are hardening! – Hear our cry![24]

The Chartist God is being called to account and to reaffirm his commitment to the oppressed and downtrodden. The hardening hearts included Cooper's; the final stanza shows him on the cusp of disbelief.

On his release from Stafford Prison in 1846, where he had just finished his well-regarded epic poem *The Purgatory of Suicides* during a two-year term for sedition, Cooper resumed work compiling hymns. He was once again appointed editor of a forthcoming collection, the *Chartist Song and Hymn Book*; in his intense, autocratic style, he quickly assumed total quality control, issuing the public fiat: 'That I have licence to reject the whole or any part of what you send'. This ruling brought outcry from at least one would-be contributor, who complained of Cooper's 'despotism' which neither the critic 'nor any other man of thought' could 'approve of'. The detractor deemed it 'anti-Chartist' and asked for a more democratic committee to assume editorial control. The *Northern Star* came out in full support of their poet laureate's 'excellent project'. The expression of confidence had come too late; Cooper had taken serious umbrage at the public rebuke. 'Under the circumstances of objection,' he complained, 'I positively decline the project altogether' (although he noted somewhat peevishly that it remained 'much wanted').[25]

Notwithstanding the fact Cooper had purportedly sworn off music after this clash, his Leicester comrades, as he recounted in his autobiography, 'so often indulged in singing' that he encouraged them to 'compose hymns for our Sunday meetings'.[26] Two of these budding Chartist hymnodists (possibly the members he alluded to) were John

Henry Bramwich and William Jones, both framework knitters. Jones was a busy member of Leicester Chartist Society's music section, copying, composing and performing music. He was also the editor of the second and third editions of the *Chartist Hymn Book* (presumably the one issued by Cooper in 1843). Bramwich contributed fourteen hymns to Cooper's *Shakespearean Chartist Hymn Book* and Jones sixteen. Hymns such as Bramwich's *Britannia's Sons, Though Slaves Ye Be* and *Great God! Is This the Patriot's Doom?* and Jones's *Sons of Poverty Assemble* struck a resounding chord throughout the Chartist movement. On the death of Bramwich, Cooper penned a memoir for the *Northern Star* in which he characterised his lieutenant as the 'pauper-poet' and 'author of the immortal hymn, "Britannia's sons, thou slaves ye be"'. 'Poor Bramwich has not lived in vain,' wrote Cooper. 'The thousands with whom I was accustomed to sing his noble hymns in Leicester market-place, on Nottingham forest, and in the Staffordshire Potteries will not forget such thrilling poetry.'[27]

Cooper's hymnbooks have not survived the passage of time; fortunately, a literary scholar, Michael Sanders, has recently unearthed a copy of the *National Chartist Hymn Book*.[28] Published in Rochdale in 1845 by the NCA, the slim volume comprises a mere sixteen hymns. A comparison with a far more substantial collection published in Leeds a couple of years later, *Democratic Hymns and Songs*, edited by Joseph Barker, a preacher-cum-journalist and Chartist, reveals a significant overlap between the two.[29] In fact, the *National Chartist Hymn Book* is virtually subsumed into the later volume; eleven of the sixteen hymns reappear in Barker's collection. What we can see clearly here is a discrete repertoire of original compositions that was in common use by Chartists. Among these were the aforementioned hymns by Bramwich and Jones as well as Ebenezer Elliott's *God of the Poor! Shall Labour Eat* and William Sankey's *Men of England, ye are Slaves*. The latter, popular among the Leicester Chartists, was invoked in evidence used against Cooper during his Stafford trial.[30]

Hymnbooks were widely used in political agitation: at numerous open-air meetings, in the law courts and for celebrations of various kinds. They were clearly widely distributed and often used as a reference point. Cooper had famously read *Britannia's Sons* to Judge Erskine at his second trial at Stafford so that all Chartists 'may learn it by heart', and directed them to page seven of the *Shakespearean Chartist Hymn Book*.[31] It was sung at Stafford Prison to celebrate the release of John Richard, when seven cars 'filled with friends of liberty came to welcome him'. As the procession was formed, some 'mounted one of the cars and gave out the fourth hymn in the Chartist hymn book'. It was 'sung in good style, making the air ring again'.[32] Some months later a vivid description of a camp meeting on Norland Moor in Yorkshire described how 'pleasing' it was 'to behold the groups of earnest and devoted friends of liberty ascending the stupendous hills in all directions, accompanied by their wives and daughters' to the 'truly romantic' meeting place, whereupon 'the mountaineers' sang Jones's *Sons of Poverty Assemble* in 'good style with stentorian lungs'. This was followed by two more hymns from the *Shakespearean Chartist Hymn Book*.[33] At a lecture in Stockport 'the singers ... opened the business of the night by singing the 36th hymn in the Chartist Hymn-book'.[34] The same hymnbook was used years later in 1850 at a camp meeting at Mountsorrel Hill where 20,000 gathered to hear Ernest Jones and Feargus O'Connor. Once again it was the 'fourth hymn' that was called into action.[35]

Camp meetings had become an important part of Chartist culture from the late 1830s, gaining particular purchase after 1839 when mass demonstrations were banned. It owed a considerable debt to the revivalist camp meetings of Primitive Methodism, which had developed close ties to British radicalism since arriving in Britain from America in the early years of the nineteenth century. Reputedly, the first revivalist camp meetings had been held in Staffordshire in 1807. Other Primitive Methodist techniques such as singing in the streets and weekly class meetings were also absorbed into Chartism. (To some extent also Cooper's hymnbooks could be understood as a re-articulation of practices he learnt as a young Methodist). It was a vibrant participatory tradition of all-day meetings based around evangelical preaching and the collective singing of folk hymns. Often set to popular tunes, in Chartist hands these folk songs were transformed into what Yeo has described as 'original democratic hymns'.[36] By mid-1842 'Hymns for Camp Meetings' began to appear in the *Northern Star* and *English Chartist Circular*,[37] and William Jones supplied his own *Hymn for a Chartist Camp*.[38] Singing added to the feverish and spontaneous atmosphere of the revivalist camp meeting. The music-making and natural settings of the meetings were often described in colourful detail. Cooper recalled one Chartist camp meeting he held at Mountsorrel where 'the exhilaration' created in great part by the 'enthusiastic singing' was such that it was 'often spoken of afterwards'.[39]

Yeo has discerned elements of the Primitive Methodist camp meeting at the massive rally held on Peep Green in West Yorkshire in May 1839, notably the collective singing of a hymn that opened the meeting.[40] The hymn had been carefully and democratically selected by a committee of delegates who had met the week before. It was determined that the text be included in the *Northern Star* to allow the people to familiarise themselves with the words.[41] Although

unacknowledged, the hymn was in fact none other than Eliza Flower's
The Gathering of the Unions, written, as we have seen, for the
Birmingham Political Union's 'monster meeting' of 1832. The third
stanza found a place in the shared memory of the Chartists:

> God is our guide, no swords we draw,
> We kindle not war battle fires;
> By union, reason, order, law,
> We claim the birthright of our sires;
> And hark! We raise from sea to sea,
> The glorious watch-word liberty!

The catchphrase, 'This is our Charter, God is Our Guide', was printed
on the membership cards of the NCA. Again showing the fluid relationship between orality, aurality and visual culture, the slogan began
to be seen quoted in full on silk banners in processions, a pattern
which continued well into the nineteenth century.[42]

With a keen sense of theatre and spectacle, and partaking in the
Romantic embrace of the sublime, the Chartists took advantage
of the potential for drama and effect in open-air settings, often
finding natural amphitheatres for mass meetings. The importance
of nature and their predilection for impressive natural locales spoke
to a strong connection with the land. It not only reinforced their
sense of true patriotism but was also part of an ongoing struggle for
a stake in the soil. As Anne Janowitz has observed, the Chartists
took advantage of the 'sublime landscape' to emphasise the 'orator
as romantic freedom-fighter, who aimed to remind the mass of its
rights to the land'.[43] Nor were they immune to the possibilities of
these locations as evocative soundscapes; to the drama and affective
power of massed human voices raised in song in such surroundings.
Their accounts often describe the way music and singing resounded
through these spaces. Among many 'sacred sites' (to borrow Engels's
words), Blackstone Edge, an escarpment in the Pennines on the border
between Lancashire and Yorkshire, was especially important for the
Chartists. It certainly held a particular place in the heart of the man
who, as we have seen, would become the last of the Chartist leaders:
Ernest Jones. In August 1846 Jones was among the speakers (who also
included O'Connor and Peter McDouall) here at what would become
a famous camp meeting. The *Northern Star* hailed the event as no less
than 'the resurrection day of Chartism'. The 'bleak, wild mountain'
was alive with movement as the 'THE BACKBONE OF ENGLAND',
30,000 strong, wound their way three miles up to what was 'a beautiful amphitheatre'. This was where Jones gave his 'maiden' speech to
his new coadjutors; an experience he immortalised in his song, *The*

Blackstone Edge Gathering On the 2nd of August, 1846, set to *The Battle of Hohenlinden*.[44]

Jones's *Blackstone Edge* was published less than three weeks after the Chartists had trudged home.[45] The first three stanzas give an immediate and vivid sense of place captured in music. Away from the incessant spewing from the forest of chimneys of the factories and mills characteristic of the industrial city, out in the 'broad sunlight', there was 'sung, that morn, with trumpet might/ A sounding song of liberty'. This 'glorious music' penetrated to the towns below:

> How distant cities quaked to hear,
> When rolled from that high hill the cheer,
> Of – hope to slaves! To tyrants, fear!
> And God and man for liberty!

The following year 'the thousands of human beings' assembled once again 'under the canopy of heaven' atop Blackstone Edge. On this occasion there was an effort to create 'Merrie England'.[46] Many were 'attired in their picturesque costume' and all were 'accompanied by the merry strains of Chartist music'.[47]

The idea of Blackstone Edge as a site of resurrection stayed with Jones. After the closure of the *Northern Star* in 1852, repeated calls for gatherings at Blackstone Edge were to be found in the pages of his *People's Paper*.[48] In September 1854, during the final gasps of the Chartist movement, Jones realised his desire to stage a mass gathering once more at what he envisaged, in a moment of myth-making, as 'this time-honoured site of olden meetings'.[49] Here, up in 'the ancient mountains' covered in flowering heather and accompanied by the sound of rushing water, the large gathering had assembled, drawn together by the 'enlivening strains of music'. The meeting opened with the 'singing of a Chartist hymn'.[50] In these episodes hymn-singing served as an expression of solidarity; a sharing of common identity and a vehicle which fused democracy and God and by so doing provided the movement with a continued sense of ceremony and ritual within a new egalitarian and progressive context.

Hymn-singing also had the potential to disrupt. This potential to cause trouble had been seen earlier during the parish church demonstrations held in the late summer months of 1839 when Chartists attended churches in great numbers across Britain to the consternation, even horror, of the regular church goers. This brief efflorescence functioned as a kind of proto-occupy movement, which protested not only the established churches' hostility to Chartism but more specifically church rates, and pew rents, through which large numbers of working people were excluded.[51] Hymns were enlisted as part of the political action, and played an important role in these confrontations, as seen by the enthusiastic participation of the Sheffield Chartists. On 31 August 1839 a large crowd assembled in Paradise Square in the city centre where they strengthened their resolve with a rousing rendition of 'Mr. Elliott's hymn' before descending upon the church.[52] The police were quick to respond. They issued a public notice prohibiting assembly in the churchyard on the following Sunday and occupied the square themselves that morning. The protestors made no attempt to confront them and instead sang a hymn as they walked peacefully from the square to the church.[53] The following week they did the same. The only difference being, however, that the hymn they 'chaunted, in a solemn and affecting manner' on their way to the church had been specially 'composed for the occasion'.[54] Their forced entry was greeted with extreme hostility by the parishioners and some protesters were physically attacked inside the church. Camp meetings in the surrounding forests were sometimes held as a coda to these protests or provided a service if in fact the protestors had been unable to enter the church. This served to consolidate the movement and further defy the established order.[55]

Hymns were not always sung; on occasion they were played to great effect by bands. One such example occurred at the consecration of a new church in Norwich in 1841, two years after the parish church demonstrations, where again the hymn became a weapon, but in this context one of political agitation rather than deculturation. The Chartists had determined 'to exhibit every species of annoyance in opposition to the solemn service to be performed' and succeeded in spectacular fashion.[56] The incident was covered in detail by at least three newspapers, including *The Times*. The Chartists turned out in anticipation of the ceremony, led by a brass band and displaying what were regarded as sacrilegious banners (one carried the well-known message: 'More pigs and less parsons'). The local *Norfolk Chronicle* used the protestors' musical choices to illustrate the degree of their 'profane and shameless disposition'. 'It is only needful to mention', recounted the newspaper, 'that one of the tunes to which [the protestors] marched at quick time was the beautiful air of the Portuguese hymn of the Nativity, "Adeste fideles"' (better known by its English title, *O Come, All Ye Faithful*).[57] On reaching the church, the Chartists were refused entry by the police, who were out in force with the order to use their truncheons. When the Lord Bishop's carriage arrived, it was unable to penetrate the large crowd that had gathered in the churchyard. The bishop was required make the final leg of his journey on foot. The presence of a police escort did not deter the crowd from throwing stones. Apparently His Grace was not hit but some of the police were not so fortunate. Meanwhile, the band, presumably not consisting of any Teetotal Chartists, had removed to the nearest public house. Once the consecration service was underway, however, they 'sallied forth' once more under the direction of a well-known local Chartist, Thomas Hewett, playing *God Save the Queen*. On being refused entry Hewett proceeded to lead the band in what was obviously an energetic performance of the usually majestic psalm tune, the *Old Hundredth*, 'to the great annoyance', as *The Times* reprovingly wrote, 'of every person in the sacred edifice'. The sermon 'was very imperfectly heard on account of the noise outside and the uneasiness and distraction of the attention of those within'.[58] The proceedings dissolved into chaos and the mayor and the superintendent apprehended Hewett and several others in the ensuing fracas. An angry crowd followed the magistrate and prisoners to the courthouse and threatened to pull it down. At the same time the Lord Bishop was forced to travel back to the palace on foot, accompanied every step of the way by the band playing *The Rogue's March*.[59]

The long-metre Calvinist hymn tune the *Old Hundredth*, which formed part of the musical arsenal at Norwich, was a perennial favourite with the Chartists. It accompanied Thomas Cooper's *God of the Earth, and Sea, and Sky*, William Jones's *Why Should Not Man Be Free?*,[60] both Bramwich's *Britannia's Sons* and *Great God! Is This the Patriot's Doom?*, as well as Elliott's *God of the Poor*. As we have seen, Elliott was a prominent radical as well as a poet and closely involved in early Chartism. In addition to his famous *Corn Law Rhymes*, he also produced a volume of *Corn Law Hymns*. His hymn *God of the Poor* found a place in the *National Chartist Hymn Book*. On 26 September 1838, the day after the more famous 'monster meeting' on Kersal Moor near Manchester, Elliott opened a Chartist gathering in Sheffield with the hymn, written specially for the occasion. He clarified the process to his audience: 'It is proposed that our proceedings shall commence with a hymn, which I shall recite stanza by stanza, and which you will sing, accompanied by the band, to the tune of the Old Hundredth Psalm'.[61] The *Northern Star* reported how two months later at a demonstration in Loughborough in support of the People's Charter and National Petition, one of Elliott's *Corn Law Hymns* was 'sung by the multitude, to the tune of the Old Hundredth Psalm, the bands accompanying the singers'.[62] Bramwich's *Great God! Is This the Patriot's Doom?* was composed for the funeral of Sheffield Chartist Samuel Holberry. It was handed out – sold, according to critics – and sung to the *Old Hundredth* by the crowd of around 50,000 people in attendance.[63] In the following weeks it continued to be heard at memorial meetings across the nation.[64] The extent to which this hymn found an enduring place in Chartist culture is seen by its performance sixteen years later at what was to be one of the final expressions of mass support for the Chartist movement. Twenty-five thousand people at Heyhead Green, south of Manchester, raised their voices in song to welcome John Frost, the leader of the Newport uprising, home from Australia in 1856.[65]

As is well known, the Temperance movement overlapped with Chartism, formally and informally. Like 'Church Chartism' (to borrow O'Connor's characterisation) enthusiasm for the cause of teetotalism produced a campaign within the ranks to encourage Chartists to take the pledge and this produced some branches only open to teetotallers. In many cases religion and temperance were closely linked. Joseph Barker was one of many Chartist preachers who supported teetotalism. In some cases this commitment was reflected in musical composition. George Russell from Warwick was a Chartist hymn-writer and a temperance advocate. Moreover, tea parties became a constant recreation in Chartist life, often held in Temperance Halls. Music, particularly singing, was central to the working-class temperance agitation as it was to later middle-class manifestations such as the Women's Christian Temperance Union (WCTU). The *Teetotal Chartist Song*, sung to *We're Fighting for Our King* (again invoking religious battle), connects freedom with sobriety and self-discipline. The chorus explicitly links the two causes (with a reference to smoking thrown in for good measure):

> The Charter let all people sing;
> The Charter will our freedom bring;
> Tis now our own – we see it near;
> While Temperance guards the front and rear;
> The battle's won – our day's begun;
> The pot and filthy pipe are gone;
> Teetotalism shall be one
> With the great Charter Union.[66]

Later in the 1850s Jones devoted considerable space in his *People's Paper* to accounts of temperance activities in which music was inevitably a major component. A glance through the 'Moral and Educational' column of April 1853 provides a snapshot of typical reports: singers provided temperance melodies with a lecture in Heptonstall; in Darlington the weekly meeting at the Working Man's Teetotal Hall was 'enlivened' with a choral rendition of 'several choice melodies'. Rochdale was awash with sober musical performance: the Massey Temperance Glee Singers performed for the Rochdale Parent Temperance Society tea party; the Rochdale Progressing Washingtonian Total Abstinence Society's annual tea party enjoyed a 'grand miscellaneous entertainment' comprising 'a company of glee singers' performing 'a number of negro melodies in character with the usual accompaniments', as well as renditions from Mr Moore, a 'well-known comic singer', the Rochdale Harmonic Band and an unnamed pianist.[67] Of course, many – perhaps even most – Chartists did not take the pledge. Drink was at the core of their day-to-day lives, including their lived experience of politics, and music-making occupied a central place within it. Most Chartist meetings took place in pubs and a rollicking rendition of a political ditty – even a hymn – probably sounded better when accompanied by alcohol.

Hymns in the secular sphere

Although a favourite with many Chartists as a worthy melody for their heartfelt politico-religious texts, the *Old Hundredth* was presented in quite a different light by the secularists of Toronto. Decades later in 1909 a satirical report of a legal case appeared in *Secular Thought* in which agents of the Metropolitan Life Insurance Company sued their employer for a $100 gratuity. The centrepiece of the account was a description of the insurance company's own song of praise, *Metropolitan Doxology 1896*, which was once again set to this pillar of Anglican hymnody. The 'Doxology' was apparently sung at the morning meetings as a kind of ritual. The author's decision to include the first stanza in the account effectively ridiculed at once capitalist greed and religion:

> Be with us in our work, O Lord,
> Be here and everywhere adored,
> Our labors bless and grant that we
> May rest in Paradise with Thee.[68]

This stands as another useful reminder of music's ability to take on contradictory meanings contingent upon context and purpose. Here, we have an amusing instance when it supplied Canadian secularists with a way to pillory aspects of society antithetical to their beliefs. However, freethinkers did not uniformly use the hymn as an object of derision. Owenism, a prominent working-class movement in the first half of the nineteenth century in Britain, is a case in point. As is well known, the utopian socialist movement, which went on to make important contributions to the Co-operative Movement and trade unionism, developed out of the ideas of the industrialist Robert Owen, who had used his factory in New Lanark in Scotland as a model for a radical social experiment. Owen envisaged his 'new moral world' as fundamentally classless, but he was no democrat. In fact, he quickly lost control of his own movement, particularly in the north where

[307]

working people inculcated the fundamental principles into their sense of participatory democracy and self-help and made it their own. In addition to the development of co-operative societies, one of well-known legacies of the Owenites was the creation of Halls of Science, often built in opposition to Mechanics' Institutes in the thrall of middle-class do-gooders associated with the rational recreation movement.

Owenism had as its basis the concept of rational religion: a belief system that replaced a faith in God with what Eileen Yeo describes as one characterised by 'brotherliness and joy'.[69] Rational religion translated and transposed religious ceremonies and rituals into secular spaces. Music was crucial to the Owenites' calendar of social festivals and lecture meetings, and more generally their cultural agenda of moral improvement through entertainment. Bands, orchestras and choirs were trained to provide the music for a wide range of events. In 1835 Owen had produced a volume entitled *Social Hymns for the Use of Friends of the Rational System of Society* (a report in the *Northern Star* of a social festival in Bradford in 1838 told of Owen singing one of his own social hymns).[70] The legacy of religion was made explicit in the Owenite newspaper the *New Moral World* during a discussion extolling the benefits of congregational singing. According to one correspondent, music was considered to be 'greatly beneficial, as most individuals have, from infancy, been trained under religious tuition, they have been accustomed to the pleasing sensation which music generates'.[71] Again, it was music's affective potential, its perceived ability both to uplift and ameliorate that was seen as useful:

> when the melody of music is mixed with the benevolent and philosophical sentiments of the most sympathetic and enlightened of our species, congregational singing should be encouraged. When our finest affections, mingled with softest and sweetest vibrations shall carry man without his narrow self, and point out the means by which he may make a perfect diapason of all the jarring and conflicting interests of the great family of man.[72]

Owenism and Chartism were linked in innumerable ways: most Owenites were in fact Chartists, but not all Chartists were Owenites. As both movements declined many Chartists and Owenites looking for new articulations of radical thought gravitated toward secularism. Consequently, secularism, a more popular branch of freethought, was closely associated with political radicalism and gained a significant working-class membership. Unsurprisingly, many of its key personnel were former Owenites and Chartists. The man who founded the movement officially in 1855, G. J. Holyoake, is a case in point: not only had he been editor of the *Northern Star*, he was also the last secretary of the NCA. Charles Bradlaugh, who espoused a more extreme version of secularism, was closely involved in the Reform League – the successor organisation for many Chartists – before founding the National Secular Society (NSS) in 1866. His sustained involvement both in freethought and radical politics reflected the ongoing and close connection between the two. Many freethought lecturers such as Charles Southwell and Joseph Symes, both former Owenites and important in the secularist movement, took Owen's concept of the 'social missionary' to an extreme and extended their crusade to the distant colonies, transforming secularism, and freethought more generally, into a truly inter-colonial movement. Southwell is acknowledged as having brought freethought to New Zealand and Symes, another leading figure in the movement, played a highly idiosyncratic role in its transmission to Australia. Charles Watts, another significant figure in the secularist movement who worked closely with Austin Holyoake (George's brother), moved to Toronto in 1884.

A glance at secularist publications across these points in the Anglophone world, namely London's *National Reformer*, Dunedin's *Echo*, Melbourne's *Liberator* and Toronto's *Secular Thought*, reveals a shared culture not only through a comparison of their reading lists and booksellers' holdings but also in a more immediate sense through the ways in which music was used in their internal activities. The *National Reformer* pre-empted the founding of the NSS by six years. It had been established in Sheffield in 1860 by Bradlaugh and the former Christian Chartist-turned-infidel Joseph Barker, both active members of the Sheffield Secular Society. The periodical moved to London to become the official organ of the NSS after 1866. It functioned much as the *Northern Star* had, not only in the kinds of musical performance it reported but also in the style of the reports themselves. Every edition contained accounts of branch activity all over Britain. Monthly social meetings, tea parties and soirees almost invariably involved musical activities, many of which were described in detail. The ongoing popularity of tea parties highlights the continuing intersection between the Temperance movement and a variety of social reform and political movements. In September 1861, for example, the *National Reformer* reported that the Oldham Co-operative Society had held a tea party to celebrate the opening of its Co-operative Hall. The festivities were enlivened by the strains of the Leeds Temperance Band; the Saddleworth Choral Society provided glees, songs and duets and a certain Mr W. Haigh provided a selection of 'Lancashire dialect songs'.[73] The Sheffield Secular Society, to take another example, met at the Hall of Science for tea followed by entertainment and instruction. The attendees were fed on a musical diet including arias from Italian opera, glees, parlour songs and 'negro' melodies. The event was deemed so successful that it was decided to continue to offer these kinds of recreations as part of monthly socials and weekly meetings.[74]

Bradlaugh, or 'Iconoclast', the pseudonym by which he was known to his fellow secularists, appeared frequently at London's Hall of Science. In November 1861 he lectured twice (accompanied by John Lowry singing). Bradlaugh's lecture took as its subject the 'absurdities' of the three creeds and the Thirty-nine Articles of the Church of England, supported by Lowry's renditions of Charles Mackay's *Songs of Progress*. According to the report these 'appropriate and progressive songs ... gave much satisfaction'.[75] Bradlaugh was notoriously difficult and over the years had ferocious quarrels with many of his colleagues, including G. J. Holyoake and Joseph Barker, who gave up the editorship of the *Reformer* in response to Bradlaugh's advocacy of birth control. Chief among these disputes was his clash with Charles Watts. Watts was the son of a bootmaker and had cut his teeth as a lecturer on the temperance platform. After hearing Holyoake speak he became a committed secularist, soon becoming a full-time lecturer for the movement. In the early 1860s Watts became sub-editor of the *National Reformer* and the NSS's inaugural secretary.

By 1877, however, Watts had become embroiled in a bitter disagreement with Bradlaugh, leading to his break from the NSS. During the early 1880s he embarked upon a series of lecturing tours to Canada, ultimately settling there in 1884. Ironically, the breakdown of Watts's friendship with Bradlaugh was instrumental in the growth of secularism in Canada. The Toronto Freethought Association was founded in 1873 and renamed the Toronto Secular Society in 1881. Among its key figures were J. Ick Evans and Thomas Phillips Thompson, the latter going on, as we have seen, to become one of Canada's most influential radical figures and a leading force in later labour and social reform movements. By this time there is enough evidence to see an important place for music in their culture. For example, a report from 1878 in the society's journal, *Freethought*, described a weekly Sunday meeting operating to a familiar formula: 'The programme consists of music, ten minutes reading, generally on a scientific subject, half hour essay or lecture, followed by a debate'. 'Miss Henrietta Scadding presides at the piano,' the report tells us, adding, 'the Association is much indebted to her for the most attractive part of the programme. She is prepossessing, plays nicely, and is a general favourite with the audience.'[76]

Watts was clearly involved in the formation and production of secular culture. As we have seen, in London in 1871 he had co-edited *The Secularist's Manual of Songs and Ceremonies*.[77] Like many similar publications, it stands as a crucible of movement culture, functioning both as manifesto and propaganda. In a preface Bradlaugh argued that it would fulfil a 'need felt through the ranks of Freethinkers in this country'. The material is organised by genre and function, including songs, recitations and texts for secular christenings, weddings and funerals. The song repertoire includes many of the standard examples of moral progress and uplift, indicated by titles such as *Liberty, Reason, Nature, Knowledge and Charity, Social Regeneration* and *Truth*. The authors include many of the progressive writers of the day, including Charles Mackay, Eliza Cook, Robert Nicoll, Russell Lowell and Mary Howitt. Explicit connections to radicalism were found in the inclusion of pieces such as the popular Chartist song *Base Oppressors*, by J. A. Leatherland, the pointedly working class *Address to the Upper Classes*, set to Sir Walter Scott's renowned re-worked ballad *Jock o' Hazeldea*,[78] the *Marseillaise*, as well as a homage to the movement's progenitor, *Death of Robert Owen: 17th of November*.[79]

The opening song section is unusual in one significant respect. As was the case with Coit and Adler's *Ethical Hymn Book*, tunes are not given; instead, the hymn metre appears in abbreviated form in the right-hand margin. This recasting of Christian hymnody reveals the ongoing desire for ceremony and ritual transferred across into the secular sphere and says much about cultural expectations regarding the public proclamation of values and beliefs, or in this case, non-belief. The mutability of ritualistic forms fulfilled the continued need for a sense of the familiar. In a sense, the trenchant disavowal of religious belief that saturated secularist rhetoric was diluted by the inclusion of hymn metres in the song section of the manual. Among the cases where tunes are nominated are instances where the chosen melody supports the political aim of the text. For example, the prominent secularist George Sexton's poem 'The Old Creeds', opening with the lines 'I cannot hold the old creeds,/ We have them now outgrown', is set to the air *I Cannot Sing the Old Songs*, effectively bringing together the acts of singing and believing.

Two figures whose presence is conspicuous throughout the *Manual*'s pages are John Lowry and John Bedford Leno. The music section opens with Leno's acclaimed celebration of agricultural labour, *Song of the Spade* to 'Music, by John Lowry', proclaimed by Edward Carpenter as 'one of the best labour songs ever written',[80] and finishes with three more of Leno's poems set to Lowry's music: *The Future is Ours, Hurrah!, Let All Your Songs Be Angel-Songs* and finally *Judge Not A Man*. Clearly, Lowry was central to the production. As well as Leno's songs, his music accompanies lyrics by Ernest Jones and George Sexton and his own musing, *There Must Be Something Wrong*. Lowry's importance, not only to the *Manual* but also to radical culture more

[311]

generally, was acknowledged by Bradlaugh: 'The songs have had the advantage of the able supervision of Mr. John Lowry, whose musical talents are so well known to our London friends.'[81]

Anticipating that the *Secularist's Manual* would promote the establishment of a 'choral class at each hall to open and close the meetings with fair singing' (the words are Bradlaugh's), the manual contains a rare example of Lowry's own prose: an essay, 'A Few Words on Singing'. He began with a case for the importance of music, invoking and making personal the already famous words, 'Let *me* write the people's songs, *I* care not who makes the laws [emphasis added]'.[82] It was, in Lowry's opinion, 'an axiom, the potency of which has been thoroughly recognised by every sect; their Hymn Book is the great "open sesame" to the hearts of their flocks.' 'This magnificent gift of munificent nature', as Lowry considered it, had been 'almost ignored by the Secular party as a grand means of propaganda'. The *Secularist's Manual* was offered as a way to 'obviate this defect'.[83] In those cases where music had not been '*specially* set [emphasis added]' Lowry decided to simply 'mark the metre of the pieces', so that 'tunes may be selected from an ordinary tune book'. Significantly, however, he exhorted the readers to take 'great care and attention' as to the 'fitness' of the tunes selected, and insisted that the words, 'must be sung with greater spirit and force than they usually are, in order that those who join in the singing ... may avoid falling into the drawling, indistinct utterance so frequently heard in congregational singing'.[84] In conclusion, Lowry seized an opportunity to proselytise for his cause in which he also highlighted the importance of making music:

> Thus, then, a true appreciation and earnest enunciation of the feelings of the poet are the great essentials of a true singer; and the people in the coming future must be their own singers, for they will tire of singing the praises of red-handed warriors, who simply destroy, and will love more to sing of the warriors of labour, who produce.[85]

The 'warriors of labour' spread across the Anglophone world: emigrants and travelling lecturers extended the global network of freethought culture not only to Canada but also to the very edges of the southern hemisphere.[86] The cultural forms and material remained the same despite the distance travelled. Dunedin, perched on the lower end of New Zealand's South Island, saw the establishment of the Dunedin Freethought Association (FTA), which quickly developed a vibrant culture. The *Echo*, its official organ, was edited by the association's founder, Robert Stout, later to become premier of New Zealand. Its columns provided members with reports of freethought activities from around the globe: from lectures by the famous American freethinker

Robert Ingersoll in Chicago to a picnic enjoyed by the Australasian Secularists in Melbourne (serenaded by a Bavarian Band). There is clear evidence of communication across a transnational network, such as Bradlaugh's pleas on behalf of the Māori in the House of Commons in 1880.[87] There was individual movement. In November 1881, for example, a report announced the departure of renowned freethought lecturer Charles Bright for San Francisco and an Australasian tour in 1885 by the 'Celebrated American Orator' Dr J. L. York (known as 'The Ingersoll of the West').[88] Printed material followed the same routes as these agitators. The stock of Dunedin bookseller Joseph Braithwaite, for example, included a large section of 'Reform Literature' penned by Bradlaugh, Besant, Bright, Carlyle, Darwin, Ingersoll, Paine, Mill, Tindall, Voltaire, Blavatsky and Aveling. These connections will surprise no student of radicalism and reform during the long nineteenth century.

FTA meetings followed the pattern established by Owen; they opened with music, moved on to an address and finished with more music and dancing. Indeed, music-making was a ubiquitous feature at meetings, social gatherings, picnics, lectures and balls, often held in the customary working-class sites of the Temperance Hall, Oddfellows Hall and Working Men's Club.[89] Scattered throughout the pages of the *Echo* were numerous accounts of the manifold successes of the 'unusually excellent' Freethought Choral Union and Band, comprising 'two violins, viola, cello, double bass, two cornets, clarionette and trombone'.[90] The repertoire revolved around operatic numbers due to their uplifting qualities.[91] And they were numerous: Verdi's *Il Trovatore*, Bellini's *La Sonnambula*, Donizetti's *Don Pasquale*, as well as Daniel Auber's *Le Maçon*, the overture from Cesare Pugni's ballet *La Esmeralda* and overtures of *Le Chevalier* and *La Souveraine* by Alphonse Herman (some less known today). In addition to this lighter fare, they also dabbled in the German classical repertoire: on one occasion the performed Haydn's Sixth Symphony and excerpts from Mozart's Twelfth Mass.[92] The detail of the reporting and the musical choices for discussion suggest an educated and aspirational readership and provide another example of the confluence of musical taste and progressive thought along the spectrum of freethought culture. Popular song was not foregrounded in the pages of the *Echo*, although there was mention of a series, 'Hymns for the Times', which included the hymn parody *Buy the Truth*, set to *Hold the Fort*:

> Buy the truth, but sell it – never!
> Speak, seek, search, and spread the truth.[93]

Their musical effusions offered freethinkers an important point for smug comparison. Encomiums for their Choral Union and Band boasted that the standard of performance was better than anything heard at the local churches.[94]

One measure of talent evident to this day was that in 1881 the *Echo* proudly announced that the New Zealand national anthem had been composed by a branch member. Thomas Bracken, an Otago journalist and freethinker, had published *God Defend New Zealand* on 1 July 1876 in his own newspaper, the *New Zealand Saturday Advertiser*, under the title 'National Hymn'. Five years later the *Echo* reconfirmed this generic categorisation in its report detailing a performance by 300 singers and a band of forty.[95] This example of a song by one of the rank and file of freethought, combined with the fact that their leader was to assume the highest position in the political nation, provide two points of convergence between this fringe progressive culture and the emerging democratic nation. Little over fifteen years later, possibly in an attempt to correct his faux pas of singing *The Wearing of the Green* in transit for an audience with the Queen (discussed previously), Premier Robert Seddon presented her with a copy of Bracken's hymn. Had she known it was from the pen of a freethinker she might have found it every bit as objectionable as the Irish rebel song.

The freethought associations of New Zealand were gentler in disposition than Joseph Symes's Australasian Secularist Association (ASA) in Melbourne. In an example once again showing the importance of an individual – who today we would call a significant actor – the progress of this organisation reflected the acerbic and notoriously obstreperous personality of its leader. As vice president of the NSS in Britain, Symes was a regular contributor to the *National Reformer* and an inveterate travelling lecturer. In 1884, in response to a request from Victorian secularists, Symes was sent to Melbourne as a missionary to foster a similar enterprise.[96] He established a Hall of Science in 1884 and founded the *Liberator* along the same guidelines as the *National Reformer*. The Melbourne-based ASA developed strong links not only with an extant Sydney branch of an organisation of the same name but also with freethought activists in New Zealand. The *Liberator* often included the column 'Auckland Notes' signed by 'White Maori'. Connections to the broader radical movement were evident too: one column reported in detail a lecture tour of Gerald Massey, a well-known poet and former Chartist.[97]

Again, the familiar cultural patterns practised by earlier generations of Owenites are evident; twice daily Sunday social services, mutual improvement classes during the week and frequent social evenings were major weekly events. In the mornings there was a social service and in the evenings a lecture. Music featured at both of these. Reports from Sydney indicate the same pattern of events. The advertisement

[314]

for Sunday Evening Lectures informs the reader that a 'Grand Choral Service takes place every evening before the lecture'.[98] Somewhat ironically, given that a chief aim of secularism was to debunk religious faith, many of the patterns of Christian ritual and ceremony were adopted and adapted.

As with the Owenite social festivals, Symes's services began and ended with entertainments comprising song, recitations and musical selections performed by members of the association. The Melbourne secularists lived for the most part on a staple diet of Victorian parlour songs by composers such as Henry Russell and Stephen Adams. Other vocal items included Irish and Scottish ballads and arrangements of Italian opera. Instrumental items were mainly flute, violin or piano solos, including the *Turkish Patrol,* a march for piano.[99] On several occasions there were compositions by a member, Mr Ashworth.[100] The concertina featured on at least one occasion, as did a more unusual performance by Madam Zimmerman, who one evening 'favoured the audience with a song with zither accompaniment' entitled *La Catelur on Lac on Leurich.* The performance was deemed 'most delightful' and the performer's execution both 'brilliant and pathetic'.[101] The musical fare was not only completely conventional, it was, like the musical repertoire of its counterparts in New Zealand and Canada, conspicuous by its lack of political content. Notwithstanding the apolitical nature of the music performed, it was at the heart of Symes's clash with the authorities, resulting in a protracted legal case. What was at stake was not musical content, but the fact that musical performance occurred at all. As we have noted, anti-Sabbatarianism was a major concern for many of these alternative movements and a highly charged public issue. During the late 1860s St Martin's Hall in London had been home to the Alhambra Society, a group of 'Recreational Rationalists' (led by radical journalist John Baxter Langley), who were heavily fined for holding 'entertainments' in a 'disorderly house' on Sundays in flagrant defiance of the law. In 1875 the government again attempted to stop Sunday lectures in the hall; this time it was the proprietor, well-known composer and teacher John Pyke Hullah, who was charged.[102]

The same scenario unfolded in Melbourne. It was not unusual at these Sunday social meetings to offer both a secular entertainment and take a collection at the door. The confluence of these musical performances with a financial transaction on a Sunday allowed the authorities to argue that they constituted a paid entertainment. Symes was aware of what had transpired at St Martin's Hall and, of course, he was following a strategy employed by radicals and secularists since the late eighteenth century and developed into the nineteenth. Indeed, Symes took it to an extreme that the notorious Richard Carlile and the 'Devil's

Chaplain', Rev. Robert Taylor, would have been proud.[103] In September 1885 Symes was charged with 'keeping a disorderly house'.[104] As per usual the music performed was almost completely without a political edge, but it was the pretext on which the government mounted a case against those whose political and moral views they found deeply threatening. Symes's talent for biting satire reached new heights during this affair and found expression both in his public speaking and his journalism. He immediately exacerbated the situation by publishing an advertisement in the *Liberator* for 'divine services' to be held on Sunday evenings by Symes in the Hall of Science, renamed 'St Kerferd's Church' as a taunt aimed at the Victorian Attorney General, George Kerferd. Symes included a price for pew rents in a gibe at the Church's hypocrisy.[105]

The following week Symes produced an even more extreme sequel pillorying religious pomposity. He was now referring to himself as 'The Right Rev. Father in God, Joseph who would open the church of St Kerferd "By the Grace of God, Archbishop of Victoria, Legate a latere, and Nuncio"' and 'consecrate the same to the worship of CANT'. There were to be fumigations with incense, followed by 'orthodox' sermons after which he would '[a]dminister the Sacrament according to the New Jerusalem Rites. Halleluiah!' In an article entitled 'A New Prayer' Symes pulled no punches: 'We thank thee that thou has raised up unto thyself a pious and holy Attorney-General, a burning and a shining light in the midst of the dark and sceptical government that now rules this colony.' Befitting a church, music-making was central. 'Let us sing the doxology,' he proclaimed:

> Praise god from whom all blessings flow!
> Kerferd's the boy to go for Joe!
> He's stronger than the heavenly host,
> Or father, and son, and holy ghost![106]

The newspaper reports describe Symes enacting these proclamations to full effect. Lampooning hymns was at the core of his attacks. On 2 August he included a verse purportedly sent in from 'a wicked wight':

> For stuff a man with Wesley's hymns
> With Psalms chucked in between,
> And, pretty soon, he'll feel his limbs
> And 'bust' the whole machine.[107]

An imaginary prayer meeting in the legislative assembly saw the Speaker 'giving out the first hymn, which was sung to the lively tune of St Bride's by a Ranter'.[108]

The *Argus* followed the case in detail during September and October. The editor took pains to emphasise the secular nature of the music performed.[109] Despite the gravity of the situation, the social meetings continued unabated. Unsurprisingly, they came under close police surveillance and were the site of physical disturbances. On one occasion a scuffle broke out in the audience during which 'a respectable-looking man was ejected with great violence' by 'three or four stalwart men'.

The case was heard in late October in the Supreme Court. The presiding judge was Justice George Higinbotham – a renowned radical-liberal and, as a Member of Parliament, an advocate for secular education.[110] Again, the *Argus* followed it closely in reports whose titles pointed to the issue at hand: 'The Sunday Entertainments at the Hall of Science'.[111] The evidence included an account of Symes's 'buffoonery', trying to sing 'a parody on one hymn'. The importance of music-making to the events was evident when it was revealed that a policeman had identified 'each individual musical work performed by name, the duration of the performance and the fact that applause was given, concluding that there "was no difference between it and an ordinary musical concert"'.[112] That applause was important was realised by both sides: the policeman reported that Symes told his audience that he 'understood that applause was sometimes allowed in churches in Scotland at one time, and he would not mind if there was applause that night'. Lawyers for both sides danced on the head of a pin over the definition of entertainment but it was actually crucial to the outcome. As the increasingly conservative *Argus* concluded: the crux of the matter was whether the hall had been used 'for public amusement and entertainment' or 'for the honest purpose of mutual instruction and improvement' and, as Symes insisted, a place of worship (albeit secular), and therefore equivalent to a church.[113]

Symes's case was controversial not only in Australia but also across the Tasman in New Zealand where the outcome was reported in at least twenty newspapers. Moreover, in the papers of Robert Stout, Symes's fellow freethinker, are cuttings from the Australian press.[114] From his instructions to the jury, Higinbotham was clearly unimpressed by Symes's argument, although he upheld the central contention (relevant for us here): 'The singing of the Churches is part and parcel of the theology of the Churches. It is as much doctrinal as the prayers or the preaching. But what conceivable relation has The Turkish Patrol or Man the Lifeboat to Mr. Symes's religious views?'[115] Obviously, Higinbotham had forgotten about the long-established tradition of counter-theatre (or reversal rituals) in demotic politics in Britain. The editor of Sydney's *Daily Telegraph* had not. 'The audience is "entertained"', he lamented, by 'jovial music and free and easy debates, a mock liturgy, burlesque sacraments, and blasphemous feats, which are … worthy of John Wilkes'.[116] The jurors also remembered, or at least some of them did. Symes's fellow citizens were deadlocked as to his guilt and he was released. A second trail ended similarly in a hung jury and the prosecution was abandoned.[117]

The ASA had collapsed by 1888 in part because of the authoritarian and divisive leadership of Symes, but also because of the fundamentally different strains of political radicalism that, despite shared beliefs in secularism, could no longer coexist under one roof.[118] The major schism occurred between socialists and anarchists on the one side and staunch republicans and advocates of self-help, including Symes, on the other. The final year of the association coincided, however, with the publication of the *Australian Secular Association Lyceum Tutor*, edited by Bernard O'Dowd, a renowned Australian poet and socialist. Like so many progressive societies which sought to create a new way of life, children were of utmost importance to the ASA, who established its own Sunday School on the model we have discussed previously. O'Dowd's *Lyceum Tutor* was produced specifically to educate younger generations of secularists. Here, music was again central to the school's activities; it was seen as a way to make the secular Sunday Schools 'as attractive as possible'.[119] Like many similar undertakings, O'Dowd's *Lyceum Tutor* was conceived and structured as a practical manual. A large body of literary and song material was carefully categorised under different headings suitable for different activities. Performance was critically important for O'Dowd. He went beyond supplying the texts, many of them written by him, but also spelt out in detail the expected patterns of behaviour, demonstrating again the continued importance of ritual and ceremonial forms in new secularised contexts. The *Lyceum Tutor* outlasted the ASA and was still called into action many years later in other radical settings such as the Socialist Sunday School in Broken Hill we have seen before.[120]

Spreading the gospel of socialism: the Labour Church.

Established in Manchester in 1891, the Labour Church espoused a potent combination of non-doctrinal Christian theology with communitarian socialism. It can be found from one corner of the Anglophone world to another. Music and music-making were central to its modus operandi and the lived experience of its members and, as we have seen throughout the preceding pages, this offers us an excellent way of glimpsing a shared radical and reformist cultural tradition. Here, our account is built around the explication of four episodes, taking us on a journey across distance and time.

The *Labour Church Hymn Book* (hereafter *LCHB*) can be understood as an heir to the *National Chartist Hymn Book* and *Democratic*

Hymns and Songs.[121] This connection is evident by the continued use of earlier radical hymns and songs by the likes of Gerald Massey, Thomas Cooper and Ebenezer Elliott. We can hear of the latter by listening in on a discussion at the Seventeenth Conference of the Labour Church Union held in Bradford in early March 1908. Music was the subject, specifically the popularity of the *LCHB*, which had already necessitated a third print run of 20,000 copies. Unsurprisingly, the profit margin on sales to that date led to a consensus that a 'new edition was again required'. Here, the unanimity ended. The decision to go to press provoked proposals for revisions to the hymnbook's contents, notably a motion to excise Ebenezer Elliott's 1847 hymn *When Wilt Thou Save the People?*. The motion was not carried; but the result – seven votes to thirteen – reveals a noticeable fissure in the committee.[122]

Second, let's look over the shoulder of Louisa Blake in Christchurch as she writes an excited letter to the founder of the Socialist Church, Harry A. Atkinson, in April 1901. In addition to being an active member of Atkinson's church, Blake had been involved in the National Council of Women of New Zealand, founded in 1896. In the letter she expressed her joy at reading a report from the London *Times* of a Labour Conference. She was inspired, proposing to Atkinson that 'two triumphant sounding Socialist songs and one or two other stirring songs' be prepared at the 'Saturday fortnight rehearsal' to be performed in celebration at a 'special Socialist meeting' at Christchurch's Metaphysical Club.[123] She wondered if William Ranstead might play for them. The Labour Conference in question was the Independent Labour Party's (ILP) Ninth Conference, held a few days earlier in Leicester; Ranstead was a prominent British socialist recently arrived from Manchester intent on establishing a Clarion Colony, yet another utopian settlement scheme, this one inspired by Robert Blatchford, a prominent activist, writer-cum-journalist and editor of the widely circulated socialist newspaper the *Clarion*.

Thirdly, in July 1898 a crowd gathered in Melbourne's Temperance Hall on Russell Street, close to the heart of the colony's capital, to remember the Chartists fifty years after the movement had reached its apogee. The programme that evening included reminiscences by seventy-one-year-old Joseph Constantine, an 'Old Chartist', 'including his arrest, imprisonment, and release'. Two well-known radical MPs spoke: William Moloney, an international socialist, republican, humanist and advocate of women's suffrage who was involved in a range of political and union organisations including the Knights of Labor, the Victorian Labor Party and the Trades' Hall Council; and John Hancock, long-time trade union official, secretary of the Trades' Hall

Council and, reputedly, the first Labor member elected to the Victorian Parliament. Hancock 'delighted' the crowd at the jubilee with 'an auto-biographical history of his grandfather, father and mother, saying that no doubt the movement had much to do with his radical opinions'.[124] The newspaper accounts also noted musical selections rendered by the Bootmakers' Band and the Labour Church Choir. The organiser of the Chartist Jubilee was a radical clergyman, Rev. Archibald Turnbull, and it was his Labour Church that had provided the choir.[125]

Finally, our gaze turns to Manitoba during the bitter winnipeg General strike. Not allowed to use Winnipeg's Industrial Bureau as a venue, the Labour Church moved its Sunday services to Victoria Park, close to the Town Hall. The striking workers came to listen to the radical preacher William Ivens and other strike leaders speak in the open air. In a poetically defiant moment, Ivens went so far as to reconceive the park as his church in a vivid description published in the *Western Labor News*. The trees fringing the park were the walls, the 'greensward' was the floor (where, he noted pointedly, there were no rented pews), the rough platform in the park's centre provided the pulpit and the metaphor was completed with the sky, 'illuminated by those "forget-me-nots" of the angels, the stars', providing the 'roof and dome'. 'Such is a dim outline of the scene to which over ten thousand men and women and children flocked last Sunday night,' he concluded.[126] It was here on the hot summer evenings of 1919 during the strike that workers came together to sing the words of what they knew as the *Labour Hymn*, with its moving opening lines:

> When wilt thou save the people, Lord; O god of mercy, when?;
> The people, Lord, the people; Not crowns and thrones, but men.[127]

The *Labour Hymn* was, of course, Elliott's anthem that had divided the Bradford Committee. How many Winnipeggers knew of its provenance is a question to which we will return.

The short-lived Labour (or Socialist) Church joined a multifarious body of alternative schismatic responses as a specifically working-class reaction to the Victorian crisis of faith. These four episodes from Britain, New Zealand, Australia and Canada span two decades and vast distances. Christchurch, located on the east coast of New Zealand's South Island, is over 18,000 kilometres from Bradford, 13,000 from Winnipeg and 2,500 from Melbourne. The dates above reveal that there was no simple move from the centre out to the periphery; the networks were contemporaneous and overlapping and the connections multidirectional. Despite the differences in time and place, these instances reveal a shared labour, radical and reform culture shaped in part by music and musical behaviour, with both transnational and trans-local dimensions. Music's flexibility allowed it to be constantly adapted to the demands of new environments. The Labour Church was short-lived with little long-lasting influence; the *LCHB* was undoubtedly its enduring contribution to socialism and the labour movement more broadly – its influence covered an even more vast geographical terrain and long outlasted the church itself.

The first Labour Church was the brainchild of John Trevor. It opened on 4 October 1891 in Manchester, but Trevor's road to that day had been long and deeply troubled. A childhood blighted by the experience of an oppressive Calvinist–Baptist splinter group and a sadistic schooling resulted in what he later called the 'continual tyranny of fear' that all but extinguished his faith. Extensive travels as a young man to Australia, New Zealand and the United States helped shape his conception of the Labour Church. His exposure to a 'new world' where he 'made the most of [his] opportunities for discovering new well-springs of life and thought' was mapped in large parts on the later reach of the Labour Church, but, as we shall see, this was no simple relationship between centre and periphery. It was in Sydney in 1877 that he immersed himself in some of the most advanced literature of the day. His memoir, *My Quest for God*, details a voracious appetite for the writings of Carlyle, Owen, Ruskin, Emerson and Whitman among others; he was even able to procure a copy of Charles Knowlton's controversial book *The Fruits of Philosophy* (published by Charles Bradlaugh and Annie Besant), which had been banned in Britain for obscenity.[128]

It was also during this time that Trevor's need for some kind of spiritual succour began to reassert itself. He joined Sydney's Freethought Society and attended lectures by touring spiritualists such as fellow Briton Charles Bright.[129] On reaching America he was introduced to Unitarianism.[130] In 1879 Trevor returned to London, taking up the role of assistant minister at Philip Wicksteed's Unitarian Chapel. Wicksteed hailed from Leeds, where his family had been deeply involved in Chartism – his uncle was known as the 'Achilles of the Complete Suffrage Unions' – and he later married the daughter of well-known Chartist Henry Solly.[131] A socialist link to the early Fabians, Wicksteed would later become one of the Labour Church's most popular speakers, as well as providing financial backing for Trevor's newspaper, the *Labour Prophet*. Through his connection to Wicksteed, Trevor attended the South Place Ethical Society, which greatly broadened his intellectual and political horizons. Here, he heard the likes of Kropotkin, Edward Carpenter, J. Bruce and Katharine Glasier, and Margaret McMillan (a self-professed Christian Socialist), among many others.[132] The seeds of the Labour Church were sown in this fertile ground of radicalism and ethical socialism.

[321]

Trevor left London to take up a post at Manchester's Free Church on Upper Brook Street, but he soon left. In the heart of the 'workshop of the world' he had come face to face with the working classes' deep sense of alienation and it fuelled his desire to create a practical humanitarian religion. Trevor's resolve to provide a 'democratic faith' strengthened and he was increasingly drawn to socialism. His Labour Church held its first service in October 1891 and for the next year he threw himself into the development and expansion of the movement. Although chronic ill health forced his retirement, the church flourished: in 1893 the Labour Church Union was founded and from there it became a national movement – effectively the religious arm of the ILP, which was established the same year. At its peak in 1895 there were fifty-four Labour Churches with Manchester, Bradford, Birmingham and Bolton seen as its strongest centres.[133]

The Labour Church was Trevor's attempt to provide the working classes with an alternative to secularism.[134] From the outset it was underpinned by a synthesis between radical politics and Christian morality.[135] The church was to provide a place for workers who felt the 'cravings of the human heart for God'.[136] The industrial North remained the Labour Church's epicentre, where it found favour with many devout socialists such as Hardie, Tillett and Tom Mann, who, like Trevor, saw in socialism a kind of practical Christianity.[137]

Much as we noted in relation to a plethora of radical and reform organisations, Labour Churches also became the locus of a way of life. Sociability was built around teas, socials, entertainments, picnics, concerts, pantomimes, theatre and weekly classes. For many socialists – in particular those influenced by William Morris – music was more than a utilitarian tool for propagandising and helping to foster a sense of solidarity, it was central to the creation of a new culture for a new age. Among its numerous programmes, the Labour Church established choirs, glee clubs, orchestras, brass bands and string bands. Many churches went on to establish music committees to organise and oversee these activities. Trevor had long remarked on the power and importance of music: it was, he declared, 'calculated to uplift all those who are capable of being moved by sweet sounds into quite a new world of beauty, romance, purity and power'. He confessed to experiencing 'a passionate sensitiveness to Music' from an early age. Trevor's inclinations were shared with many fellow socialists, including his friend Robert Blatchford. Founder of the Clarion Fellowship movement and author of the hugely influential *Merrie England*, Blatchford did not believe that there was 'any art so refining, so elevating, or so delightful as the art of music'.[138]

Trevor's church was based at the People's Concert Hall in Lower

Mosley Street, the centre of Manchester's entertainment industry. It was, as Joseph Clayton recalled, 'a dingy, draughty and not overly reputable hall'. The church services were often preceded by 'demonstration parades' led through the streets by a brass band and banners, two of the iconic symbols of working-class popular culture we have seen many times.[139] Like many of its middle-class counterparts, including the South Place Ethical Society and the Australian Church, the Labour Church was determinedly creedless. Trevor declared in an address of 1896: 'In the midst of English Socialism alone do I see any sign of Religion being able to stand securely alone, without Priest, without Parson, without Creed, without Tradition, without Bible'.[140] Despite the rejection of traditional religion, however, the formal pattern of the religious service persisted (much as they did for Watts and Symes). Thus, a Labour Church service followed a familiar template: a hymn, prayer (poem) and reading (guest lecture on a range of pertinent topics), musical selections, hymn and blessing.

Of course, neither the hymn nor the reading was religious, drawing instead upon leading progressive writers of the time including many of those Trevor had encountered in Sydney: Emerson, Ruskin, Whittier, Lowell, Arnold, Morris, Carpenter, Kingsley and Whitman. Various accounts show that the musical taste was eclectic, ranging from standard hymn tunes to socialist and radical songs, popular dance music and traditional songs set to works by Donizetti, Gounod and Handel.[141] An instrumental band and choir was involved in the inaugural service. Trevor's musical offerings included an overture played by the string orchestra, a solo song and a rousing rendition of Carpenter's *England Arise*. There is a surfeit of evidence to show how musical performance went on to be a vital part of the Church's culture.

Trevor's efforts to create 'a bond of sympathy' and 'congregational spirit' through musical participation were, according to many reminiscences, largely successful.[142] Many in the congregation clearly appreciated a lively and supportive culture within the walls of their Labour Church. Joseph Clayton fondly remembered the 'singing of Socialist songs and Labour hymns' as a great feature of the meetings specifically as it invoked older traditions; he likened it to 'an old custom of the Chartists'.[143] Wicksteed's account of an early service makes much of the musical contribution to what he described as 'the most genuine and spontaneous religious service in which I ever engaged'. 'As a matter of fact', he continued:

> the hymns, prayer, solo songs, pieces of music, lesson and address had all been arranged beforehand, but one felt at the time as if each one of them came just where and when it did in response of the present want of the eager souls that were drinking in every word and sound.[144]

[323]

Importantly, he commented in almost exactly the same terms as Higinbotham's comment from the bench in relation to Symes:

> The hymns were sung with the utmost heartiness, the solo singers and musicians were felt as a part of the congregation, not as performers.[145]

An important adjunct to the musical culture of the church was an appropriate hymnbook. This need intensified as new Labour Churches began to appear. A shared hymnbook promoted solidarity and a unified outlook. As with so many of these kinds of alternative hymnbooks, the preface functions in part as a manifesto that succinctly and powerfully outlined the fundamental precepts of the Church. Trevor's idealised notion of music did not blind him to the power of the hymn as an evangelical tool to spread his gospel. He gave a clear account of their instrumentality when outlining his plans to establish a Labour Church in Oxford: first he prepared a sheet of hymns for the 'agricultural labourers' to be sung at their outdoor meetings. These carefully chosen selections were to be taught to the workers with the 'invaluable' assistance of three local fife and drum bands. After these hymns were learnt, Trevor introduced the *LCHB*. This would allow the implementation of 'regular Labour Church services'. The success of this evangelical scheme rested upon the teaching and singing of carefully chosen hymns followed by the dissemination of the *LCHB*.[146]

The general tenor of the *LCHB* is one of 'personal and social regeneration' rather than overt political propaganda and, as a number of reminiscences tell us, a copy became a prized family possession.[147] The first hymnbook was published in 1892, the tune book separately in 1893; both were subjected to many revisions in subsequent years. A balance was sought between choosing music familiar to the congregation and providing 'really good music which can be heartily sung by large audiences'.[148] The 1906 edition was substantially expanded from the original 89 hymns to 178, and was the first to consolidate the words and printed music in both notational systems (tonic sol-fa and standard) into one volume. What is immediately apparent (as other scholars have noted) is that many of these so-called hymns are unconventional. In fact, very few were in fact generally considered hymns at all. Of the first edition's eighty-nine pieces, not even half (forty-two) use overtly religious language. The majority, rather than being religious or even discernibly political, are (to borrow Chris Waters's words) imbued with a 'vague utopian yearning'.[149] Among the contents are poems by Lowell, Whittier, Samuel Longfellow, Kingsley, Mackay and offerings from an earlier generation of radicals such as Thomas Cooper, John Macleay Peacock and, of course, Elliott, as well as the younger socialists: Edith Nesbit, Havelock Ellis, H. S. Salt and Edward

Carpenter. Significantly, there is transnational element: *Fatherhood of God and the Brotherhood of Man*, which appeared first in Carpenter's iconic *Chants of Labour* (1888), was taken from the *Otago Witness* in New Zealand.[150]

Despite the emphasis on moral uplift, there are songs that commemorate earlier radical moments such as the opening *Union Hymn*, which for early editions of the *LCHB* was, as we have seen, Flower's *The Gathering of the Unions*.[151] These editions directed would-be singers to Harriet Martineau's passionate account of the 1832 'monster meeting', or more particularly the rendition of the *Union Hymn*, for inspiration: 'It never was so sung before,' she wrote, 'a hundred thousand voices pealed it forth in music which has never died away in the hearts of those who heard it.'[152] Choosing this hymn to open the collection, Trevor left no one in any doubt of the political context in which it was originally published, but he too would have been unaware of its genteel origins.

The seventeenth Labour Church Union conference in 1909 was by no means the first time the contents of the hymnbook had come under close scrutiny; in fact, it was the rule to prove the exception.[153] Individual churches were encouraged to list possible amendments to the contents and these invariably reveal a deep divide between religion and secularism within the Labour Church (one that subsequent scholars have seen as crucial to its early demise).[154] This tension was present from the inception. For example, the *Labour Prophet*'s slogan, 'God is our King' was replaced by Mazzini's 'Let Labour be the basis of civil society'. In 1894 a vote to remove God completely from the Labour Church's Principles lost by the narrowest of margins: nine votes to eleven.[155] As we have seen, a similar division was present at South Place; here, however, ideological and spiritual differences were played out through the selection of appropriate hymns. The fight over *When Wilt Thou Save the People?* was a case in point, revealing that an individual hymn could become a capsule statement for a struggle over the identity of the Church at a national level and that the control of textual meaning and musical representations of this identity was critically important.

Some individual churches were clearly identifiable as being allied with one side or the other. For example, in 1908 the strongly secularist members of the Hyde Labour Church replaced the *LCHB* with their own *Socialist Hymn Book*. The Birmingham Labour Church similarly produced the *Birmingham Labour Church Hymn Book*, which, like its Hyde counterpart, emphasised socialism.[156] The Aberdeen branch was criticised by the faithful for only singing socialist hymns.[157] Conversely, there were churches that favoured the spiritual over the secular. Initially, the Ashton-under-Lyne Labour Church regularly sang hymns with clear Christian references. They even said the Lord's Prayer until the branch succumbed to the influence of the American secularist Robert Ingersoll. The Labour Church at Bolton stood at the other end of the spectrum to Hyde and Birmingham. Originally a Congregational Church, it held onto the strong link to established religion. According to David Summers, this was reflected in part in their 'hearty singing, and in their choice of hymns'. He notes that the Boltonians had been among strongly opposed to the removal of the hymns with a 'theological reference'.[158] The Bolton Labour Church was led by Rev. Bailey J. Harker, whose devout Christianity was blended with strong support for trade unions, including the leaders of the London Dock Strike such as Ben Tillett and Tom Mann. It was through Harker's invitation to Mann to speak to his congregation that Mann met Harker's daughter, Elsie, who married him and, as we have seen, played a crucial role in Tom's many peregrinations in pursuit of a better world.

It is not surprising then that the 1912 edition of the *LCHB* was published under the supervision of a specially appointed Hymn and Tune Book Committee based in Nottingham (a move reminiscent of the Chartists).[159] An examination of the repertoire included in this edition shows that only fifty-three of the original eighty-nine hymns survived; also worth noting is the inclusion of political songs, including many of William Morris's *Chants for Socialists*, four hymns by W. J. Linton,[160] Harriet Martineau's *All Men are Equal*, Jim Connelly's labour anthem *The Red Flag*, the *Marseillaise* and *O, Help the Prophet to be Bold* from the pen of the renowned anarchist Luisa Bevington. The committee received musical advice from the composer W. H. Bell, a professor at the Royal Academy of Music. This goes some way to account for the notable increase of art music, which ranged from the Renaissance composers, Orlando Gibbons and Michael Praetorius, to Bach, Beethoven, Mendelssohn and the contemporary composer and socialist Rutland Boughton. Indeed, in terms of music, it was not dissimilar to its more 'highbrow' counterparts in the ethical movement.

Despite the addition of overtly political songs and art music in the 1912 edition, there are attributes of the collection that maintain a strong connection to religion; indeed, the abundance of hymn tunes adds a sonic religiosity to the collection. Even when a particular tune was specified, the hymn metre was often also included at the top of the page, which allowed for the use of other metrically suitable hymn tunes. Furthermore, the simple four-part settings that necessarily dominate, whether known hymn tunes or not, intensify the religious sound. The musical texture and harmonic language evokes church music even if it is an arrangement of a traditional folk melody or an original composition: they sound like hymns. The South Place composer E. J. Troup's setting of Gustav Spiller's secular poem *Raise Your Standard* is a case in point.[161] The aural effect of the hymn tune emphasises the sense of the religious over the secular (and even the political). In certain instances the music subverts the secular nature of the words. Bevington may have been an atheist and anarchist, but when her poem exploring man's treatment of man is set to the standard hymn tune *York* it sounds like a hymn. The lyrical sentiment has been co-opted by religion. The same process happens to Martineau's *All Men are Equal* in its setting to *Dunfermline* from the Scottish Psalter. The examples go on.

What becomes clear is that an individual hymn, or the hymnbook taken as a whole, was a capsule statement of identity. If we return to the 1909 dispute among the delegates over inclusion of Elliott's *When Wilt Thou Save the People?*, we can see the importance of music – in this case as expressed in the pages of a hymnbook – in demotic politics. On the one hand, the dispute centred on the lyrics, and the terms of that argument reveal much about a significant fracture in views and values. On the other hand, we can see that the musical setting was crucial. Irrespective of text the hymn sounded religious. In this sense it was easy for secularists to waste their words. For fervently religious socialists, however, the music could achieve what otherwise could be endlessly debated: the sacralisation of socialism.[162]

'Brother Socialists of all nations'

Notwithstanding the fact the Labour Church had failed to make any significant progress in the south of England, Trevor's vision extended beyond national borders. He was determined that it should become an international movement: 'Brother Socialists of all nations,' he wrote, 'I appeal to you to organise yourselves for the emancipation and development of your religious life, as you have organised yourselves for the emancipation and development of your social and industrial life.'[163] To bring this about he put out repeated calls for missionaries and pioneers 'willing to help in the spread of the movement'.[164] At this time he already knew of the success of Herbert Casson, a Canadian journalist, socialist and lapsed Methodist minister, who had established Labour Churches in Massachusetts and Rhode Island. Trevor also knew of proposals to establish a Labour Church in Melbourne, and, indeed, subscriptions from 'Melbourne' and 'Australia' were recorded in the 'Pioneer' column of the *Labour Prophet* in 1892.[165]

Among the first of Trevor's transnational missionaries was a New

Zealander, Harry A. Atkinson. Like Trevor, the young Atkinson had been introduced to radical ideas in the southern hemisphere.[166] While training to become a mechanical engineer in Wellington he had been exposed to the writings of the Fabians, the Russian anarchists and the American transcendentalists. In 1890 he travelled to Britain, looking both for employment as an engineer and a role in the British labour movement. Atkinson met Trevor in Manchester and became the inaugural general secretary of the Labour Church. After returning to New Zealand in 1893 he established his own church in Christchurch, distinguishing it from Trevor's by adding the word 'Socialist' to its title. The surviving records show that the Socialist Church was officially connected to the British churches. Like Trevor, Atkinson saw socialism as a religious movement: 'The Socialist Church', he declared, 'has been formed of people of all classes in life, who realize the necessity for a Church preaching the Gospel of Socialism.'[167] Like the Labour Church, Atkinson's promoted a 'free' and 'practical everyday' religion; it sought to restore religion 'to its true meaning'.[168] Atkinson saw his church as a 'link in a great chain' of what he hoped would become a unified socialist front; from trade unions to the Fabians.

The Socialist Church became a small but dynamic radical association and its weekly pattern of activities reflected the broader transnational radical culture. There were evening meetings, Sunday meetings, lectures and outdoor speeches, entertainments, socials and fundraisers for the needy; delegates were sent to major labour events and a monthly leaflet was issued. Moreover, it kept its members informed of radical activities across the Anglophone world by disseminating key socialist publications from the Unites States and Britain, including the American publication *Appeal to Reason* as well as the *Labour Prophet*, Blatchford's *Clarion* and various Fabian publications.[169] The venues were also similar and included the Oddfellows Chambers, the Metaphysical Club and the WCTU Rooms.[170]

The contents of the *Monthly Leaflet* from 1897 clearly show the Labour Church culture.[171] Familiar names appear throughout: Ruskin, Morris, Blatchford, Carpenter, Massey and Whittier. The *LCHB* was drawn upon heavily for the songs that scatter the pages: Morris's *March of the Workers*, Mackay's *There's a Good Time Coming, Boys*, Kingsley's hymn *The Day of the Lord is at Hand*, Hosmer's *O Beautiful My Country*, Peacock's *Sons of Labour* and New Zealand's *Brotherhood of Man*, which had returned home with Atkinson. While the evidence does not point to the same public dimension of the musical activities as in northern England, such as the demonstration parades led by brass bands, it is clear that music-making was a regular part of the church's activities. As New Zealand's foremost

Labour historian, Herbert Roth, wryly pointed out, 'the only seem-ingly religious feature [of the Socialist Church] was the singing of Labour Hymns'.[172] Atkinson had in fact compiled the *Socialist Church Hymns*, comprising nineteen hymns drawn directly from the *LCHB* with the original numbering (see figure 7.1).[173] The first hymn in the collection was, unsurprisingly, *When Wilt Thou Save the People?*. The connections with the British labour movement were direct, personal and sustained. When Ben Tillett toured New Zealand in 1897 he stayed with the Atkinsons.[174] The Socialist Church was listed in a Labour Church directory of 1898, as well as featuring in correspondence with the Bradford Labour Church in 1904.[175]

There was also an Australian Labour Church, headed by the redoubtable Rev. Archibald Turnbull. While there was no direct personal relationship between the leaders of the Australian and British Labour Churches, as there was between Trevor and Atkinson, Turnbull's pivotal role in the 1898 commemoration of Chartism could nonetheless be understood as an instantiation of Trevor's desire to fuse political and religious activism. However, there was a prehis-tory of interest in Trevor's experiment among Australian radical circles in the years before the Jubilee. Only seven months after its inaugural service in Manchester (and before Atkinson had returned to New Zealand), Melbourne's *Commonweal and Workers' Advocate* published a lengthy and incisive report under the prosaic title 'Labor Church'. The newspaper was edited was George Prendergast, a social-ist, trade unionist and later premier of Victoria.[176] At the time of the publication of the article he was a member of the Free Church of England, a schismatic Anglican sect based in the Melbourne working-class suburb of Collingwood since the 1860s. Prendergast's article noted 'considerable attention' on a 'recent movement of the above nature in the mother country' and then unleashed a ferocious attack on the established church, vilifying the clergy as the 'hireling mouth-pieces of oppressors who had alienated the poor from the congrega-tions by their blind self-interest'. Again, there was an emphasis on the need for a creedless church that spoke a spiritual truth not available in the established churches; one that understood the needs of the working people. There was a clear understanding of the basic premises of Trevor's Labour Church seen in the strong support for a 'broadly independent labour church which would free those workers' who held 'religious convictions ... from the trammels of religious bigotry'. As in Manchester, this 'purified church', underpinned by a creedless reli-gious philosophy, would be governed by committee, and a hired hall would replace the cost of a church.

Prendergast went on to make suggestions for possible speakers to

THE SOCIALIST CHURCH.

HYMNS.

1. L.C.H., No. 2.   *Air*—COMMONWEALTH.

WHEN wilt Thou save Thy people?
 O God of mercy! when?
Not kings and lords, but nations!
 Not thrones and crowns, but men!
Flowers of Thy heart, O God, are they;
Let them not pass, like weeds, away—
Their heritage a sunless day!
 God save the People!

Shall crime bring crime for ever,
 Strength aiding still the strong?
Is it Thy will, O Father,
 That man shall toil for wrong?
"No," say Thy mountains; "No," Thy skies;
"Man's clouded sun shall brightly rise,
And songs ascend instead of sighs!"
 God save the People!

When wilt Thou save the People?
 O God of mercy, when?
The People, Lord, the People!
 Not thrones and crowns, but men!
God save the People! Thine they are,
Thy children, as Thy angels fair;
Save them from bondage and despair—
 God save the People!
 EBENEZER ELLIOTT.

2.   L.C.H., No. 3.

THE Day of the Lord is at hand, at hand!
 Its storms roll up the sky!
The nations sleep starving on heaps of gold;
 All dreamers toss and sigh;
The night is darkest before the morn;
When the clouds are heavy, then breaks the
 dawn;
 And the Day of the Lord is at hand!
 The Day of the Lord is at hand!

Gather you, gather you, angels of God—
 Freedom and Mercy and Truth!
Oh, come! for the earth is grown coward and
 old!
 Come down, and renew us her youth.
Wisdom, Self-sacrifice, Daring, and Love,
Haste to the battle-field, stoop from above,
 To the Day of the Lord at hand!
 The Day of the Lord at hand!

Gather you, gather you, hounds of Hell—
 Famine and Plague and War;
Idleness, Bigotry, Cant, and Misrule,
 Gather, and fall in the snare!
Hireling, Mammonite, Bigot, and Knave,
Crawl to the battle-field, sneak to your grave,
 In the Day of the Lord at hand!
 The Day of the Lord at hand!

Who'd sit down and sigh for a lost age of gold,
 While the Lord of all ages is here?
True hearts will leap up at the trumpet of God,
 And those who can suffer can dare.
Each old age of gold was an iron age too,
And the meekest of saints may find stern work
 to do,
 In the Day of the Lord at hand!
 The Day of the Lord at hand!
 CHARLES KINGSLEY.

3.   L.C.H., No. 5.

Now sound ye forth with trumpet tone,
 Let all the nations fear,
Speak to the world the thrilling words
 That tyrants quail to hear;
And write them bold on Freedom's flag,
 And wave it in the van—
They are THE FATHERHOOD OF GOD,
 THE BROTHERHOOD OF MAN.

Upon the sunny mountain brow,
 Among the busy throng,
Proclaim the day for which our hearts
 Have prayed and waited long;
The grandest words that men have heard
 Since ere the world began,
They are THE FATHERHOOD OF GOD,
 THE BROTHERHOOD OF MAN.

Too long the night of ignorance
 Has brooded o'er the mind;
Too long the love of wealth and power,
 And not the love of kind;
Now let the blessed truth be flashed
 To earth's remotest span,
Telling THE FATHERHOOD OF GOD,
 THE BROTHERHOOD OF MAN.

4.   L.C.H., No. 6.

MEN whose boast it is that ye
 Come of fathers brave and free,
If there breathe on earth a slave—
 Are ye truly free and brave?
If ye do not feel the chain
 When it works a brother's pain,
Are ye not base slaves indeed—
 Slaves unworthy to be freed?

Is true freedom but to break
 Fetters for our own dear sake,
And with leathern hearts forget
 That we owe mankind a debt?
No, true freedom is to share
 All the chains our brothers wear,
And with heart and hand to be
 Earnest to make others free.

They are slaves who fear to speak
 For the fallen and the weak;
They are slaves who will not choose
 Hatred, scoffing, and abuse,
Rather than in silence shrink
 From the truth they needs must think;
They are slaves who dare not be
 In the right with two or three.
 JAMES RUSSELL LOWELL.

5.   L.C.H., No. 7.

ENGLAND, arise! the long, long night is over,
 Faint in the East behold the dawn appear;
Out of your evil dream of toil and sorrow—
 Arise, O England, for the day is here;
 From your fields and hills,
 Hark! the answer swells—
 Arise, O England, for the day is here!

7.1 Specific references to the *Labour Church Hymn Book* appear at the head of each hymn. Front page of *The Socialist Church Hymns*.

spread the 'gospel of labour'. Among those names he put forward – men of 'advanced thought and high aims' who 'could be relied upon for sound and earnest speaking' – included Samuel Mauger and Charles Strong.[177] Unsurprisingly, an article on the Labour Church soon appeared in Strong's organ of the Australian Church, the *Australian Herald*.[178] Among offerings by Catherine Spence on the electoral system, Gerald Massey's poems, essays on Whitman, addresses by Mann on the moral and religious basis of the labour movement and Symes's contributions to the Australian Church Literary Society, was a report on recent interest in founding a Labour Church 'on the lines of that in Manchester carried on by Mr. Trevor'.[179] It was presented as one possible way to '[break] down ecclesiastical barriers' and to provide 'a platform for men of different religious types'. Strong suggested the working-class suburbs of Collingwood of Fitzroy as appropriate sites for the establishment of such a church. These were the two main places where the Australian Church ran their social welfare pro- grammes. Unlike his more radical counterparts, Strong never entirely repudiated the need for clergy or theology; nevertheless, he had long been interested in providing for a broad range of religious belief. In an article exploring the 'ethics of creed conformity' from the same year, he had even proposed the hymnbook as one 'truer' symbol of 'union and unity than all the creeds'.[180]

Hereafter, however, the interest of Prendergast and Strong in Trevor's venture appears to have come to an abrupt end. Subsequent references in the press to the Labour Church movement are sporadic and invariably brief. Over a period of two decades between 1892 and 1912, Brisbane's *Worker* included passing references to the Labour Church in Britain and New Zealand and gave the occasional tantalising hint of plans to form a Labour Church in Brisbane. Nevertheless, as the account of the Chartist jubilee celebrations – described at the begin- ning of this section – makes clear, there was a Labour Church active in Melbourne. This group of determined individuals was driven by the indefatigable enthusiasm of Archibald Turnbull. Turnbull is a fascinat- ing if little-known reformer.[181] Born in Adelaide, he moved as a child to Sydney where his father's shoemaking shop became a 'meeting-place for radicals and protectionists'. In Sydney he became an Anglican min- ister and subsequently worked for various Christian bodies, including in his native Adelaide, Melbourne slums and amongst the poor in Sydney's working-class suburb of Balmain. Later he moved to Hobart to take up a post at the Church of England People's Mission, where his combination of a political sermon with 'light musical items' was similar to Trevor's approach. His 'militant Christian Socialism' and political activism had long been problematic for the church elders and when he established the Labor and Liberal Political League, based on a radical platform, his licence to preach was revoked and he was expelled from the Anglican Church. This precipitated a move to Melbourne where he established his Labour Church in Carlton, another working-class suburb. From this base he developed close links to the Victorian Socialist League that endured until his death in 1901. Fittingly, Charles Strong presided over his funeral.

Although the newspaper accounts do not divulge the particulars of the selections sung by Turnbull's Labour Church choir, there is plenty of evidence that the *LCHB* had made it to Australian shores. Early in 1894 the *Ballarat Star* – edited until recently by a former Chartist – published a song from it; as did the *Prahran Chronicle*, a suburban newspaper in Melbourne and the *Bunyip*, a newspaper in a country town north of Adelaide.[182] Over the next couple of years it turns up in reports from Port Augusta (South Australia); Broken Hill (New South Wales), Adelaide, Sydney and Quorn (South Australia).[183] We have seen how many veteran agitators in Britain treasured their copy of the *LCHB*; many clearly took theirs with them when they migrated to Australia. Over a decade after Melbourne's Chartist Jubilee, radical Sydney newspaper, the *Watchman*, published a comprehensive review of the revised 1906 edition.[184] The writer offered many insightful observations on both the state of the British Labour Church and the contents of the hymnbook. He noted, for example, that the Labour Church was already considered to be 'out of touch' in Britain, further remarking upon an unfortunate consequence of the Church's gener-ous platform being that 'almost everything distinctive of a Church as commonly understood, has disappeared'. The high standard of verse was commended and individual authors singled out for praise, namely Whittier, Lowell and Morris. *Wilt Thou Save the People?* was counted among the highlights along with Kingsley's *The Day of the Lord is at Hand*, Shelley's *Men of England*, the *Marseillaise* and Martineau's *All Men are Equal*.

The thoughtful analysis of the *LCHB* included a detailed examina-tion of the idea of the hymn. The writer goes so far as to say that 'many compositions, not commonly classed as hymns, are to be found here'. It was understood that the 'chief requisites' of 'a colourless theology and a universal emotion' had shaped the hymnbook in important ways. He effectively invokes the ongoing division between the religious and the secular within the ranks of the movement: 'Theological hymns have no place in the Labour Hymn Book, and the tendency to fight shy of even theistic hymns is also marked.' The hymnbook as a whole was deemed impressively 'cosmopolitan' and showed 'the high level of education present in the Labour movement'. The author again revealed a clear knowledge of the movement in the identification of hymn-singing as one of the strongest aspects of Labour Church culture. '[I]n the Labour Church the hymn has undoubtedly caught on,' he announced, going on to note that apart from the political address, most of the service was dominated by hymn-singing. He continued: 'It is the aspiring and inspiring part of the service – its most worshipful feature. To hear for the first time a large Labour congregation, led by a trained choir, sing "The Red Flag", or, better still "England arise!" is to be thrilled with sympathy for the great heart of democracy, to be impressed with the conviction that this plaintive and determined cry of a burdened people must grow and grow until it becomes irresistible.'[185]

The brief efflorescence of the Labour Church movement in Canada is the most removed from its British precursor, both chronologically and by the fact that the Canadians failed to acknowledge their British forebears. William Ivens, the leader of the Winnipeg Labour Church, appears to have never alluded to the earlier Labour Church movement in print (in stark contrast to Herbert Casson, his predecessor and compatriot, who had crossed the Atlantic to witness the British Labour Church in action). This is all the more curious because many of the local labour, trade union and radical leaders, including Ivens himself, were British-born and it is generally understood that many of them had (to borrow the words of Arthur Lowers, writing in 1946) 'had their views formed in British left-wing Labour circles'.[186] Undoubtedly, many of them, like their Australian counterparts, had carried their copies of the *LCHB* with them on the journey to Canada. The absence of explicit references to the earlier British Labour Church is even more surprising given the statement of Canadian principles explicitly recognises their church's place in a 'larger world-wide movement'.[187] Despite this odd lacuna, it is possible to find strong connections between the Canadian example and its counterparts in the guiding principles, the repertoire of action and musical culture.

Ivens's Labour Church was galvanised by the 1919 Winnipeg General Strike, itself a key moment in Canadian political history.[188] Of the four case studies, this is most bound up with direct political action. Ivens became one of the major strike leaders and was ultimately arrested and imprisoned for this role. The effects of the strike on the Labour Church were not lost on contemporary commentators. The strike newspaper, the *Western Labor News* (of which Ivens was editor), commented that whereas the church had previously served as 'a sort of cave of Adullam in which revolters from the orthodox churches found refuge', it was transformed by the onset of the strike into a 'spontaneous movement of the people – an insistence upon a social code of ethics – a revolt against denominationalism and formality and commercialism in the

[333]

church – a hunger after righteousness and spiritual truth, a sense of fellowship in suffering and inspiration'.[189] The strike may have transformed the Labour Church; conversely, the Labour Church had given the strike 'the spirit of a religious revival'.[190]

Ivens was originally a gardener before studying theology. He began his religious service as a Methodist minister but, like Turnbull and Strong before him, had been expelled for his radical political views. According to one account, he was the 'best known man in Canada west of the Great Lakes'.[191] The Winnipeg Labour Church held its first service in the Labour Temple on 8 July 1918. Like its forerunners across the seas, it allowed for a broad range of religious beliefs and appropriated and adapted existing 'religious forms and ceremonies'.[192] Like the British Labour Church it also experienced tension between secular and religious elements within the broader congregation. This fissure only became acute once the unifying force of the strike had dissipated.

There were important local dimensions to the Canadian Labour Church movement, the foremost being its close connection to the Social Gospel movement that had gained considerable purchase across Canada.[193] Its supporters came from the Nonconformist churches, including Wesleyan Methodism, who put social issues and the plight of the labouring poor at the centre of their agenda.[194] For example, the Canadian Labour Church unashamedly founded itself on 'the teachings and spirit of Jesus of Nazareth' and, in a North American echo of Atkinson's Church in Otago, 'the Fatherhood of God and the Brotherhood of Man'.[195] According to David Summers's calculation, the brief flowering of the movement in Canada amounted to around sixteen churches.[196] Thus, the Canadian example is comparable to Britain in terms of scale. Moreover, like their earlier British counterparts, the Canadian Labour Churches provided a suite of weekly classes, societies, guilds and Sunday Schools, as well as choirs, bands and orchestras. In Winnipeg as in Manchester, 'excellent' bands both provided the 'appropriate' music that opened the Sunday services and played a key role in leading public demonstrations. Opened since 1900, Victoria Park functioned not only as Ivens's outdoor church – in May 1919 an estimated 7,000 attended a service – but also as the departure point for many of the strike's massive parades accompanied through the streets by music: 'a fine martial swing, whistling and singing the old familiar tunes '.[197]

Sympathetic commentators on the strike well understood the capacity of communal hymn-singing to represent and communicate the power of the movement. Hymn-singing was used as a symbol of solidarity in the newspaper accounts. According to the *Western Labor*

News, the hymn sung by a crowd of approximately 5,000 'expressed the deepest longings of the workers, and the volume of harmony that rose in those thousands of throats was a sound for the Gods to rejoice over'.[198] Towards the end of the strike, after many of the leaders were in jail and public meetings had been banned within the city limits, meetings were still held beyond the urban boundaries where again hymn-singing was used to demonstrate power and defiance. According to one commentator, the opening lines of the 1849 hymn *Faith of Our Fathers, Living Still*, dedicated to the Catholic martyrs that suffered at the hands of Henry VIII, were sung at one such meeting:

> Faith of our fathers! Living still,
> In spite of dungeon, fire and sword.

The hymn, he remembered, 'rang out with a new meaning to those who during the preceding fortnight had been behind the bars or shot at by the soldiery or otherwise deprived of the rights of free citizens'.[199]

Ivens, too, understood the power of the hymn, and was acknowledged as the movement's anthem writer as well as its leader. His hymns sought to capture the objectives and spirituality of the movement and to provide his followers with their own repertoire. Contributions such as his *Labour Anthem*, published at the end of 1919, were sung with enthusiasm.[200] As we can see, it reflected his Social Gospel beliefs and their celebration of the emancipation of the working classes resonated with much of the content of the *LCHB*:

> Hasten Thy Kingdom, Lord,
> When men of one accord
> Shall do the right;
> When profits curse no more,
> Strife, hate and war are o'er,
> Love's banner goes before,
> God bless our cause.[201]

But on that hot summer night in Victoria Park, where we first encountered Ivens and his massed comrades, it was another *Labour Hymn* that was ringing in the air. It is impossible to know how many of those thousands singing knew its provenance. They were actually singing what was arguably one of the most famous songs in the *LCHB*: Elliott's *When Wilt Thou Save the People?*. However, the fact that they knew it at all points to a shared radical and reform culture. While there is no ready acknowledgement of the British antecedent in the reports, there is other evidence of a shared repertoire present in Canadian radical print culture in the decades leading up to the strike. In 1903 the *Voice* (the previous iteration of the *Western Labor News* to which Ivens also contributed) ran a series of 'Labor Campaign Songs'. Amongst the offerings are many canonical socialist songs also found in the *LCHB*, notably Elliott's hymn, but also Lowell's *Freedom*, Shelley's *Song to the Men of England*, Carpenter's modified *Toilers Arise!*, H. S. Salt's *Hark the Battle Cry* and Joseph Whittaker's *Lift Up the People's Banner*.[202] This provides some context for what may have also been sung in Victoria Park and on the streets of Winnipeg in 1919. This repertoire persisted. The undated song sheet, *Hymns and Songs* of the Edmonton Labour Church, features much of this repertoire, including a hymn by Ivens, as does the *Songs and Hymns* of the Religion-Labour Forum of 1942. This songbook, which opens with a Labour Church Prayer by J. S. Woodsworth, includes among its musical offerings *When Wilt Thou Save the People?*.[203]

The Labour Church in Britain was relatively short-lived and the few that were still operational in 1914 had become almost completely secular. It was virtually defunct when the Winnipeg movement began, which itself did not survive long after the strike. Whereas the connection between Britain and New Zealand was direct and personal and the Australian socialists were aware of the British movement, the connections to Canada were attenuated although undeniable. Even if the actors were no longer conscious of the connections, the underlying principles and philosophies were the same. They were revealed in the ways that the culture was constructed and the political agendas implemented. The Labour Church's most enduring contribution to the international labour movement was the *LCHB*. It became, along with Edward Carpenter's *Chants of Labour* and the *Clarion Song Book*, one of the main sources for future radical, socialist and reformist song collections. Long after the demise of the Labour Churches in Britain, the *LCHB* provided content for countless other socialist and labour songbooks across the radical Anglophone world. In short: music and music-making in the Labour Church provided a connective tissue that crossed both time and distance.

The musical repertoires and practices that have been explored in early nineteenth-century radical working-class movements from Chartism and Owenism through to the secular and freethought associations and the Labour Church movement in later decades point to music's central role in both the creation of distinct internal cultures and identities as well as transnational and what were in many cases actually trans-local networks. The hymn in particular was reconceptualised by various segments of the radical working-class world and for many it operated as a political tool with which to resist oppression and work for change.

Moreover, hymns and hymnbooks of all persuasions provided capsule statements of core beliefs. They evangelised, exalted, denounced, unified, divided, reminded and constructed. They sounded out a belief system. Through a process of appropriation and adaptation in combination with the production of original works, a discrete radical hymnody was produced; one that offers a profoundly different picture of Victorian hymnody than has been commonly assumed. The hymn, which as Michael Sanders has noted, has been overlooked as a subject of scholarly investigation due to an assumption of its inherent conservatism, went on to take its part in the musical cultures of the later nineteenth-century movements of secularism and schismatic religious bodies such as the Labour Church, which themselves were inter-colonial and transnational.[204] The malleability of music and music-making allowed for adaption to new environments and new demands. But the contents of hymnodies and songbooks, as well as modes of their performance, allow us to see threads of connection, often overlapping, which might otherwise be missed. Even when the actors were seemingly no longer wholly conscious of these connections, we can hear them.

Notes

1 John Lowry, 'A Few Words on Singing', in Austin Holyoake and Charles Watts (eds), *Secularist's Manual of Songs and Ceremonies* (London: Austin, 1871), p. 8.
2 *Liberator* (4 October 1885).
3 See Mark A. Noll and Edith L. Blumhofer (eds), *Sing Them Over Again to Me: Hymns and Hymnbooks in America* (Alabama: University of Alabama Press, 2006).
4 David Nash, 'Reassessing the Crisis of Faith...', *Journal of Victorian Culture*, 16:1 (2011), p. 79.
5 *Northern Star* (13 July 1839).
6 *Northern Star* (2 March 1839).
7 See *Northern Star* (13 July 1839); *Northern Star* (2 March 1839); *Northern Star* (10 April 1841).
8 *Northern Star* (6 March 1841), quoted in Eileen Yeo, 'Robert Owen and Radical Culture', in Sidney Pollard and John Salt (eds), *Robert Owen, Prophet of the Poor: Essays in Honour of the Two Hundredth Anniversary of His Birth* (Lewisburg: Bucknell University Press, 1971), p. 104.
9 Yeo, 'Robert Owen', p. 107.
10 See Paul Pickering and Alex Tyrrell, 'In the Thickest of the Fight: The Reverend James Scholefield and the Bible Christians of Manchester and Salford', *Albion*, 26:3 (1994), pp. 461–82. See also Eileen Yeo, 'Christianity in Chartist Struggle 1839–1842', *Past and Present*, 91 (1981), pp. 109–39.
11 *Northern Star* (10 April 1841).
12 *Northern Star* (20 May 1843).
13 *Ibid.*
14 James Scholefield, *Select Hymns For The Use Of Bible Christians; By The Late Rev. W. Cowherd, With An Appendix By The Rev. Jas Scholefield, Christ Church, Every Street, Ancoats*, 7th edn (Manchester: Bradshaw and Blacklock, 1841).
15 See *Northern Star* (28 December 1844); *Northern Star* (1 March 1845); *Northern Star* (5 July 1845) and *Northern Star* (6 December 1845).
16 *Northern Star* (30 June 1849).
17 *Northern Star* (3 September 1842).

18 *Northern Star* (1 July 1843).
19 Thomas Cooper, *The Life of Thomas Cooper Written by Himself* (London, Hodder and Stoughton, 1897), p. 110.
20 *Ibid.*, p. 107.
21 *Ibid.*, pp. 110–11.
22 *Ibid.*
23 Ned Newitt, *The Anthology of Leicester Chartist Song, Poetry and Verses* (Leicester: Leicester Pioneer Press, 2006), p. 18.
24 *Ibid.*, pp. 9–10.
25 *Northern Star* (24 January 1846).
26 Cooper, *Thomas Cooper*, p. 165.
27 *Northern Star* (4 April 1846).
28 *National Chartist Hymn Book* (Rochdale: National Chartist Association, 1845). The place of hymns within the Chartist movement has gained increased notice in recent years, in particular with Michael Sanders' discovery and his subsequent scholarship in the area. See Michael Sanders, '"God is Our Guide! Our Cause is Just!": The National Chartist Hymn Book and Victorian Hymnody', *Victorian Studies*, 54:4 (2012), pp. 679–705.
29 Joseph Barker, *Democratic Hymns and Songs* (Wortley: J. Barker, 1849).
30 See Newitt, *Chartist Song, Poetry and Verses*, p. 45.
31 *Northern Star* (4 April 1846).
32 *Northern Star* (11 May 1844).
33 *Northern Star* (14 September 1844).
34 *Northern Star* (1 November 1845).
35 *Northern Star* (30 June 1849).
36 Yeo, 'Robert Owen', p. 104.
37 Thomas Cooper's 'We are Many, They are Few' in *Hymns for Chartist Camp Meetings III* appeared in the *English Chartists Circular*, 2:75 (1842). See Newitt, *Chartist Song, Poetry and Verses*, p. 11.
38 First published in *English Chartist Circular* (4 July 1842). See Newitt, *Chartist Song, Poetry and Verses*, p. 29.
39 Cooper, *Thomas Cooper*, p. 174.
40 Yeo, 'Christianity in Chartist Struggle', pp. 121–2.
41 *Northern Star* (18 May 1838). This hymn is also sometimes attributed to George Loveless, the 'Tolpuddle Martyr', who was transported to Australia in 1834 for trade union activities. He wrote down the third stanza for his friends and family prior to his departure, although he did not compose it.
42 *Northern Star* (24 July 1841); *Northern Star* (4 September 1841); *Northern Star* (4 December 1841).
43 Anne Janowitz, 'Ernest Jones: Who is he? What has he done?' *History Workshop Journal* 57 (2004), 283–8, at p. 284, quoting James Vernon.
44 For a discussion of Jones's appropriation of *The Battle of Hohenlinden*, see Kate Bowan and Paul Pickering, '"Songs for the Millions": Chartist Music and Popular Aural Tradition', *Labour History Review* (UK), 74:1 (2009), p. 58.
45 *Northern Star* (22 August 1846).
46 *Northern Star* (17 July 1847).
47 *Northern Star* (3 July 1847).
48 *People's Paper* (21 May 1853); *People's Paper* (4 June 1853).
49 *People's Paper* (16 September 1854).
50 *Ibid.*
51 These idiosyncratic episodes have received attention from Chartist historians, notably by Eileen Yeo. See Eileen Yeo, 'Christianity in Chartist Struggle', pp. 109–39.
52 *Northern Liberator* (31 August 1839). 'Mr Elliott' is Ebenezer Elliott.
53 *Northern Liberator* (7 September 1939).
54 *Northern Liberator* (14 September 1839).
55 *Leeds Mercury* (17 August 1839).

56   'Chartist Disturbances', *The Times* (19 November 1841).
57   'Disgraceful Conduct of Chartists', *Norfolk Chronicle and Norwich Gazette* (20 November 1841).
58   'Chartist Disturbances', *The Times* (19 November 1841).
59   *Ipswich Journal* (20 November 1841).
60   Newitt, *Chartist Song, Poetry and Verses*, p. 28, first published in *English Chartist Circular* (8 August, 1842).
61   *The Sheffield Independent* (29 September 1838).
62   *Northern Star* (17 November 1838).
63   *Northern Star* (2 June 1840).
64   *Northern Star* (9 July 1842); *Northern Star* (16 July 1842).
65   *People's Paper* (30 August 1856).
66   See *Northern Star* (27 March 1841).
67   *People's Paper* (2 April 1853). Another manifestation of working-class temperance was the Band of Hope movement founded in Leeds in the late 1840s, which was aimed specifically at educating children. Bands of Hope sprang up across the Anglophone world. Again, singing was central to their educational programmes and songbooks were produced to promulgate their aims. Editions of *Hymns and Songs for Bands of Hope* appeared in Britain as early as 1855, and many variants continued to be published into the early years of the twentieth century. See Christopher Newman Hall (ed.), *Hymns and Songs for Bands of Hope* (London: William Tweedie, 1855). They appeared across the Anglophone world; see, for example, *The Victorian Band of Hope Union Hymn Book* (Melbourne: Edwin Wilson, 1860) and David C. Cook, T. Martin Towne (eds), *Band of Hope Songs* (Chicago: David C. Cook, 1881).
68   'The New Bible – The Insurance Man', *Secular Thought* (1909), p. 379.
69   Yeo, 'Robert Owen', p. 96.
70   *Northern Star* (3 March 1838).
71   *New Moral World* (30 July 1836), quoted in Yeo, 'Christianity in Chartist Struggle', p. 98.
72   *Ibid.*
73   *National Reformer* (14 September 1861).
74   *National Reformer* (28 September, 1861).
75   *National Reformer* (9 November 1861); *National Reformer* (16 November 1861).
76   *Freethought*, 1:6 (1878), p. 88.
77   See Holyoake and Watts (eds), *Secularist's Manual*.
78   See Charles G. Zug, 'Scott's "Jock of Hazeldean": The Re-Creation of a Traditional Ballad', *The Journal of American Folklore*, 86:340 (1973), pp. 152–60.
79   Holyoake and Watts (eds), *Secularist's Manual*, p. 59.
80   'Mr. John Bedford Leno', *Commonwealth* (6 October 1866).
81   Holyoake and Watts (eds), *Secularist's Manual*, p. 4.
82   This is Lowry's variant of Scottish writer and politician Andrew Fletcher of Saltoun's famous words: 'if a man were permitted to make all the ballads he need not care who should make the laws of a nation', taken from 'An ACCOUNT of A CONVERSATION concerning A RIGHT REGULATION of GOVERNMENTS For the common Good of Mankind: In A LETTER to the Marquiss of Montrose, the Earls of Rothes, Roxburg and Haddington, From London the first of December, 1703' (Edinburgh: n.p., 1704).
83   Lowry's appropriation was not an isolated occurrence. Royle cites a later instance where T. E. Green produced a 'penny Secular-Hymn-book' in 1898. See Royle, *Infidel Tradition*, p. 87.
84   Holyoake and Watts (eds), *Secularist's Manual*, p. 7.
85   *Ibid.* p. 8.
86   Harry Hastings, a historian of New Zealand freethought, has noted that 'travelling lecturers' including Charles Bright, Gerald Massey and Moncure Conway 'invaded' New Zealand and 'found it a fruitful field'. See National Library of Australia, Papers of Harry Hastings Pearce (1897–1984), MS 2765, Series 12, Box 63, MS

2765/12/24, Handwritten history of rationalism in New Zealand, 'Unbelief in N.Z.' [typewritten manuscript].

87 *Echo* (12 November 1880).

88 *Echo* (4 March 1882); *Echo* (30 December 1882), *Echo* (12 November 1881). Reports of meetings in Melbourne and Adelaide appear throughout. See, for example, a report from Adelaide on 8 April 1882 and Sydney on 18 July 1882. For York see *Liberator* (2 August 1885).

89 See *Echo* (20 August 1881); *Echo* (24 July 1880); *Echo* (10 April 1880).

90 *Echo* (23 July 1881); *Echo* (20 January 1883).

91 *Echo* (18 June 1881).

92 *Echo* (2 October 1880). It was actually composed by Wenzel Müller.

93 *Echo* (24 July 1880).

94 See *Echo* (4 September 1880).

95 *Echo* (21 October 1881). Although *God Defend New Zealand* was generally considered New Zealand's unofficial anthem alongside *God Save the Queen* for many years, it was not officially recognised as such until 1976, a century after its composition.

96 For Symes and an account of secularism in Melbourne more generally see F. B. Smith, 'Joseph Symes and the Australasian Secular Association', *Labour History*, 5 (1963), pp. 26–47.

97 *Liberator* (30 August 1885).

98 *Liberator* (31 May 1885). Orchestral and choral selections were a common feature of these Sydney meetings. See *Liberator* (14 June 1885); *Liberator* (2 August 1885); *Liberator* (13 September 1885).

99 *Liberator* (13 September 1885).

100 *Liberator* (28 June 1885); *Liberator* (25 October 1885); *Liberator* (8 November 1885).

101 *Liberator* (28 June 1885).

102 See *Era* (25 August 1867); *Lloyd's London Weekly* (19 January 1868); *Westminster Review* (July 1876), quoted in the *Liberator* (20 September 1885).

103 See Iain McCalman, *Radical Underworld* (Cambridge: Cambridge University Press, 1988); Christina Parolin, *Radical Spaces: Venues of Popular Politics in London, 1790-c.1845* (Canberra, ACT: ANU E Press, 2010).

104 *Argus* (14 September 1885).

105 *Liberator* (13 September 1885).

106 *Liberator* (2 August 1885).

107 *Ibid*.

108 *Liberator*, (27 September 1885).

109 *Argus* (14 September 1885); *Argus* (21 September 1885).

110 See Gwyneth Dow, 'Higinbotham, George (1826–1892)', *Australian Dictionary of Biography*, National Centre of Biography, Australian National University, available at http://adb.anu.edu.au/biography/higinbotham-george-3766/text5939 (accessed 23 September 2016).

111 See *Argus* (23 October 1885); *Argus* (24 October 1885); *Argus* (26 October 1885).

112 *Argus* (23 October 1885).

113 *Argus* (27 October 1885).

114 New Zealand Electronic Text Collection, Pamphlet Collection of Sir Robert Stout, Vol. 59, available at http://nzetc.victoria.ac.nz/tm/scholarly/name-209352.html (accessed 23 September 2016).

115 New Zealand Electronic Text Collection, Pamphlet Collection of Sir Robert Stout, vol. 59, Cutting, available at http://nzetc.victoria.ac.nz/tm/scholarly/name-209352.html (accessed 23 September 2016).

116 *Daily Telegraph* (26 October 1885). For reversal rituals see John Brewer, 'Theatre and Counter-Theatre in Georgian Politics: The Mock Elections at Garrat', *History Today*, 33:2 (1983), pp. 14–23; E. P. Thompson, 'Patrician Society, Plebeian Culture', *Journal of Social History*, 7:4 (1974), pp. 382–405.

117 *Evening Star* (11 December 1885).

118 See Smith, 'Joseph Symes', pp. 38–44.
119 See *Liberator* (5 July 1885).
120 See Sandra Bloodworth, 'Militant Spirits: The Rebel Women of Broken Hill', available at www.anu.edu.au/polsci/marx/interventions/rebelwomen/militant.htm (accessed 23 September 2016).
121 *Labour Church Hymn Book* (London: Office of the 'Labour Prophet', 1892).
122 See David Fowler Summers, 'The Labour Church and Allied Movements of the Late Nineteenth and Early Twentieth Century', vol. 2 (PhD dissertation, University of Edinburgh, 1958), pp. 491–2.
123 Alexander Turnbull Library, Wellington, NZ, Herbert Otto Roth Papers, MS-Group-0314 (hereafter Roth Papers), Socialist Church Records, 94–106–14/14, Louisa Blake to Mr Atkinson, 11 April 1901.
124 *Worker* (23 July 1898); *Argus* (23 November 1899); *Argus* (10 February 1890); Geoffrey Serle, 'Maloney, William Robert (1854–1940)', *Australian Dictionary of Biography*, National Centre of Biography, Australian National University, available at http://adb.anu.edu.au/biography/maloney-william-robert-nuttall-7470/text13015 (accessed 23 September 2016).
125 *Argus* (12 July 1898); *Worker* (23 July 1898).
126 *Western Labor News* (10 June 1919).
127 Anna Penner, 'Politics in the Park: Winnipeg's Victoria Park during the General Strike', *Manitoba History*, 40 (2000–2001) available at www.mhs.mb.ca/docs/mb_history/40/parkpolitics.shtml (accessed 23 September 2016).
128 John Trevor, *My Quest for God* (London: Office of the 'Labour Prophet', 1897), pp. 78, 91–2.
129 *Ibid.*, pp. 91–2.
130 *Ibid.*, p. 129.
131 For Philip Wicksteed, see Ian Steedman, 'Wicksteed, Philip Henry (1844–1927)', *Oxford Dictionary of National Biography* (Oxford University Press, 2004) available at www.oxforddnb.com/view/article/38802 (accessed 24 September 2016); For Henry Solly, see Owen Ashton and Paul A. Pickering, *Friends of the People: Uneasy Radical in the Age of the Chartists* (London: Merlin, 2002), chap. 2.
132 Trevor, *My Quest for God*, p. 195.
133 See Summers, 'Labour Church and Allied Movements', vol. 2, p. 311. Henry Pelling and Kenneth Inglis give the number at around thirty. See Henry Pelling, *The Origins of the Labour Party 1880–1900* (London; New York: St Martin's Press, 1954), p. 144; Kenneth Inglis, *Churches and the Working Classes in Victorian England* (London: Routledge and Kegan Paul, 1963), p. 216.
134 This endeavour took its place among many other similar initiatives advanced particularly by key Christian Socialists such as Stewart Headlam. See, for example, Stewart D. Headlam, *The Socialist's Church* (London: George Allen, 1907).
135 Trevor, *My Quest for God*, p. 219.
136 *Labour Prophet* (October 1893), p. 100, quoted in Inglis, *Churches and the Working Classes*, p. 240.
137 Ben Tillett, *Memories and Reflections* (London: J. Long, 1931), pp. 188–9.
138 Quoted in Chris Waters, *British Socialists and the Politics of Popular Culture 1884–1914* (Stanford: Stanford University Press, 1990), p. 101.
139 *Labour Prophet* (February 1892), p. 100; Joseph Clayton, *The Rise and Decline of Socialism in Great Britain 1884–1924* (London: Faber & Gwyer, 1926), p. 95; a reprint of a leaflet advertising the first anniversary called 'Labour Church Demonstration' is included in Pelling, *Origins of the Labour Party*, p. 142.
140 Roth Papers, Labour Church Papers, 94–106–15/21, John Trevor, 'The Labour Church in England', p. 52. See also Mark Bevir, 'The Labour Church Movement, 1891–1902', *Journal of British Studies*, 38:2 (April 1999), pp. 217–45 (especially pp. 221–4).
141 From *Labour Prophet* (June 1893), p. 609, quoted in Summers, 'Labour Church and Allied Movements', vol. 1, p. 97.

142   Summers, 'Labour Church and Allied Movements', p. ii; Inglis, *Churches and the Working Classes*, p. 237.

143   Clayton, *Rise and Decline of Socialism*, p. 95; Summers, 'Labour Church and Allied Movements', p. ii. Kirsten Harris recently singled out the singing of 'social-ist hymns' as an example of the Labour Church's appropriation of the 'institu-tional structure of Christianity'. See 'The "Labour Prophet"? Representation of Walt Whitman in the British Nineteenth-Century Socialist Press', *Walt Whitman Quarterly Review*, 30 (2013), pp. 115–37.

144   *Labour Prophet* (February 1892), p. 10.

145   *Ibid.*

146   Roth Papers, Labour Church papers, 94–106–15/21, John Trevor, 'The Labour Church. Manchester and Salford', 8 November 1892, p. 3.

147   Trevor, Preface, *Labour Church Hymn Book*; Summers, 'Labour Church and Allied Movements', vol. 2, Appendix: Correspondence concerning Labour Churches, p. 699.

148   John Trevor and Eliza Trevor (eds), *Labour Church Tune Book* (n.p.: Labour Church Institute, 1893).

149   See Waters, *British Socialists*, p. 114. Carpenter was not trying to produce a hymn-book and thus they only share nine songs.

150   See 'The Fatherhood of God, and Brotherhood of Man', Edward Carpenter (ed.), *Chants of Labour: A Song Book of the People with Music* (London: Swann Sonnenschein, 1888), p. 74.

151   See, for example, '1. – Union Hymn', *Labour Church Hymn and Tune Book*, 2nd edn (London: Office of the 'Labour Prophet', n.d.). By the expanded 1912 edition, Flowers's words remained – still unattributed – but her music had been replaced by a setting by W. H. Bell. See *Labour Church Hymn and Tune Book* (Nottingham: Labour Church Hymn and Tune Book Committee, 1912).

152   Harriet Martineau, *The History of England during the Peace 1816–1846*, 2 vols (London: Charles Knight, 1849), p. 58. It is important to remember that Martineau was closely involved with Flower during the time she wrote this hymn. Kathryn Gleadle suggests that Martineau in fact wrote the words. See Kathryn Gleadle, 'Flower, Eliza (1803–1846)', *Oxford Dictionary of National Biography* (Oxford: Oxford University Press, 2004), available at www.oxforddnb.com/view/article/9762 (accessed 24 September 2016).

153   For example, the Tenth, Twelfth, Thirteenth and Sixteenth Labour Church Union Conferences had seen resolutions passed for the hymnbook to be revised and expanded. See Summers, 'Labour Church and Allied Movements', vol. 2, pp. 487, 489–90.

154   See, for example, Pelling, *Origins of the Labour Party*, p. 147–50; Inglis, *Churches and the Working Classes*, pp. 240–2.

155   The losing faction preferred the words 'moral and ethical'. See Inglis, *Churches and the Working Classes*, p. 239.

156   See Summers, 'Labour Church and Allied Movements', vol. 2, p. 333.

157   *Ibid.*, p. 325.

158   *Ibid.*, p. 346.

159   *Labour Church Hymn and Tune Book.*

160   Linton drew upon the hymn tradition in his 'Spartacus' songs, which were serially printed under the title *Hymns for the Unenfranchised*. See Janowitz, *Lyric and Labour*, p. 205.

161   The American secularist Gustav Spiller was an important figure in the develop-ment of the ethical societies.

162   The *LCHB* was surely the longest lasting legacy of the Labour Church. The ILP made this debt explicit in its *Labour's Song Book* (1924), including the subtitle: *With Additional Pieces from the Labour Church Hymn Book and Other Sources*. Many subsequent socialist songbooks across the Anglophone world also borrowed heavily from it.

163   Roth Papers, Labour Church Papers, 94–106–15/21, Trevor, 'Labour Church in England', pp. 62–3.

164   Roth Papers, Labour Church Papers, 94–106–15/21, Trevor, 'Labour Church. Manchester and Salford', October 1892, p. 4. For other instances see, *Labour Prophet* (June 1898), p. 48, quoted in Inglis, *Churches and the Working Classes*, p. 246; Roth Papers, Labour Church Papers, 94–106–15/21, Trevor, 'Labour Church', 8 November 1892, p. 2.

165   *Labour Prophet* (May 1892); *Labour Prophet* (September 1892); *Labour Prophet* (January 1898); Roth Papers, Labour Church Papers, 94–106–15/21, Trevor, 'Labour Church in England', p. 56; *Labour Annual 1895* (Manchester: Labour Society Press, 1895), p. 166. There was also notice of a church being established in the Netherlands. For an account of Herbert Casson's visit to English Labour Churches in 1897 see Inglis, *Churches and the Working Classes*, p. 236.

166   For a detailed account of Atkinson and the Socialist Church see James Taylor, 'Harry Atkinson and the Socialist Church, 1896–1906' in Melanie Nolan (ed.), *Labour History and Its People* (Canberra, ACT: Twelfth Australian Society for the Study of Labour History Canberra Region Branch, 2011), pp. 271–81.

167   Roth Papers, Socialist Church Records, 94–106–14/14, *Socialist Church Monthly Leaflet* no. 1, February 1897; *Labour Annual*, 1895, p. 166.

168   Roth Papers, Socialist Church Records, 94–106–14/14, *Socialist Monthly Leaflet* no. 4, May 1897.

169   See Roth Papers, Socialist Church Minute Book, 94–106–07/02 and Socialist Church Minute Book, 94–106–07/03.

170   This is not surprising. Not only was Blake involved in both organisations, but so was Atkinson's wife, Rose. Both women with their interest in the labour movement and feminism typify the forward thinking, politically progressive New Zealand woman.

171   Roth Papers, Socialist Church Records, 94–106–14/14, Socialist Monthly Leaflets nos 1–5, February-June, 1897; Hocken Library, University of Otago, NZ, Stewart, William Downie: Personal, Political and Family Papers, MS-0985–031/084.

172   Herbert Roth, 'The Labour Churches of New Zealand', *International Review of Social History*, 3 (1959), p. 363.

173   Roth Papers, Socialist Church Records (1897–1903), 94–106–14/14, *Socialist Church Hymns*.

174   Tillett's visit is mentioned in the *Monthly Leaflet* as well as in his memoir. See Tillett, *Memories*, p. 199.

175   Summers, 'Labour Church and Allied Movements', vol. 2, p. 385. Taylor has noted both the transnational and trans-local dimensions of the Socialist Church, observing that they 'thought globally, but acted locally'. See Taylor, 'Harry Atkinson', p. 281.

176   See Geoffrey Serle, 'Prendergast, George Michael (1854–1937)', *Australian Dictionary of Biography*, National Centre of Biography, Australian National University, available at http://adb.anu.edu.au/biography/prendergast-george-michael-8103/text14145 (accessed 23 September 2016).

177   'A Labor Church', *Commonweal and Workers' Advocate* (7 May 1892).

178   'Labour Church', *Australian Herald* (June 1892), p. 191.

179   For Spence see *Australian Herald* (July 1892), pp. 200–1; for Massey see *Australian Herald* (May 1892), p. 171; for the essay series on Whitman see *Australian Herald* (May 1892), pp. 172–4; *Australian Herald* (June 1892), pp. 186–9; *Australian Herald* (August 1892), pp. 220–2; for Mann see *Australian Herald* (September 1892), pp. 234–5; for Symes see *Australian Herald* (October 1892), p. 245.

180   Charles Strong, 'The Ethics of Creed Conformity', *Australian Herald* (October 1892), p. 242.

181   For an account of Turnbull's life, see Diane Langmore, 'Turnbull, Archibald (1843–1901)', *Australian Dictionary of Biography*, National Centre of Biography, Australian National University, available at http://adb.anu.edu.au/biography/turnbull-archibald-8880/text15595 (accessed 23 September 2016).

182   *Ballarat Star* (7 April 1894); *Prarhan Chronicle* (7 July 1894); *Bunyip* (29 June 1894).

183   *Quorn Mercury* (6 August 1897); *Port Augusta Dispatch* (30 July 1897); *Weekly Herald* (6 August 1897); *Worker* (9 February 1895).

184   'The British Labour Movement. The Labour Church. A Democratic Hymn Book', *Watchman* (25 March 1909).

185   *Watchman* (25 March 1909).

186   Arthur Lowers, *Colony to Nation: A History of Canada* (Toronto: Longmans, Green & Co., 1946), p. 499, quoted in Joanne Carlson Brown, 'The Form without the Power? Wesleyan Influences and the Winnipeg Labour Church', *Canadian Society of Church Music* (1994), p. 71.

187   J. S. Woodsworth, *The First Story of the Labour Church and Some Things for Which It Stands. An Address in the Strand Theatre, Winnipeg, 5 April 1920* (Winnipeg: Labour Church Office, 1920), p. 16.

188   The Winnipeg General Strike of 1919 is still considered one of the pivotal moments in early twentieth-century Canadian labour history.

189   *Western Labor News* (11 July 1919).

190   Woodsworth, *Labour Church*, p. 8.

191   *Red Bluff Daily News* (9 December 1920).

192   'Labor Day at Brandon', *Western Labor News* (5 September 1919).

193   For accounts of the Canadian Social Gospel movement see Tom Mitchell, 'From the Social Gospel to "The Plain Bread of Leninism": A. E. Smith's Journey to the Left in the Epoch of Reaction after World War I', *Labour/Le Travail*, 33 (1994), pp. 125–51; Oscar-Carne Arnal, 'The Prairie Labour Churches: The Methodist Input', *Studies in Religion/Sciences Religieuses*, 34:1 (2005), pp. 3–26.

194   Woodsworth, *Labour Church*.

195   *Ibid.*, p. 12. In 1892 the American William Rauschenberg founded the Brotherhood of the Kingdom based on Social Gospel thought. The Golden Rule Movement that grew out of this was also based on the edict of the Fatherhood of God and the Brotherhood of Man.

196   Summers, 'Labour Church and Allied Movements', vol. 2, p. 311.

197   *Western Labor News* (5 June 1919); Anna Penner, 'Politics in the Park: Winnipeg's Victoria Park during the General Strike', *Manitoba History*, 40 (2000–1), available at http://www.mhs.mb.ca/docs/mb_history/40/parkpolitics.shtml (accessed 23 September 2016).

198   *Western Labor News* (20 May 1919).

199   Woodsworth, *Labour Church*, p. 9.

200   Carlson Brown, 'Form Without the Power?', p. 75. See also Oscar L. Cole-Arnal, '"Street Preaching" in Strike Mode – Winnipeg 1919', *TST Homiletics Seminar*, 1:2 (2007), p. 4.

201   William Ivens, *Western Labor News* (12 December 1919), quoted in Carlson Brown, 'Form Without the Power?', p. 75.

202   See 'Labour Campaign Songs' in the following issues of the *Voice*. For Carpenter, see *Voice* (13 March 1903); for Elliott see *Voice* (3 April 1903); for Lowell see *Voice* (10 April 1903); for Shelley see *Voice* (8 May 1903); for Salt see *Voice* (29 May 1903); for Whittaker see *Voice* (12 June 1903).

203   University of Toronto, Thomas Fisher Rare Book Library Robert S. Kenny Collections, MSS 179 (hereafter Kenny Collections), Box 62A, Folder 1, Songs Sheets, *Hymns and Songs of the Labour Church* (Edmonton: n.p., n.d.); Kenny Collections, Kenny can pam 0374, *The Religion-Labour Forum. Songs and Hymns* (Toronto: n.p., 1942).

204   Sanders, 'National Chartist Hymn Book', p. 680.

CONCLUSION

'And they sang a new song'[1]

The people's flag is deepest red,
It shrouded oft our martyred dead;
And ere their limbs grew stiff or cold,
Their hearts' blood dyed its ev'ry fold.

Then raise the scarlet standard high!
Within its shade we'll live and die.
Though cowards flinch and traitors sneer,
We'll keep The Red Flag flying here.

Words: Jim Connell (1889). Tune: *The White Cockade* (traditional).[2]

On Sunday, 20 May 1906, the members of the Victorian Socialist Party
gathered for their weekly 'Propagandist Meeting' in the Bijou Theatre.
The Bijou was a commodious building located at 225 Bourke Street,
a bustling thoroughfare in the heart of 'marvellous Melbourne' in
Victoria.[3] By the time the socialists had taken up their residency in
April of that year the theatre had been open for thirty years.[4] It had a
capacity of 1,500 to 2,000 and the socialists attracted bumper crowds
for Sunday evening events featuring a potent admixture of ideology and
entertainment familiar to any student of oppositional politics during
the long nineteenth century. We have encountered the same many
times during the preceding pages.

Fortunately, a photograph of the meeting on that evening in May
appeared on the front page of the party's newspaper, *The Socialist*, published on 2 June (see figure 8.1).[5] The photographer's vantage point was
the stage and the panorama through the camera aperture shows extensive stalls and two steep circular balconies.[6] Thanks to a comment in an
earlier edition of the newspaper we know exactly what the assembled
crowd was doing at the moment the photograph was taken: singing the
international anthem of the socialist and labour movements, *The Red
Flag*.[7] Jim Connell, an Irish-born socialist, political activist and trade

[345]

"WORKERS OF THE WORLD UNITE."

The Socialist

An Exponent of International Socialism

[Registered at the General Post Office, Melbourne, for Transmission by Post as a Newspaper.]

No. 5. Vol. I.   MELBOURNE, JUNE 2, 1906.   [ONE PENNY.

THE SOCIALIST PARTY OF VICTORIA
—HOLD—
A Propaganist Meeting Every Sunday Night
—IN THE—
BIJOU THEATRE, MELBOURNE.

THIS PICTURE SHOWS THE AUDIENCE AT THE MEETING ON MAY 20
TOM MANN, Lecturer.   A. P. JONES, Chairman.

8.1 Members and supporters of the Victorian Socialist Party gather at Bijou Theatre in Melbourne. A comment in an earlier edition of the party's newspaper indicates that the photograph would show the assembly singing *The Red Flag*. *The Socialist* (2 June 1906), p. 1. NLA MS3939 Series 11.

unionist, had written the song lyrics during the London Dock Strike in 1889, but, as we have argued elsewhere, it was an act of many commemorations, referencing the Paris Commune, the Russian Nihilists, the Irish Land Leaguers and the Chicago anarchists.[8] The tune Connell chose was a powerful historical gesture: the well-known traditional song named for the emblem of the Jacobites, *The White Cockade*. 'There is only one air which suits the words of "The Red Flag,"' he declared, 'and that is the one which I hummed as I wrote it. I mean "The White Cockade".' Much to his chagrin, by the mid-1890s *The White Cockade* had been substituted with the tune of an American Civil War song, *Maryland, my Maryland*, which was itself a contrafactum of a traditional German Roman Catholic hymn, *Tannenbaum*. 'I never intended "The Red Flag" should be sung to church music to remind people of their sins!' Connell fumed, his pen dripping with sarcasm.[9] George Bernard Shaw agreed with Connell's assessment on aesthetic grounds, insisting that the anthem had become 'the funeral march of a fried eel'.[10] The Scotsman Keir Hardie made a concerted effort to remain faithful to Connell's wishes and preserve the direct link to the Jacobites, taking the trouble while touring South Africa, for example, to give some Cape Town socialists 'a few lessons' on how to sing it to *The White Cockade*.[11] Tom Mann, at the time of the meeting the leading light of the Victorian Socialist Party, was fully aware of the dispute and, notwithstanding the fact that he later celebrated the song's 'magnificent popularity', it is notable the Melbourne *Socialist Songbook* issued in 1907 listed *The White Cockade* as the tune.[12]

The direct and deliberate link with the past Connell intended by his musical choice was not uncommon. *The Kellys are Coming*, which rang out in the mountains of central Victoria in the 1880s, had been *The Chartists are Coming*, echoing through the streets of Leeds in the 1840s. In the preceding pages we have peeled back layers even when the transmission of meaning and significance was encoded, as was the case with *Sing a Song of Sixpence*. We have highlighted the considered choice of repertoire to link past and present through sound and to press it into political purpose with its original meaning intact. Listen again to Edith Brand singing *The Wearing of the Green*. At the same time, our study shows that there was often little sense of discernment when it came to musical style or genre. *The White Cockade* was ditched on the grounds that *Tannenbaum* was easier to sing. Its prehistory mattered less than its utility. We have seen throughout this study a generous eclecticism. All kinds of music was performed and heard in an equally diverse range of settings: traditional airs from England, Ireland, Scotland, Wales, Germany, France and Austria, broadside ballad tunes, popular and sentimental song, drinking songs, French revolutionary songs, Civil War songs, hymn tunes of all persuasions, African American spirituals and different kinds of classical music from glees to Italian opera. We have heard music from those composers that have long been taken into the canon, such as Beethoven, Mozart, Bach, Weber, Spohr, Mendelssohn and Gluck, and other more marginal figures that have not. In some cases the choices reflected the different tastes of the middle and working classes; in others it cut across class reflecting society at large.

Accordingly, we have not limited our focus to one genre; to do so would have given a skewed view of the past. For example, we have not been listening for, or indeed looking for: folk music, classical music, popular music, industrial folk, trade union songs, labour anthems, work songs, hymns or broadside ballads within radical and reform culture. We have engaged with music and music-making as it appeared in our sources and what we have found includes examples from all these generic types. To have surrendered to a taxonomic urge – to the desire to categorise – would have obscured what actually happened.

As multifarious as the musical genres were, so were the venues and contexts – public and private – in which they were played. The format at the Bijou was a familiar one, discussed often in the preceding pages, but we have also reported on music and music-making at tea parties, soirees, banquets, dinners, picnics, *conversazione*, fundraisers, benefits, 'smoke' concerts, commemorations, lecture series, religious and quasi-religious services, street corners, town squares, parades, various forms of mass meeting, elections, demonstrations, strikes, rebellions and riots. Time and distance mattered little here. We have seen that this panoply of events might have taken place among radicals and reformers anywhere across the Anglophone world from Glasgow to Toronto to Dunedin to Brisbane. In his memoir, published in 1868, Thomas Wright, the well-known 'journeyman engineer'-cum-social commentator, meditates on the institution of the trade union 'Club-House'. 'Its members are numbered by tens of thousands, and it is, so to speak, ubiquitous,' he noted. 'I can turn it into any part of England, Ireland, Scotland or Wales,' Wright continued. 'And if I go farther afield – to Australia, New Zealand, Canada, or the United States – it still awaits me with open doors and brotherly welcome.' Here, a labourer 'on tramp' was guaranteed to find food, drink, shelter, a good fire and a song.[13] Notwithstanding the impact of new technologies, in some respects we have seen time stand still. A liberal election parade through the streets of Maitland in New South Wales in 1843, where the band played *See, the Conquering Hero Comes*, was much the same as a liberal parade in 1879 in Dalkeith, Scotland, where the musicians hammered out the same tune; a dinner among the Spenceans in late eighteenth-century London – punctuated by raucous renditions of radical songs – was not unlike a boisterous celebration in Sydney in 1860 where Daniel Deniehy and his fellow republicans chirruped the *Marseillaise*.[14]

We have observed the presence of music and music-making then in a multitude of different contexts and, within them, we have seen it play a multitude of roles. To summarise these it is useful to return to the photographic record of that May evening in Melbourne's Bijou theatre. Ostensibly, as with Wright's trade union 'Club-House', the walls of the building provided a structure for their assemblage – in Manuel DeLanda's sense[15] – that was replicated by the photograph's border. In it we can see the outlines of a rich movement-culture. A banner on the facia of the lower balcony bearing the rallying cry made famous in the pages of the *Communist Manifesto*, first published in English in 1850, 'WORKERS OF THE WORLD UNITE', immediately catches the eye. The fact that the first edition in English was serialised in a Chartist newspaper in London in 1850 is worthy of note.[16] The auditorium is packed to the rafters with women and men; even the standing room at the back is full. We can see that many among the crowd sport their Sunday best clothes: starched collars and bonnets abound. The majority of the outfits would have been made with trade union labour advertised elsewhere in the columns of the paper and in countless more we have read in the pages of this book.

On a rostrum we can see the familiar piercing expression of Tom Mann, the party secretary, notorious the world over for his stentorian oratory, as we noted in our introduction and numerous times since. As contemporary accounts make clear, the promise of his weekly 'Sermon' draws many.[17] Mann's hands rest on the shoulders of two children, undoubtedly students of the flourishing Socialist Sunday School, which by February 1907 was operating twelve different classes per week. As we have seen, dedicated Sunday Schools for the children of radicals and reformers were a feature of their political culture the world over. Among the crowd were the teachers 'specialising in child culture'; also present were the many patrons of the socialist 'library and literary depot', the repository of the 'world's best printed matter in the area of sociology' and, of course, the *Socialist Songbook*. This slim, thirty-page volume, like the many dozens of song and hymn-books we have dipped into in this study, both reflected and fostered identity, revealing affinities and like-mindedness and sometimes bitter divergences across a range of political and reform movements. We have browsed the shelves and stock-lists of several radical publishers, from John Catnach to William Swan Sonnenschein, who produced reams of political literature as well as musical scores, songsters, slip ballads and song sheets. Members of the Socialist Party Co-operative and depositors of the Socialist Savings Bank were surely captured in the photograph too, as were vendors and consumers of Red Flag Tea – 'none better'.[18] We can undoubtedly see members of the Socialist Gym, and many that had participated in splendid Socialist Party picnics – a staple of radical and reform movements throughout the Anglophone world – in the countryside around Melbourne.[19]

Clearly visible in the foreground of the photograph is an orchestra pit; several musicians can be seen in it. These were members of the Socialist Choir, Orchestra and Brass Band, or some combination thereof. The band was officially constituted in 1907 and continued to operate successfully into the 1920s, eventually becoming the official band of the Trades Hall Council.[20] These players must stand in here for the countless bandsmen we have heard: some with battered and tarnished instruments, others with their trumpets, cornets and euphoniums gleaming and new; some resplendent in uniforms with shiny buttons, others scrimping and saving for theirs. We have found them in cities, towns, villages and hamlets as well as on reservations and missions among English, Scots, Welshmen, Australians (colonials and Aborigines), North Americans (indigenous and non-indigenous) and New Zealanders (Māori and Pākehā). Melbourne's Socialist Choir must represent the tens of thousands choristers – women, men and children – we have listened to in this book. In this case it comprised women only, described by one commentator as 'more inclined to extreme political action than the men';[21] they are a reminder that the musical life of radicalism and reform was often generated and sustained by women.

This point was fully evident a few days after the photograph was taken when twenty or so women from the choir headed a protest march to Parliament House singing 'labour songs'. Facing arrest for singing – a pattern we have seen before – Tom Mann intervened to defuse the situation. One chorister – Mrs Kirk – was, however, taken into custody. Having made their point the procession marched off, singing as they went, conducted by a woman sporting a blue sash.[22] She was very likely Elsie Harker (Mann). Her complete absence from the pages of Tom's memoir could not be more misleading as an indicator of her essential contribution to the multifarious causes they participated in together from one corner of the Anglophone world to the other. Formally trained as a musician, Elsie was described as a 'pensive blond little lady' – an 'entire contrast' to Tom – but she was every bit as important as him. Her exact place in the photograph is not clear, but she was there and she stands for the many women we have encountered whose central role in driving radicalism and reform we have sought to rescue. Indeed, by focussing on music and music-making we seized an opportunity to throw light onto some of the key roles played by women in reform and radical movements both in the public and private sphere: from Edith Brand on the hustings and the menacing women outside John Bright's house to the South Place composers, Eliza Flower and E. J. Troup, and the Māori women singing temperance hymns in an attempt to rehabilitate their men; from imprisoned suffragettes and Lady Stout to Georgia Pearce, editor of the *Clarion Song Book*, Eliza Cook, Harriet Martineau, Ivy Trigg and Melbourne's Margaret Strong.

We know that Elsie Mann was present at the Bijou precisely because we can be certain that the moment captured by the photographer's flash on that Sunday night in Melbourne was of the sight *and* sound of *The Red Flag* sung to the tune of *The White Cockade*. The fact that they chose to photograph a moment of sound is worth lingering over. We can hear as well as see it as it happened. On the one hand, the walls of the building, overlain by the photograph's frame, gave definition to what was effectively a dynamic way of life; it was, as Christina Parolin has put it, a radical space.[23] At the same time, despite the ostensible hard shell provided by bricks and mortar, the Bijou was ephemeral and the part it played in the cultural formation illusory. The Melbourne socialists insouciantly used other halls and meeting places upon which they – like many reformers and radicals we have encountered – only temporarily imprinted their culture. In this sense the photograph is misleading. What defined their social culture as the camera flashed on that day in May was music-making. As we have seen elsewhere, the strains of the music – in this case singing *The Red Flag* – provided an auditory cover, helping to create a cultural space to live a way of life. Under a blanket of sound, the sounds of liberty were vital to reaffirming common purpose, renewing commitment and nourishing solidarity. We have seen the ways music-making was central to inspiring, entertaining, commemorating and mourning. We have seen how music provided agency and was dialogic, an effective means of communication from and to the platform, between leaders and led. We have suggested that it is no accident that political meetings – large or small, public or private – were almost invariably bookended by music-making. Moreover, we have seen music at the core of social action. Music and music-making sent activists, with renewed defiance for the challenges ahead, into the public sphere where it served as a highly effective precis of a cause – whatever that might have been – and as a potent weapon to taunt, disrupt, intimidate and, as we have observed many times, to precipitate violent confrontation.

Cataloguing the multitude of ways that music and music-making served radicals and reformers also points us to broader conclusions. If studying music and music-making tells us much about those who made it, what else does it reveal? What we point to is quintessentially a shared inter-colonial, transnational and even trans-local culture; we suggest that the contours of this culture can be mapped onto an Anglophone world (as opposed to a strictly 'British world'). Music and music-making were central elements in the repertoire of popular politics for those who never ventured far from kith and kin, but they also sustained and nourished ties across space and time. The many examples we have cited cover more than a century and tens of thousands of kilometres. They cross-cut and respond to many significant changes in the political ground rules and thus the actual objectives of reform. The rituals associated with electioneering – to recall the most obvious episodes discussed – persisted long after they had become meaningless in the processes of formal politics. Whether in Aberdeen, Ontario, Auckland or Sydney, throughout the long nineteenth century radicals and reformers could recognise in the sound of the music (as well as the ways they made it and the uses to which they put it) a common cause. As noted throughout the preceding pages, the past was often mobilised to advance a wide range of political and reform agendas.[24]

In many instances, past and present were connected not only by flesh and blood but also by music. Before they dispersed at the conclusion of their march on Parliament, for example, the Melbourne Socialist choir from the Bijou gave a rousing rendition of the *Marseillaise*, led by an 'old white-bearded man of about 80 years of age'.[25] In that moment we can hear music and music-making as a connective tissue. Following in the footsteps of the legions of reformers and radicals who moved freely and often relentlessly around the Anglophone world opens our eyes to transnational and inter-colonial perspectives. Perhaps our old, white-bearded socialist can stand in for tens of thousands of others. As the choir marched back to their headquarters on Elizabeth Street, however, they encountered Vida Goldstein in a doorway and cheered her as they went. As we have seen, Goldstein can certainly represent the peripatetic radicals and reformers we have meet in the preceding chapters who, in turn, were typical of a form of globalisation from below.[26] Nevertheless, tracking the music that wayfaring radicals and reformers carried with them is a way of hearing connections and histories that otherwise might still remain discrete and even out of earshot. At the core of this process was the replication of cultural practices and repertoires of political action. By recounting stories we have seen the multiple ways that music and music-making facilitated continuities; it helped to prevent that which was 'experience-near', in Geertz's terms, from becoming 'experience-distant' even from afar.

[352]

But nowhere do we suggest that the shared culture of radicalism and reform we have mapped onto the Anglophone world by centring music and music-making was either monolithic or canonical. On the contrary, as well as self-replicating, the cultural formation it throws into sharp relief was organic and changeable. Indeed, we have shown signs of growing impulses to provide new music reflected in a quest of originality both in terms of lyrics and melody. Of course, the desire for new music to better support the imagined new socialist utopias burned brightly in Britain too. In the introduction to his *Chants of Labour*, Edward Carpenter emphasised the significance of the fact that much of the music was new, 'composed by friends expressly for this volume'. Moreover, he drew attention to the fact that the 'accompaniments and arrangements of old and standard airs have been re-cast and adapted'. This would, he insisted, 'help to give voice to those who have so long been dumb!' He had done so, he wrote, from a 'sense of respect for the actual movement'.[27] Georgia Pearce, the *Clarion Song Book's* editor, similarly highlighted the forty new tunes written 'expressly for the song book', a point enthusiastically endorsed by Robert Blatchford in his foreword.[28] John Bruce Glasier, a Scottish-born activist of many allegiances on the Left, teased out the point further in the introduction to his songster published in 1895. 'Surely we may hope that the spirit of Socialism which has already given us so many excellent lyrics', he wrote, 'will also yet gift to us new and beautiful melodies.'[29] What we see here – and what we have noted elsewhere – is inter alia that the sounds of liberty were often underpinned in a sense by a potent admixture of historicism, taste, independence, self-reliance and in some cases what we might crudely call class consciousness, which helped to motivate the spilling of gallons of ink. Moreover, a sense of national identity – variously British, English, Scottish and, less frequently, Welsh – was evident in these collections. Carpenter's most famous song was, after all, *England Arise* (often adapted to *Workers Arise* outside England).

It goes without saying that tonnes of these songbooks produced in the Old World – and the many more like them considered in the preceding pages – spread across the broader radical and reformist world where they were treasured, tattered and torn, stuffed into pockets or drawers, studied, ignored and or passed down through the generations (as they were in Britain). It will be self-evident from our discussion here and elsewhere that the printing presses in Auckland and Adelaide churned out local books at a similar rate. It goes without saying that an assertive commitment to self-reliance and in some cases class animated radicals and reformers outside Britain with equal enthusiasm. Nevertheless, what distinguished many song collections published

[353]

in the wider Anglophone world was an increasing sense of discrete national identity. We have shown that as the century wore on many expressions of musical culture, particularly song repertoire, underwent a kind of 'nativising' as it put down deeper roots in the soils of the Anglophone world. This process saw content and approach adapted to suit the local context and in some instances to the very particular physical attributes of the new environments. The huge corpus of new lyrics produced over the long nineteenth century is one outcome of this desire to build on a shared heritage, but there were also, albeit in a less abundant way, efforts to produce new music to accompany the new lyrics.

On one level *fin de siècle* Australian and New Zealand socialist culture, to take a fruitful example that we have touched on many times, was entirely derivative of its British counterpart. Apart from the individuals themselves this can be seen most glaringly in the form of songbooks. In the early years of the twentieth century, however, home-grown compositional efforts began to appear in the pages of local publications. Notably, these often specifically essayed local themes. For example, the *Barrier Socialist Songster*, published around 1910, included *Sons of the South*, penned by the well-known anarchist-journalist J. A. Andrews, which, as we have seen in an earlier chapter, referred explicitly to 'our native land'.[30] A palpable sense of nationalist fervour appeared elsewhere in collections such as John H. Nicholson's *Rouse Australians* and *The Song of Australia*, which had been composed over fifty years earlier in 1850 by Caroline Carleton and the German-Australian composer and erstwhile European revolutionary Carl Linger.[31] The well-known Australian poets and socialists Bernard O'Dowd and Marie E. J. Pitt contributed *Our Country* and *A Marching Song* to socialist songbooks published in Melbourne and Sydney. Original music was supplied for these poetic efforts by fellow socialist and amateur composer Frank Vernon, whose musical contributions, notably, can also be found supporting such staples as Thomas Cooper's Chartist song *Truth is Growing*.[32] In *Our Country* O'Dowd, like Andrews, begins to equate freedom with the iconic symbols of Australia. After an unabashed declaration of patriotic love in the first line – 'We love our fair Australia' – O'Dowd makes explicit references to the landscape, the Southern Cross and other 'totems of Australia', including emus and kangaroos.

In 1901 in Wellington the newly formed Clarion Colony held a meeting chaired by Robert Hogg, recently arrived from Edinburgh. The evening featured both a rousing rendition of Carpenter's 'great Socialist hymn' *England Arise*, and, notwithstanding the fact that he had barely reached dry land, Hogg's original composition *Beneath* the *Wattle Bough*, written in 'praise of colonial life'.[33] His comrade, London dock clerk-cum-shoemaker John Brooks Hulbert, who travelled to New Zealand by way of Hobart to become the Socialist Party secretary in 1906, also contributed actively to local musical culture. In addition to his political work, Hulbert organised entertainments and produced his own songbook with music. His collection reveals a considerable crossover with ethical and secularist song literature (including songs by Gustav Spiller and Felix Adler as well as musical accompaniments composed by E. J. Troup), but Hulbert put his own musical abilities to work to produce an alternative musical setting for *The Red Flag*.[34] Several years later, Hulbert's original setting appeared in the *Maoriland Worker* above a letter of explanation, 'The Composer to the Comrades', in which he justified his decision on the basis that 'all the songs of the Socialist movement should have their own musical settings' and a fellow socialist had pointed out that 'Maryland was unworthy of such grand lines'.[35]

Another example spanning the Anglophone world illustrates the way that a mutable transnational culture could both promote the ties that bind and reinforce the continuities built around a shared sense of the past and also gave rise to a sense of national exceptionalism built on a form of political-cum-cultural amnesia. On the other side of the coin of continuity was originality combined with a form of forgetting. One of our aims has to been see both sides of the same coin. In Chicago in 1899 Charles Kerr published the first of several editions of a socialist songbook that in terms of content closely mirrored the ones being produced in Britain and Australasia. He acknowledged the debt to 'our English comrades', noting that 'only a few' of his pages contained original material: 'We American Socialists are only beginning to sing,' he confessed.[36]

Members of the Knights of Labor may well have taken issue with Kerr's humble confession. Over a decade before the appearance of Kerr's *Socialist Songs*, the Knights were energetically creating a vernacular song culture seen, for example, in J. D. Tallmadge's *Labor Songs Dedicated to the Knights of Labor* (also published in Chicago).[37] The late Victorian socialist song literature that pervades Kerr's collection is well nigh absent from this collection, and there is a noticeable increase in songs with a clear nationalist character. Again, original music was evident; Emily Tallmadge wrote accompaniments to several of the more patriotic items such as *Rouse Americans Rouse*.[38] In 1892 Phillips Thompson put together a Canadian collection for the Knights. While drawing more noticeably than Tallmadge upon the pre-existing radical song tradition, it included a significant number of his original contributions.[39]

As we noted in the introduction, the subsequent historiography of the Knights has perpetuated the narrative of the movement's distinctive 'indigenous' culture. Philip Foner in 1975, Clark D. Halker in 1991 and Robert Weir in 1996 have all drawn attention to one particular song, *Song of the Proletaire* by local New York songwriter Tom O'Reilly.[40] It first appeared in 1876 in the *Socialist*, but was introduced to the movement in 1887, from which time it was used to close the general assemblies.[41] The song, according to Weir, 'created a stir', quickly becoming a 'minor sensation' and ultimately a 'showpiece' for the order. It was, Weir determined, a 'local song that passed into general use'.[42]

But this was only part of the story and the silences speak volumes. In 1848 the *Northern Star* turned its attention away from the revolutions spreading through the capitals of Europe to report on a tea party and ball in Oswaldtwistle, a village in Lancashire. During the proceedings one of the revellers gave a rousing rendition of *Base Oppression* [*sic*] '(from the Chartist hymnbook)' with the 'assembled multitude' joining him in the chorus.[43] Better known as *Base Oppressors*, this song was written by J. A. Leatherland, the minor poet and erstwhile Chartist. Although later in life Leatherland was to claim he was 'never a thorough-going Chartist', he nonetheless admitted a grudging pride in the success of his song.[44] The song quickly established a place in British radical culture, appearing in several collections, including Joseph Barker's *Democratic Hymns and Songs* in 1849 and later in John Bedford Leno's *Reformer's Book of Songs and Recitations*, as well as Austin Holyoake's and Charles Watts's *The Secularist's Manual of Songs and Ceremonies*.[45]

Even as the Knights of Labor were enthusiastically singing *Hymn of the Proletaire* across the Atlantic, British reformer H. S. Salt was including details of Leatherland's song's reception along with the song itself in his carefully historicised collection *Songs of Freedom*.[46] A glance at the first stanzas of both O'Reilly and Leatherland's songs shows that it was in fact the same song. Listen to the Chartists of Oswaldtwistle:

> Base Oppressors, break your slumbers;
> Listen to a Nation's cry;
> Hark! United, countless numbers
> Swell the peal of agony!
> Lo! From Britain's sons and daughters,
> In the depths of misery–
> Like the sound of many waters–
> Comes the cry 'we will be free!'[47]

Now hear the Knights in New York:

Base oppressors, cease your slumbers,
Listen to a people's cry,
Hark! Uncounted, countless numbers
Swell the peal of agony;
Lo from Labor's sons and daughters,
In the depths of misery,
Like the rush of many waters,
Comes the cry, 'We will be free,'
Comes the cry, 'We will be free.'[48]

Whether O'Reilly appropriated, plagiarised or simply forgot is not the point. The issue is that historians have missed the point. What this example shows is a transnational process of transmission – based on music and music-making – giving rise to a nationalist anthem.[49] This instance serves as a telling example in that not only does it again highlight connections across time and space, many of them in need of recovery and repair, but also in a broader sense it underscores the importance of extending the historical gaze beyond borders when seeking to understand the sight and sound of a shared culture. 'Experience-near' cultural forms and practices, to invoke Geertz's framework again, could sometimes be both near and far. Thus, through the lens of music and music-making, we have seen that the trajectory of the women and men who set out for Australia, New Zealand and North America with reform – sometimes radical reform – in their hearts were affected by their multifarious experience of the different political, social and physical landscape they encountered in the years after they arrived. For all that they were seduced by the impulse to shape new nations, however, in some important respects they had not gone anywhere. Indeed, we began our introduction with Tom Mann on a stage in London participating in a festival of music for the people; we begin our conclusion with him on a podium twenty years earlier at the other end of the Anglophone world, leading a rousing chorus of *The Red Flag*. It is likely that Tom and Elsie were the only people to actually share both stages, but, in a sense, everyone did. Perhaps this should not surprise us. As Keith Hancock put it famously in 1930 in relation to those he called independent Australian Britons, 'a country is a jealous mistress and patriotism is commonly an exclusive passion; but it is not impossible for Australians, nourished by glorious literature and haunted by old memories, to be in love with two soils.'[50]

The living, dynamic tradition of music and music-making was fuelled by and depended on repetition. For us this has been both methodology and finding. We have approached our subject on the basis that in stories are explanations, which, in turn, offer shards of understanding. We offer no conclusions about the persistence of music-making as

[357]

a form of social-cum-political action beyond our chronology – although the extensive list of choirs on stage with Paul Robeson in the late 1930s suggested that it was not finished yet. We do, however, suggest possible lines of inquiry into the future. Throughout the long nineteenth century one of the most common impulses, which reflected the importance of music and music-making in sustaining and transmitting reform culture, was to rush to the printing press to produce a songster as part of a repertoire of action. The handful of later twentieth-century songsters we have dipped into, however, share two important features: first, the songs are typically grouped under national headings; second, they are almost invariably accompanied by extensive historical explanations. Paradoxically, the headnotes provided for older songs suggest that in order to reify a tradition and a shared heritage songbooks had to become history books.

Without postulating a grand narrative beyond the chronology studied here, this at least suggests that, in a transnational context, repetition and replication of the ways of doing things began to fade over time just as the period of what has been called free trade globalisation after 1850 receded between the wars. Does the rise of iTunes, Spotify and the constant expansion of Europe (even to include Australia) for the purposes of the Eurovision Song Contest signify a perpetual age of technologically enabled cultural transmission beyond borders – the triumph of the digital – or will it too fracture and fade on the back of Brexit and the next global financial crisis? The significant revival of protest music in the 1960s and 1970s undoubtedly captured the hearts and minds of a generation, but its music was overwhelmingly original. Pete Seeger's entire oeuvre comprises songs of his own composition. Again, however, originality sat alongside forgetting. The claim that Crosby, Stills, Nash and Young's *Ohio* was the 'first' protest song to provide an instant response to a political crisis is, as we have seen many times, nonsense.[51] The fact that the main theme of the hippie apotheosis, *Godspell*, is an unattributed rip-off of a radical song of the 1830s – Ebenezer Elliot's *When Wilt Thou Save the People?* – is the *ne plus ultra* of cultural amnesia. A handful of academic commentators have historicised the later efflorescence of protest music during the British 'Rock Against Racism' campaigns of the 1970s and early 1980s, and among performers Billy Bragg has explicitly asserted a left-wing claim to a proud tradition. Not surprisingly, he has not only recorded *The Red Flag* but he did so to the tune of *The White Cockade*.[52]

The tribulations of *The Red Flag* within the formal labour movement in Britain over the past hundred years serve as a capsule statement for much of what we want to say by way of conclusion. In 1923 the defeat of Bonar Law's Tory government on the floor of the House of

Commons (over a minor public service bill) provoked a lusty chorus of *The Red Flag* from the Labour members. 'Not since Cromwell's time', enthused the editor of the *Maoriland Worker*, has that 'sacred and venerable hall ... felt so palpably the shock of revolution'.[53] A year later, as a meeting to celebrate the election of the first Labour government came to a tumultuous end, the 'whole assembly rose in chorus' (David Granville has noted) and 'raised the roof of the mighty building, as together they sang the most fervent of all socialist anthems ever, "The Red Flag".' Nevertheless, the following year Ramsay MacDonald, Labour's first prime minister, initiated a competition (ultimately unsuccessful) to replace it as the party's anthem.[54]

By 1945 further cracks in the cultural edifice appeared. Famously, when Winston Churchill entered the Commons chamber for the first time since his ignominious defeat his colleagues in the Tory ranks began to sing *For He's a Jolly Good Fellow*. This prompted the Labourites to begin a 'counter demonstration' by singing *The Red Flag*. As one observer quipped, however, even at this moment of epochal triumph the likes of Hugh Dalton and Herbert Morrison – the antecedents of New Labour – had appeared to struggle with the words.[55] Fifty years on the denouement of Tony Blair's systematic attempt to stamp out the last embers of 'old Labour' involved the banishment of the red rose from the party's iconography and ceasing the ritual rendition of *The Red Flag* at the end of party conferences. The reintroduction of the practice a few short years later in 2011 as part of Gordon Brown's attempts to reconnect the party with its core constituency necessitated handing out lyric sheets.[56] Apparently, it didn't catch on. When current Labour leader Jeremy Corbyn was first elected in 2015 he adjourned with his coadjutors to a London pub to celebrate. The beer flowed and the putative renaissance of democratic socialism was marked by a rendition of *The Red Flag*. Even here, bathed in the luminosity of renewed red, the warbling was characterised by an obvious uncertainty over the lyrics and an excruciating butchering of the tune.[57] Here, we bear witness to a very faint echo of an Anglophone political culture nourished by music and music-making among radicals and reformers chronicled in this book, which had long since faded along with the strains of the sounds of liberty themselves.

Notes

1   *Socialist Songs* (Melbourne: Fraser & Jenkins, n.d.), cover. The quotation is from the New Testament (King James Edition), Revelation 5:9.
2   *Socialist Songs* (Melbourne: Socialist Party Press, 1907), Song 1.
3   Graeme Davison, *The Rise and Fall of Marvellous Melbourne* (Melbourne: Melbourne University Press, 1979).

4 Ralph Marsden, 'Bijou Theatre', available at http://theatreheritage.org.au/on-stage-magazine/stage-by-stage/item/52-bijou-theatre (accessed 24 September 2016). It had been rebuilt following a fire in 1889.

5 *Socialist* (2 June 1906).

6 Several other placards are not legible.

7 *Socialist* (19 May 1906).

8 Jim Connell, 'How I wrote the "Red Flag"', *The Call* (6 May 1920); Kate Bowan and Paul Pickering, 'Singing for Socialism', in Laurajane Smith, Paul Shackel and Gary Campbell (eds), *Heritage, Labour and the Working Classes* (New York: Routledge, 2011), pp. 192–215.

9 Connell, 'How I wrote the "Red Flag"'.

10 Winston Churchill, *Great Contemporaries* (London: T. Butterworth, 1937), p. 53.

11 J. van Wyk, '"Volcano Needing Constant Watching": South African White Labour and Socialist Culture 1900–1924', *Journal of Literary Studies*, 14:1 (1998), p. 123.

12 Tom Mann, *Memoirs* (London: Labour Publishing Company, 1923), p. 97. Later editions of the songbook recommended *Maryland*.

13 [Thomas Wright], *The Great Unwashed* (London: Tinsley Brothers, 1868), pp. 152–8. Interestingly, Wright also included France in the places where trade union clubs were open to him.

14 *Maitland Mercury* (4 March 1843); *Sydney Morning Herald* (20 March 1860); *The Scotsman* (27 November 1879).

15 See David Worrall, *Celebrity, Performance, Reception: British Georgian Theatre as Social Assemblage* (Cambridge: Cambridge University Press, 2013); Manuel DeLanda, *A New Philosophy of Society: Assemblage Theory and Social Complexity* (London: Continuum, 2006).

16 *Red Republican* (June–November 1850). Behind the cameraman was a large screen upon which images could be projected, although reports do not make clear what they were on this day.

17 See *Punch* [Melbourne] (30 July 1908).

18 See the weekly editions of the *Socialist* during 1906–7 for details of this rich way of life from which the above information has been drawn.

19 See Bertha Walker, *Solidarity Forever! A Part Story of the Life of Percy Laidler* (Melbourne: National Press, 1972), p. 29.

20 Walker, *Solidarity Forever!*, pp. 35–6.

21 *Punch* (28 June 1906).

22 *Argus* (28 June 1906).

23 See Christina Parolin, *Radical Spaces: Venues of Popular Politics in London, 1790–c.1845* (Canberra, ACT: ANU E Press, 2010).

24 Ron Eyerman and Andrew Jamison consider the 'mobilisation of tradition' as a central social process in their study of social movements. See Ron Eyerman and Andrew Jamison, *Music and Social Movements: Mobilizing Traditions in the Twentieth Century* (Cambridge: Cambridge University Press, 1998), p. 1.

25 *Argus* (28 June 1906).

26 *Ibid.*

27 Edward Carpenter (ed.), *Chants of Labour: A Song Book of the People with Music* (London: Swan Sonnenschein, 1888), p. vi.

28 See Robert Blatchford's 'Foreword' and the 'Editor's Preface' in Georgia Pearce (ed.), *Clarion Song Book* (London: The Clarion Press, 1906), pp. vi–viii.

29 John Bruce Glasier, 'Preface', in *Socialist Songs* (Glasgow: Labour Literature Society, 1895). See also Chris Wrigley, 'Glasier, John Bruce (1859–1920)', *Oxford Dictionary of National Biography* (Oxford: Oxford University Press, 2004); online edition, available at http://www.oxforddnb.com.virtual.anu.edu.au/view/article/38468 (accessed 24 September 2016).

30 J. A. Andrews, 'Sons of the South', *Barrier Socialist Songster* (Broken Hill: Truth Print, n.d.), pp. 14–15. It also appeared in his collection. See *Labour Song Book* (Melbourne: Tocsin Print, n.d.), pp. 32–3.

31 John H. Nicholson, 'Rouse Australians' and Caroline Carleton, 'The Song of Australia' (music by Carl Linger), *Barrier Socialist Songster* (Broken Hill: Truth Print, n.d.), p. 17 and p. 19, respectively. See also [Caroline Carleton], 'The Song of Australia', *Social Democratic Song Book* (Broken Hill: 'Barrier Truth', 1908), p. 20. Linger, who had been a staunch supporter of the 1848 revolutions in Europe, left Germany the following year to pursue a better life in South Australia.

32 These songs appear in the songbooks published by the Victorian Socialist Party from c.1907 into the 1920s. See, for example, *Socialist Songs* (Melbourne: The Socialist Party, 1907); *Socialist Songs with Music* (Melbourne: Fraser & Jenkinson, [1906–1923]); *Socialist Songs* (Melbourne: The Socialist Party Affiliated with the Socialist Federation of Australasia, [1909–1912]); *Socialist Songs*, 10th edn (Melbourne: The Socialist Party Affiliated with the Socialist Federation of Australasia, n.d.).The contributions of O'Dowd, Pitt and Vernon also appear in Sydney's *Socialist Song Book* (Sydney: Social Democratic League, 1917).

33 Alexander Turnbull Library, Wellington, NZ, William Ranstead Papers, 1859–1944, MS-Papers-0071, folders 1–26, 'Scrapbook of miscellaneous newspaper cuttings', 'An Evening with the Ranstead Party', *Wellington Post* (2 May 1901). During his subsequent years in New Zealand, when he was the secretary of the Socialist Party and editor of both the *Maoriland Worker* and the *Commonweal*, Hogg made more contributions to the song literature, including *Workers of the World, Unite* (which appeared in songbooks in Melbourne and Sydney as well as New Zealand) and *Demos is Our King*. See *Songs of Revolt*, no. 1 (Wellington: 'N.Z. Times' Co., Ltd., for the Publisher, the Editor of the 'COMMONWEAL', 1909). For Australian publications see: *Socialist Song Book* (Sydney: Social Democratic League, 1917); *Socialist Songs with Music* (Melbourne: Fraser & Jenkinson, [1906–1923]); *Socialist Songs*, 10th edn.

34 J. B. Hulbert (ed.), *Socialist Songs with Music* (Wellington: J. B. Hulbert, 1906). He had already achieved a measure of notoriety with an earlier song, *The Scab*, written for the Maritime Strike of 1890.

35 *Maoriland Worker* (27 December 1912).

36 Charles H. Kerr (ed.), *Socialist Songs with Music*, 4th edn (Chicago: Charles H. Kerr & Co., 1906). For *Your Work, My Work*, see p. 7; for *Hymn of the Toilers*, see p. 13.

37 J. D. Tallmadge (ed.), *Labor Songs Dedicated to the Knights of Labor* (Chicago: J. D. Tallmadge, 1886).

38 Tallmadge, *Labor Songs*, p. 3.

39 Thomas Phillips Thompson (ed.), *The Labor Reform Songster* (Philadelphia: Journal of the Knights of Labor, 1892). As we have seen, across the border in Canada there was a version of the song, *Rouse Thee, Canada!*, which entreated English, Scottish and Irish voters to support the Liberal cause during the 1882 Presidential Election.

40 Philip S. Foner, *American Labor Songs of the Nineteenth Century* (Urbana: University of Illinois Press, 1975), pp. 159–61; Clark D. Halker, *For Democracy, Workers and God: Labor Song-Poems and Labor Protest, 1865–95* (Urbana: University of Illinois Press, 1991), p. 38; Robert E. Weir, *Beyond Labor's Veil: The Culture of the Knights of Labor* (Pennsylvania: Pennsylvania State Press, 1996), p. 114.

41 Tom O'Reilly, 'A Labor Song', *Socialist* (6 May 1876). Cited in Halker, *For Democracy, Workers and God*, p. 46.

42 Weir, *Beyond Labor's Veil*, p. 114. See also, Phillips Thompson, *Labor Reform Songster*, p. 27.

43 *Northern Star* (15 January 1848).

44 J. A. Leatherland, *Essays and Poems, With a Brief Autobiographical Sketch* (London: W. Tweedie, 1862), p. 17.

45 Austin Holyoake and Charles Watts (eds), *Secularist's Manual of Songs and Ceremonies* (London: Austin, 1871), p. 10.

46 H. S. Salt (ed.), *Songs of Freedom* (London: W. Scott, 1893), p. 118.

47 Leatherland, *Essays and Poems*, p. 17.

48   1887 *Proceedings of the Knights of Labor General Assembly*, quoted in Weir, *Beyond Labor's Veil*, p. 114.

49   Leatherland's song did appear in at least one American publication in its original form, but paradoxically there is no mention of it in connection with O'Reilly's appropriation. See, J. A. Leatherland, 'Base Oppressors, Leave Your Slumbers (No. 35)', in D. M. Bennett, *The Truth Seeker Collection of Forms, Hymns and Recitations, Original and Selected, for the Use of Liberals* (New York: Liberal and Scientific Publications, 1877), available at www.hymnary.org/hymn/TSCF1877/d35 (accessed 22 May 2016).

50   Keith Hancock, *Australia* (Melbourne: Jacaranda, 1930) p. 68.

51   Dorian Lynskey, 'Neil Young's Ohio – The Greatest Protest Song', *The Guardian* (7 May 2010).

52   See Billy Bragg, *The Internationale*, Elektra – 60960–2, 1990, compact disc, track 6; Billy Bragg, *The Progressive Patriot* (London: Black Swan, 2006). The song was also recorded in 1987 by Scottish 'alternative-indie' band Aztec Camera.

53   *Maoriland Worker* (18 April 1923).

54   David Granville, 'The Song for All Socialists', *The Irish Democrat* (3 November 2002), available at www.irishdemocrat.co.uk/features/red-flag (accessed 23 September 2016); 'Labour and The Red Flag', *The Radical Read Project* (22 September 2015), available at www.radicalread.co.uk (accessed 23 September 2016).

55   *Sydney Morning Herald* (2 August 1945); *Western Advertiser* (20 September 1945).

56   Simon Hoggart, 'Labour Brings Back The Red Flag, Melodious and Neutered', *Guardian* (30 September 2011).

57   Lizzie Dearden, 'Jeremy Corbyn Celebrates Election as Labour Leader by Singing The Red Flag at Victory Party', *Independent* (12 September 2015), available at www.independent.co.uk/news/uk/politics/jeremy-corbyn-celebrates-election-as-labour-leader-by-singing-the-red-flag-at-victory-party-10497938.html (accessed 24 September 2016). The article includes an embedded YouTube clip of the rendition.

INDEX

Aberdeen (Scotland), 2, 86, 123, 325, 352

Adams, Sarah Flower, 233, 234, 239, 240, 241, 253

Adams, Stephen, 250, 315

Adams, W.E., 167

Adams, William Bridges, 234

Adelaide (Australia), 24, 106, 180, 192, 214, 288, 331, 332, 353

Alfred the Great, 122, 198, 199–200

Alhambra Society, 315

Alma Band (Broken Hill), 117, 185

Amalgamated Miners' Association (Australia), 100, 107, 181, 182, 185, 187, 193, 206
  AMA Band, 100, 101, 110, 185–6, 193, 206, 207

Andrews, John A., 52–3, 131, 133, 354

Anti-Corn Law League, 54, 81, 173, 191, 231, 236

appropriation, 13, 37, 38, 39, 40–1, 55–7, 59, 65, 115, 117, 127–9, 178, 190–1, 199, 200–1, 216, 256, 275, 337

Argyle (Australia), 153

Arnot, John, 49

Ashton, John, 85, 152

Ashton-under-Lyne (England), 215, 217, 326

Atkinson, Harry, 10, 319, 328–9, 334

Auckland (New Zealand), 84, 158, 176, 185, 209, 213, 314, 352, 353

Australasian Secularist Association, 313, 314

Australian Church, 229, 246–58, 264, 282, 285, 294, 323, 331

Australian Socialist League, 84

Aveling, Eleanor, 313

Bailey, Jim, 192, 193

Ball, Edward, 165

ballads, 7, 8, 24, 32, 33, 34, 38, 39, 41, 45, 56, 57, 59, 62, 63–5, 71, 73, 77, 82, 85, 140–1, 144, 145–7,

150, 151, 152–3, 157, 170, 187, 196, 210, 214, 216, 245, 250, 251, 266, 311, 315, 348, 347, 349–50
  as journalism, 151, 152, 272
  see also election ballads and song; songs

Bamford, Samuel, 194–5, 198–9, 205

bands
  collective identity and, 104–5
  instruments, 109–10, 111, 113, 169, 194–5, 251, 274, 275, 279, 298, 350
  named
    Alma Band (Australia), 117, 185
    Amalgamated Miners' Association Band (Australia), 100, 101, 110, 117, 184, 185, 193, 207, 208
    Army and Navy Veterans' Association Band (Canada), 111
    Bartley's Barrier Band (Australia), 184, 185–6
    Battersea Socialist Band (England), 124
    Bavarian Band (Australia), 313
    Bootmakers' Band (Australia), 320
    Burnham Industrial School Band (New Zealand), 111
    City Band (Australia), 185
    Cobar Town Band (Australia), 100, 106, 109, 120
    'Combined Band' (Australia), 184, 185
    Elite Band (New Zealand), 107, 109, 111–12, 117
    Engineers Band (New Zealand), 107, 109
    Excelsior Band (New Zealand), 102, 112
    Freethought and Choral Union Band (New Zealand), 313–14
    Garrison Band (New Zealand), 107
    Heretaunga Band (New Zealand), 177

EU authorised representative for GPSR:
Easy Access System Europe, Mustamäe tee 50,
10621 Tallinn, Estonia
gpsr.requests@easproject.com

www.ingramcontent.com/pod-product-compliance
Lightning Source LLC
Chambersburg PA
CBHW051948270326
41929CB00015B/2574